THE
DARK
TREE

THE
DARK
TREE

JAZZ AND THE COMMUNITY ARTS IN LOS ANGELES

STEVEN L. ISOARDI

WITH ARTISTS OF The Pan
Afrikan Peoples Arkestra and
The Union of God's Musicians and
Artists Ascension

WITH AN Appendix by
Roberto Miranda

DUKE UNIVERSITY PRESS
Durham and London   2023

All rights reserved
Printed in the United States of America on acid-free paper ∞
Project Editor: Jessica Ryan
Typeset in Warnock Pro and Helvetica Inserat
by Westchester Publishing Services

Library of Congress Cataloging-in-Publication Data
Names: Isoardi, Steven Louis, [date] author.
Title: The dark tree : jazz and the community arts in
Los Angeles / Steven L. Isoardi.
Description: Revised and updated. | Durham : Duke University
Press, 2023. | Includes bibliographical references and index.
Identifiers: LCCN 2022061117 (print)
LCCN 2022061118 (ebook)
ISBN 9781478025283 (paperback)
ISBN 9781478027416 (ebook)
Subjects: LCSH: Jazz—California—Los Angeles—History and
criticism. | African American jazz musicians—California—Los
Angeles. | Artists and community—California—Los Angeles. |
Jazz—Social aspects. | BISAC: MUSIC / Genres & Styles / Jazz |
SOCIAL SCIENCE / Ethnic Studies / American / African
American & Black Studies
Classification: LCC ML3508.8.L7 I86 2023 (print) |
LCC ML3508.8.L7 (ebook) | DDC 781.6509794/94—dc23/
eng/20230525
LC record available at https://lccn.loc.gov/2022061117
LC ebook record available at https://lccn.loc.gov/2022061118

Cover art: (*top, left*) Azar Lawrence, alto sax, and Ray Straughter,
tenor sax, at the Sun, early 1970s. (*top, right*) Concert at
South Park, late 1960s. Photos by Kamau Daáood. (*bottom*)
The Arkestra at the Watts Towers Jazz Festival, 7 July 1979.
Photo by Mark Weber.

TO

the memory of
Horace Tapscott

the Brothers and Sisters of
The Underground Musicians Association
The Underground Musicians and Artists Association
The Pan Afrikan Peoples Arkestra
The Union of God's Musicians and Artists Ascension

and

UGMAAgers everywhere

"The Dark Tree" has to do with the tree of life of a race of
people that was dark,
and everybody went past it and all its history.
The whole tree of a civilization was just passed over and left
in the dark,
but there it still stood.

—HORACE TAPSCOTT, *Songs of the Unsung*

CONTENTS

The first edition of *The Dark Tree* appeared in 2006 and went out of print some ten years later. In the years since, it seems to have become a collector's item, fetching three-figure sums on the internet, much to my regret and to the chagrin of the younger sisters and brothers who have emerged recently in the community arts movement in African American Los Angeles and who have been drawn to this story, wish to know more, but don't have the means to acquire a copy. They have provided the motivation to bring this back in print and I hope it serves them well. With renewed vigor an impressive new generation is emerging, and I hope this effort again stimulates and inspires.

This is a lightly revised edition, which does not go beyond Horace Tapscott's passing in 1999. Since then, the Pan Afrikan Peoples Arkestra (or "Ark") has continued on its mission through good times and bad, satisfying and challenging. Veteran Ark saxophonist Michael Session led the band until his son, drummer Mekala Session, took over the helm in 2017, supported by a strong cadre of veterans and an increasing number of novices recruited recently. Aside from the brief update in the Epilogue, it will fall to another historian in the future to chart the course of the Ark since 1999.

Not a great deal of additional information has surfaced since the first edition, but I have been able to track down and interview some important members who earlier eluded me and whose voices I am pleased to add to the text. It also affords me the opportunity to add a few stories, correct errors, and clarify a couple of points and events. Otherwise, the text remains the same as the first edition.

The book's origins trace to our final taping sessions for Horace Tapscott's autobiography, *Songs of the Unsung*.[1] Horace talked about additional research that needed to be done in documenting the African American community's cultural life in Los Angeles. He had a way of pushing you to do more. Dance was a particular priority, as he remembered other influences during his formative years on Central Avenue. It was typical of him not to focus on his own involvements and contributions, but given my interests and passions I had to ask, "What about the Ark and UGMAA?" Horace smiled and said, "Yeah, well, that needs to be done, too." He later added emphatically, "Yeah, you can do it, man, because it should be told." Assured of his support, I planned to start researching as soon as Horace's book was completed. To collaborate on his autobiography was a special gift, and now the opportunity to work on an oral history of the Arkestra with Horace was more than I could have hoped. And so it turned out to be.

One Sunday evening in October, bassist David Bryant called with word that Horace had had a seizure hours earlier and been rushed to the hospital. A few days later, he was out of intensive care. As I walked into his hospital room, he looked up from a composition in progress and, nonchalantly, greeted me with "Steve, they give me six months to live." Horace had been diagnosed to be in the final stages of lung cancer. One week later he was home and with the time remaining continued his work, making plans with fellow musicians and supporters for the future of the Arkestra and its related organization, the Union of God's Musicians and Artists Ascension (UGMAA). He also arranged my first interviews for the history. Horace would not live to see its completion, but he did set it in motion and I promised him that it would be finished and that it would preserve the story for future generations.

By the time of Horace's passing in February 1999, I had become a strong supporter of the movement. While working with Horace on his autobiography, he told me one day, "Now you're one of our wordsmiths," which I considered and consider a great honor and responsibility. Consequently, I felt a sense of immediacy to offer something inspirational that would assist everyone involved after such a great loss, to take some satisfaction in what they accomplished, and to continue the movement. By holding their work, their history, their words, effort and commitment over the previous forty years up to them, I hoped that this oral history would act as a mirror, reflecting the contributions and achievements of their lives back at them, and inspiring further efforts on their part and others in this post-Horace period.

The Dark Tree is not simply the history of a band, nor of a music school. It is not a story of young artists seeking their first exposure as musicians and then emerging into the professional realm spurred by sage elders, though this occurred in some cases. It is a story of the struggle by many artists to rediscover and rebuild community, to forge an ethic of community involvement and to create an aesthetic derived from and part of that involvement.

Under Horace's guidance this movement spanned forty years of African American history in Los Angeles to the end of the twentieth century, but its roots reach back to an even earlier L.A. history and deep into the traditions of this country, ultimately extending in part to the cultural beliefs and practices of West African peoples. During those four decades some three hundred UGMAA artists offered hundreds of free performances and other services to thousands throughout their community. As instigators and key participants in the vibrant community arts movement in South Central Los Angeles, Horace and the Arkestra crafted and offered related arts and music—"African American classics" in Horace's words—as a vital part of the everyday life of their community. In so doing they also presented an expansive, inclusive, noncompetitive vision of the arts and the role of the artist that offered an alternative to that of the commercially oriented music world.

It is also a story largely unknown throughout the American mainstream, much of the jazz world, and even within parts of Horace's community. One of the earliest *Los Angeles Times* reviews of a Tapscott-led UGMAA ensemble, almost twenty years after the organization's founding, refers to Horace as "a somewhat invisible fixture on the L.A. jazz scene for some time now."[2] The theme of invisibility echoed for the remainder of Horace's life and followed his passing. After the graveside service for Horace in March 1999, his longtime friend and collaborator, the actor William Marshall, arrived late with his companion, writer Sylvia Jarrico. As they approached the freshly covered grave, they noticed the temporary I.D. tag for a "Harold Tapscott."[3]

The *Times'* observation of Horace's invisibility suggests more about the jazz scene than it does about Horace, the Arkestra, or the music. The failure to recognize such movements is more a comment on the inability of much of the jazz and mainstream media to see beyond commercial venues and into the areas that birthed this art form. Much of the African American audience is where it has always been, in their communities and not in higher-priced clubs, halls, and festivals far removed from those neighborhoods and their working-class populations. While most of jazz journalism, history, and commerce have focused primarily on these typical venues, they've become increasingly removed from African American communities and the music emerging there over the last sixty years, such as that of the Pan Afrikan Peoples Arkestra. Performances at parks, schools, social centers, and cultural festivals continue to attract substantial audiences.

With Horace at the helm the Arkestra performed in those spaces for almost forty years and during that time built a dedicated following. Horace's
last public appearance was before hundreds, filling the streets of his community in September 1998 to see the Ark and other ensembles in the Leimert
Park Jazz Festival. The annual Central Avenue Jazz Festival has taken place
since 1996 on the streets of South Central Los Angeles to an ever-increasing
audience. Spectators to the 2003 edition, who arrived on Saturday at noon
for the opening panel discussion, found every seat taken as hundreds came
early just to listen to the reminiscences of a few veteran musicians. Every
year the community pulses to many such celebratory cultural gatherings.
Horace and the members of UGMAA knew where their audience was and
they reveled in four decades of honest and undiluted artistic communion.

Focused on their community, well under the radar of the mainstream
media, the Arkestra was rarely documented in standard sources, making this
in some ways a difficult book to research. Unlike my experience in researching the African American community along Central Avenue in the first half
of the twentieth century, there was little coverage even in the local black
press.[4] At the time of Horace's passing the entire collection of writings on
Horace and the Ark—newspaper reviews, magazine articles, and references
in a few books—could be easily accommodated in one file folder. A small box
would suffice for the community arts movement of South Central Los Angeles, perhaps the largest and deepest of the last half century that included, in
addition to the Arkestra and UGMAA, institutions such as ARTWORKS 4,
the Brockman Gallery, Compton Communicative Arts Academy, Crossroads
Arts Academy, 5th Street Dick's Coffee Company, the Gathering, Inner City
Cultural Center, Kabasa Drum and Arts Studio, KAOS Network, Mafundi
Institute, Malcolm X Center, Performing Arts Society of Los Angeles, Project
Blowed, St. Elmo Village, Studio Watts, Watts Happening Coffee House, Watts
Towers Arts Center, Watts Writers Workshop, and the World Stage. Fortu-
nately, this situation has improved in the last few years, more writings have
appeared, but there is still much to be done.

Given the paucity of written documentation, history, and analyses, I found
myself relying—exclusively in many cases—on oral histories to tell the story.
Some one hundred brothers and sisters shared their thoughts with me to
make this book possible, not one person refusing an interview request. Without their willingness, even eagerness to remember and the richness of their
reminiscences, this history could not have been written, and it is through
their voices that the story of the Ark and UGMAA unfolds. They are invaluable as sources of information for much of the history, but they are more. In

their language and phrasing, their ideas and hopes, and in their emotion is also contained much of the explanation of that history.

Consequently, rather than relying mainly on my summaries, I have elected, as much as possible, to present their words in the belief that the closer the reader can get to the individuals involved, the more clarity and insight will follow. Secondhand iterations, no matter how competent and empathetic, must always diminish; they are not the ground itself. The story of the Arkestra is one of hundreds of individuals gathering around, supporting, and living a vision of the arts in their community, each story unique and part of this larger picture. Many did not achieve renown outside of their areas and were just recognizable to their neighbors as part of the band—musicians, poets, dancers, visual artists, or archivists—as they went about their daily lives on the streets of South Central Los Angeles.

Those involved never doubted the validity and the historical importance of their movement. They worked to preserve it and we are richer for it, though there have been the usual quotient of disasters. For many years, Linda Hill, one of the originators of the movement, kept extensive, handwritten journals of concerts—including personnel and pieces performed—anecdotes, and random stories of the people and events in and around the Arkestra. Sadly, all of these were lost, consigned to the garbage bin in the 1980s by her estranged husband.

Fortunately, over the years Ark members assiduously preserved musical compositions and taped performances and rehearsals. The Horace Tapscott Archive, now in the care of UCLA's Performing Arts Special Collections, contains more than seven hundred tapes dating to 1960, and, in whole or part, sheet music for hundreds of compositions, most original. It is a valuable musicological documentation of a grassroots movement and a monument to the hundreds of artists who contributed their artistry to their community. Combined with my interviews and a few boxes of ephemera and paperwork in the Archive, this constitutes the sum of available source material on the Pan Afrikan Peoples Arkestra.

Originally conceived as the history of a musical aggregation, this project has expanded considerably beyond its initial scope to include aspects of both West African and African American cultures in the United States, as well as the history of the community and the city of Los Angeles. As I learned from Horace and my many interviewees/teachers, the story of the Arkestra, its ethos and aesthetic, can only be fully understood when set against patterns of West African cultures and African American cultural history, which shaped their enterprise, and in the history of a community and its social and arts movements, from the culturally expansive days of Central Avenue to the more recent devastations of parts of South Central Los Angeles.

More particularly, it quickly became apparent that the arts movement, especially after the Watts upheaval of 1965 and the subsequent cultural resurgence, was not only multifaceted but that many of the component parts were inextricably connected. The story of the Arkestra, though possessing its own trajectory and integrity, branched into many other areas and organizations. Consequently, other stories, groups, and individuals are also presented as part of the social and cultural fabric. Even so, given the treelike nature of this movement—in terms of the organizations, geographic spread, and sheer number of individuals involved—I have only explored those branches that bear directly on the history of the Arkestra. A more thorough consideration of this movement as a whole must await another book, if one volume could do it justice. Such is the scope and the depth of the commitment of the community artists of South Central Los Angeles.

Note on Documentation

Interviews conducted as part of my personal research for this book are not individually noted in the text. Readers are directed to the first section of the bibliography, titled "Interviews Conducted for This Book," for a listing of those sources. All other material, including additional interviews, are documented in endnotes.

ACKNOWLEDGMENTS

When performing within his South Central Los Angeles community, Horace Tapscott would occasionally forego introducing a particular composition by title and simply announce to the audience, "This is one more you wrote through us." I offer this book as one written through me by dozens of artists and supporters of the Pan Afrikan Peoples Arkestra and UGMAA. Approximately one hundred members generously spent hours with me telling their story of this history. To them, my profound thanks. I stand in awe not only of their accomplishments but also of the fire that still burns, fueled by passions and values of the noblest kind.

Undoubtedly, I have missed many others and to them I can only offer my sincerest apologies. I have tried to discover and contact as many people as I've learned of, but I also realize the difficulty, if not impossibility, of trying to locate everyone involved in a movement of this magnitude over a forty-year period. I only hope that they see in this history an accurate reflection of what they experienced.

This project could not have been carried out without the support of Horace Tapscott and his family. Horace set the research in motion and since his passing the family has been an essential support in bringing this work to a conclusion. Cecilia Tapscott, Michael Dett Wilcots, Renée Tapscott Wilcots, and Raisha Wilcots not only embraced this project, providing guidance and support at every stage, but insisted, without reservation, that I tell the story as I found it. They also welcomed my partner Jeannette Lindsay and me into their family, an honor we shall always cherish.

The first time I saw Roberto Miranda he was on a bandstand with Horace. Witnessing the two of them in full cry was an experience I'll never forget, one that altered my understanding of and reinforced my awe for this music when it achieves such a level of consummate artistry. My lengthy interview with Roberto was key in understanding much of this history. His willingness to then write an analysis of the music of the Arkestra and Horace in an appendix was an added bonus. To you, my brother, a thousand thanks.

I am indebted to the corps of readers, who spent time on various drafts and who will recognize their handprints throughout this text. This project benefited enormously from their knowledge and willingness to assist in my journey through this history. For their time and effort, I thank Chris Abani, Fuasi Abdul-Khaliq, Adam Bush, Kamau Daáood, Larry Dilg, Ron Gottesman, Robin D. G. Kelley, Steven McCall, Mimi Melnick, Roberto Miranda, Cecilia Tapscott, Michael Dett Wilcots, Renée Tapscott Wilcots, and three anonymous readers. The research assistance of my former student Adam Bush was an important support. Mimi Melnick contributed the index to the first edition, a Herculean effort, while I modified it for this edition. Errors and omissions are solely mine.

I have also benefited from the willingness of a few vital community institutions and individuals to share their resources. Mark Greenfield and Muffet at the Watts Towers Arts Center, and Sarah Cooper, director of the Southern California Library for Social Studies and Research, for making their archives available to me and for providing generous assistance. Harold Hambrick, director of the Mafundi Institute, provided me with documentation on the early years of the Mafundi. Steve Buchanan, formerly a program host with radio station KCRW in Santa Monica, generously provided me with a copy of his interview with Arkestra member Adele Sebastian. George Lipsitz kindly supplied a copy of his revised paper on the Black Artists Group of St. Louis.

For permission to use photographs, I am grateful to the Tapscott family, particularly to Michael Dett Wilcots for making many of his available, and to Larry Clark, Kamau Daáood, Marla Gibbs, Patricia E. Hill, Tamar Lando, Otis O'Solomon, Mark Weber, Michele Welsing of the Southern California Library for Social Studies and Research, and Jared Zagha.

My fourteen-year association with the UCLA Oral History Program (now the Center for Oral History Research) from 1989 to 2003 yielded forty-seven life-history interviews documenting Los Angeles's African American community through its secular music history. Organized into two projects, "Central Avenue Sounds" and "Beyond Central," they have been an important aspect of my continuing education on this vibrant community and have been essential in writing this book. My thanks to former director, Dale Treleven, my mentor of many years, who first shaped these projects with me in 1989;

to former administrator Alva Moore Stevenson, an advisor, colleague, supporter, and friend since the day I first walked into the Program; to former director Teresa Barnett, and editor Alex Cline. My thanks to the Center for Oral History Research, Charles E. Young Research Library, UCLA, for support throughout.

The Horace Tapscott Archive is now securely ensconced in the Performing Arts Special Collections at UCLA. Due to the original efforts of Music Librarians Gordon Theil, Stephen Davison, and Tim Edwards, the collection was preserved and made available to researchers. I am grateful to them for their awareness of the importance of this material, providing such an exceptional home for the Archive, and also for their readiness to pack their already overworked schedules with my requests for digital transfers of old reel-to-reel tapes.

The completion of the first edition of this book was invaluably assisted by a year's fellowship from the National Endowment for the Humanities in 2003–4, which enabled me to take a one-year sabbatical leave from my teaching responsibilities. Any views, findings, conclusions, or recommendations expressed in *The Dark Tree* do not necessarily reflect those of the National Endowment for the Humanities.

It was a very pleasant surprise when Ken Wissoker of Duke University Press expressed immediate enthusiasm at the prospect of publishing a second edition of *The Dark Tree*. Ken had signed Horace Tapscott's autobiography, *Songs of the Unsung*, to Duke over twenty years ago and our work together was a completely satisfying experience. To collaborate again with him and the excellent staff at Duke couldn't have been more professional and satisfying. Thanks to Ken, Ryan Kendall, Kate Mullen, Jessica Ryan, and Courtney Leigh Richardson.

Finally, my soulmate, Jeannette Lindsay, has lived with this project since its inception and contributed to it in ways numerous and varied. She filmed my first dozen interviews, worked on the photographs, critically read every draft, immeasurably improving each, and even suggested the title. As I worked on the first edition of this book, she was steadfastly engaged in her documentary film project of the African American community arts scene. The feature-length *Leimert Park: the Story of a Village in South Central Los Angeles* was released on DVD in 2008 and is an invaluable visual preservation of a vital community movement. In preparing this revised edition she has been, again, an essential advisor and editor, despite being immersed in writing her L.A. mystery trilogy, partially set in Leimert Park. She has always been an inspiration—*a Jeannette, due cuori battendo all'unisono.*

ANCESTRAL ECHOES

Roots of the African American Community Artist

I've known rivers:
I've known rivers ancient as the world and older than the
flow of human blood in human veins.

LANGSTON HUGHES

Early one morning, not very long into 1961, Horace Tapscott, a twenty-six-year-old trombonist, pianist, and arranger with Lionel Hampton's orchestra, took his seat on the band bus as Hamp's troupe was preparing to leave Hollywood on a grueling journey of cross-country performances. It was a routine the promising young musician had come to know well over the past two years with Hamp's band, but this morning was different. A growing disillusionment with the state of black music, the lack of respect accorded it by a commerce-oriented society, and the continuing exploitation of artists and art had led to his questioning the purpose of the music and his position within it. No sooner had he boarded the bus that morning than he re-emerged, waved goodbye to a bandmate declaring, "This is it, brother. I've had it," and walked home to his family in South Central Los Angeles, jobless but with a new artistic purpose forming in his mind.[1]

His decision was an ending, but also a beginning, a rejection of one set of values and the embracing of another, a turn to African American and African tradition, and an act of rebellion against a music business dominated by commercial concerns. The commercial dictates and pressures, which increasingly shaped the content and direction of the music and under which musicians struggled to survive, were opposed to his conception of the music, the reasons and conditions for its creation, its artistic and social purpose. Creative authenticity, an essential artistic value to Horace, meant following one's own vision and not the dictates of industry executives and the fluctuating marketplace. Also, the time and travel demands placed upon a professional musician, especially one in a high profile big band, forced a choice between that life and parenting. By August 1961 he was the father of five young children. Horace's presence at home was much needed and he committed himself to it.

Horace had been confronted with the injustices of racism and exploitation at an early age while growing up in the black areas of Houston and Los Angeles in the 1930s and 1940s. But he had also experienced the nurturing social and cultural centers of those communities, which drew from a heritage that reached back through the slave era to West and West Central Africa, where the arts and the importance of communal life shaped the individual and the artist. By the end of 1961 and with the support of his family, Horace resolved to remain within South Central Los Angeles to develop his music and to foster the arts and artists within his community, believing that this would raise the quality of life for his family and his people. No longer the itinerant artist, he started gathering musicians for a band and organization that would evolve over the years, through a number of incarnations, ultimately becoming by the early 1970s the Pan Afrikan Peoples Arkestra (PAPA) and the Union of God's Musicians and Artists Ascension (UGMAA). For Horace it represented a return home and to the more communal past, as well as the embracing of a vision of an alternative homeland in the future.

A forerunner of the movements of the late 1960s and early 1970s and in many ways a unique cultural organization, the Arkestra became part of a larger pattern of cultural groups that flourished in the heated political atmosphere of those times. Accompanying this period of political activism was a search for communal values, goals, and organizations, which many African Americans deemed necessary and yet missing, to some extent, from their lives by the 1960s in allegedly post-segregation America. In part, this was typical of any people's desire to understand and assimilate their past, but it was also a reflection of continued economic exploitation and their denial of full integration into American society.

While the passage of the Civil Rights Act of 1964 and the Voting Rights Act of 1965 seemed the successful culmination of a political process that began with the Supreme Court's unanimous 1954 decision on *Brown v. The Board of Education* and the Montgomery Bus Boycott of 1955, the manifest failure of the civil rights movement to change the severely unequal social and economic status quo of capitalist America fueled a confrontational stance within most African American communities and a search in African American and African history not just for their past, but for alternatives to the exploitation and self-aggrandizing commercialism of the United States.

What political equality had been realized through the civil rights movement did not foster tolerance, understanding, and sharing among the cultures but rather the dissolution of black culture into white America. Upon leaving segregated schools that featured some exposure to their culture and history, African American children found the new integrated environs devoid of any consideration of their past, while for those who had always attended integrated schools, there was a lack of historical awareness.[2] Segregated black schools had had severely inadequate resources, but they had also been populated by African American teachers, who were somewhat at liberty to determine many aspects of the school environment and curriculum.[3] Horace Tapscott recalls the Frederick Douglass Elementary School he attended in Houston's segregated Third Ward:

> They taught us about Frederick Douglass and Countee Cullen, and other black writers, the educators of our race. As you walked down the hallway at school, you'd see these big pictures of Frederick Douglass, Booker T. Washington, Harriet Tubman, all these black people. And we just accepted it. That was the way it was supposed to be, and it was just natural to us. It was only later on, when I went to the integrated schools in California, that black people disappeared from the history being taught.[4]

Horace's autobiography does not simply offer fond memories of early local influences, but he begins his story by describing the community into which he was born. The social involvement of his pastor and church, the close interactions of family, neighbors and friends, the steadfast support for and role of music and artists, the strength of ethnic pride and historical awareness, all are among his strongest memories and, indeed, he uses them to explain his own development. For many artists the recent, odious period of de jure segregation also offered an important example of the benefits of a community focus.

By the early 1960s, Horace and other artists concluded that an alternative value system and aesthetic that drew from the most positive aspects of their past history and addressed contemporary needs were necessary. They sought inspiration in the wisdom of shared historical experiences, which ranged from traditional West and West Central African cultures, through the social bonding required to survive the depredations of slavery, to communal values developed during the period of de jure racial segregation. The roots of "The Dark Tree" run deep.

Communal Arts and Artists in West and West Central African Traditions

In the ancient kingdoms of Western Africa, it was common practice for disputants or their intermediaries to clearly and cleverly state in sophisticated word play their claims to each other before engaging in warfare. In the thirteenth century, before the climactic battle that determined who was to be ruler of the kingdom of Mali, the usurper king, Soumaoro, and Sundiata, the rightful heir, confronted each other with their claims to the kingdom:

> "I am coming back, Soumaoro, to recapture my kingdom. If you want peace you will make amends to my allies and return to Sosso where you are the king."
>
> "I am king of Mali by force of arms. My rights have been established by conquest."
>
> "Then I will take Mali from you by force of arms and chase you from my kingdom."
>
> "Know, then, that I am the wild yam of the rocks; nothing will make me leave Mali."
>
> "Know, also that I have in my camp seven master smiths who will shatter the rocks. Then, yam, I will eat you."
>
> "I am the poisonous mushroom that makes the fearless vomit."
>
> "As for me, I am the ravenous cock, the poison does not matter to me."
>
> "Behave yourself, little boy, or you will burn your foot, for I am the red-hot cinder."
>
> "But me, I am the rain that extinguishes the cinder; I am the boisterous torrent that will carry you off."[5]

Many participants, observers, and historians recognize the roots of rap in the African American tradition of oral jousting, manifest in such games as "the dozens." It is not difficult to discover the antecedents of those verbal contests in various West African rituals, such as Sundiata's confrontation with Soumaoro or in the traditional songs of recrimination.[6]

From its inception the movement initiated by Horace Tapscott and his colleagues also drew heavily from and was inspired by communal aspects of traditional West and West Central African cultures. Some of this was the result of formal studies, particularly among the generation that would emerge in the late 1960s, but just as often, particularly in the organization's early years, it was as much a result of members sharing family traditions and oral histories. While it is not possible to trace the specific origins of much of the Arkestra's ethos and aesthetic, it is possible to identify aspects of West and West Central African cultures that were incorporated into their worldview and artistic practice or at least served as a validation of their methods and objectives. They perceived West African art as both an integral part of social life and an outlet for individual creative expression.[7]

In traditional West and West Central African societies, the arts were integral to communal rituals. To the Akan-speaking peoples of Ghana, according to J. H. Kwabena Nketia, "The enjoyment or satisfaction which a social occasion gives to the participants is directly related to its artistic content—to the scope it gives for the sharing of artistic experience through the display of art objects, the performance of music, dancing, or the recital of poetry."[8] In his study of the Fang people of Gabon, James Fernandez observes art to be essential to political rule: "Among the highly egalitarian politically unstructured Fang it is impossible to impose order without art. The leader had to be proficient in expressing himself artistically, creating thereby a moving aesthetic spectacle."[9] To the Yoruba, art connected them to spiritual forces and validated religious ceremonies. "Art's presence and visual power," write Henry Drewal, John Pemberton, and Rowland Abiodun, "therefore help to make an altar or ritual efficacious. It literally and figuratively shapes religious thoughts and practice."[10] Although there was a rich social and cultural diversity among the many peoples of West and West Central Africa, art was an essential part of communal experiences that served to express, validate, and preserve worldviews.[11]

Among the various art forms, music was present at virtually every community event. Laure Meyer explains, "Most traditional African religious rituals involved music, chants and masked dances. Village life without such events is inconceivable."[12] Indeed, the hundreds of deities in the Yoruba religion each had its own musical expression through percussion instruments, dances, and songs.[13] Every event in Ashanti society involved the participation of drum choirs.[14] Among the Igbo, write Herbert Cole and Chike Aniakor, all festivals "involve music and dancing. Drumming and other musical forms marshal participants, set the mood, and provide dramatic focus for rituals, processions, wrestling matches, masquerades, and all other special features."[15]

Not only were the arts central, but in one form or another were all-inclusive. Frequently, communal gatherings, especially festivals, dissolved the distinction between artist and observer, between participants and audience, involving and empowering everyone. Musicologist Fred Warren observes, "The solo singer draws a spontaneous reaction of singing, handclapping, and dancing from those who stand nearby. Everyone takes part in what is going on."[16] Whether through dress, masking, dances, preparing foods, or any of the wide variety of activities that became this expression of national life, everyone created.[17]

To ensure social continuity, artists and musicians took seriously the responsibility of passing along their knowledge and skills to the next generation. This was accomplished primarily through the craft and family structures and through participation in the communal process, involving absorption, adaptation, and imitation. In Hausa society instruction involved a student watching an instructor, usually an older family member, perform, and then trying to imitate what the elder had done.[18] In Akan society, Nketia observes,

> As far as it is known, the principle of musical education has always been that of slow absorption through exposure to musical situations and active participation, rather than formal teaching. The very organization of traditional music in social life enables the individual to acquire his musical knowledge in slow stages, to widen his experience of the music of his culture through the social groups in which he is progressively incorporated and the activities in which he takes part.[19]

This invariably meant a wide range of ability within various musical associations, which was expected, and the most talented members took the lead. Through this interaction of young and old, inexperienced and talented, the musical tradition was nurtured and passed along, an approach that was to be an essential element of Arkestra pedagogy in Los Angeles.

In many West African societies, among the most significant guilds of artists were the griots and griottes or djelis, those most responsible for maintaining the history of their people. In Djeli Mamoudou Kouyate's telling of the epic of Sundiata, the great king is reliant upon and served by his griot, Balla Fasseke. When Sundiata's father bestows the griot upon his son, he tells the young prince, "Be inseparable friends from this day forward. From his mouth you will hear the history of your ancestors, you will learn the art of governing Mali according to the principles which our ancestors have bequeathed to us."[20] Balla Fasseke soon reveals other talents, such as his skills as a singer and as a balafon player, which assist Sundiata in reclaiming his kingdom from the sorcerer Soumaoro.

The griot was a pervasive figure with as many different incarnations as there were cultures embracing him or her. From the most important political figure next to the king, to a singer of praise songs for hire, the griot's role and status varied from nation to nation and over time. In his study of griots, Thomas Hale lists their tasks as genealogist, historian, adviser, spokesperson, diplomat, mediator, interpreter and translator, musician, composer, teacher, exhorter, warrior, witness, praise-singer, and ceremony participant.[21] Nevertheless, the common denominator, according to Hale, was verbal art, spoken and sung, captured in such synonyms as *"bard, wordsmith,* and *artisan of the word."*[22]

Given the centrality of the arts in the life of a nation, artists may be seen as essential to the cohesion of a community, most importantly in the interplay between the individual artist and his or her society, and the consequent demands placed upon an artist's creative capacity to interpret a complex and changing world. According to Nigerian scholar Wande Abimbola, "The artist is, therefore, historian, critic, messenger, and even at times, prophet. The artist seeks to understand and record the world in which we live. Hence, the artist is indispensable in our own efforts to know ourselves and our culture. He enables us to sense and respond to the multiple rhythms that shape our lives."[23]

Artists worked within the value structure of their people, but were also expected to produce a creation that was their expression of those values in the context of a changing world. Among the Yoruba this sense of change was captured in their description of their culture as "a river that is never at rest."[24] Similarly, among the Igbo the world was seen as always in motion with powerful forces and gods rising and falling, appearing and disappearing.[25] Artists were expected to respond to new developments in their world and, thereby, help their people understand and assimilate these changes. In their study of Yoruba art, Drewal, Pemberton, and Abiodun conclude, "Hence, ritual art both shapes and is shaped by the imagination of the artist who seeks to reveal the interrelatedness of the divine and the human through sculpted image, song and dance."[26]

Creativity in individual expression was, therefore, essential and the mere repetition of previous work not acceptable, since it would not be responsive to new developments. After the conclusion of Igbo festivals, the artistic products were relegated to the past, but the process kept. "When the product is preserved or venerated," explains Chinua Achebe, "the impulse to repeat the process is compromised. Therefore the Igbo choose to eliminate the product and retain the process so that every occasion and every generation will receive its own impulse and experience of creation."[27] At their creative best artists were not simply craftsmen, who skillfully, if not imaginatively, fit an unwavering form to timeless function. There was a dialectic of preservation and transformation, of reaffirmation and re-evaluation, as individual artists, shaped by their nations and reacting to changes around them, in turn gave shape to the world in which they lived.

West and West Central African art is creative, nuanced, complex, and diverse. Though the names of most traditional artists are unknown, much of the history of this art is stamped by individuality. Among the Hausa, the more artistically inclined, improvising musicians, according to David Ames, "are conscious of, and proud of their originality and inventiveness, and their virtuosity is recognized and rewarded."[28] In her careful study of the royal arts of West and West Central Africa, Suzanne Preston Blier argues, "Royal power bound up with artistic innovation was a particularly prevalent feature of various African kingships."[29] The exceptional creativity of much West and West Central African art is even evident from the earliest examples we possess, that is, the stunning Nok terra-cotta statuary from Nigeria, dating as far back as 1000 BCE.[30]

For many African American artists in search of an alternative during the 1960s, their focal point became the role of the arts and artists in West African societies, and, most particularly, that of the griot. Through their studies of African cultural history, some members of the Pan Afrikan Peoples Arkestra embraced these aspects of West African cultures, from the more general understanding of the relation between art and society, to the role of the griot and the specifics of mentoring the next generation. To other members, lacking a formal background in African studies, these ideas resonated with the communal traditions they had acquired within their families and growing up in America's segregated communities. From these diverse sources, the members would then shape their approach to the music, organization, and community.

Communal Aspects of African American Culture in Slavery and Segregation

When a distinct African American culture began emerging during the eighteenth century, it drew upon an extensive and diverse heritage of African cultural tradition, and evolved its own communal values and practices. Fostered by the social needs of different peoples thrown together and also by the grouping of ethnically similar slaves, as well as expanding kinship groups, crossing plantations and generations, this culture grew.[31] According to Lawrence Levine, "The slaves' expressive arts and sacred beliefs were more than merely a series of outlets or strategies; they were instruments of life, of sanity, of health, and of self-respect. Slave music, slave religion, slave folk beliefs—the entire sacred world of the black slaves—created the necessary space between the slaves and their owners and were the means of preventing legal slavery from becoming spiritual slavery."[32]

The prohibitions against literacy among the slave population forced a reliance on African-derived oral tradition that was manifest not only in their religious practice and preaching but also in everyday gatherings and in the thousands of tales, aphorisms and jokes which were created and passed on throughout the slave world. Horace Tapscott's mother, Mary Lou Malone, was not only a devoted parent and pianist of some renown on the East Texas chitlin' circuit, she was also an important link in a chain of family oral history. To her daughter, Robbie Tapscott Byrd, she passed on the ability to speak "tut," a language formed generations earlier in the South. According to Robbie, it is "a patois that evolved among the slaves, when they didn't want the masters to know what they were talking about." A skill passed only through female members of the family, Mary Lou had learned it from her mother, Pearlina, who had been tutored by Robbie's great grandmother, Amanda, an enslaved African American.

Arriving without cultural artifacts, these enslaved Africans recreated some of their own. These included a variety of instruments to accompany vocalizing, which was the primary means of achieving artistic expression, with storytelling, dance and music the dominant forms. As in West Africa, these were all communal arts. The roles of a griot were circumscribed to that of song leader, storyteller, preacher/exhorter, diviner/conjurer, or simply an elder or council of elders, who settled disputes and passed along historical and/or genealogical information. As such the griot continued to be the preserver of a people's history and, perhaps, its conscience through the few limited forms available.[33]

In the most immediate sense, those with musical abilities were at one with their fellow slaves in the daily routine of their lives, contributing their cries and songs to a common task, at times easing the burden, at times giving voice to a range of emotions, reflecting back to the others their condition and that of the world around them. According to Eileen Southern, "Slaves recorded the circumstances of their daily lives in song just as assuredly as if they had kept diaries or written biographies."[34] Music, according to Levine, was "created or constantly recreated through a communal process."[35] It was also a medium uniting people. In his study of the Igbo basis of slave life in Virginia, Douglas Chambers writes, "The Quarter of the slaves was also the scene or stage of collective performance. This is where African and Afro-Virginian slaves sang and danced and where they held their 'frolics' and 'plays.'"[36] In areas where the ethnic diversity of slaves was greater, Peter Wood argues that music was their initial point of reference: "Recognizable African harmonies, intonations, and rhythms sounded familiar to strangers from different regions who could not converse with one another. This shared musical background drew together people who still spoke different languages."[37]

It was in performance that the communal aspect was most manifest. Southern writes, "The single most important element of the slave music was its performance as, indeed, is true of black folk music in the twentieth century. It was the performance that shaped the song into an entity that finally determined its melody, texture, tempo, rhythmical patterns, text, and effect upon listeners."[38] Performances were as multi-dimensional as circumstances allowed, involving music, dance, storytelling, and the participation of everyone there.[39] The line separating audience and performers was absorbed into the communal aspect of the performance. In slave-era storytelling, Levine notes, "through the entire performance the audience would comment, correct, laugh, respond, making the folktale as much of a communal experience as the spiritual or the sermon."[40]

The end of slavery inaugurated a period of social construction, as black schools, churches, and various social organizations emerged to replace community life in slave areas, which held ninety percent of the African American population. Before emancipation, free African Americans in northern and a few southern cities had already organized fraternal organizations and benevolent societies, which continued on a massive scale after emancipation within African American areas, along with newer organizations such as black women's clubs.[41] The churches, in particular, came to represent and house much of community life, from its spiritual core to everyday needs. W. E. B. Du Bois wrote at the turn of the twentieth century, "The Negro church of to-day is the social centre of Negro life in the United States, and the most characteristic expression of African character."[42] More particularly, Noralee Frankel explains, "Services sometimes lasted two hours, during which ministers read letters from former slaves wanting to know about family members separated during slavery. Church buildings also provided school classrooms and places for meetings and lectures."[43]

Emancipation opened lives to a fuller participation in the rapidly developing capitalist economy and to more diverse and idiosyncratic experiences, such as travel and exploration, which were reflected in the wider substantive content of the music. Artists took advantage of what professional opportunities there were, performing initially in minstrel shows, and then in vaudeville, theater circuits, and dance bands.[44] Although their art was suffused with African American culture, they were moving in a more professional direction that set them somewhat apart from the traditions established during slavery.

However, theirs was not the only course and there were other artists who taught and performed within their communities. Southern terms them "itinerant and community musicians," those who "provided essential music services for the newly established ex-slave communities, playing organ or piano in the churches, playing in the opera houses for musical events staged by local groups, playing in the dance halls, beer parlors, and saloons."[45] Itinerant and/or local musicians also provided ongoing commentaries on life in communities throughout the South and in practically every social setting. Drawn from musicians' lives, those were experiences that were shared broadly and understood by most African Americans, who provided an exclusive audience. As the blues spread through the South and jazz emerged from New Orleans, many seminal artists were part-time performers, who worked other jobs to survive but were essential to every local function, performing in parades, public spaces, clubs, social organizations, and thereby providing more to their communities than an occasional musical accompaniment.

Though far less encompassing than in traditional West African societies, black arts and artists played a strong role in their North American communities. The growing importance of the professional artist, seen in the prominence of the classic blues divas of the 1920s and in the separation of the jazz soloist from the ensemble beginning with Louis Armstrong later in the decade, were reflections of African Americans' increasing movement into the individualism of American capitalist society in the post–World War I era. According to Levine, "The blues were solo music not only in performance but in content. The persona of the individual performer entirely dominated the song which centered upon the singer's own feelings, experiences, fears, dreams, acquaintances, idiosyncrasies."[46]

Nevertheless, even in so individual a form as blues singing, the common bond with the audience remained. "Thus although blues songs were individual expression they were meant to be shared, they were meant to evoke experiences common to the group, they were meant to provide relief and release for all involved. And, the point is, all present *were* involved for black musical performances properly speaking had no audience, just participants."[47] Consequently, Levine concludes,

> Within all the varied components of black music and throughout all the changes it underwent, it remained a group-oriented means of communication and expression. Acculturation to the tastes and standards of the larger society was undeniably taking place but the continued existence of a flexible, creative, and distinct Afro-American expressive culture indicated that the group itself remained alive, creative, and distinctive.[48]

Even those artists who pursued a more commercial path remained bound to their communities. Throughout the first half of the twentieth century, segregation forced all African American musicians of whatever genre preference and of whatever class into being community artists. Those few who attained national renown and toured a good part of every year spent most of their time within African American communities around the country, leaving only to play commercial gigs in white theaters and clubs. In urban areas, it was important for black musicians to gain a union card, but they were confronted by a segregated American Federation of Musicians, which maintained separate black locals in most cities.[49]

Consequently, even the most commercially successful artists remained very much a part of the larger African American community, physically, emotionally, and artistically. Whether sharing day labor in the fields, rambling from town to town, juke joint to juke joint, or traveling in buses from theater to theater, musicians carried and drew from a common reservoir of social experience and cultural attitudes. As visible members of their communities, no matter what degree of renown achieved, they provided not only inspiration and their art to the community but also everyday accessibility to the succeeding generations, those young people gathered outside the hotels, theaters, union halls, diners, and boardinghouses waiting to meet their heroes.

Post-Segregation Inequalities and Cultural Movements

By the early 1960s, Horace Tapscott and other artists concluded that an alternative value system and aesthetic that drew from the communal aspects of their history and addressed contemporary needs was necessary. As white flight led to de facto segregation, as the African American "talented tenth" left their former communities, and as those communities, overwhelmingly working class, bore the economic brunt of the downside of capitalist America, they lost much of their social cohesion and support structure. The absorption into monocultural integrated schools, the elimination of distinct black organizations across the cultural and social spectrum, and the failure to achieve meaningful social and economic equality for most of the black population left these communities with less of their cultural and spiritual cement.

The movement to eliminate segregated Locals within the American Federation of Musicians, commencing with the amalgamation of Locals 47 and 767 in Los Angeles in 1953, provided more opportunities to a few black musicians and offered expanded union benefits for all. But this movement also sacrificed the cultural and social centers that the black Locals offered without providing a replacement. The newly integrated Locals were essentially business institutions, not sociocultural gathering places occupying a central place within the community. Political integration provided greater strength for the labor movement and meant more interaction among a minority of artists, but it did not offer a significant sharing of cultural experiences. Instead, it meant further sublimation of African American history and traditions. The problem of how to defeat segregation and strengthen the labor movement, while maintaining the most beneficial aspects of community life, was never solved.[50]

Artists who then remained within their old neighborhoods were either forced there by persistent racism and economic necessity, or chose to stay closer to their roots and traditions. Some artists, such as Horace Tapscott, made the community the focus and inspiration for their work and provided the basis for the emergence of local arts organizations.

While the full flowering of the community arts movement in the 1960s would reject a commercial ethos, some of the first artistic movements in the post–World War II period were more limited, involving efforts to mitigate the exploitation of artists by controlling the conditions of artistic production and distribution within the marketplace. By the early 1950s artists were attempting to alter the circumstances under which their music appeared in recorded form. Composer/bassist/bandleader Charles Mingus and drummer Max Roach started Debut Records and Chazz-Mar Inc. publishing company in 1952 at a time when other artists were doing the same, including Dizzy Gillespie and Duke Ellington.[51] In 1955 alto saxophonist Gigi Gryce, joined by Benny Golson, formed Melotone Music to control their music, inspiring other musicians, including Horace Silver and Quincy Jones, to form publishing companies.[52]

Trumpeter Bill Dixon, organizer of the 1964 October Revolution performances in New York City, shortly thereafter organized black and white artists into the Jazz Composers Guild, a collective organization to protect musicians and foster their music. "By now it is quite obvious that those of us whose work is not acceptable to the Establishment are not going to be financially acknowledged," Dixon argued. "As a result, it is very clear that musicians, in order to survive—create their music and maintain some semblance of sanity—will have to 'do it themselves' in the future."[53] The initial core group included Paul and Carla Bley, Burton Greene, Michael Mantler, Sun Ra, Roswell Rudd, Archie Shepp, Cecil Taylor, John Tchicai, and Jon Winter. The Guild members codified their purpose: "To establish the music to its rightful place in the society; to awaken the musical conscience of the masses of people to that music which is essential to their lives; to protect the musicians and composers from the existing forces of exploitation; to provide an opportunity for the audience to hear the music; to provide facilities for the proper creation, rehearsal, performance, and dissemination of the music."[54] The Guild was short-lived, rent by internal dissension over such problems as gender issues and members pursuing individual recording contracts, but provided an important multiracial example of artists attempting to control the conditions and circumstances in which they work.[55]

By the early 1960s organizations were emerging that not only tried to control the conditions of employment and recorded output, but more importantly were offering artistic alternatives to the commercial marketplace and to some extent the Western aesthetic. By refocusing their art and lives within their communities via collective bands, orchestras, associations, and non-profit organizations, and by drawing upon the rich artistic and communal heritage of African American, West African, and to some extent avant-garde Western musical culture, they sought to achieve a range of goals, from supporting their artistic integrity and creating performance spaces, to participating in the preservation and betterment of their culture and communities.

Sun Ra, who formed his Arkestra in Chicago in the mid-1950s, was the first to establish an organization considerably outside the Western mainstream.[56] The focus of the organization was Sun Ra's conception of music and his elaborate worldview, which included an early appreciation of North African influence in the beginnings of Western civilization, ancient Egyptian metaphysics, and of the place of humans throughout the galaxy.[57] According to David Such, "Sun Ra is the first musician to fuse a spiritual awareness with his worldview and style of musical performance. . . . The underlying theme in Sun Ra's metaphysics is the exploration of the cosmos through the mediums of music, the imagination, or other means; for instance, Sun Ra claims to practice astral projection."[58]

Ultimately, the goal was achieving spiritual freedom. Progressive music, he felt, was "supposed to stimulate people to think of themselves as modern freemen."[59] To achieve this end, Sun Ra insisted on an iron discipline from those around him. "When the army wants to build men they isolate them," according to Sun Ra. "It's just the case that these are musicians, but you might say they're marines."[60] Those who lived with Sun Ra did so in communal fashion and had to scrupulously abide by his ban on women, drugs, and alcohol. In return the members of the Arkestra participated in an intense experience that stretched the boundaries of twentieth-century music, a veritable academy of the avant-garde, yet steeped in the history of black music as well.[61]

While Sun Ra's Arkestra revolved around one individual's music and philosophy, it was also an important participant in the community arts movements, offering a dramatic example of artistic control through the musical integrity his Arkestra maintained—not least through their record label, Saturn—as well as through a unified conception of the arts. Arkestra performances were usually multimedia affairs, involving costuming, dance, image projections, chants, and spoken word. During the 1960s, while in residence in New York, Ra participated in the Jazz Composers Guild and the Arkestra was an important musical component of Amiri Baraka's black arts movement in Harlem.[62] After the band relocated to the Germantown section of Philadelphia in the fall of 1968, some of the Arkestra members opened a small grocery store—the Pharaoh's Den—to service the needs of that community.[63] However, this was never the band's focus, which remained a vehicle for one man's worldview.

A more community-oriented organization was the Association for the Advancement of Creative Musicians (AACM), formed in Chicago in 1965 as a music cooperative under the guidance of pianist Muhal Richard Abrams, with a core group of outstanding young musicians to nurture the black arts and artists within the South Side community. They sought to improve job prospects, offer performances within the community, and provide an opportunity for music education and a space in which artists would be free to fully develop and express their creativity. Rules of etiquette were formulated and a manifesto issued, which also stressed individual development: "Superimposed over our training framework is our keen desire to develop within our students the ability to value *self*, the ability to value *others* and the ability to utilise the opportunities they find in society. It is felt that such values should be based on the cultural and spiritual heritage of the people involved."[64] The connection to past culture was an important element. According to musicologist Ronald Radano,

An African-inspired cultural nationalism became the official position of the AACM, whose membership—particularly those aligned with [Muhal Richard] Abrams—envisioned an immutable, pan-African musical legacy transcending cultural and historical categories. "Creative music" or, less euphemistically, as later defined by the Art Ensemble of Chicago, "Great Black Music," was a dialect of the mother tongue, a creation with African origins that had been spiritually preserved in the slave culture of the United States. Evoking images of the musician-seer of tribal Africa, many AACM musicians spoke in priestly terms of black music's spiritualism, which, they believed, revealed a kinship with the ancient myth-makers, the original cultural guardians of the black people.[65]

In 1967 they started a school, and, according to John Litweiler, "invited all, especially young, black, inner city students, who wanted to learn music to attend."[66] Providing regular instruction and at times instruments without charge to students in need, the AACM not only has produced a number of important bands, including Air, the Roscoe Mitchell Quartet, the Art Ensemble of Chicago, and the Braxton-Jenkins-Smith Trio, but has trained hundreds of musicians. The school continues to this day, led by the AACM's next generation of artists.[67]

During the following decade other AACM-inspired organizations formed. Roscoe Mitchell founded the Creative Arts Collective of Detroit in 1976. In New Haven, a group coalesced around Fred Anderson, Anthony Davis, George Lewis, and Leo Smith. Perhaps the most important was the St. Louis-based Black Artists Group (BAG) formed in 1968 and including musicians Hamiet Bluiett, Julius Hemphill, Oliver Lake, and Bakaida Carroll, as well as artists working in other media. According to historian George Lipsitz, "BAG brought together musicians, dancers, poets, actors, and visual artists for mixed media performances in unlikely spaces—ranging from housing project multi-purpose rooms to school classrooms, from private lofts to public auditoriums."[68] In so rooting their creative expressions within the community, they were offering an alternative conception of art, drawing on their communal needs as well as on a tradition that stressed the interrelatedness of the various arts and of the use of public and local spaces. BAG's tenure was all too brief, lasting only until 1972 before succumbing, according to Lipsitz, "to inadequate funding, internal dissension, and external opposition."[69]

In New York City, the Jazzmobile, beginning in Harlem in 1964 under the impetus of pianist Billy Taylor, brought the music to the streets via musicians performing on flatbed trucks. With government and corporate sponsorship it developed a year-round performance schedule for people in black and Latino areas of the city and offered music classes in various schools as well.[70] A more ambitious organization, the Collective Black Artists (CBA), was founded by Reggie Workman in 1970. According to historian Eric Porter, "The group operated for several years as a collectively run clearinghouse for support services for musicians, as a vehicle for artists' activism, and as a locus for the production of socially relevant music."[71]

Finally, Tribe, a Detroit collective formed by Phil Ranelin and Wendell Harrison, lasted from 1972 to 1977 functioning as a record label and a self-help organization for musicians. In 1974 they added a quarterly magazine, *Tribe*, to their productions, proclaiming it to be "Detroit's First Magazine for Black Awareness" in their masthead. Inspired by a very egalitarian interpretation of West African tradition, they drew a direct link to their purpose and functioning: "The Tribe is an extension of the tribes in the villages of Africa, our mother country. In Africa everyone had a talent to display. There were no superstars: just people and collectively all the people of the village played a vital role in shaping that culture."[72]

Through their recordings and publications, they sought to present issues of social importance to the African American community of Detroit, but underlying that was a felt need to preserve African American culture through self-help organization. In the liner notes to an early Tribe LP, Ranelin, who would later join Horace Tapscott and the Pan Afrikan Peoples Arkestra in Los Angeles, proclaims, "This recording itself, is part of the revolution, and the whole purpose behind this self-determination venture is survival; survival for the musician, his music, and thus, survival for you, the listeners and demanders of this creative Black Art form that has been labeled 'Jazz.'"[73]

Among the most important of the community arts organizations was the movement begun by Horace Tapscott in 1961. Probably the least known outside of the black community of Los Angeles, more than any other organization it offered the fullest expression of an alternative art. In 1985 saxophonist/composer Anthony Braxton, one of the AACM's luminaries, wrote, "It is clear however that when the proper documentation arrives it will focus on the work of musicians like Horace Tapscott, whose dynamic activity has shaped a whole region of alternative functionalism."[74] That documentation started arriving with the publication of Horace's autobiography in 2001. It shows that his notion of the community artist and the role of arts within the community evolved from his early life experience in segregated African American communities, from the music that surrounded him, and the stories that passed through his family, friends, elders, and teachers in his neighborhoods. From those sources he forged an alternative ethos and aesthetic, forward-looking within the Western world yet also strikingly West African in many respects, which would situate the arts at the center of community development and inspire hundreds of artists to create a remarkable cultural process and body of work. The story continues, therefore, not with the organization's beginnings in 1961, nor with Horace Tapscott, but rather with the community that shaped him and his fellow artists, the Central Avenue scene in Los Angeles during the first half of the twentieth century.

BALLAD FOR SAMUEL

The Legacy of Central Avenue and the 1950s
Avant-Garde in Los Angeles

Hand me Down
my Silver Trumpet

ARNA BONTEMPS

After visiting Los Angeles in 1913, W. E. B. Du Bois wrote, "Nowhere in the United States is the Negro so well and beautifully housed, nor the average efficiency and intelligence in the colored population so high."[1] It was an opinion widely shared. Lured by an expanding economy and the prospect of jobs, the relatively low cost of real estate, a mild climate, and a seemingly less overt racism, African Americans began moving to Los Angeles in large numbers after 1900. For the next forty years their numbers doubled every decade and by 1940 represented slightly more than 4 percent of the total population. Part of a general population growth in southern California, they came primarily from the South and the Southwest. Texas, Arkansas, and Louisiana were important departure points and Creoles were an important part of the populace, their many organizations occupying a prominent place in the area's social life.

A segregated African American community was also an early twentieth-century creation, the result of a rising tide of racism, legally maintained until the late 1940s through racially restrictive housing covenants in property deeds. An oppressive political establishment, hostile Los Angeles Police Department, separatist social structure, and racist organizations, such as the Ku Klux Klan, all contributed to the grotesquely unjust social order, which forced most African Americans to live around Central Avenue.

Arkestra bassist Roberto Miranda is fond of quoting pianist McCoy Tyner's observation that "pressure creates diamonds." The history of Central Avenue would seem to bear that out. Because of segregation, the community was forced to discover its own resources and resolve, and despite the hardships and indignities, it responded with a vibrant social and cultural scene that would contribute substantially to shaping twentieth-century American culture, nurture hundreds of artists, and encompass many different arts and styles. In its final years it offered creative soil for musical explorers and explorations that would lay the groundwork for the avant-garde of the 1950s and inspire the community arts movement from the 1960s to the present in Los Angeles.

The Community Setting and Artistic Foundation

Extending southward from the downtown area, South Central Avenue was the African American economic and social center in Los Angeles. As the population grew through the pre–World War II era, the community expanded along Central from First Street to Slauson Avenue, some four miles south—an area that came to be known as the Eastside. It then jumped some forty blocks of white housing, whose boundaries were militantly defended by the Ku Klux Klan and various ad hoc racist gangs, to the Watts area, seven miles from downtown. By 1940 approximately 70 percent of the black population was confined to the Central Avenue corridor and relied upon the Avenue to meet all of its social needs. One longtime resident reminisces, "If you wanted to meet any of the people you went to school with or had ever known, you could walk up and down Central Avenue and you would run into them." Consequently, according to another, "You didn't want to hit the Avenue with dirty shoes."[2]

Supported by the citywide electric-trolley system, the Avenue served the community's shopping and business needs; grocery stores alternated with department stores, beauty parlors, cafes, funeral houses, insurance companies, banks, restaurants, and barber shops. Yet, despite the changing demographics, many of these businesses remained white-owned. Fueling discontent was the practice of not hiring African Americans, a policy protested by the Urban League and Leon Washington, the founder and editor of the *Los Angeles Sentinel.* Early in 1934, under the slogan "Don't Spend Your Money Where You Can't Work," they organized demonstrations and protests along Central Avenue, forcing many stores to open their doors to equality in hiring.[3] Nevertheless, a significant number of black enterprises flourished, such as the Dunbar (originally the Somerville) Hotel, Golden State Mutual Life Insurance Company, the *California Eagle* and *Los Angeles Sentinel* newspapers, theaters, clubs, restaurants, and dozens of small retail stores.[4]

As the sun set, the bustle of shoppers, clerks, and businessmen was replaced by the swagger of the night crowd. Dressed in the sharpest clothes and groomed to the nines after a session with the barber or hairdresser, the denizens of the Avenue hit the streets sartorially splendiferous and prepared to participate in the night-long social and cultural scene. As reed-player and lead alto with the Count Basie Orchestra, Jackie Kelso, remembers the scene, "Suddenly, there's an aura of mysterious wonderfulness. . . . There's a new, special magic that comes, a type of paintbrush that paints all of the flaws. New glamour comes to life. It's almost as if special spirits of joy and abundance bring special gifts at night that are not available in the sunshine."[5] With a non-stop, vibrant club scene, the Avenue not only produced some of the major voices in jazz and rhythm and blues (R&B), but was the only integrated setting in Southern California during that period, as all races and classes gathered to enjoy the community's finest artists and entertainers.

As the center of a substantial black community, approximately one-third of which were homeowners, Central Avenue's music scene was not dependent upon or characterized by one particular style or by one particular generation of musicians. For the first fifty years of the twentieth century it was home to all African American styles and musicians, an omnipresent, essential part of the community, which, in turn, supported the art in myriad ways. To those visiting, it offered performance venues, continuous jam sessions, and some of the finest hotel accommodations for African Americans in the country. For those making their homes in the Eastside and Watts, support for artists, both aspiring and established, could be found in the extensive public school music programs, many talented private teachers, generations of musicians spanning the history of the music, Local 767 of the American Federation of Musicians, a plethora of local venues, social organizations and public spaces, and even a few, small, black-owned record companies.

Formal classes in music were available at all levels of the public education system. At Jefferson ("Jeff") and Jordan High Schools, the curriculum included courses in music theory, music appreciation, harmony, counterpoint, orchestra, band, and choir. One of Jefferson's music teachers, Samuel R. Browne, sought to incorporate new trends in African American music, creating a big band class. "I didn't bring jazz in; it was already there," Browne recalls. "I just met it head-on and I put my arms around it. I salvaged it and tried to make it respectable because it was here to stay. I personally had a classical background and was trained in European music. But jazz music, that's what they wanted."[6] For aspiring musicians, sixth period each day at Jeff in Bungalow 11 was Jazz Band class, which included writing, arranging, and performing, as well as occasional visits by musicians from the Avenue and renowned composers, including W. C. Handy and William Grant Still. "I invited into the classroom some famous black performers for them to hear and talk with. I brought in, for example, Jimmie Lunceford. He came over to Jefferson and took the school by storm. I had Lionel Hampton there, Nat King Cole, and others."[7] Soon the band was offering regular evening concerts. According to Browne,

> In 1951 . . . we charged as much as 75 cents for admission and the place was filled. At night! At Jefferson! In the auditorium! Those were the days of Horace Tapscott and Frank Morgan, and Gay Lacey, and those people. Dexter Gordon was there, yes. Dexter and Sonny Criss. And Cecil "Big Jay" McNeely. And Chico Hamilton, Jack Kelson, and Donald Cherry. They were all there. They were the guys I spent so much time with, you know, standing around talking and going to the Avenue, going to the sessions.[8]

Samuel Browne's hiring in 1936 broke new ground and represented the beginning of an integrated faculty in Los Angeles public secondary schools. African Americans had been hired at the elementary level but remained excluded from the high schools along the Central Avenue corridor, despite their mixed enrollments of African, Latin, Japanese, Chinese, and European Americans. The faculties were solidly white even though college-educated blacks lived in the community. None had been hired until Browne was contracted to teach music at Jefferson, his alma mater, a few blocks east of Central Avenue at Forty-first and Hooper. Years later Browne recalled in an interview with the *Los Angeles Times* that upon his hiring he was "called into the office of an assistant district superintendent who cautioned him: 'Remember,

Brownie, now that you've got the job, you're going to have to do the work of three white men.'"[9]

Samuel Browne remained at Jeff for over two decades, created a model program in jazz education, and directly and positively influenced the lives of many musicians, in and out of the classroom, who subsequently became major contributors to the art and culture. Horace Tapscott, a former student, who remained a close friend and collaborator of Browne's until the older man's death in 1991, performed and recorded some of his mentor's compositions, "Blue Essence" and "Perfumes in the Night," as well as composing a piece in his honor, "Ballad for Samuel."

Browne's perception of his job and his contribution stretched beyond the confines of the Jefferson High School Music Department. As he writes in the liner notes to *Flight 17*, the first LP record of the Pan Afrikan Peoples Arkestra, "Many celebrated musicians had their roots in our community. . . . However, if we are to realize a full return from those to follow, those whose roots are now dormant, spreading, or undiscovered, we must provide opportunities for constant economic and musical growth through mutual effort and total involvement."[10] An important element in his pedagogy was an involvement with students and their families. He not only routinely spent after-school hours with his students, but was with them in the clubs on Central and at the various sessions. "The students were about the best friends I had. Most of the faculty didn't take too kindly to me, but those kids—I lived with them. I was on Central Ave. with them half the time, at my house half the time. We'd go to clubs together, go out on gigs together, eat together."[11] He also made a point of visiting the elementary and junior high schools to meet with and encourage the younger students. Horace remembers visits and mentoring from Browne and renowned composer William Grant Still, a friend of Browne's, at rehearsals of the Lafayette Junior High School band. It was also not unusual to have Mr. Browne turn up on your doorstep. According to Horace,

> When he drove down the street, everybody would say, "Hello, Dr. Browne." He would come to certain musicians' houses to see that they were taking care of business, and was at my house and Frank Morgan's house all the time. He'd stop by all the cats' pads and he knew your family. They knew him. He knew that the family was important in inspiring the youngsters and he was making sure the foundation was being correctly set from the family on up. He was able to come in and to teach

or to inspire, just come and talk with you. He made sure he kept an eye on you and he really dug you.

"I dig you, man."

That's what he'd tell you.

"You don't understand that yet. But I dig you."[12]

From its earliest years, the community was awash in private music instruction, from institutions such as William Wilkins's Piano Academy and John Gray's Conservatory of Music, to dozens of individual teachers.[13] When the first New Orleans jazz musicians settled in the Los Angeles area before and immediately after World War I, they passed on some of their skills to local aspirants. According to former Watts resident and Harlem Renaissance writer Arna Bontemps, Jelly Roll Morton found it necessary to teach accompanying local musicians, such as Ben Albans, Jr., the new music: "Jelly patiently taught the young cornetist, as well as the other musicians he had found in the community, the style of playing he required."[14] Pianist Buster Wilson, whose family had moved to Los Angeles in 1904 when he was six, benefited directly from Morton, who "coached the young pianist."[15] Perhaps along with his other accolades, Jelly may be credited as one of, if not the first jazz teacher in Los Angeles. According to Morton scholar Phil Pastras, "It was evidently a role that Morton played with some relish. . . ."[16]

During the 1920s and 1930s there was an array of private teachers for those students interested in jazz and showing promise, as well as those professionals in need of "post-graduate" work. Willis Young, Lester and Lee's father, not only led the family band but also taught students in the community, as did Marshal Royal, Sr. and Ernest Royal, the father and uncle of alto saxophonist Marshal and trumpeter Ernie. Trombonist William Woodman, Sr., whose sons Coney, William, Jr., and Britt, formed an important pre–World War II band in Watts ("The Woodman Brothers Biggest Little Band in the World"), maintained a busy performance schedule, operated a performance space in Watts with Jelly Roll Morton, managed his sons' band, and offered instruction.

By the 1940s Alma Hightower, Lloyd Reese, and Percy McDavid had started teaching the legions of musicians who would make their names, and Samuel Browne's, legendary in the community. Alma Hightower, the aunt of early Central Avenue drummer Alton Redd, and the grandaunt of alto saxophonist and vocalist Vi Redd, taught privately for more than two decades. She also led a big band, the Melodic Dots, which rehearsed in Ross Snyder Park, a few blocks east of Central Avenue near Jefferson High School, had a few gigs, and also performed for the community in open lots along

Central Avenue. Its membership included at various times alto saxophonists Anthony Ortega and Vi Redd, trumpetiste Clora Bryant, and trombonists Melba Liston and Lester "Lately" Robertson, later to be one of the founding members of the Pan Afrikan Peoples Arkestra.[17]

Before the decade was out, reed and flute masters Buddy Collette and Bill Green had begun their teaching careers on the Avenue, which would last for the next fifty years, as well as organizing jam sessions for younger musicians at the Crystal Tea Room near Forty-eighth Street and Avalon Boulevard. With the help of a few like-minded artists, including bassist David Bryant, also to become a founding member of the Arkestra, they formed the Progressive Musicians Organization to oversee the sessions and encourage the art form among younger artists, who included saxophonists Walter Benton, Hadley Caliman, Sonny Criss, Eric Dolphy, Big Jay McNeely, Frank Morgan, and drummer Billy Higgins.[18]

Young musicians also benefited from the casual instruction and friendship of visiting artists, as well as local heroes. Forced into the confines of the Central Avenue area, African Americans of unique talents and abilities, who might otherwise have gone elsewhere, were a visible, every day presence. Young people did not have distant heroes or role models, who might appear for a gig or lecture only to disappear upon its conclusion, never to be seen again. Central's artists were accessible and could be approached daily on the streets, in the stores, or in the diners, eateries, and clubs, which allowed a great deal of contact and, therefore, a more direct influence on their lives and budding artistry. Not only were most members of the leading bands, such as Duke Ellington's, Count Basie's, and Jimmie Lunceford's, accessible, but many would befriend the kids gathered around stage entrances, the hotels, and union building. Gerald Wilson and Snooky Young from Lunceford's trumpet section might be seen relaxing in the lounge at the Dunbar. At the 54th St. Drugstore, Johnny Hodges and Harry Carney could be approached as they consumed an afternoon meal of burgers. Louis Armstrong could be hailed as he crossed Seventeenth Street on his way to the musicians union at 1710 South Central Avenue.

To meet the needs of this expanding music scene, Creole cornetist and Joe "King" Oliver's teacher in New Orleans, bandleader and recent transplant Thomas R. LeBlanc in 1919 organized the Colored Musicians Union of the Pacific Coast. In 1920 it became Local 767 of the American Federation of Musicians, serving as a meeting place, clearinghouse, and rehearsal space for African American musicians denied membership in white Local 47, housed a few miles northwest in Hollywood. A gathering place for generations of musicians, 767 also served as a social and cultural center and offered a range of activities from casual affairs to barbeques and parades that brought the varied membership and people in the community together. Clarinetist Joe Darensbourg, who moved to Los Angeles in the 1920s, recalls in his autobiography: "A nice thing about our local was the celebration we'd have every year. The bands would get on wagons or floats and parade down Central Avenue. All the good bands and musicians, they'd end up at the Musicians' Union and have a lot of drinks."[19]

Local 767 was also a favorite hangout for young, aspiring artists wanting to be a part of the scene and to meet their heroes. If the year was 1944, Gerald Wilson could be heard rehearsing his unique sounds and harmonic innovations with his new band in one of the upstairs rehearsal rooms. There was usually an open invitation to the Avenue's serious young musicians to follow the music, ask questions, and get involved. Horace Tapscott was a regular at rehearsals: "I've been looking at Duke Ellington's writing since I was thirteen. When his band rehearsed at the union, I'd walk right through the sections and look at the music, ask a question if I wanted. And they let me sit-in during the rehearsals. It was cool."[20] Friendships developed, some becoming lifelong; wisdom was imparted. In this informal manner the culture was passed along. Horace's memories are vivid: "Every black musician in the world would pass by there, slap you upside the head, and say something smart to you. . . . Me, Eric Dolphy, Don Cherry, Frank Morgan, Hadley Caliman, Leroy 'Sweet Pea' Robinson, Clyde Dunn, and the other young guys, were sitting there all the time, during all those years. . . . It was just rich, very rich."[21]

Aspiring artists also had outlets for their passions, places where they were able to express their artistry and grow. Central and its environs offered block after block of clubs as well as public spaces in which musicians could shape their own voices interacting with spirited and involved audiences. Many of the artists recollect working regularly in the clubs by their midteens. Big bands, some led by Percy McDavid, spanning the generations and including some of the finest musicians on the Avenue, performed in parks on Sunday afternoons. Among the performers were future members of the Pan Afrikan Peoples Arkestra.

Their music was the community's music, shared across generations and at the center of community life. It was neither marginalized nor underground. Playing the blues, jazz, or R&B was not an act of rebellion against staid cultural norms, as it was for young white musicians, nor was it an imported

One of Mingus's performance opportunities for his music was in a short-lived, cooperative band, The Stars of Swing, which he formed with reed and flute virtuoso Buddy Collette in the spring of 1946. It also included trombonist Britt Woodman, trumpeter John Anderson, tenor saxophonist Lucky Thompson (replaced by Teddy Edwards after their first performance), pianist Spaulding Givens (later known as Nadi Qamar), and drummer Oscar Bradley. Offering new music built on subtle dynamic shadings, melodic inventiveness, use of counterpoint, and a tight ensemble sound, the band's brief existence during a six-week stay at the Downbeat Room on Central Avenue attracted serious audiences that included Charlie Parker and a young Eric Dolphy.[39]

A few years younger than Mingus, Eric Dolphy was studying with Lloyd Reese and Buddy Collette during this period, as well as playing lead alto in Roy Porter's 17 Beboppers band. Although firmly grounded in the bop idiom, hints of Dolphy's adventurous nature were evident early on. Alto saxophonist Anthony Ortega played with Dolphy in Reese's rehearsal band and remembers Eric's "far-out" sounds, "bird calls" to some band members.[40] Legendary are the stories of Dolphy playing with birds and delving into microtonality in these trans-species collaborations.[41] Tenor saxophonist Clifford Solomon, also a member of Porter's band, recalls, "He was lead player, and he was precise, and he was good as lead player. His soloing left a lot to be desired because he was sort of disjointed. He played the same way then as he did later on in years, but later on in years what he was doing was more accepted. . . ."[42] According to Buddy Collette, "He loved the outside notes, being different, altering chords. . . . I'd give him a couple of melodies and he would alter everything. He loved it, using different notes, even with a lot of his flute stuff. He used to get some interesting density in a few things that would be far out. That's the kind of thing he liked. He wasn't just a one-three-five kind of person."[43]

Collette, not generally known as an avant-garde musician, but rather as an artist with a gift for melodic improvisation, maintained an interest in a wide range of musical innovations, from Schillinger's teachings to Arnold Schoenberg's twelve-tone system, and studied with challenging teachers, including George Trembley, one of Schoenberg's students. His 1956 debut album as a leader, *Man of Many Parts*, includes "Jungle Pipe," which he describes as "a weird one that is written in Lyle Murphy's 12-Tone System of equal intervals."[44] A few years later, at Trembley's request, he also composed a Schoenbergian twelve-tone blues, based on notes taken from "Basin Street Blues."[45]

As subsequent chapters will illustrate, one of those who best carried the communal and musical legacy of Central Avenue was Horace Tapscott, a contemporary student of Lloyd Reese with Dolphy. Horace was coming of age on Central along with Earl Anderza, Hadley Caliman, Don Cherry, Billy Higgins, Anthony Ortega, Lester Robertson, Guido Sinclair (formerly Sinclair Greenwell), and others who would subsequently live near the musical boundaries. According to Horace,

> Eric was about four years older than me, but musically we were tight. Whenever we could, we hung out with Gerald Wilson's band when they were rehearsing. Eric also had his own group by this time with Lester Robertson and a few of the cats, and I had a band, also. Eric was looking outside even then, but he wasn't the only one. Before him there was a cat named George Newman, a saxophonist, who used to be with Don Cherry a lot. He was the first cat that Mr. Browne called, "This guy's out."[46]

As these musicians evolved along their own musical paths during the 1950s and 1960s, they carried the lessons learned on the Avenue and have been virtually unanimous in crediting their teachers for their artistic integrity, growth, and, for some, commitment to their community. Two aspects of their pedagogy seem to have been especially important in supporting those with a more musically adventurous bent: an encouragement to master all the dimensions of music, while bearing in mind that it was open, continuously evolving, and a receptivity to individuality by encouraging students to find their own voice, in some cases, regardless of formal rules. Percy McDavid at Lafayette Junior High School and Samuel Browne at Jefferson High School not only instilled a strong sense of discipline and technical command, but also encouraged students to arrange and compose. Horace remembers playing an early composition, "The Golden Pearl," for McDavid while in junior high school with Browne and William Grant Still looking on. "On a certain night every week there was a rehearsal at the junior high school. I met the composer William Grant Still and Mr. Browne there. . . . Still . . . told me that he liked the line and the undercurrent, but he wanted the sound corrected. He was there listening and was approachable."[47] In fact, Still would follow Horace's musical evolution, attending performances and offering advice and encouragement to the younger composer into the 1960s.[48]

Lloyd Reese, whose father had come to Los Angeles from New Orleans, was renowned for the many students who passed through his studio and Sunday rehearsal band, including Dexter Gordon, Collette, Dolphy, Mingus, and Tapscott, as well as for his demanding musicianship. According to Buddy Collette,

> All of his students had to play piano, which I thought was good, because then all the students had a pretty good foundation for whatever they wanted to do. You'd also be reading better; you'd be blowing all your tunes; you could transpose. He was covering everything. Most of us could write, most could conduct. You were getting all that other knowledge; he was not just grilling you on technique. . . . This guy was preparing you to be a giant. He was opening our minds to being very musical.[49]

Reese not only insisted that his students be complete musicians, he fostered creativity by encouraging them to seek their own solutions to musical problems. For Horace Tapscott, it served as a clear demonstration that technique must ultimately be shaped by creative content: "Reese would give me something to work on for maybe two weeks, like getting some kinds of sounds. He wouldn't tell me how to work on this, but for me to find a way to do it. He knew there was more than one way to do something, more than one way to play, and he wanted me to find my way to get a sound, to find a way that physically suited me to make these sounds. That approach was so important and opened up a lot of creativity." He even gave Horace an early and unorthodox appreciation of tone clusters. "He really focused on how to make sounds and his ear was incredible. He had one of those terrible ears that would hear everything. One time, he told me to sit on the piano and put my hands, my ass, all over the keyboard. Then he called all the notes."[50]

Students were also encouraged to explore the possibilities inherent in their instruments, even to go beyond the conventional range of an instrument. Earl Anderza was an emerging alto saxophonist, a student of Samuel Browne's, who also studied with Reese, and a contemporary of Horace's at Jefferson High School. Horace recalls, "Earl Anderza was bad. He was one of the cats when Frank Morgan and Ornette Coleman were in Los Angeles playing alto sax. But Earl was the outest, the one everyone said played that 'crazy sound.'"[51] Although Anderza's career was side-tracked in the 1950s by personal problems, in the notes to his first album as a leader in 1962, he states that Reese "taught us to play above the range of the horn."[52]

While Reese's students ranged across the stylistic spectrum, the number of seminal figures among them in the later Los Angeles avant-garde and community arts movement is impressive, and, in part, attributable to his exploratory attitude. This is not to suggest that they emerged from Reese's studio as outside players in the 1940s, but rather that those of his students who became explorers of musical boundaries in the 1950s and 1960s found support during important, formative years of their lives. "There were just so many cats around here then," according to Horace, "and everybody was working on their own thing, bringing their own shot at the music. Everybody played different and there was always somebody trying to do something different. And most of them came from under the tutelage of Samuel Browne and Lloyd Reese."[53]

The Avant-Garde of the 1950s

When Mingus left for New York in 1951, an influx of musicians, open to pushing artistic boundaries, would merge with like-minded local artists, some of whom would found the Pan Afrikan Peoples Arkestra, to create a varied and dynamic avant-garde musical scene in 1950s Los Angeles. As Mingus was departing, alto saxophonist Ornette Coleman and drummer Ed Blackwell arrived. In the next few years, pianists Carla Bley, Paul Bley, Andrew Hill, and Don Preston, tenor saxophonist Charles Brackeen, trumpeter/cornetist Bobby Bradford, and bassists Charlie Haden, Scott La Faro, and Gary Peacock would settle in the City of Angels for varying stretches. The end of de jure segregation in Los Angeles in the late 1940s and the emergence of integrated performance spaces across the greater L.A. area, also served to bring together many black and white musicians pursuing the muse beyond the boundary of conventional musical practice.

Ornette Coleman's years in Los Angeles and his concurrent musical development has been the most studied aspect of the 1950s L.A. avant-garde.[54] Interviews with and reminiscences of many artists have left a picture of a young Coleman challenging society's lifestyle and musical conventions, and forging a new direction in melodic improvisation. During his stay, according to Horace, "He had these long dreads that went down to his ass. One day he came by Jefferson. Mr. Browne looked out at him and said, 'Ah! Here come black Jesus!' Ornette had hooked up with Don Cherry, who was at Jeff rehearsing with us, and had come by to hear some music. But before Ornette, Don, and George Newman had a great group [the Jazz Messiahs] with Billy Higgins and Bill Pickens, until George went out of his mind and out of music."[55]

Coleman was ubiquitous at clubs and jam sessions throughout Los Angeles County. From Watts to the San Fernando Valley northwest of L.A., from El Monte, a few miles east, to the west side, Coleman rarely missed a session. In the early 1950s he had friends from Texas with whom to work, most notably Ed Blackwell and Bobby Bradford. After their departures in the mid-1950s, he hooked up with bassist Charlie Haden and some of the community's most promising young musicians, including Don Cherry and Billy Higgins.

There are many reminiscences of the opposition Coleman encountered on the bandstand, from being shunted into the early morning hours before he could play, to musicians refusing to play with him and rhythm sections walking out. "He'd go to the jam sessions by himself and get run off the stage," Bobby Bradford remembers. "You know, he'd try to go and sit in with Dexter [Gordon] when he was in town, and Curtis Counce and those guys would run him off the bandstand."[56] Charlie Haden first heard Coleman one Monday at the Haig club: "He starts playing, man, and it was so unbelievably great I could not believe it. Like the whole room lit up all of a sudden, like somebody turned on the lights. He was playing the blues they were playing, but he was playing his own way. And almost as fast as he asked to sit in, they asked him to please stop."[57] After being stopped by one bandleader, Coleman recalls, "I had no money left, so I walked all the way home again in the rain. That sort of thing happened a lot. Some musicians would promise me I could play, but they'd keep me waiting all night."[58]

Undoubtedly, Coleman's new sound was a problem for many players, and was partly, if not largely, responsible for the hostility he encountered. But his quiet self-confidence also created a feeling of entitlement that would have been off-putting to other musicians whatever his approach. As Bobby Bradford explains,

> He was the kind of guy that was trying to make his mark, and he'd go to whoever it was at the club and say, "I want to play." You know, guys like myself. . . . We'd see Dexter Gordon up there, we wouldn't get up there. Ornette would get right up there and say to him, "What do you want to play?" Not "Can I sit in?" Ornette would say, "Well, yeah, we're just two saxophone players up here."[59]

Nevertheless, what seems more interesting than the opposition Coleman encountered, is the number of musicians who were listening and recognized his vision, and the years he remained in Los Angeles, rehearsing and still finding a few open venues, and his first recordings with Contemporary Records. Not long after he arrived, there were opportunities to play with Sonny Criss, Teddy Edwards, and Hampton Hawes, who appreciated his playing, and he also earned the approval of other local artists, such as alto saxophonist Joe Maini, pianist Don Friedman, pianist/bassist Don Preston, and bassists

Eugene Wright and Putter Smith.[60] "Eugene would always say to him, 'Come on, man. I hear you got something there,'" Bobby recalls. "I remember him saying to Ornette a couple of times, 'Now, don't forget me when you get up there.'"[61] Eric Dolphy was similarly inclined. In 1960 he told interviewer Martin Williams: "I heard about him and when I heard him play, he asked me if I liked his pieces and I said I thought they sounded good. When he said that if someone played a chord, he heard another chord on that one, I knew what he was talking about, because I had been thinking the same things."[62]

Future Frank Zappa collaborator and Mothers of Invention keyboardist, Don Preston, arrived in L.A. in 1957 and soon became friends with Paul and Carla Bley and the other members of Bley's band. While attending their performances at the Hillcrest Club, Don became acquainted with Coleman and also heard him and Don Cherry in late-night, weekend jam sessions at Georgia Lee's Caprice, a club just east of Los Angeles in the city of El Monte:

> I was very excited by his music. . . . I thought he was a true innovator. . . . And, you know, all through my life that's been one of the most important aspects of music to me: innovation, carrying on change, you know, like going forward another step [further] than what has been done before and trying to be original. Or not trying to be original but just being original. . . . And he filled all those qualifications for me because he was. He was an exceptional player, and his sound was very unusual, and his ideas also were extremely unusual.[63]

Bobby Bradford remembers their band playing gigs in one of the seediest parts of downtown L.A.: "We used to play at a little club down there called The Victory Grill, and another The Rose Room. Ornette, me, Eddie Blackwell, and a piano player named Floyd Howard. . . . We played Ornette's tunes and some jazz standards. We didn't get that much work but we were playing often enough to be playing some of Ornette's tunes."[64] The tenor saxophonist with the Jazz Messiahs, James Clay, recalls inviting Ornette to the bandstand at a club date: "He went out and played, and the next thing I knew he got them *goin',* Jack! He played and blew their brains out."[65]

According to Buddy Collette, "In the early fifties they had jam sessions every weekend at places like Normandie Hall, with Eric [Dolphy] and Ornette Coleman. Walter Benton and a bunch of the young players, who we met through that period, used to go there and jam every Friday or Saturday night. Eric and Ornette were just two players. We didn't know that they'd get as good as they did and no one else knew."[66] Buddy recognized that Coleman "had these sounds in his head that he wanted to explore. He was very talented and was trying to do quarter tones on his horn. A little later on, when his group got together with Don Cherry and a few people, the tunes were, at first, a little strange. Even the intonation was weird. But they began to make some of us believe that they knew where they were going."[67]

The story of the 1950s Los Angeles avant-garde involves more than the story of Ornette Coleman. There were other musicians, who were also stretching out and not necessarily in the same direction as Coleman. Dolphy led a bopish sextet at the Oasis on Western Avenue but had also organized a rehearsal band with trombonist Lester Robertson to stretch bop's approach to harmony.[68] By early 1958, Dolphy was leading another ensemble at the Oasis, which included Lester Robertson and Billy Higgins, and that had a distinctly adventurous sound, despite being primarily a house band.[69] Saxophonist Curtis Amy, who settled in Los Angeles in 1955, met Dolphy at the club and was in attendance at every opportunity to hear him play: "But he was out. He was playing out then. . . ."[70]

Lester Robertson, already a veteran of Gerald Wilson's and Lionel Hampton's big bands, would soon join with Horace Tapscott to form the Underground Musicians Association (UGMA), the original name of the Arkestra. In addition to Robertson, alto saxophonists Guido Sinclair and Jimmy Woods, bassists Al Hines and David Bryant—all among the founding members of UGMA—were also a part of the scene, as well as Bobby Hutcherson and Charles Lloyd. Not long after arriving in Los Angeles around 1956, Al Hines was studying with a Philharmonic bassist and gigging around town with similarly inclined players. "At a place in the [San Fernando] Valley I played with Don Cherry," Al recalls, "but I played with Ornette at Shelly's [Manne-Hole]. They used to have sessions there and we'd just go and play. Their style never changed that much; they just played like that. Their conception was there regardless of what their knowledge was."

Paul Bley had been leading the band at the Hillcrest on Washington Boulevard for some time prior to Coleman joining, and had added saxophonist Anthony Ortega, who had studied with Lloyd Reese and come up in Watts in the 1940s. After a stint with Lionel Hampton's band and a few years in New York, he returned to Los Angeles and by the later 1950s was already displaying the musical adventurousness that would result in his 1966 album, *New Dance,* awarded the Prix de la Redecouverte in Paris in 1992 for best album reissue on hat ART Records. When Anthony returned to Los Angeles in 1958, Paul Bley asked him to join his band. He remembers that "the further out, the more Paul liked it . . . it all seemed to gel well because he played such extensions and everything. And then I was getting off into some things."[71]

Profoundly influenced by Asian musics and soon to achieve renown in the Western classical world as the initiating force in "minimalism," La Monte Young was a high school student in Los Angeles in the early 1950s and studying saxophone at the Los Angeles Conservatory of Music with Central Avenue veteran Bill Green, a master of technique, who inculcated in his students the value of long tones. He then attended L.A. City College and immersed himself in the local avant-garde jazz scene. He won the second alto chair in the school dance band over Eric Dolphy (the first chair going to Lanny Morgan), but played second clarinet in the orchestra next to Dolphy's first.

Outside of school Young had his own jazz quartet, which included Don Cherry and Billy Higgins. He also frequented jam sessions and performed with Dolphy and Ornette Coleman, as well as with the Willy Powell Big Blues Band. A favorite spot was the Big Top on Hollywood Boulevard, "one of the most creative session spots in the whole L.A. area. As soon as they saw me walk through the door, they knew I was going to play for a long time. Other guys would go on the stand and take a couple of choruses, but I would never stop. I was just playing and playing. And somehow, something began to flow through me. Improvisation helped me understand this process."[72] He privately recorded with Billy Higgins during this time and also met saxophonist George Newman, whom he thought "just incredible. He could play all of these Charlie Parker solos right off the record and he was a sensation." For Young, whose music was already exhibiting polytonality and fragmented beats, "It was really exciting growing up in L.A. because there was so much going on in music, and so many young talents."[73]

When Horace Tapscott returned to Los Angeles in 1957, following a four-year hitch in the US Air Force, he found the scene vital as well: "There were a lot of the out cats in town. Ornette Coleman was giggin' with his band at the Hillcrest Club on Washington Boulevard. All the out cats came by there. The It Club and the Black Orchid also opened nearby. The It Club had John T. McClain running it and all kinds of shit went on there. McClain had a house behind the club for Phineas Newborn, so he could keep him in tow. It was out. And all the cats played there."[74] Across the street from the It Club was the Metro Theater, originally a movie house that had been turned into a black playhouse. After the other clubs closed at 2 A.M., devotees could walk across the street and enjoy jam sessions in the three hundred seat Metro until the sun came up. According to Cecil Rhodes, one of the theater organizers, "We started having jazz on Saturday night and we used to pack people in. And this was money we could use to put on plays, because at that time there was not really a black theater going on in Los Angeles." Doug Westin's Troubadour club featured a group led by Horace Tapscott and attracted many similarly inclined musicians. By the early 1960s, according to Horace,

> All the people that [FBI Director] J. Edgar Hoover was against in those days, white and black, would all come through that club. All the so-called discards from society would always be there, the creative people, like Ava Gardner and Lenny Bruce. That's why I enjoyed that gig, because it attracted creative people and I got to play exactly what I wanted to play. I had control of the music, and we fed them the new music. And all kinds of people came down and played with us, including Bill Pickens, Bobby Hutcherson, Albert Stinson, Roy Ayers, Walter Benton, Rafmad Jamal, Elmo Hope, Guido Sinclair, Charles Lloyd, Jimmy Woods, and King Pleasure.[75]

The year Horace returned to Los Angeles, saxophonist Paul Horn arrived as well. He remembers, especially, the open quality of the scene:

> When I moved from New York to Los Angeles in 1957, I quickly realized the East Coast was extremely conservative. California was wide open—an experimental, innovative and exceptionally creative environment. People felt free to try new ideas, anything at all. If it was new and interesting, they went for it. This kind of atmosphere produces its share of kooks, weirdos, and psychotics, but it also produces brilliant concepts in science, art, business, education, and spiritual matters.[76]

As vital as the jazz scene was, this activity remained below the radar of most artists and the national media. If California was considered at all, "West Coast Cool" defined the range of their inquiries. According to Horace,

> All these out cats were here, a lot of them from Central Avenue days, but nobody followed anyone in particular. Everyone had an individual approach with a lot of people doing different things, but all of it helping the music to grow. It was happening out here, even if all people ever heard about the West Coast was tiptoe-through-the-tulips music. Cannonball Adderley once said in an interview, "Wait a minute, man, have you been out on the West Coast? Have you been to the bush? You've got to go to the bush. Not downtown. They've got a lot of cats out there playing." That was a time when the music was popping out here, and nobody was paying any attention to it.[77]

In his masterful history of jazz on the West Coast during this period, Ted Gioia writes, "the truth was that no other place in the jazz world was as open to experimentation, to challenges to the conventional wisdom in improvised music, as was California during the late 1940s and the 1950s."[78] From piano-less quartets to various bop and hard bop stylings, from the Brubeck quartet's cool sound and the Chico Hamilton Quintet's swinging chamber jazz to Ornette Coleman and big band writing as diverse as Roy Porter's bop band, Gerald Wilson's harmonically rich and Latin-influenced charts, Shorty Rogers's and Stan Kenton's drawing upon the Western classical tradition, and the, at times, atonal, serial-inspired music of Bob Graettinger, California offered a broad palette of sounds without any one gaining hegemony. Gioia concludes, "Indeed, if one thing should stand out in this account of music in California during the postwar years, it is the enormous diversity of the music, the ceaseless, churning search for the different and new. It is this characteristic that unites a Stan Kenton and an Ornette Coleman, a Charles Mingus and a Jimmy Giuffre, a Shelly Manne and an Eric Dolphy."[79]

Explanations for this range of creativity are many, but tend to focus primarily on the area's climate, its dispersed urban settings and lack of dominating centers, particularly in Los Angeles, and the absence of a weighty critical establishment. However, other influences have shaped the music—jazz, Western classical, and pop—emanating from the West Coast, perhaps none more significant than the area's distance from the East Coast and Europe and proximity to non-Western sounds as part of the Pacific Basin. More than any other part of the United States, it has been awash in a wide range of cultural influences, from African and Asian to Latin and Native American, which have given some of the Coast's arts their diversity and distinct regional flavors. Perhaps more accurately than in the jazz world, in the early twentieth century Western classicists applied the term "West Coast Sound" to the unique music that drew from these varied cultural influences and started emerging during and shortly after World War I in California. Composers Henry Cowell and Harry Partch, followed by Lou Harrison and John Cage, would carve out alternative music and inspire succeeding generations (including La Monte Young) in a movement Cowell referred to in 1940 as "Drums along the Pacific."[80]

Harry Partch drew from the microtonality of Asian, African, and Native American sources as well as ancient Greek musical and dramatic practice, which led him to reject not tonality but the European system of equal tempered scales. Western tempered theory dictates even distances between each of the twelve tones of an octave. Since the actual distances are not the same—equal temperament being a compromise widely accepted in European music during the nineteenth century to facilitate key modulation—Partch devised octaves, one consisting of forty-three tones, based on real or just intonation, preserving the mathematically correct distances or ratios between each note. He also devised some two dozen instruments to perform his music. For the most part a mixture of string and percussion, they were sculptural works of art in their own right. His masterpiece, *Delusion of the Fury*, is structured in two parts, one drawing on a common theme in Japanese Noh plays and the other an Ethiopian folk tale.[81]

Among Henry Cowell's early influences as a child in San Francisco were the sounds of the various ethnic groups then populating the City. Living in Chinatown, he was exposed to Asian instruments, music, and drama. In some of his earliest works from 1913 to 1920, he was already creating music outside the boundaries of much of the Western framework. Heavily percussive early piano works, including "Adventures in Harmony," "Dynamic Motion," "The Banshee," and "The Tides of Manaunaun," feature widespread use of riffs, percussive effects, simultaneous multiple meters, pounding piano clusters, and plucking the piano strings. Cowell's interest in and incorporation of Asian instruments and forms of musical organization into his music continued throughout his life and lent his music "an extraordinary breadth of style," according to biographer Michael Hicks. "A thoroughly abstract, dissonant piece may follow a simple diatonic one. The same piano piece may harbor modernist noise in one hand and a modal folk tune in the other. Or an ensemble piece built with traditional harmonic materials may exhibit radically new formal concepts."[82] In some ways it is also an apt description of aspects of the music of two subsequent West Coast jazz pianists and composers— Horace Tapscott and Jon Jang, whose artistries would be similarly expansive.

Cowell was attuned to the music of Africa and African American composers, such as William Grant Still. In his edited 1933 collection of essays, *American Composers on American Music*, he featured a piece by Still on African American composers, which reflected Still's turn toward folk material and away from the influence of his earlier work with Edgard Varese in New York.[83] Cowell also published Still's composition *Dismal Swamp* in his *New Music Quarterly*, a journal devoted to new music.[84]

Cowell's intersection with William Grant Still and through him perhaps Samuel Browne, whose musical training was also in the Western classical tradition, is intriguing, as is that of La Monte Young with the jazz avant-garde in Los Angeles. Yet, these rather tenuous links are more revealing when seen as parts of a larger picture of diversity and cross-influences in the California arts scene, of the emergence of new sounds, approaches, techniques, and content that drew from a wide range of the world's cultures. As Cowell wrote in 1963, two years before his death, "I present myself to you as a person who realized from his own experience that the music of Japan, as well as that of China and other oriental countries, is part of American music."[85]

Within Los Angeles' African American community the jazz and R&B stylings that emerged grew from the common stock of national black music but at the same time exhibited regional flavors that reflected the black experience in this culturally diverse part of the country. This would be even more in evidence in the music of the Pan Afrikan Peoples Arkestra, which at times would offer a Latin and Native American tinge.

By the early 1960s many of the musicians, who had contributed to the dynamic and varied 1950s jazz scene had departed, most leaving for the East Coast, the most celebrated being the Ornette Coleman Quartet's arrival at the Five Spot in New York in 1959. This eastward migration and the unrelenting decline of Central Avenue left the African American community artistically poorer and without the supportive, communal atmosphere of Central Avenue's best days. On April 1, 1953, Local 767 of the American Federation of Musicians ceased to exist, as the membership of the former black local traveled to Hollywood to merge with Local 47. Though former members continued to gather at the old house on Central Avenue for a few more years, many would never be heard from again and a community center was lost.

To some of those artists remaining in Los Angeles, the challenge now was to rekindle that atmosphere by reinvigorating the arts in the changed conditions of the community in the early 1960s. Among those involved in creating new sounds, Horace Tapscott soon gathered together many of them to form an alternative music collective that blended avant-garde approaches with traditional African American sounds, and to forge a movement with an aesthetic and ethos deeply rooted in the communal values of Central Avenue, in the expansiveness and variety of West Coast sounds, and in the rich cultural heritage of West and West Central Africa. Under the banner of community arts, they would become a force for advancing the music and for the social and cultural enrichment of their community.

LINO'S PAD

African American Los Angeles and the Formation
of the Underground Musicians Association

Find your own voice & use it
use your own voice & find it

JAYNE CORTEZ

In 1961 Samuel Browne left the music department at Jefferson for a teaching position at the newly opened Palisades High School in an affluent part of Los Angeles, just a short walk from the Santa Monica beaches. During the 1950s Jeff and the community around it were changing and in a manner that did not suit Browne. By the end of the decade, the rising tensions in the community that would explode in the Watts upheaval of 1965 were palpable, and the influx of drugs into the music scene also fed his growing disillusionment. "The whole social fabric began to change," Browne reminisced many years later, "and I no longer had the kind of students that I once had: talented, motivated, able to concentrate their minds on an objective. . . . Other trumpets were being blown, other drums were beating somewhere else. There were distractions and unrest. The breaking of bonds."[1]

A few years earlier, Browne had abandoned the Jazz Band class, a staple of the Jeff curriculum, and was teaching only music theory and appreciation. Students during the later 1950s, including drummers Bill Madison and Carl Burnett, remember learning of his and Jeff's past and then pleading with him for more instruction. But the best Bill could get from Browne was a promise: "'If you ever get yourself together and decide what you're going to do, I'll send you to study with Lloyd Reese.' I'd never played a note, but he knew how I felt about the music. He'd always say, 'I don't want you to grow up to be a goof.'" Carl remembers when he and classmate, vibist Roy Ayers, discovered Browne's history: "We said, 'Well, man, why don't you just form a band? You could help us, man.'" It was to no avail, as Browne's disillusionment was not to be overcome. Carl also recalls the perception among many young musicians that you could only play at your best with the aid of drugs, and Browne's frustration with this attitude: "And people actually felt like that, man. They really thought that. So a lot musicians began to go in that direction. And when he couldn't stop them, and he saw what was happening with that, I think it just kind of broke his heart, man, and he decided, 'No, I don't want to teach the band no more.'"[2]

Browne's gradual withdrawal and then departure from the music program at Jeff meant the end of a long and wonderful musical tradition. It also was indicative of a growing cultural void within the community—"the breaking of bonds" as Browne put it—since the demise of Central Avenue as the community's centerpiece. Dozens of small clubs, corner bars, and other such performance spaces remained: the 5–4 Ballroom, Memory Lane, the California Club, the Oasis, Hillcrest, It Club, Black Orchid, Adams West, and the Metro Theater, among others. Western Avenue, the new center about four miles west of Central, as well as its successor in the 1960s, Crenshaw Boulevard, a further three miles beyond Western, did encompass many businesses and music venues. But they were faint imitations of Central during its best years, and the sense of community and community arts fostered along Central Avenue was evaporating. Especially to those artists beginning their careers during the 1950s, African American Los Angeles had changed and not necessarily for the best. "The Watts riots were only a few years away," Browne told an interviewer in 1979, "and I could see the handwriting on the wall."[3]

African American Los Angeles by 1960

By the early 1960s, more than a decade after the Supreme Court had decreed racially restrictive housing covenants unenforceable in the 1948 *Shelley v. Kraemer* decision, the African American community had expanded west from Central Avenue and come to occupy a forty-eight-square-mile area that would be commonly referred to as "South Central Los Angeles," partly in homage to the community's earlier "main stem." This did alleviate the serious overcrowding problem along Central Avenue, which had reached critical proportions by the end of World War II, but the westward expansion of the community was not simply an exhaling of a pent-up Central Avenue population. The 1950s also saw a continued migration of African Americans into California, more than any other state, and the black population in Los Angeles increased eightfold.[4] As had been the case since the turn of the century, California continued to be a magnet, supposedly offering economic opportunities that few other areas could match.

However, for many African Americans moving into previously all-white areas, struggle accompanied the expansion and white flight would transform these areas by the mid-1960s. The migration came with a heavy price as many faced vicious, and at times violent, racist opposition in their new neighborhoods. Writing of this opposition to black movement beyond the community's traditional boundaries, historian Josh Sides notes, "While the postwar period brought unprecedented gains for African Americans, it also brought a crushing wave of virulent anti-black racism the likes of which the city had never known."[5] The pages of the *California Eagle* in the early 1950s are replete with stories of real estate agents and white owners blatantly violating Court rulings, of white mob actions, arson attacks, house bombings, and cross burnings. Many African Americans fought legally to assert their rights; others armed themselves and stood their ground, when necessary.[6]

The African American community was also not exhibiting the signs of prosperity that other regions of Los Angeles so clearly enjoyed. Two-thirds of African American L.A. was blue collar, but black workers were denied employment in the higher-paid industrial jobs in Commerce, Vernon and other areas just east of the black community. The 1950s expansion of the American economy produced only a steady increase in unemployment in South Central L.A. According to historian Gerald Horne, "By 1960 unemployment in Black L.A. officially was 12.5 percent and most likely was higher. By 1960, 44.5 percent of Watts' families were at the poverty level, earning under $4,000 annually."[7] In the black community as a whole, the percentage of those living at or below the poverty level was lower but still over one quarter, and just under 40 percent of those were less than fifteen years of age.[8]

Almost half of the black population had grown up after the end of de jure segregation. Yet, Los Angeles remained one of the most segregated cities in the country and the expansion of the population did little to alter that. A combination of affordable housing, white flight to the San Fernando Valley and the southern rim of Los Angeles County, Los Angeles Police Department (LAPD) hostility, and continued racial exclusion from the suburbs maintained a now almost mono-racial, separate, though geographically enlarged community in South Central, comprising some 90 percent of Los Angeles's African Americans. Those few who crossed the boundary paid a price. Poet Jayne Cortez, soon to collaborate with Horace Tapscott and UGMA during the mid-1960s, grew up in Watts and attended junior high school just a few blocks beyond the area's boundary, which put her in the middle of an all-white school and in the midst of a "miserable" situation.

> Miserable simply because of the attitudes of both the white students and the white teachers. Almost every book we read was about their lives, their history, their values, their culture. Things would really get tense when we got to the slave era. It was repulsive. They taught such lies about Africa. I tell you I had to fight every day. I mean when a white kid called me "nigger," I had to jump up and beat the hell out of him or her. And I did that constantly. My mother was always at the school.[9]

The communal bonds were further weakened by the acceleration of gang activity during the 1950s, as an increasingly dismal economic situation left fewer options for young people. Gangs had been a presence practically since the community's inception. Pianist Coney Woodman recalls them as part of his childhood in Watts of the 1920s: "We'd go where there was boxing, and we'd have fights all the time with different people. You know, this was our territory, and when guys came from Los Angeles down here, we'd roll them back. One group was called the Twenty-second Street Gang. And they'd come down here and want to take over, so we'd have to run them back. We were called the Tarzans."[10] Saxophonist Anthony Ortega, who grew up in Watts during the 1930s and early 1940s, remembers conflicts, restricted to gang members, using fists and knives, that might occasionally pit a Watts Latino gang against one from East L.A. "There used to be some gangs, but the area was so much lower-key than it is now. I mean, maybe they would just have fights with each other, or some guys from La Colonia would have a fight with the guys from 103rd Street or something like that."[11] These rather typical, neighborhood aggregations, underwent a more serious shift in direction by the late 1940s. Historian Mike Davis suggests that gangs emerged during that time as more tightly organized, almost military organizations in a defensive reaction to the racism they encountered in the schools and on the streets from white youths.[12]

The worsening economic conditions of the 1950s, in particular the dwindling prospects for young people, and the racist offensive against minorities by Chief William H. Parker's Los Angeles Police Department broadened the gangs' appeal and their numbers grew. According to historian J. K. Obatala, "The fathers, through their struggle to escape from the South and make a new start in L.A., found a sense of black manhood that had been lost for centuries; the sons, out of school and out of jobs and trapped in the inner city, found only powerlessness and frustration. What began as a pilgrimage of hope for the parents became a parody of hell for the offspring." Without a promising economic future and stripped of any sense of cultural heritage in the schools, through their involvement in gangs they "tried to find . . . a sense of power and prestige and a substitute for the lack of genuine meaning in their lives."[13] The Daddy Rolling Stones, then the Slausons, Businessmen, Gladiators, Orientals, Flips, Low Riders, Twenties, Rabble Rousers, and the Blood Alleys emerged as much of South Central was subdivided among the rivals.[14]

The end of de jure segregation and the geographical expansion of the community had not resulted in a greater access to economic benefits, nor had there been any change in the political status quo. Political scientist Raphael Sonenshein characterizes Los Angeles in 1960 as "one of the most backward cities in the nation in African American political representation. Los Angeles Blacks had yet to elect a city council member or a congressperson. Their only political representative at any level was State Assemblyman Augustus Hawkins."[15] On the streets tensions were rising. The period of the late 1950s and early 1960s witnessed some demonstrations and activities in support of the civil rights struggles in the south, in addition to the many protests and confrontations that grew from local issues. Conflicts between citizens and the LAPD provide evidence that the upheaval, which would erupt in 1965, could have occurred in any of the few preceding years.[16]

Since 1950, the Police Department had operated under the direction of a virulent anticommunist and white supremacist, Chief William H. Parker, free of any effective political or civilian control.[17] His mission was to clean up a notoriously and historically corrupt department and to impose his concept of modern police professionalism. Drawn in part from the Marine Corps training regimen and his involvement in policing postwar Europe with the US military, Parker's approach was to turn the LAPD into a paramilitary organization with a style of policing termed "pro-active." "Simply put," according to journalist Joe Domanick, "pro-active policing calls for officers not to wait for a crime to happen, but to seek it out, stop it before it happens. And if a violation of the laws does occur, straighten it out right away.

Keep things orderly, and always make it clear who's in charge."[18] According to a former LAPD commander, "The entire essence of an L.A. officer's training and development at the academy was that we were the centurions, the people who had responsibility for eliminating the lice from the community. It was a responsibility that was taken very seriously, more so than in most other police agencies."[19]

Nothing less than the future of society was at stake, according to the delusional Parker. "We're the most lawless nation on earth; an overriding reason is our tribunals—which create a Shan-gri-La for thugs and murderers."[20] Historian Bruce Tyler notes that "Parker demanded, actually, police martial law to stem the crime wave he perceived taking place. He did not want any legal safeguards between the L.A.P.D. and suspected criminals and the public. . . . He demanded that homes, or anyplace, where crime was suspected, should not have any protections whatsoever."[21] Not surprisingly, according to Tyler, "Parker's brand of police professionalism made him not only contemptuous of meddling politicians, courts and the public, but of the law itself. The L.A.P.D., under Parker, became a law unto itself."[22]

In Parker's mind even the growing civil rights movement was part of an international communist conspiracy trying to destroy American society. Any movement against the status quo, and certainly any movement that was critical in any way of the LAPD, was subversive. Every attempt to establish even minimal control by a review board was castigated by Parker and his minions as communist plots.[23] And throughout Parker's reign, according to Domanick, the department found little opposition "outside of L.A.'s powerless black and Latino communities. It was, in fact, very popular. L.A. was still a city with a small-town mentality run by conservative descendants of Midwestern farmers. The prevailing morality was still straight Victorian. It was Bill Parker's world."[24]

Given the segregationist, racist views of the political establishment and Parker in particular, this set the stage for the virtual criminalization of Los Angeles's minority communities. Under Parker the LAPD did lose the stigma of corruption, only to have it replaced with that of racism and systematic brutality. Almost from the moment Parker assumed command, his department was under a constant drumbeat of criticism for attacks on the citizenry, particularly minority groups.[25] Reports of police brutality were routine, at least in the black press, and protested vigorously by the community. So desperate had the situation become by the early 1960s, that a group of religious leaders representing the United Clergymen of Central Los Angeles told Mayor Sam Yorty, "We call on you to take immediate steps to investigate the activities of the administrative officer (Parker) of the Police Department in order to avoid dire consequences in the community."[26] Selectively targeting African Americans and Latinos in particular, using harassment, verbal and physical intimidation, and handling minority crime in a harsher manner than identical instances of white crime, the LAPD had become, in essence, an army of occupation—all that Parker had dreamed for a modern, professional police department.

One of Parker's first aims was to break up the integrated social scene on Central Avenue, and in the early 1950s his "troops" were a visible presence, warning and threatening any whites to be found there, routinely harassing and arresting interracial couples. Mike Davis recounts one such campaign: "In 1954 John Dolphin, owner of Los Angeles's premier R&B record store near the corner of Vernon and Central, organized a protest of 150 Black business people against an ongoing 'campaign of intimidation and terror' directed at interracial trade."[27] The *Los Angeles Sentinel* reported,

> Intimidations began, according to Dolphin, Halloween night when 12 police officers, allegedly led by Sgt. George Restovich, paraded the store's entrance and formed a human block to the store's entrance during a three-hour vigil of terrifying Caucasian cutomers of the store and routing them from the neighborhood.
>
> Observers said at one interval the officers parked a patrol wagon near the store's entrance while other officers stopped all white patrons on the sidewalk and allegedly advised them to "buy your records outside the Central avenue area."
>
> Dolphin said the officers entered his store and ordered several teenage patrons to leave and offered to escort them to their automobiles, "because Central avenue was too dangerous for white people."[28]

By the mid-1950s, after dissipating the interracial aspect of the Avenue, Parker had instituted a heavy deployment of police and aggressive patrols throughout the African American community. Among other justifications, he went after the black community as a primary source for the spread of drugs throughout Los Angeles, arguing that this was communist inspired.[29] According to Tyler, "Parker fervently believed that the mob and Communism would make its entrance through the backdoor of the Black community. He decided to station . . . police at the doors of the Black community. They put, in effect, the Black community under 'house arrest.'"[30] So outlandish were the policies of the Parker regime that even a judge complained in 1959, "I feel when police officials instruct their subordinate officers to arrest only Negroes on given charges it will not be long before this newly gained power will prompt them to enforce other statues [*sic*] against only certain other groups."[31]

To the generation emerging in the 1950s there was little within their community to instruct them in and validate their past and even less hope for the future offered by the political and economic situation. The population of South Central Los Angeles was a near majority of young people, who had grown up in this area during the post–World War II era and were emerging with little sense of who they were in the midst of an economic and cultural area in decline, patrolled by a hostile occupying army in blue.

Origins and Early Growth of the Underground Musicians Association (UGMA)

When Horace Tapscott encountered Samuel Browne at Jefferson High School, he recalls that the teacher offered him a deal. He'd give Horace the magic, if he promised to pass it on.[32] Browne's recollection of the incident, though slightly different, contains the same commitment: "When I was quite young someone said to me . . . 'Remember, if you have a kindness shown, pass it on.' One day I repeated these words to my pupil, Horace, who resolved as I had years before to put these words into action."[33] The end of Browne's tenure at Jeff in 1961, coinciding with the weakening socio-economic situation within the community, the increasing commercialization of the music, and the departure of much of the 1950s jazz avant-garde, suggested to a young Horace Tapscott, then in his mid-twenties, that now was the time to take up the task. In his autobiography, Horace observes, "During the 1950s, there wasn't much cultural activity going on in the African American community of Los Angeles. . . . Communication was missing; the social contact that people used to have on Central Avenue was gone. So there was a sense of searching for something better, resetting things now that segregation was over."[34]

When Horace returned to Los Angeles in 1957 from his four-year hitch in the Air Force, he and his wife Cecilia moved in with her parents near 120th Street and Avalon Boulevard, just below Watts, in a house they rented from trumpeter Don Cherry's mother-in-law. Within a year they relocated their growing family to an apartment in the midst of South Central L.A., near Sixty-sixth Street and Avalon. In 1959 they moved into a home with Horace's mother on Fifty-sixth Street, also near Avalon, which they would occupy for the next seven years. Horace quickly appropriated the garage and converted it into a rehearsal room, one that soon became an important space for local artists pursuing new music.

For as long as anyone could remember, Horace seemed to attract people. When he was six in Houston, Texas, he was already organizing neighborhood children, who wanted to play music.

> I always used to have a gang of cats that would follow me. We got some old furnaces, buckets, tin pans, skillets, some sticks, and I'd play these like they were drums, setting the rhythm. The other cats would be up front blowing into some things or whatever instruments they had. It seemed like everybody had instruments or wanted to. We thought we were playing music. And we always had an audience, because the whole family would sit down and listen sometime during the day.[35]

When he took over the garage on Fifty-sixth Street, it quickly became a gathering place for musicians. Although the garages changed whenever the family moved, the sessions continued for the rest of Horace's life, also attracting musicians not involved with his band but with a strong creative bent and desirous of perfecting their craft. Carl Burnett, soon to be one of the leading and most recorded jazz drummers on the West Coast, was one such artist who frequented the garage sessions. When he started learning to play vibes, he mastered them at Horace's. "He taught me all kinds of songs. We'd go over to his house, have a little party, and then play," Carl recalls. To his surprise, this became a learning experience that encompassed more than just mastering standards. "His whole playing was total creativity. . . . He wasn't like any other piano player. People would look at him like Thelonious Monk. He'd do some things and play some chords that I'd never heard before."[36] Bassist Henry "Skipper" Franklin was another participant. "We would play in the garage. And that's where I first met Don Cherry. He was there with Horace."[37]

Opportunities for jam sessions may have been dwindling in the post-Central years, but the music and musicians found a way regardless of circumstances. Skipper was also participating in garage jams at drummer Bruz Freeman's home, along with tenor saxophonist Herman Riley and pianist Andrew Hill, then living in Los Angeles. "We were stretching out a little bit there. I think at that time we were mostly trying to play tunes, but I'm sure we took it out quite a bit."[38]

In 1961, after a two-year stint, Horace left Lionel Hampton's band and by the end of that year had returned to the garage full-time to begin organizing a community ensemble. He soon attracted a regular core of musicians, including trombonist Lester Robertson, alto saxophonists Guido Sinclair and Jimmy Woods, bassists Al Hines and David Bryant, and drummer Arnold Palmer. Horace had known Lester and Guido years before while in high school. Lester was a few years older and a close friend of Eric Dolphy, who had recently dedicated "Les" to him, a composition recorded on Dolphy's first album as a leader, *Outward Bound* (Prestige, 1960). Guido was close to Horace's age and while at Jefferson they had formed a small band. Jimmy, Al, and Dave had been acquaintances in the 1950s, and Arnold had gigged around town with Eric Dolphy in the mid-1950s and then with Horace.

Most had experienced the Central Avenue scene during its last full days and all had embarked on careers as professional musicians. But they also were searching for something more than the mainstream professional and commercial worlds offered to artists, and most were involved with Los Angeles's avant-garde of the 1950s. Horace was looking to surround himself with musicians with just that sensibility, an artistically exploratory attitude with roots in the community.

> I started by looking for different kinds of personalities who were involved in the music. And every person I brought in was an outsider, so to speak. They leaned a little bit, you dig? They didn't walk a straight line; they leaned as they walked . . . didn't like what they were doing, or were trying to find something different in the music. There were players around, perhaps working in bands across town, who approached the music in an out way for the bands they were in. They'd end up with no solos and not being used very much. So I sought out those kinds of people, those who weren't a part of the studio cliques, a part of the group of people who worked a particular area all the time . . . , because I figured that they had much more to offer and that was something very precious.[39]

From the beginning Horace attracted musicians and artists who were different. Drummer Donald Dean, soon to come around, remembers meeting Jimmy Woods through UGMA: "I loved Jimmy and I loved his way of playing. He was out there. Jimmy's kind of weird too. Looked like everybody I knew was weird, everybody in UGMA." Woods, a veteran of Gerald Wilson's big band and a Contemporary Records recording artist (*Awakening!* [1961–62] and *Conflict* [1963]), possessed a fierce originality and masterful technique that appealed to Horace.

> I'll never forget an incident one Sunday at Larry Hearns's club off Central Avenue at Avalon and Forty-second, across from the old Wrigley ballpark. Sunday was the day of the fast gun, seeing who could play the fastest. There were the junkies, the non-junkies, the weed heads—everyone there was categorized. But Jimmy was off on the side by him-

self, in his old blue suit and glasses. When he got on stage, the cats looked at each other and said, "Man, who is this guy?"

"I don't know, man. I ain't never seen him."

"Okay, 'Cherokee' . . . up! One, two . . . One-two-three-four!"

One of them looked at Jimmy and said, "Okay, man, you take the bridge."

They figured they'd just blow him off. But when they got to the bridge, Jimmy Woods just blew through it. He *ate* the bridge up!

"Who the fuck is this?"

"Where'd he come from?"

They had to come out of their act and from then on the cats gave him respect. You had to pay attention.[40]

By the end of 1961 the rehearsal group formed as a band with a purpose, to preserve and create music that reflected their experiences and those of African Americans in mid-century America. Horace was already composing prolifically and the band rehearsed his music, as well as that of other members. According to David Bryant, the group's elder statesman and Central Avenue veteran, "We were playing some of Duke and Monk, but mostly originals. A lot of guys in the group were writing and they had a chance to hear their music. A lot of musicians, especially in L.A., if you ask them to come to a rehearsal, they say, 'Where's the gig?' But we would get together and play with no gig in sight. Just play. It was like when I was growing up. We just wanted to play."[41]

The return to core values involved a turning away from commercial music and a focus on creating jazz that resonated with their sense of self and the African American experience. According to Bryant, "I'd turn down gigs so I could play with UGMA, but I kept my sanity. I got so tired of playing commercial music." Bassist Al Hines, a protégé of Bryant, who had been rehearsing on-and-off with Horace since 1957, echoes that sentiment: "We wanted to preserve the black arts, to keep them alive. When I was playing gigs, I wasn't preserving my arts. I had to play the way they wanted me to play so I could work the gig. That's how I got fired from Hanna Barbera, because I was bringing musicians in to do things that they weren't up to."

The performance of original music was only one aspect of what Horace and his cohorts envisioned. Another was bringing that music to the South Central community to help fill an increasing cultural void, a role that Horace seemed fated to play. Samuel Browne's encouragement to pass it on and Horace's own experiences growing up in Houston's Third Ward and Los Angeles's Central Avenue shaped his purpose, and to his family and friends it was his destiny. One childhood friend, Wendell Lee Black, remembers, "He always had the dream that he wanted to have a big band spread out all through the community. He used to tell me about it, and that he wanted to get involved in the community."[42] To his sister, Robbie, "Here was a kid, who was not an ordinary kid, because he had a dream that he held on to, and people who trusted and believed and supported him—family—and that's important. And he was the king of the world. He was Ace, and there was nothing he couldn't do." In his memoir, Horace writes,

> I've always thought that music gets people's attention and brings people together. It's a focal point. And I felt that having the Arkestra—which had a message to give, playing original music, dances and poetry—would give us an opportunity to open up all the areas in our culture that had been stopped. That was the chore that we took off on. The Arkestra would allow the creativity in the community to come together, would allow people to recognize each other as one people and ask, "Now what can we do to make this community better? What can we do for this community together?" So I figured that would be the best move to make, while realizing that it was going to take some time. It's going to take a little time to do anything, but you can plant the seed and nurture it and watch it.[43]

Calling themselves the Underground Musicians Association (UGMA), in 1962 the group shifted their base of operations to the home of Linda Hill, a nurse's aide and aspiring artist, who had met Horace a few years earlier, while he was being treated for kidney stones at Los Angeles General Hospital.

> I come in one midnight and check patients names, new and discharges and see Tapscott's name. Horace, can't tell whether it's a brother or not, so I go through my rounds in the middle of the night enter this room and look over there and Horace is sitting up in the bed "is there anything you need Mr. Tapscott?" I could see that whatever they used to sedate him didn't work cause he was holding on to keep his pain down. Got so I end up half of every night talking with him. Four years later I walk into General's building—go into this room and here's Horace standing there "hey where you been, you have a piano?, you mind if I come over some time?"[44]

Linda's house, a smallish, two-bedroom structure at 1222 East Seventy-fifth Street, just east of Central Avenue, offered fewer distractions than the Tapscott home, and the band rehearsed on a daily basis. "First he came over and played the piano," Linda wrote twenty years later, "then he would bring the drummer over, Arnold Palmer, then he would bring bassists David Bryant and Al Hines, then he brought a whole orchestra over, all in one little room, horn players reading sheet music on each other backs."[45] Soon to be known as "Lino's Pad" after Linda's nickname and memorialized by Horace in his composition of the same title, the building was a "shotgun house," notes drummer Bill Madison. "You could almost see from the front straight through to the back, and then rooms were off of it. The room to the right is where the piano was, barely room for piano, bass and drums. People were almost hanging out the window with horns trying to play." According to David Bryant, "The guys would just get together and have sessions. We'd play and then just hang out. Some cats would spend the night there, then wake up and play. It was strictly music. Just a bunch of musicians getting together and playing each other's music, not just Horace's, although he was doing the bulk of the writing." His colleague, Al Hines, remembers, "We hung out together all the time. Horace wouldn't get no job and I wouldn't get no job. Our old ladies were running us crazy because we wouldn't do nothing but play." Lino's pad had become the first in what would be a series of UGMA houses.

A single mother in her mid-twenties with a young son, Leland, in elementary school, Leila Marian "Linda" Hill had grown up along the southern rim of Watts at 120th Street and Central Avenue in the 1940s and 1950s with five brothers and two sisters, most of whom played music, a few professionally on Central. Though she had embarked on a career as a nurse's aide, her dream was to spend her life in the community involved with music and the arts. She had studied piano with her mother, a piano teacher, voice and cello at Willowbrook Junior High School, and then viola and modern dance at Compton High School.[46] Music had not been a particular focus and when she met Horace, who was one year and a half her senior, Linda did not have a career-oriented musical background.

Nevertheless, within a year or two she had become a musical mainstay of UGMA, both as an instrumentalist and as an arranger under Horace's tutelage, devoting all of her free time to her and UGMA's musical development. Leland remembers that "she'd be up writing all night, writing the parts for all the instruments." She also developed a facility with most instruments. Within a few years, vocalist Amina Amatullah witnessed her facility with virtually every instrument in the band. "They'd be playing something, and she'd sit down and just start playing on the vibes. Then she'd put that down and pick up the bone and play on that. Then she put that down and went to play on the bass. I've seen her do that. She could play every one and sound good. I've watched her learn how to write lead sheets."

Within a year of its inception, UGMA was attracting more musicians, including saxophonists Arthur Blythe and Stanley "Chico" Roberson, bassist Eddie Mathias, and drummer Bill Madison. "Dudes started coming around," according to Al Hines, "because they knew we had something going on that they wanted to be part of." During 1962 Blythe, then twenty-two years old and recently relocated to Los Angeles from San Diego, was living in a rooming house with saxophonist Vernon Crane, a friend of Linda, who occasionally visited the house on Seventh-fifth Street. One day, Arthur accompanied his friend and walked in on a Tapscott-led rehearsal. "It was very inspiring to hear that. That's what I wanted to hear. 'Yeah! Yeah, man! Let me hurry-up and get my saxophone!' I jumped right in there. It was beautiful. The communication was right off." That connection extended beyond the musical realm and was the basis for a collaboration that would continue on an almost daily basis until Blythe left for New York in 1974 and then intermittently until the day Horace died.

> We had like feelings musically and about political things, spiritual things, social things. We were young men trying to develop who we were, thinking about trying to be better, trying to do the best. We were drugged with the black people's situation and our history, not being racist about it, but feeling the injustice being done and speaking out about injustice. We weren't soapbox people, so we did it with our music. That was part of the connection, love for self and family, and wanting the best that we could possibly provide for them. But at the same time we were learning how to be young men, how to do this the best that we could do it, and hoping to make it a positive expression.

Arthur's worldview meshed perfectly with Horace's vision of a community band and their artistic and social role. "I got exposed to Elijah Muhammad, Malcolm and Dr. King and Adam Clayton Powell. There were certain black men out there who seemed to be working for the betterment of the whole country. We were feeling that if we were together, we'd be an asset to our environment rather than a liability." The discussions within the group, prodded by Horace's suggestions and observations, focused on shaping UGMA as an organization dedicated to performing music from the community for the community. According to Linda, "The thoughts and conversations became more and more about this dream, 'if this was happening and that was happening we would be able to . . . , that can be real.' The dream kept growing."[47]

By the early Sixties, a group of drummers had arrived in Los Angeles from Kansas City, Missouri, looking for careers in music, most of whom would play with UGMA and embrace its purpose. Jimmy Lovelace, Donald Dean, Leroy Brooks, and Everett Brown, Jr. were all in their early twenties and in search of richer, more diverse musical pastures. In Kansas City, Everett felt he "wasn't playing enough, and every player was the same. I thought I should get away." With the exception of Lovelace, who would subsequently relocate to New York, the other three drummers would play important roles in the history of UGMA and its successor organizations. Donald Dean quickly established himself in L.A. and was soon working with many artists, including Teddy Edwards, Dexter Gordon, Hampton Hawes, Harold Land, and Gerald Wilson. Not long after arriving, he struck up a personal and musical friendship with Horace. Although his commitments to other artists, particularly Les McCann and Jimmy Smith, kept him on the road a great deal into the 1990s, when in Los Angeles he rehearsed and performed with UGMA. As was the case with Blythe and the other members, the connection transcended the musical realm. "Most of the things we did were rehearsals and special concerts," recalls Donald. "There wasn't a whole lot of money to be made, but it was a whole lot of fun and there was a whole lot to learn in the challenges that he put out there for us. It was different, very avant-garde, and the music had a way of making a statement, so to speak, as far as black culture was concerned. That made me feel good, being my background was from Kansas City, which was not the most liberal place."

Leroy Brooks and Everett Brown, Jr. were both protégés of Dean, each possessing prodigious talent. Leroy quickly became a regular, and, although he later struggled with psychological problems, was on the scene until the late 1960s, when he committed suicide. "Fuck could this guy play! Just a natural!" Donald exclaims. "And he ended up killing himself. He was very depressed. He'd come by my house at two, three o'clock in the morning, crying and saying different things. Horace and I were almost like his daddies, so to speak. All of a sudden, he just started the motor up in his garage. Why, I don't know. He never thought he was as good as he was, but this guy could play up a storm, I'm telling you." Guitarist Avotcja remembers him as "an amazing drummer. He wasn't a basher. He was a melodic drummer like Max Roach is a melodic drummer. Leroy would make traps sound like talking drums." Amina Amatullah witnessed Leroy at a subsequent UGMA house playing simultaneously on two drum kits: "He had two sets of drums set up in the living room. He looked like a ballet dancer, when he played these simultaneously, left foot on this bass drum, right foot on that bass drum. He would just play and both his feet would be moving, and then he'd work the cymbals. It was very unreal. Two sets of drums!"

Perhaps the most important drummer in the organization's history was Everett Brown, Jr. Horace's version of their meeting describes a chance encounter on a street near the musician's union.[48] Everett tells a different story of Horace dropping by one of his gigs. "He'd just watch me. So I asked him once, 'Man, why are you watching me all the time?' He said, 'Well, I got a jazz orchestra, and I want you to play in it.' So that's what I did." At first sight it was evident that Everett was exceptionally talented. "He could play anything, any type of drumming" according to Blythe. "He could carry four different grooves and get intricate with them, be able to have an overview of them and then choose as he was going along his way." Stanley Crouch, a recent graduate of Jefferson High School, who would play a major role in the black arts movement in Los Angeles as a writer, spoken word performer, avant-garde drummer, bandleader, and teacher, concurs, "They had this great drummer with them, Everett Brown. He should have gone to New York. I mean he was one of the great drummers. This cat could really, really, really play. He could *really, really* play. It's hard to describe his style, because he didn't sound like anybody. The only one that he reminded me somewhat of was [Ed] Blackwell, but he didn't play like that either. He just had his own way of playing." When asked if he had ever drummed with UGMA, Stanley replied,

> Oh no, no, no, no, no, no, no, no. With Everett Brown in that band? Are you crazy? They didn't need anybody but him. He was special. I mean, he was one of the great drummers, man, for real. They had another guy [Leroy Brooks] out there, who committed suicide and played like Elvin [Jones], but Everett Brown was something. He could play in four different meters at the same time. I saw him do that. He had that kind of independence. He was incredible and had a beautiful, beautiful sound.

Other musicians and artists passed through for shorter periods of time, but made important contributions and, in turn, were affected by UGMA. Pianist Stanley Cowell was in town pursuing a year of graduate studies in music at the University of Southern California during the 1963/1964 academic year and visited the house. Bill Madison muses, "Stanley had and has a lot to say; writes good tunes, plays excellent, good background. He used to come to my house a lot. He and Linda got together and did some writing. We used to play at his house." Cowell remembers Horace's impact on him: "In a pleasant way, he was a pianist who pushed my development by 'dueling' with me on several friendly playing occasions. I admired him and felt a kinship with him in that neither of us was interested in the musical status quo. He was further on the cutting edge at that time than I was."[49] Those friendly duels occurred during sessions at the UGMA house and also while Horace was working with Curtis Amy's band at the It Club on Washington Boulevard, where Stanley also worked, playing six A.M.-to-noon Sunday sessions.

UGMA emerged without a formal leadership and organizational structure. There were no rigid requirements and only an ad hoc division of labor. Shared musical and socio-political values brought the musicians together, while Horace provided much of the musical direction. Rehearsing was continuous, primarily at Linda's UGMA house, but also throughout the community, in whatever garages, houses and public spaces were available and in whatever configurations could be assembled. Early performances, featuring line-ups ranging from trio and quartet settings to big band size with as many as twenty musicians, took place in various community spaces, from parks and schools to small local clubs and social organizations.

"We were all UGMAgers"—The Second UGMA House

By 1964 as the Association grew and the walls of the first UGMA house— Lino's Pad—were being stretched, Linda found another residence and moved about two miles northwest to an old, two-story, wood-frame house near the corner of Fifty-sixth and Figueroa Streets. Along with a bohemian and cultural activist named "Brother" Percy Smith, they set up what would serve as an arts center and the second UGMA house for the next four years. Set back from the intersection and hidden behind a U-shaped collection of medical offices, the secluded building enhanced UGMA's underground mystique and became an intense round-the-clock gathering and rehearsal space for dozens of artists, cultural and political activists, and an assorted gallery of hangers-on.

The aging house had a large living room, dining area, and kitchen downstairs, and three bedrooms upstairs. They installed a piano in the living room, which became the main rehearsal space. Formal rehearsals under Horace's direction occurred two or three times a week, but the music was non-stop. "We'd play all day and all night in different configurations," according to drummer Bill Madison. "Every day, man, every day," Arthur Blythe confirms. "That's what I loved. 'Let's go!' Sometimes I'd be scuffling to get the rent for a little room. Sometimes it'd be difficult to get fifty dollars a week. But I would be playing all the time, every day, and that was a good feeling, a good learning period." Recent arrival Danyel Romero concludes, "Basically, it was a place you could go to and there'd always be some music happening, and if not, you could make it happen because there was always somebody there."

The older members of UGMA were not in residence at the house, but would appear to play and rehearse. David Bryant resided in Watts, in the same house on 115th Street that his mother had built, when she moved her two young sons to the West Coast in 1923. Lester Robertson lived with his wife, Esther, a dancer, who worked in Hollywood and recently had performed in *The Ten Commandments.* Horace had his wife, Cecilia, and a growing family of five children. To support them, he took jobs when he could, arranging charts for pop singers with Marion Sherrill at the Script House above Grant's Music Center on Third Avenue near Venice Boulevard. Backing vocalists such as Lorez Alexandria and Juanita Cruz, he also took occasional sideman gigs with Curtis Amy, Lou Blackburn, and Onzy Matthews, and even played in a brothel.[50] In the intervals his family remained supportive and Cecilia worked steadily in administration at the County Hospital.

The second UGMA house was soon welcoming new members. Brother Percy hailed from East St. Louis, where he had been a community organizer, and was older than most of the artists in residence. He and his friends weren't musicians, but loved jazz and the arts in general. In his role as philosopher, supporter, muse, and enthusiast, Brother Percy was responsible for finding places to play in the community and for recruiting new participants, some musical and some simply artistic and/or just in search of an alternative scene. Trumpeter Danyel Romero, discharged from the Army in 1963, hung out with friends at a donut shop on Slauson Avenue, a few blocks from the UGMA house, which also offered jazz on its jukebox. Percy was another regular customer and invited Danyel back the House. "It was my first taste of playing with some really creative people," Danyel recollects. "I got my start in playing professionally with them, although I had been working with a group in the Army band. They really helped me to find myself, to get inside and relax, to be one with the music."

Billy Boyd and Carmel Crunk became regulars at the house. Billy was a pianist and vibes player, a classmate of Billy Higgins at Jacob Riis High School, the local reformatory, and recently discharged from the army after overseas service in the Pacific. Carmel, a friend of Linda in his thirties and a civil servant with an office job, became a regular presence at the house piano, vocalizing and writing songs and lyrics. Some of his spirituals-influenced compositions, such as "Close to Freedom" and "Many Nites Ago," became an essential part of the UGMA book. "Close to Freedom" captured UGMA's support for the ongoing civil rights struggles.

We're almost there,
Close to freedom—we ain't no more slaves—
We're almost there,
Close to freedom—we gonna take it to our graves.[51]

Guitarist Avotcja was a recent transplant from New York City, when she met Bill Madison and immediately developed a strong and, for her, unusual friendship. "I just remember that Bill and I used to have these long, long conversations about music and all kinds of stuff, and it was such a pleasure to be around a guy who was just a friend and a musician who was talking some serious music." In the male-dominated jazz world this was unusual, as it was in UGMA during its early years.

> Like a lot of things, including a lot of the guys in UGMA, most men have a real difficult time being friends with women on any kind of real level, and Bill was a friend and that impressed me. So when he started talking about Tapscott, I figured it was worth a gamble because I was sick of getting shoved in all these little corners and categories with folks, and I just wanted to play and be able to try some of my stuff and be pushed by somebody else in different directions.

Through Linda there had always been a strong female presence in the organization, but particularly early on gender relations were rather typical. Many of the musicians in the mostly male band depended on support from family, wives, or partners, especially in the beginnings of their careers. Donald Dean recalls a conversation with Horace: "We were sitting up on my balcony one day, and he said, 'Doubles, you know I've never had a woman that I made more money than her.' Like this joke that goes around: 'What is homeless?' 'A musician without a wife.' So we all had our wives or girlfriends and they had steady jobs, which enabled us to play, practice and do the things that we did." Avotcja recalls the typical male attitudes of the time: "In that day everybody thought that way about women. And the guy who was different, was really different. The guy who broke that mold was really an oddity in those times." She also remembers Linda,

> She was a brilliant musician and she was definitely an organizer. She was the kind of woman that UGMA liked. I was not. She was a care-taker and in Horace's case she could play follow the leader. As much as I loved Horace, I wasn't the follow the leader kind of sister. And those were the kind of sisters they wanted. I didn't sleep with them. I was just interested in music, which is why I liked Bill [Madison] and Arthur

[Blythe] and a couple of the folks I was really close to there. But I wasn't part of the inner workings and all that stuff, because I thought it was pretty scandalous and sleazy to tell you the truth. She was a great musician. I think that she never got the play that she was due.

Nevertheless, perhaps more than most organizations of the time, some women, including Amina, Avotcja, and Linda, played important roles in UGMA's early years. Given the bleak history of women in jazz organizations, this was significant, despite the fact that there were still relatively few. Donald Dean remembers, "A lot of the things we played were from Linda Hill. She was a poet, I guess, and she was a very strong woman. She was the first woman I'd ever met like that in my life. These women that were a part of UGMA, I'd never experienced like that. Their strength and their involvement with the culture and everything, that really took me."

As word of the UGMA house spread, it also attracted musicians who were active in more mainstream circles but also interested in new sounds, as well as others who had a passing acquaintance with the organization and who occasionally visited to rehearse or perform with the band. Bassist and cellist Walter Savage remembers, "UGMA was also a lot of people who didn't publicize the fact that they hung out and played around with UGMA. There were a lot of good musicians that came around and hung out, that you never would have thought were UGMAgers. As Leroy [Brooks] used to say, 'Are you an UGMAger?' So we were all UGMAgers. [Saxophonist] Hadley Caliman used to hang out there a whole lot and there are a lot of guys whose names I can't even remember." For a few years in the mid-1960s Caliman, a Central Avenue veteran then known as "Little Dex" both for his skills and his admiration for tenor saxophonist Dexter Gordon, and recently returned to Los Angeles, was a regular. "We used to go over there every day and play what we thought was the coming new music. Every day. All these people would come, some from my early childhood that were maintaining their musical careers."

Avotcja remembers the excitement, including some of the remarkable artists who passed through the house: "Some of my greatest heroes came through there. It was such an honor to be able to play with them, like Eric Dolphy and all that. Dolphy came through there a couple of times. Art Pepper came through there. None of those folks were regulars there, but so many people walked through there." Sonny Criss began a musical relationship with UGMA that would last until his death in 1977. Amina recalls, "That's where they would come, even if they didn't hang out. If they got off a gig at two in the morning, and they'd be in town two or three days and didn't really have nothing to do, they'd come by the house at two in the morning and stay there until the sun came out."

Percussionist, trumpeter, and vocalist Juno Lewis, who would soon record *Kulu Se Mama* (Impulse, 1965) with John Coltrane, had settled in Los Angeles and was part of the scene. Bassist Jiunie Booth and saxophonist Pharoah Sanders visited when in town. Members of Gerald Wilson's orchestra were also regulars. Edwin Pleasant recalls, "Thurman Green used to come through and just look. We were very avant-garde, and it was pretty wild there." According to Linda's son, Leland, "People were over all the time, on the weekend and during the week, and Linda used to cook. She'd just fix big pots of chili, chicken soup, whatever. She was always cooking meals for the cats."

Methods of survival for those at the house varied greatly, from typical nine-to-five jobs for a few, to the many who crashed at the house and lived off of Linda's nurturing and cooking. Continuing to work as a nurse's aide, Linda and a few others covered the rent and most of the household expenses. Bill Madison held clerical jobs for the State of California and lived in the house until he married. Danyel Romero worked for a lamp manufacturer on Slauson and Billy Boyd took a job with the railroad.

Linda was also becoming the UGMA therapist. According to Leland, Linda "cared about everybody. She always lent an ear." If Horace was becoming known as "Pops," later to be affectionately known as "Papa" (also the Arkestra acronym), Linda was emerging as the UGMA matriarch. She offered a motherly or older sister influence to the predominantly male aggregation and ran the house, but the source of her authority rested more in her artistic abilities, vision, unique worldview, and strong personality. Linda's sister-in-law, Edith Hill, recalls, "I do remember that she was never happy on any 9-to-5. I believe it was because she was such a free spirit, who was so instilled with her African heritage and her love of music. She hated having to straighten her hair, wearing shoes and stockings, and doing the things required to conform to so-called society's standards. These requirements made her uncomfortable. She had great courage in that she dared to be different."[52]

In this new setting a more bohemian lifestyle was evolving, which definitely set a broader underground tone. The lifestyle at the house was "out," to use one of Horace's favorite words, too out for some, who would appear each day for the music and then leave, such as Avotcja. "There was a lot of stuff that went down that I was not part of and I'm so grateful for that. Too out for me." Linda, however, remained at the center of it. Alto saxophonist Will Connell remembers, "Linda was calling James 'Semaj.' She used to call people's names backwards. She had all the names like a family tree written on the wall in her room. Linda was full of ideas like that." According to Danyel, "Linda was like a big flower. She was great; she was mystical. She was connected to some spirits or sources of the unseen world that most of us were not at that time dealing with the way she was. She had a rock, a mojo stone. She was a very spiritual person and very for real. She was somebody who wouldn't BS you, a down-to-earth realness. She was very loving." Stanley Cowell, who knew her just as she was embarking on her career as an artist, looks back fondly on Linda as "a big, loving soul, who took care of the musicians and wanted to compose. I did compose a piece called 'LA Dance' in her memory, but never announced it."[53]

As was typical in most underground environments, drugs were also part of the lifestyle. A few of the artists were heroin users, but for most, Horace included, the experience was limited to marijuana. What hard drug use there was, remained somewhat concealed. "That was not an open scene. You wouldn't go in there and see people shooting up—that was not it. Cats would go get high in the bathroom. It wasn't like 'Let's all get high,'" Danyel remembers. "Most of the people just smoked herb. . . . I practically learned how to smoke weed there. Hold your nose, puff out your cheeks when you're taking a hit, so that they can get carefully high. That was the first time I experienced that kind of getting high on herb. I thought, 'Wow, is that how you do it?' So I tried it, and it worked!" Some of those with serious addictions found support from members. Guitarist Tommy Trujillo, who became a member in the mid-1960s, recalls the situation of one much admired and beloved artist:

> When I lived with [name deleted], he was shooting up every night. He was basically a full-time junkie, but [he] was so spiritual. He had the deepest spiritual understanding of any artist that I had met up to that time. When he would get sick, because we loved him so much, we would go out and cop him some dope, and we weren't even into it. We just cared about him so much. He was just so inspiring as a person, and that's the way he was his whole life. He represented the real spirit of the music and the people in UGMA did as well.

Despite varied distractions, UGMA's focus was a commitment to free artistic expression and the development of a social consciousness about its community. Most participants had just begun forging a conscious worldview and developing their own identity as African Americans and as artists. Emblematic of this was the transformation of saxophonist Arthur Blythe into "Black Arthur Blythe" or "Black Arthur" or even "Black."

I had been reading . . . about musicians at the turn of the century. There was one particular musician, Jim Europe, and I was amazed at what he was doing with all those instruments. We were drinking a little bit, and I was expressing my newfound understanding or newfound validation of black people's efforts. I said, "Yeah, that's really valid!" I was just talking and talking, and they were saying, "Okay, okay, we believe you." I just kept on. . . . Then Linda Hill said, "Please, Black Arthur, will you shut up!" And it stuck. I didn't mind. I was glad. The image was a little recognition from my peers. Also I was recognizing that I didn't want to be a part of the older psyche of black people that at one time meant being ashamed of who we were, of our lips, our nose, our skin, of being black. So I chose, "Yeah, this is who I am. I'm Black Arthur." It didn't mean that I hated white people. I was just acknowledging myself, because we had not been acknowledging ourselves. It was a way of being honest and that was part of the association with Horace and the others, Linda, Lester Robertson.

Linda Hill's quest involved a search for roots in African culture, well in advance of the movements of the late 1960s and early 1970s, manifested both in her historical studies of African arts and in her adoption of African personal styles. According to Arthur, "She would look like an African, very early on, when nobody else was doing it at all. She looked like those African women with the shaved heads and earrings."

The range of interests and values—personal identity, family, community, politics, African American and African history—within UGMA was exemplified in the music. Carmel Crunk's politically conscious work is still a staple of the band. Horace's early compositions ranged from celebrations of family—"Isle of Celia" (wife Cecilia), "Golden Pearl" (grandmother Pearlina), "Sandy and Niles" (son Niles)—to assertions of the African American musical tradition in "Why Don't You Listen," with lyrics by Linda Hill.

Why don't you listen to sounds of truth
    Why don't you listen
Why didn't you listen to Bird and Trane
    Why didn't you listen
Why didn't you listen to Lady Day
    Why didn't you listen
Why didn't you listen to what they say
    Why didn't you listen

Why didn't you listen, why didn't you listen

Now listen[54]

Internationally, they covered ruminations on Africa with "Thoughts of Dar es Salaam" and on the anti-colonial struggle in "Lumumba," Horace's homage to Patrice Lumumba, the first prime minister of the newly independent Congo, who was assassinated at the behest of the US CIA and the Belgian government in 1961. Lyrics were co-written with Linda Hill.

Your dream still lives
Freedom now—
The death of Lumumba was not in vain
Freedom now—[55]

UGMA was also aligning with more politically conscious artists and political figures. Horace met poet and activist Jayne Cortez, then planning her first one-woman show. Raised in Watts during the 1940s and married to saxophonist Ornette Coleman in the 1950s, she had spent 1963 working in Greenwood, Mississippi, with the Student Nonviolent Coordinating Committee (SNCC) in voter registration drives. She returned to Los Angeles that same year to coordinate support work by organizing the Friends of SNCC and also to pursue her poetic art. When she met Horace, she was looking for musicians to perform with her and in support of SNCC. There was an immediate bonding, musically and politically. Jayne remembers, "Clearly among the musicians, Tapscott was the one with the most consciousness and dedication to the black freedom struggle." She worked with UGMA backing, perhaps three to five performances a year, from clubs to schools, from Sunset Boulevard to 103rd Street in Watts, until she left for New York in 1967. The show evolved during that time, largely as a reaction to events around them and throughout the world.

We were always expanding the show. I remember once that Tapscott added something about Lumumba. This had words and we did that. We were always expanding as we went along. As things happened in the world, we would include whatever. The level of consciousness was pretty high. We had a lot of conversations about music, about the daily rhythms of life, about family, friends, but we also talked a lot about liberation movements in Africa and around the world, about political situations. I think Horace was a very political thinker. He talked about racism, police brutality, discrimination—job discrimination, housing discrimination, and also about making the African American community stronger, what could happen, which is why he organized UGMA and then his Arkestra. And which is why he stayed in Los Angeles and the community and didn't come to New York, when the rest of us left. I used to say, "Well, Horace, it's something to be able to do your music in an atmosphere where people are doing the same thing, so that you would have a fuller response, just to bring it up to another level." He said, "Well, if I leave, who's going to be here?"

From the schools and parks to the growing swell of protest movements, Horace and UGMA moved through the community offering an undiluted, noncommercial artistic expression of their experiences and evolution as African Americans, aligning themselves with a broad spectrum of political movements, from civil rights activists to revolutionaries. As artists it was something they all were seeking to express and in their coming together created an outlet for it. In Horace the members found a fellow artist who embodied that perhaps better than anyone else. According to Arthur Blythe,

> When I first met him, we just had a connection about certain attitudes, ideas, some belief system that was in us. I acknowledged it in him and he acknowledged it in me. And I was a supporter of his efforts and he was a supporter of my efforts. But he was more organized within himself than perhaps I was at the time. I hadn't grown to that point. He was a spiritual supporter, an emotional supporter. Cats could see that about him and go along with him on his efforts.

There is, perhaps, no better assessment of what Horace expressed during these years than that offered by John Outterbridge, sculptor and assemblage artist, and the former director of the Watts Towers Arts Center. At thirty years of age, he moved to Los Angeles in October 1963. A few months later, he attended a concert that featured an artist unknown to him.

> Shortly after arriving—it had to be early- or mid-1964—I attended an event somewhere on Broadway downtown, in a theater building I think. A program was being presented by—I don't know the organization, but it was featuring the Watts Symphonic Orchestra and they had a guest. The guest was a young man named Horace Tapscott, pianist. I was very impressed by the sound of the orchestra, which at that time numbered about thirty people, a rather small orchestra, but just a great sound, a real stout sound. And they introduced this young man, Horace Tapscott, who came out and sat down at the piano.
> As best I can say this, when everything is new and you know nothing about where you are, the intangibilities sever any notion of what is

being presented to you. I didn't know anything about the history of the orchestra. I didn't know anything about Horace Tapscott. So it was a brand-new, fresh pulse that was being introduced to me.

When he was introduced, not very much was said about what would be presented. He simply started to play, and what was coming at us was the story of the history of America in sound. It was so colorful and so vivid that people were crying. I'm serious. On this Sunday afternoon I found myself staring in space at the piano and at this young man, who I didn't know anything about, and raving within myself about the discipline within this small orchestra. And Horace did a very classical rendition of the color of this country's legacy. From the slave era to whatever we had experienced as human beings in our lives was part of the color of his presentation. I can't explain it other than that, but I knew I was meeting some gigantic, stout musical personality.

4

THE GIANT IS AWAKENED

The Watts Uprising and Cultural Resurgence

We have removed the cataract
from history's impartial eye

OJENKE

While a high school student in the early 1950s, Horace Tapscott rode the electric streetcars down Central Avenue to Jordan High School in Watts to attend an evening class taught by jazz musician and Jordan alumnus Buddy Collette. Having grown up in Watts during the 1920s and 1930s with fellow musicians David Bryant, Joe Comfort, Bobby and Big Jay McNeely, Charles Mingus, and the Woodman brothers, Buddy appreciated the cultural richness of the community and realized the importance of fostering creativity and passing on the best of that tradition. For Horace, it was the beginning of an involvement with that area that would last until his death almost fifty years later. Some of the first performances of the Underground Musicians Association took place there, and by the mid-1960s UGMA would be an important and constant presence in the heart of the community.

A small working-class enclave tucked into south central Los Angeles County, Watts would play a leading role in the life of the African American community in 1965, when African Americans took to the streets en masse in response to growing social and economic inequalities. The Watts uprising was part of a national experience between 1964 and 1968 in which over one hundred cities experienced upheavals, many provoking military responses. However, in terms of its dimensions—the level of ferocity, fatalities, and destruction—as well as its subsequent cultural resurgence, it was unique.

Though associated with Watts, the precipitating event happened just west of it, while the uprising far exceeded the boundaries of that community, ultimately consuming much of South Central Los Angeles. Nevertheless, Watts was engulfed in the fighting and in the years that followed became a focal point for many of the social, political and cultural movements that emerged. It was also to serve as the hub of a grassroots arts movement that spread throughout the African American community, in many ways exemplifying ideas about the role of art and artists in the community that had been germinating in the Underground Musicians Association.

Watts's Cultural Legacy

By 1960 Watts was still a relatively young community, having been subdivided from a former Mexican land grant in the latter half of the nineteenth century and only incorporated as a city in 1907. Within a few years it had a thriving business center with more than forty commercial enterprises on Main Street, later renamed 103rd Street, and a population of approximately 2,000. Primarily a blue-collar town, it was racially mixed, though groups tended to live within their blocks, characterized by small, family homes, many built by the original occupants. At this early stage the majority was European derived, with a heavy German component, but there were also Latino, black, and Japanese American populations. African Americans were concentrated in the southwest portion of the city, below Main Street and east of Central Avenue. By 1920 the population of Watts had increased to 4,529 of whom 14 percent were African Americans, a percentage four times greater than in Los Angeles. This trend, which would create an African American majority within the area shortly after the end of World War II, prompted the Ku Klux Klan and other residents to seek Watts's affiliation with the city of Los Angeles to prevent the possibility of African American elected officials. In 1926, Watts voted to annex itself to Los Angeles.[1]

Watts offered a culturally rich environment practically from its inception. Arna Bontemps, an important writer of the Harlem Renaissance, was raised in Watts and there composed his first novel, *God Sends Sunday* (1931). The first black-owned film company, the Lincoln Motion Picture Company (1916–1921), filmed throughout the greater Los Angeles area, including Watts.[2] By the early 1920s Italian immigrant Simon Rodia had begun crafting his *Watts Towers*, which would consume him for the next three decades. He devoted his free time to the project before walking away from his magnificent creation in 1955.[3] Throughout this time the rising structures stood to puzzle, confound, amaze, and inspire the neighborhood, particularly the young people, some of whom would soon emerge as artists. In *Beneath the Underdog*, Charles Mingus writes, "Tig Johnson and Cecil J. McNeely used to gather sacks full of pretty rocks and broken bottles to take to Mr. Rodia, and my boy hung around with them watching him work. . . ."[4] McNeely remembers, "Oh yeah. We used to go down there all the time and watch him build it."[5]

Perhaps most important, especially for improvising artists, was the object lesson of Rodia's restless exploration. According to Mingus, "He was always changing his ideas while he worked and tearing down what he wasn't satisfied with and starting over again, so pinnacles tall as a two-story building would rise up and disappear and rise again. What was there yesterday mightn't be there next time you looked, but then another lacy-looking tower would spring up in its place."[6] In his autobiography, Buddy Collette recalls, "Simon knew what he was doing with it, but we had no clue. Most people thought, 'That crazy guy, what's he building?' We had never seen anything like that before, and he just kept adding to the structures. It wasn't until later that we could see that the guy was very artistic and knew where he was going."[7]

Watts's musical legacy predates the arrival of the Collette-Mingus generation. By the end of World War I, just a few years after the city's inception, it was an important outlet for late night, after-hours entertainment with many small clubs and one somewhat extravagant venue in Baron Long's Tavern (later the Plantation Club), populated by the wealthy and Hollywood elite.[8] One of the most significant, if somewhat short-lived venues was at Leake's Lake, a pond and surrounding lands owned by real estate investor Charles C. Leake, who farmed fish commercially there.[9] In the early 1920s Central Avenue musicians and entrepreneurs Reb and Johnny Spikes, created a pavilion, bandstand, and picnic area, offering day and evening entertainment. Shortly thereafter management was taken over by Jelly Roll Morton and William Woodman, Sr., who called it Wayside Park, which became the site of regular performances by Jelly Roll Morton, Kid Ory, and their respective bands, as well as King Oliver's Creole Jazz Band on a few occasions in the spring of 1922.[10] These were some of the most important New Orleans musicians in the creation of jazz and they could all be heard in rural Watts.

The testimony of attendees celebrates not only the musical richness of the scene, but also its peacefully integrated character. Some fifty years later a white business executive reminisces, "We'd drive down from Los Angeles and stay as long as they'd pick up a horn. Out there at night, the music coming over the water was like the only thing in the world. Nothing interfered. You could get drinks. Lots of people brought bottles. Black and white came there. Some people danced, but most of us stood around and listened to that crazy jazz."[11] According to a black member of the Watts community, "Jazz bands played at Leake's Lake. He had a bandstand and place to dance overlooking the water. There was also the Plantation Club and others around 108th and Central. Liquor was definitely a problem, but the clubs had good music and entertainment. They were places where black and white mingled. In the twenties there were a lot more activities together."[12]

By the mid-1930s Bryant, Collette, Comfort, Mingus, and the McNeely and Woodman brothers were emerging as artists, performing in the two theaters, the Largo and the Linda, on 103rd Street and other small venues throughout the community. The strong cultural tradition of Watts did not end with that generation, and Collette spent some of his time at mid-century grooming the next generation, including alto saxophonist Sonny Criss and Horace Tapscott. Watts also became a major center of the new R&B sound in 1948, when band leader and drummer Johnny Otis opened The Barrelhouse at 106th Street and Wilmington, across the railroad tracks from the Watts Towers, perhaps, according to historian George Lipsitz, "the first night spot in the world to feature rhythm and blues music exclusively."[13] "At that time," Otis recalls, "Simon Rodia was still building the towers and we were building rhythm and blues with Etta James, Pee Wee Crayton and Big Jay McNeely, among others."[14]

For the five years of its existence, The Barrelhouse was an incubator of R&B talent, including Little Esther Phillips and the Robins (later known as the Coasters), as well as featuring Otis's various bands. According to Jayne Cortez,

> Watts in the late forties, 1948 to 1952, was very vital. There was a lot more cultural activity. In the Fifties there was a lot of music in the African American community in most of the parks, like South Park on the

Eastside, and Wrigley Field, Will Rogers Park in Watts. There were always concerts, jazz concerts, at those places on Sunday afternoons, or on some Saturdays or special holidays. And there were always people playing music in their garages, in little cafes, and little music clubs. I remember going to teen-age dances, where bands like Johnny Otis's would be playing with Big Mama Thornton singing. Little Esther Phillips would sing, and the Robins. All around Watts there were about four or five little places they played. I got into the Barrelhouse as a teenager. It was always very exciting to me.

Cortez's poetry also grew from the fertile soil of her community, where oral street tradition and more formal poetics were part of everyday life. "Poetry had always been recited in churches, in homes, in the street and in all other public events in the African American community," she recalls. "As a child, I remember playing the dozens, sounding on my playmates, and making up rhymes, and somewhere along the line I guess I was just attracted to words and poetry. . . . I remember Langston Hughes, James Weldon Johnson, Paul Laurence Dunbar—their poetry always seemed to be recited in different churches and places."

Such was the vitality that new arrivals from more congested urban cities or impoverished southern fields could miss the growing socioeconomic problems plaguing the area. Not long after arriving in Los Angeles in 1963, artist John Outterbridge and his wife made a point of driving through various communities to explore and acquaint themselves with their new city. He remembers vividly their first drive through Watts:

> What I was discovering was a very unique, manicured community with white picket fences and bright lawns, and a community called Watts. We drove down 103rd Street and there was a shopping center, theater, and then I spotted out of the corner of my eyes, to my left, some strange structure that I didn't know anything about. That was the Watts Towers. I said, "Wow! What is that?" I turned off of 103rd and went down Graham Street to 107th Street and turned into 107th Street. I couldn't take my eyes off the structure. I said, "Man, that is a magic thing!" And I met at that time two artists who were part of what was then the Watts Towers Arts Center, like a little row house. The people that I met that Sunday afternoon were Noah Purifoy and Judson Powell. I think Noah Purifoy and Judson were both co-founders of the Watts Towers Arts Center program. So here I am meeting a person that would become a mentor, a friend, both of them, and introduce me to the tapestry of a

very, very beautiful, unique community—Watts. It had a kinship right away. And there were artists and musicians. There was a real vibrant, pulsating thing there.

The Uprising of 1965

Though culturally rich, by 1960 every socioeconomic indicator pointed toward increasing immiseration for the black community. The years of civil rights support work and demonstrations, of protestations by the local NAACP, CORE, and Urban League, had not altered the living conditions of most African Americans. The area was almost 85 percent African American, overwhelmingly working class, and segregated at the bottom of that class. "The 1965 Special Census indicates that the entire South Central Area was severely disabled socially and economically according to all of the criteria measured, and Watts was one of the most disabled of the communities studied," according to sociologist Nathan Cohen. "Unemployment was over 13 per cent; the median income was below the poverty line defined by the Federal Government; over 10,000 families were headed by females."[15]

In 1961 the last electric streetcar line was terminated. Although increasingly in disrepair, the cars had been an important source of transportation for many working outside the black community. Many basic public services were becoming either ineffectual or nonexistent. Historian Patricia Rae Adler graphically illustrates the intolerable situation: "The never-adequate sewers stank in the summer, there was not enough water to flush the toilets, not enough pressure to fight fires. Health facilities were inadequate."[16] Stanley Crouch would take the title of his spoken word LP of 1969 from the response one community member received when telephoning for medical assistance: "Ain't no ambulances for no nigguhs tonight."[17]

Especially glaring was the failure of political movements to have any impact on halting the campaign waged by the police department against minority communities. "Police violence also rose dramatically in ghetto neighborhoods," notes historian Martin Schiesl. "Sixty blacks were killed by patrolmen from 1963 to 1965, of whom twenty-five were unarmed and twenty-seven were shot in the back."[18] Not one of them was considered unjustified by review boards. The only visible impact was the use of this issue as an electoral ploy by politicians, most notably Sam Yorty in the mayor's race of 1961, to win African American and Latino votes. With Yorty's election nothing was done to deal with Chief Parker's department, which continued to maintain the boundaries of a segregated Los Angeles. The election in 1963 of three

African Americans to the city council—Tom Bradley, Gilbert Lindsay, and Billy Mills—may have offered some critical voices, but they did little to alter the status quo. Meanwhile, tensions were escalating. All that was needed was a spark to set South Central afire.

The uprising of 1965, then the largest and most destructive in American history, was provoked by a confrontation between law enforcement and residents of South Central. Marquette Frye and his brother, Ronald, were pulled over by two California Highway Patrol officers at the corner of 116th Street and Avalon Boulevard, barely one-half mile west of Watts, on the evening of August 11. A crowd quickly gathered and the LAPD showed up in force. The situation rapidly escalated into a confrontation, fueled by a report that a woman in a maternity dress had been struck by one of the officers. It was later learned that the woman in question had been wearing a smock that appeared like a maternity dress but that she was not pregnant. Given the Department's history, such a story was instantly believable to the people who had gathered and news of it spread rapidly.

A spontaneous, mass uprising against the police ensued, in essence an expression of rage and opposition to decades of systematic abuse and brutalization. As novelist Chester Himes, a resident of Los Angeles in the 1940s, notes, "The only thing that surprised me about the race riots in Watts in 1965 was that they waited so long to happen. We are a very patient people."[19] The response of the police department to these developments further validated the outrage of the protestors and fanned the flames. Chief Parker's explanation was that "one person threw a rock, and then, like monkeys in a zoo, others started throwing rocks."[20] His racist views were again trumpeted two weeks later, when he told a national television audience on *Meet the Press*, "It is estimated that by 1970 45 percent of the metropolitan area of Los Angeles will be Negro; if you want any protection for your home and family . . . you're going to have to get in and support a strong police department. If you don't do that, come 1970, God help you."[21]

While the fighting subsided by August 18, it was merely the end of the main event, not of police assaults on citizens and confrontations, which would keep the level of tension high during the next year particularly, and beyond it as well. Historian Gerald Horne concludes, "It reached a crescendo in the spring of 1966 when South LA almost exploded again."[22] UGMA bassist Wilber Morris, a recent Air Force veteran who grew up in San Pedro and on the streets of Watts with drummer Billy Higgins, witnessed one confrontation in early 1968: "I remember one time, turning a corner on 103rd and Central, and being caught in a crossfire. The police were on one side and a group was on the other side, and they were shooting across the street in Will Rogers Park. I had an old Pontiac Chieftain and I had to duck down and had my hands up above holding the steering wheel." That same year vocalist Amina Amatullah was working on a film, *The Voice of the People*, and witnessed the LAPD attack on the Watts Summer Festival that resulted in three deaths and dozens injured:

> I was holding the light bar, sitting on the top of an Austin Healey with the top down, and we were filming the festival. All of a sudden one of them said, "Look! Shine the camera over there." I shined the light over and there they were, a couple of policemen crawling on their bellies through the park, getting ready to come up and start some stuff. Right when I did that, of course they see us. We're in an Austin Healey in the park. When they saw us do that, the one who was the driver took off. I'm holding onto this light bar, the camera is rolling, and they're on foot, trying to get to the car to radio in to try and get them to stop us, but we're filming the whole while. We drive this Healy through the trees, down the sidewalk, off the curb, go up a road somewhere and vanish. And sure enough there was a riot in the park. They invaded and, of course, it ended up with people looting and stuff like that, but they started it. When it came on the news, they did it like the festival got out of hand, but that's not what happened. They started it. They started it.

The Watts upheaval and subsequent confrontations were uprisings, hardly mere riots. Not so much the lessons of Martin Luther King and the civil rights movement, but rather the teachings of Malcolm X for aggressive self-defense took root in the streets of South Central. Such sentiments were not new within the community, when confronted with an intransigent racism. Los Angeles also experienced a resurgent Ku Klux Klan in the 1920s and blacks armed themselves in their own defense. One resident remembers being approached by a group of neighbors organizing community self-defense: "They asked my husband if he had a gun and he said he had. They told him to keep it loaded and handy, just out of reach of the children. Negroes were all armed in Watts in the early twenties."[23] The level of exasperation and the resolve to offer resistance was clearly stated in the weekly *California Eagle*, Los Angeles's most important black paper at the time, which called for integrated self-defense in a series of front-page articles in October 1921. The final piece of the three-part series, "How to Kill the Ku Klux," declares,

The Eagle is going to be a bird of "Rapid motion" and isn't going to sit down any longer "Meditating" about this damnable Ku Klux Klan propaganda. It is now going to tell you in hot and strong words "what it is going to do about it," in the way of Killing these Klanners. . . .

He is tired of writing about the regeneration of the Negro or a new Republic, or giving long-winded messages to the New Negro world. The Ku Kluxers have made him blood-thirsty—for a taste of the Klanner's blood. . . .

I will tell you the way to find these humanized rodents in their Invisible Empire. Go after them just as you do when you all join in a great Rat Hunt. . . .

Klan-rat campaigns should be organized and directed by astute officers familiar with the best methods and thoroughly trained in such work, all Jews, Japs, Negroes, Aliens and Roman Catholics co-operating as far as possible.[24]

Nevertheless, the upheaval of 1965 and the confrontations that followed over the next few years were no more than uprisings. They lacked the political focus to challenge, in any meaningful way, the ruling class in Los Angeles and its armed fist, the LAPD. There was tremendous anger and militancy, but there was no organization with the strength and political program to represent that, to organize it into a force that could change the racist status quo. The government attacks on the left during the right-wing Cold War period of the 1950s and early 1960s had seriously weakened left-wing organizations and the labor movement in Los Angeles. This weakening was coupled with the failure of liberalism and the civil rights movement to improve most African Americans' living conditions. As Adler writes, "The civil rights demonstrations of 1963 and the proud new expressions of a black identity produced only feeble echoes in the housing projects and parking lot social centers of Watts. Voiceless and isolated, the community absorbed the civil rights victories as news from a distant battle and kept to its private concerns."[25] The African American community was thrown back on its own resources to fill a leadership void and offer political and social alternatives.

The experience of fighting back, in Los Angeles and around the country, led to an outburst of activity within South Central Los Angeles and particularly within Watts, which became a focal point for political and cultural movements. People came together to sort out what had happened, to become more politically involved, to discover and celebrate African American culture, and to express "Black Pride." Black nationalism grew rapidly and came to dominate both political and cultural discourse. The Black Panther Party for Self-Defense, the US Organization, and the Nation of Islam were the main beneficiaries of and advocates for some form of political and/or cultural nationalism. What separated them was their attitude toward the state. When faced with the firepower of a fully mobilized LAPD, supported by departments from other areas and the California National Guard, the problems were posed point blank. Only the Panthers, inspired by Maoism and struggles for national liberation throughout Asia and Africa, raised an urban guerrilla strategy that, while brave, was doomed by posing the African American community, actually unemployed street youth, against the force of state power. No matter how courageous and self-sacrificing, unemployed inner city youth, some Vietnam veterans, were no match for the state. Most other nationalists, for all their militant rhetoric, focused on cultural issues and the carving out of space based on black self-determination, essentially capitalism as usual, but black control of it, something much more congenial to the ruling class.

There were a number of Marxist organizations, representing tendencies from Trotskyism to Soviet-style and Maoist Chinese-style Stalinism, that did intervene in the struggles in an attempt to win supporters to a broader revolutionary vision, but whose numbers and social weight remained small. Civil rights groups, including the Student Nonviolent Coordinating Committee (SNCC) and the Southern Christian Leadership Conference (SCLC), were there as well, and procapitalist organizations, like The Sons of Watts, emerged to gain greater access for African Americans to the existing order.[26] Attempts were made to coordinate many of these local organizations, the most significant being the Black Congress, an umbrella organization of almost two dozen political, social and cultural black groups and not a cohesive, programmatically based political movement. They were short-lived.[27]

While the political currents that flowed through the African American community of South Central Los Angeles were many, varied and often ideologically conflictual, there were commonalities in an awakening of black pride and a sense of community, as well as a strong opposition to the LAPD and the economic exploitation of the black community. These would be reflected in the various arts movements and artists that emerged in the years following the uprising as well as in the approach and activities of the Underground Musicians Association, which sought to further develop a community-based aesthetic and ethos through their artistic practice and social involvement.

The Watts Arts Resurgence

As the fires were still smoldering in the business district of Watts on 103rd Street, artists Noah Purifoy, Judson Powell, John Riddle, John Outterbridge and others picked their way through the charred remains, pulling up whatever bits of scarred debris caught their eyes. Within a few weeks they had accumulated over three tons of material and with the wreckage of the uprising started creating dramatic assemblages to make sense of what had happened, to explore their emotions, and to offer a positive vision of the community and its potential, this last sentiment being widely aspired to within the community. Elaine Brown, later chair of the Black Panther Party in the 1970s, captures this feeling: "What I saw in Watts at the time, and I was pretty much in tune with it, which was why I liked it, is that people were really floundering around trying to find some meaning in all this shit. People were just trying to figure out what the hell do we do now, and who are we." Within the few months following the uprising, other artists and people within the community came together to sort out the events of August 1965 and to explore through art their situation and future. According to Elaine, "At that time there was no voice for this. The voice had to be in the poems, the music and the cultural things."

Although the uprising began just west of Watts and ultimately engulfed much of South Central Los Angeles, Watts became the focal point for cultural and social movements, many of which had offices and performance spaces around 103rd Street, or "Charcoal Alley No. 1" as it came to be called in the wake of the summer's devastation. Sadly, Central Avenue was designated "Charcoal Alley No. 2," as the fires consumed many of the structures that had housed the community's earlier cultural center. There quickly emerged a core group of organizations that offered not simply artistic outlets, but movements that stretched the boundaries of artistic as well as social conventions with innovative creations, performances, and productions. In so doing they not only offered reflections upon their lives and the community experience, but they challenged artistic boundaries in terms of the type of art produced and the purpose and role of art and the artist within the community. These were Studio Watts, the Watts Towers Arts Center, Watts Writers Workshop, Watts Happening Coffee House, and the Mafundi Institute.

One of the first organizations to appear was Studio Watts. During 1964, James Woods, an accountant who moonlighted as the doorman at Shelly's Manne-Hole, a Hollywood jazz club, called a meeting of friends to discuss creating a multiracial artists' collective. At the suggestion of Jayne Cortez, he scouted Watts and by the fall of 1964 had found a place at 10311 Grandee Avenue, just off of 103rd Street next to the railroad tracks. Soon Studio Watts was offering programs that ranged across the arts, attracting hundreds of artists and local students. Cortez became director of the acting and writing workshop. "We recruited right from the community, actors, young people who came in," she recalls. "And we did a lot of improvisational work and scenes from plays." They also utilized the streets and parks to host classes, art gatherings and festivals. By August 1965 Studio Watts had been in operation for almost a year. The uprising provoked a heightened sense of commitment. According to Cortez,

> The community came, and other people from Los Angeles came out to see what we were doing. It was a very small space, but it was enough to build a set and do things there. There were some visual arts programs—I think painting—that went on there. A lot of painters came down. Carmencita Romero used to teach dance there, and Bob Rogers taught design. Guy Miller was a sculptor, who taught sculpture and painting. Horace [Tapscott] came and played.[28]

Stanley Crouch worked with Cortez at Studio Watts and then in her Watts Repertory Theater Company, a development from Studio Watts. "We did theater pieces and there was some art that was done in there. We did original plays, and toured around L.A. and some parts of northern California." Jazz musicians John Carter and Bobby Bradford were in the process of forming a band with bassist Tom Williamson and drummer Bruz Freeman, soon to be called the New Art Jazz Ensemble, and by 1966 were rehearsing regularly at Studio Watts. Combining Carter's intricate command of harmony and Bradford's Ornette Coleman–influenced improvisations, they brought another dimension to the avant-garde music scene of South Central.[29]

Woods's vision also included developing community housing, initially by establishing accommodations for artists but also using artists to help design buildings and spaces, as well as represent the people in residence. According to Woods, "Each of the artist-occupants—some of whom will have taken part in the planning—will get a stipend in return for a commitment to community participation, offering lessons, organizing art events, and acting as 'the resource for the expression of needs, joys and desires of their neighbors.'" In so doing, Woods addressed the question of the relation between art and society, and found in the notion of community arts, "the most exciting arts thing happening in the country today."[30] To John Outterbridge, "He saw art as a social tool, a vehicle, to really make some changes. He made some big changes. And he was one of the first people that I started to hear that from when I came to California, he and Noah Purifoy, community involvement through the arts, and using your creativity as a way to reestablish and to extend the whole concept and notion of community. That's what we were all about at that time."

Of equal importance was how community involvement would challenge an artist's creativity. In the visual arts, the direction of Noah Purifoy's work at the Watts Towers Arts Center offered a dramatic demonstration of that dialectic. Noah combined an assemblage approach to art, drawn from his studies of the Dada movement and artists such as Marcel Duchamp, with a concern that art should be rooted in the community. In 1964, the Committee to Save the Watts Towers hired Purifoy as the first director of the Watts Towers Arts Center, located next to Simon Rodia's creations on 107th Street. With educator Sue Welsh and fellow artist Judson Powell, he established a Towers art school and set about recruiting students from the surrounding area from pre-schoolers to late teens. "Well, as a rule, black kids, particularly poor black kids, have low self-esteem, a low self-image," Noah explains. "The object here was to raise the self-image. We believed that an art experience was transferable to other areas of their activity and so forth and that if they could come to the Towers and have a good experience, a positive experience, they could take this experience with them wherever they go."[31]

When Purifoy first moved to Los Angeles a decade earlier, armed with a master's degree in social work, he was employed at the county hospital. Disillusionment with social work led him to art school and the unorthodox approach of Dada, especially as it related to the use of found objects. However, he was not to find his direction until the uprising of 1965. "The debris from the riot is what finally launched me on my own course."[32] He recalls how he and Powell, "while teaching at the Watts Tower[s] Art Center, watched aghast the rioting, looting and burning during the August happening. And while the debris was still smoldering, we ventured into the rubble like other junkers of the community, digging and searching, but unlike others, obsessed without quite knowing why."[33] Artist John Riddle, a recent acquaintance of Noah's, was also rummaging on 103rd Street. "I liked assemblage, too, but I was getting ready to like it more than I have ever liked it. Because when the riots came, all these burned-out buildings were there. There were charred remains and this and that. What was really weird was I met some black artists poking through the ruins."[34]

With over three tons of debris collected, Noah and his fellow artists set about shaping their sculptures. Eight artists collaborated on *66 Signs of Neon,* a collection of sixty-six assemblages that were first exhibited at The Simon Rodia Commemorative Watts Renaissance of the Arts from April 3–9, 1966, at nearby Markham Junior High School. It was also shown at the Watts Summer Festival that year before touring nationally. Noah produced such signature pieces as *Watts Riot* (1965), *Six Birds (Flew Past My Window)* (1966), and *Sir Watts* (1966). In this last piece, he combined wood, metal, and glass with safety pins and old drawers to form the torso and head of a knight-like figure, an indelible image that is at once universal and a triumphant symbol of a proud people aroused.[35]

For Purifoy the uprising and then the work on *66 Signs of Neon* crystallized his thinking on the role and purpose of art. "It can make people there realize," Noah told an interviewer, "that their junk, their lives, can be shaped into something worthwhile."[36] The exhibit was also meant to stress the importance of art as a means of communication and as a vehicle for change. As he explains in the catalog to the exhibit,

> If junk art in general, and *66* in particular, enable us only to see and love the many simple things which previously escaped the eye, then we miss the point. For we here experience mere sensation, leaving us in time precisely where we were, being but not becoming. We wish to establish that there must be more to art than the creative act, more than the sensation of beauty, ugliness, color, form, light, sound, darkness, intrigue, wonderment, uncanniness, bitter, sweet, black, white, life and death. There must be therein a ME and YOU, who is affected permanently. Art of itself is of little or no value if in its relatedness it does not effect change. We do not mean change in the physical appearance of things, but a change in the behavior of human beings.[37]

Noah created art and encouraged art in others as a street-level activity accessible to anyone. "Oftentimes we'd take the children on trips to pick out objects—junk and etc.—and bring it back to the Towers, to the Art Center, to do assemblages and collages and so forth," he recalled many years later.[38] According to art historian Lizzetta LeFalle-Collins, "Purifoy remembers the period as a great artistic awakening throughout the community: dropouts found a voice through street theater; preschoolers accompanied the artists on junk hunts down the railroad track; amateurs and professionals did backyard paintings together; senior citizens learned to tie-dye; people of all kinds learned to dance and make musical instruments."[39]

Unfortunately, Noah's tenure at the Watts Towers was short-lived. He served as director for only two years, before being forced out by a board that wanted a more "sophisticated" arts program, and remembers with some disgust and disappointment, "They wanted to be known as something profound, some advanced art school of some echelon, I don't know what. It made me very unhappy about their attitude, because they didn't fully realize that that was Watts. That you can't get to know a community by having a sophisticated arts school there that did not include the community."[40]

In his brief time as director, Noah offered an important example of an artist who rejected commercialism and the trappings of success, and instead pursued excellence in his community. He also became a mentor to an emerging generation of artists, including Nathaniel Bustion, Mel Edwards, David Hammons, John Outterbridge, John Riddle, and Betye Saar, who all, to varying degrees, absorbed his teachings. Betye Saar grew up not far from the Watts Towers, which also exerted a strong influence on her work. According to art historian Samella Lewis, she "feels that her memory of their construction contributed measurably to her artistic expression. The towering spirals, created from such castoff items as broken glass and bottle tops, in addition to steel and cement, apparently made a lasting impression on Saar's artistic imagery."[41] In her *The Liberation of Aunt Jemima*, she positions what was once a plastic mammy memo-and-pencil holder from the 1930s against a backdrop of stereotypical images derived from a box of pancake mix. She places a rifle in the figure's left hand and superimposes a clenched black fist in the foreground, thereby transforming a stereotypical racist image into an assertion of dignity, strength, and rebellion.

Noah's vision was continued at the Watts Towers Arts Center by John Outterbridge, who became director in 1975 and remained there until 1992. John had been teaching at the Towers since the mid-1960s and shared Noah's worldview, experiencing a similar transformation after the uprising of 1965 expressed in *The Containment Series*. According to John, "Junkyards illustrate to me much of what the society that we live in really is all about—discarded materials. Materials that have related to human experience in a very profound way. You go into a junkyard and you can pull these things out. You try and give them life again. This is realness, this is truthfulness to me from a people point of view, from a folksy point of view."[42]

Before his tenure at the Watts Towers, John directed another important community arts center that expanded his conception of the field of art. In 1968 he was invited to generate an arts program in Compton, just south of Watts, at an old two-story house donated by the Salvation Army to the Compton-Willowbrook Community Action Agency, a federally funded organization. Within a year he established and became the director of the

Communicative Arts Academy and relocated it to a larger structure, an old arena no longer in use. This was a stimulating challenge that opened new vistas and resonated with previously acquired values about community.

> That challenge also extended the language of relationship and relationships within the levels of community. You started to see community, first of all, as a piece of material that started with the individual and the individual family and the agencies. Like here was a composition that you could unravel and you could relate to. But I think the heavy edge of the challenge was to say something about who we were and how it might fit and how it might assist.[43]

Despite persistent financial problems, Outterbridge remained until 1975, when he became the director of the Watts Towers Arts Center. In that time, he made the Academy a community institution. From their music workshop, he created a large jazz band that performed original music at monthly concerts and other venues, such as local prisons. There were also dance, photography, and various visual arts programs and workshops, all open to the community with the results on display. Through it all, John expanded his notion of art to accommodate his new gig.

> Well, that became the art. The environment of the Communicative Arts Academy became my process. I created a lot of environmental influences for other artists. It was very stimulating to young artists to come into the space and see what had been built, to see what had been rendered on the walls, and to have an opportunity to paint on the huge walls of the Academy itself. Like the young woman who is now director of the Studio Museum in Harlem, which does really fine programming nationally—Kinshasha [H. Conwill. She] was one of those artists. . . . [44]

The Watts Writers Workshop, nationally the most visible symbol of the burgeoning arts scene after the uprising of 1965, was initiated by novelist and screenwriter Budd Schulberg (*What Makes Sammy Run, Waterfront*). Shaken by the images of the uprising while watching the news in his Beverly Hills home, days later he was driving to Watts to learn for himself. The experience led him to offer a Creative Writing Workshop at the Westminster Neighborhood Association building, a run-down two-story house off of 103rd on Beach Street. The association had been established in 1960 by the Presbyterian Church as a social service agency for the community, and it provided some basic educational and arts classes as well. By the time of

Schulberg's visit its budget and staff had grown considerably and would continue to do so over the next few years with substantial government support.[45]

Schulberg's first notice for the class went up on the Association bulletin board at the end of August and after a few lean months the Watts Writers Workshop had some two dozen members. By the end of 1965 a larger space was required and in the following spring they relocated to the Watts Happening Coffee House around the corner on 103rd Street and initiated a regular program of readings, titled "From the Ashes." Using imagery that also inspired the visual artists who created *66 Signs of Neon*, Schulberg's Workshop had a similar purpose. "The writers of Watts were expressing the hope not only of their twenty-odd voices but of the entire community," explains Schulberg. "From the ashes, out of the rubble, out of apathy, despair, neglect, and hopelessness might rise a black phoenix."[46]

Within two years the Workshop had an international reputation and a few shows on national television: *The Angry Voices of Watts* and Harry Dolan's two pieces, *Finders Keepers* and *Losers Weepers*. During 1967 two anthologies of writings appeared both edited by Schulberg: *From the Ashes: Voices of Watts* and the fall issue of the *Antioch Review* titled "The Watts Writers Workshop."[47] Among the writers and poets included were Harry Dolan, Guadalupe de Saavedra, Alvin Saxon, Jr. (soon to be Ojenke), Johnie Scott, Jimmie Sherman, and Jeanne Taylor. One year later, new member Quincy Troupe edited the next collection of material, *Watts Poets: A Book of New Poetry and Essays*, drawn from the workshop and other local writers, including Robert Bowen, Elaine Brown, Stanley Crouch, K. Curtis Lyle, Ojenke, Eric Priestley, Linda Hill, and Troupe.[48] Encompassing poetry, short stories, plays, essays, commentary, and autobiographical portraits, the writings offer honest, at times searing reflections upon self-identity, individual lives and families, the community, and political and social struggles. As journalist Erin Aubry so aptly summarizes the contribution of the Workshop, "It was a greenhouse of ideas and friendships and spiritual alliances, a point of social and artistic convergence that spawned a theater, a coffeehouse, stage productions, a poetry anthology and innumerable dreams of far greater things for L.A.'s black arts community."[49]

One of the early members, who would soon become a part of UGMA, Ojenke Saxon graduated from high school in 1965 and first encountered the Workshop at the Coffee House. "I was working full time at Douglas Aircraft in Long Beach, and somehow I heard about the Watts Writers Workshop. I went down there and after the first session I knew that was the place for me.

That's when I quit my job." Ojenke was to be instrumental in recruiting a number of other members. He met poet and novelist Eric Priestley, a former student of Samuel Browne's at Jefferson High School, over the piano at Studio Watts and invited him to the workshop, beginning a life-long friendship. Not long afterward Ojenke performed at Los Angeles City College (LACC) along with Bunchy Carter, Ron Karenga, Horace Tapscott, and UGMA, where he met journalism major Quincy Troupe, who was covering the performance and who would soon be a mainstay of the Workshop and an UGMA collaborator. According to Ojenke,

> I took him down there one Wednesday evening, when we'd have this circle of expression. People would get together and just share their work. So the thing about Quincy was that he had these poems, but he didn't know how to read them, how to express them. That was the thing that really attracted him to me. I had this way of expressing, using Coltrane as my model and my father was a minister; I had this oratory thing. So Quincy would come up to me and ask me, "Man, I want you to read this poem for me, because I can't read." So for the first few sessions, I would read Quincy's poems, until he got enough confidence. And once he got going, he was gone.

Troupe reminisces,

> I got to be good friends with Ojenke and Bunchy, and Linda, who was in UGMA. I met Horace, and Arthur Blythe was in that band. So they said, "Well, we're out in Watts." Everybody was out in Watts on 103rd Street. So I started to go out to Watts with Ojenke and then I discovered the Watts Happening Coffee House on 103rd Street. The actor, the great actor, William Marshall, was there. I started going to Watts all the time and going to the Watts Writers Workshop.

While relocating to the Coffee House on 103rd Street solved an immediate need for space, the workshop was also faced with the problem of homelessness, unsettled lifestyles among many, and political rifts. In the fall of 1968, some members moved to a dilapidated, nine-room house a few blocks away at 9807 Beach Street. Dubbed The House of Respect, a small stage was built in the backyard and soon they were giving readings and concerts, and living a decidedly social, but still bohemian existence. Quincy's memories are vivid:

> I won't say we were crazy, but I felt definitely the freest I've ever felt in my life. . . . We were just irreverent. . . . For us to walk down the street in the

daytime was a spectacle. There would be like seven or eight of us. I'd have on these weird clothes and sunglasses. And Emory Evans, who was about six foot seven, had on a blue navy overcoat, high topped tennis shoes and shorts, little bitty sunglasses with yellow rims. And he was real jet black, a weird looking cat, looked like a Watusi. And we'd be walking down the street and then Ojenke, Curtis Lyle, Eric Priestley, and Cleveland Sims, and these painters with paint all over them—we were strange. When we would walk down Beach Street, everybody would say, "Here they come! Here they come!" And everybody would come out on their porches and watch us. It was like the parade of the lunatics.

Lifestyle issues aside, the focus always remained on their work and the community. If the Workshop can be seen as spawning differing styles, they are probably best illustrated in the work of Ojenke, Troupe, and Kamau Daáood, who all reflected more of an Amiri Baraka approach, strongly influenced by the charismatic church tradition and the music of John Coltrane, and that of the Watts Prophets, whose street-wise lyrics were an important predecessor of rap.[50] According to Father Amde (formerly Anthony Hamilton), "The Watts Prophets were one school, and you could say that our school went into the HipHop thing. Ojenke and his thing went into the Kamaus and the Quincy Troupes. But Ojenke is the papa of those styles there, that preacher kind of thing." Ojenke credits the early influences of his father and a love of the power of communication in shaping his approach to poetry. "My interest in poetry relates to my love of the power of communication, which I got first hand from observing my father, who was a minister, delivering sermons. The African American form of preaching sometimes can be very poetical, employing metaphors and all type of beautiful similes and refrains. All type of poetic devices are part of it, which I didn't realize when growing up that it was poetry, but I think that is what led me to a fascination and love of words."

Within their poetry and lifestyle, the commitment to community was strong. According to Troupe, "The neighborhood loved us. We used to give classes for the kids in the neighborhood. I'd teach English and writing, and Ojenke would do that and teach science. Everybody taught different kinds of things. They'd give us food and we'd teach the little kids after school. Because we were definitely broke. We didn't have any money." For Otis O'Solomon literary gatherings began by dealing with the daily problems of survival: "You could always talk to people about writing, but it wasn't always about writing. Even when I became the poetry/creative writing instructor at the www—I did that for about six years—a lot of times when I would hold my workshop and classes, we might spend an hour or two talking before we got into any reading or anything. Somebody would say 'my rent's due' or 'my lights have been turned off' and they had serious problems."

The Workshop later managed to get access to a burned-out Safeway building at 1690 East 103rd Street near Graham Avenue and set about repairing it. By this time some of the early members had moved on, such as Quincy Troupe and Johnie Scott, but some remained, including Harry Dolan, who became the director of the new facility. Meanwhile, others were arriving. Fr. Amde, Richard Dedeaux, and Otis O'Solomon, who would shortly come together as the Watts Prophets, met at the Workshop during this time. According to Richard, "Bit by bit, piece by piece, we pieced it together. We had a legitimate huge stage. We had a slanted floor with the theater. We had a real theater with offices, whereas at the Douglass House it was just a little stage in back and mainly a place for the artists to crash temporarily."

Each of the Prophets had developed an interest in writing earlier but had yet to take it much further. Otis had been working on poetry from an early age, but Richard had only started writing in his mid-twenties. When they drifted into the workshop, they became much more focused on their art. According to Fr. Amde, "That's when I started writing. I just happened to be walking through Watts, 103rd Street, that was my street. I was looking for a job and I used to go by this poverty program on 103rd. I met a writer there who saw me scribbling on paper and throwing it away. I'd done that for a lot of years. His name was Odie Hawkins and he brought me to the Watts Writers Workshop."

Under Dolan's directorship and in this new facility, the workshop took a more theatrically oriented direction, offering dance and acting classes as well as writing workshops. According to Richard, "There were plays constantly going on. . . . We opened the Watts Writers Workshop with a play called *The Poor Boy*, which was about an unemployment thing. Then we did another one, *My Tears Are My Train Fare Home*. We did *The Iron Hand of Nat Turner* that Ted Lange directed." Under Lange's direction, the Theatre literally threw open its doors to the community. He recalls, "I'd have the rehearsal doors open and anybody in the neighborhood could come in, sit in the back of the theater, and watch the rehearsals. That's how you keep the energy going." His community orientation was propelled by an encounter at the Mark Taper Forum in downtown Los Angeles with Polish director Jerzy Grotowski, the founder of the Polish Laboratory Theatre and the author of *Towards a Poor Theatre*:

He [Grotowski] talked about "Towards a Poor Theatre," politicizing the theater, what the artist's relationship is to theater, to the people, to the establishment. So I jumped up and I said, "Shouldn't the Music Center do more black plays. They don't do any black plays down here."

He said, "No. They don't owe you any black plays. They don't owe you nothing."

I said, "What?!" Because we had always said, "The establishment owes us." We were used to that.

He said, "They don't owe you nothing. Why do you have to do a play down here? Do it in the community. As a matter of fact if you do it in the community, it makes more of a statement about what the establishment is not doing. That's what 'Towards a Poor Theater' is."

I went, "Wow! We don't have to ask nobody for nothing?"

"No, you shouldn't be asking nobody for nothing. Do it yourself."

That was the moment that changed my life as a theater person, talking to Grotowski. From then on I never asked for nothing. I did plays in garages. I did them in the street. I did them in PASLA, Mafundi, Watts Writers Workshop.

The Watts Writers Workshop was ultimately brought down by one of the FBI's COINTELPROS (counterintelligence programs). An FBI-sponsored infiltrator, Darthard Perry (aka Ed Riggs), spent years disrupting programs and equipment, torching the stage and rear area of the House of Respect, and then setting fire and burning to the ground the 350-seat theater on 103rd Street in 1973.[51] For Richard Dedeaux, the memories are still fresh:

We were always a compassionate group at the Watts Writers Workshop. One day this bum [Perry, aka Riggs] came to the Workshop, all nasty and smelly, said he was hungry and shit. So we took up a collection and got him something to eat. He told us how he was down on his luck a little bit and asked us if he could stay at the Workshop a while. So we let him stay on the couch there. After a while, he became kind of like the keeper of the Workshop. But what it was, he was sent there by the FBI, part of that COINTELPRO thing. And so things started really happening, like all of a sudden one day a bunch of seats would get cut up in the workshop. When we got ready to film things, the camera equipment worked, but things would break and we'd lose that. Sometimes when mailing out flyers for our events, we'd find them in the sewers, in the drains. So all kinds of things, and we never once had any suspicion, until this guy got on Pacifica Radio and confessed.

Financial problems had been mounting, some of that due to Perry's actions, but the coup de gras was the torching of the Theater. The Workshop never recovered from this terrorist act, perpetrated by an agency of the US government. They gained access to office space near 103rd and Central and managed to keep some sessions going for a few years. Otis O'Solomon continued his creative writing classes, which at one time were attracting as many as seventy-five students. But by the mid-1970s, the Writers Workshop had become another part of Watt's rich, but past cultural history.

The Watts Happening Coffee House opened in October 1965, when young people from the community took possession of an abandoned furniture store and turned it into a performance space and arts center. Located at 1802 East 103rd Street between Wilmington and the railroad tracks, it was supported by the Department of Housing and Urban Development, as well as the Southern California Council of Churches, which paid the rent.[52] Under the direction of Otis Williams and his staff initially, its beginnings promised a federally funded payroll, but little more. Elaine Brown, an early employee, remembers,

> I'm telling you that man [Otis Williams] didn't have program one. He had seventy-five people on the payroll and there wasn't but four people coming in. What did they do? We don't know. That's why they liked me, because I could invent this crap every week. . . .
>
> This was what they called a field office of the OEO [Office of Economic Opportunity]. That's what they loved to name this shit. And I was like the administrator. I had one typewriter, an IBM electric. I made up the payroll and I wrote out the reports. And that was really all that ever happened at the Watts Happening Coffee House, until . . . suddenly there was Horace and these microphones and this stage. I said, "Where'd this shit come from?"[53]

The person responsible for "this shit" was a bass player, Walter Savage. Just returned to Los Angeles from overseas after an eight-year hitch in the Air Force, Walter was hired at the Coffee House and took on the task of organizing performances. In search of some musicians to start jam sessions, he approached pianist Harold Land, Jr., who recommended UGMA. With his jazz experience limited to the few clubs he frequented while in Europe, Walter was not prepared for that first night.

> So I invited UGMA, the whole group, down to the Coffee House. I expected to have a jam session and did all I could to get people in there. They [UGMA] sort of straggled in, one or two or three at a time . . .

turned out to be about twenty-five of them. I never got to speak to any-body. They just started playing, and they weren't playing a song. I was kind of in shock. They just set up and started to going at it. I'm thinking, "Are they going to play a song or what?" I wanted to hear "So What?" or "Milestones," or anything. "What the hell is going on here?" But it was all free stuff. They never played a tune the whole time they were there.

UGMA became a mainstay at the Coffee House, as the members got in-volved not only in performing but in maintaining the space and offering classes as well. Amina Amatullah remembers bringing crates and pillows to make the place habitable and creating wall space for artists to hang their work. "We closed off the windows completely. There was a big plate glass window and we boarded it up. The only way you know what's going on in there, you have to go in. You know they didn't like it. The police didn't like it. None of them liked it, but we built it." Budd Schulberg recalls the look of the Coffee House in 1966: "There are home-made paintings on the wall, a few of them fascinating, a lot of them promising, some of them god-awful. There is a stage where poetry readings and self-propelled plays like Jimmie Sherman's *Ballad from Watts* and musical entertainments are performed weekly. There are happenings and political discussions that lean toward extreme Black Na-tionalism, and a record player that swings everything from the Supremes and Lou Rawls to grand opera."[54] Quincy Troupe's memories are still vivid:

The Coffee House on 103rd Street was beautiful. It was dark and I re-member the stage. I never remember that place being light. It had dark walls. I remember they used to have these workshops there. People used to be just hanging out there and doing different things, what they do in coffee houses, people get high and shit. They'd have some pro-ductions. And William Marshall was running the acting workshops and then they'd have concerts on the weekends. I can't remember any-thing being planned. And I just remember the great music that was there being played. Bobby Bradford and all these people would come and play. You gotta remember one thing. Everybody was loaded at this time. So it was like a fog, man. You just go in there and say, "Oh, this is hip." And you're looking for women and the drugs and listening to the music and hanging out. That's what it was and it was like one day went into the next day.... The days and nights were indistinguishable.

The Coffee House was used by and gave birth to other organizations, serving as the initial home for the Mafundi Institute. During the summer of 1966, the Charles F. Kettering Foundation, through the Brooks Institute in Santa Barbara, supplied funds for a filmmaking class and project for local high school dropouts. By the end of that year, the students successfully completed a forty-five-minute film, *Johnny Gigs Out*, starring Paris Earle, a young actor. Ojenke recalls the film as "about this brother who wanted to be a jazz musician and it talks about the struggles that he had to go through and what eventually leads to his succumbing to the system, all the pressures that cause a brother to more or less fold."[55] This experience inspired discussions over the next few months among local artists—including writers, poets, dancers, filmmakers, and actors—meeting at the Coffee House to establish a permanent arts program under community control, which led to the founding of the Mafundi Institute.[56]

The combination of a growing need for additional space and declining funding at the Coffee House led the Institute to seek its own space, and with the financial assistance of the Kettering Foundation they found offices at 1772 East 103rd Street. A short while later, success in winning city and federal grants led to the construction of a new building to house the Mafundi. In 1970, ground breaking was held at 1827 East 103rd Street near the corner of Wilmington Avenue, accompanied by a performance of UGMA, but now the Underground Musicians and Artists Association (UGMAA).[57]

In Swahili *mafundi* means "artisans" or "creative people" or "craftsmen." In Dar es Salaam, Tanzania the *mafundi* are street artists, who work in a manner strikingly similar to that of assemblage artists, though in most cases out of economic necessity in a resource-scarce environment. In an exhibition of this art the Fowler Museum of Cultural History describes, "Floorboards from old buses reborn into locks or hoes; oil drums metamorphosed into barbecue grills, coffee pots, or gleaming, melodious steel pans; these and other material conversions are the art of the resourceful, urban artists known as mafundi, people who give new shape and life to cast-offs, or, those who have the 'knowledge of their hands.'"[58]

Inspired by these East African artisans and the expanding aesthetic of community arts emerging in Watts, artists gathered to form an arts center embracing a wide range of artistic activity and performers. For the next five years the institute offered courses and performances. Its schedule for mid-winter 1970 included classes in acting, Afro-American literature, dance, painting, sculpture, art history, set design and lighting, music, vocalizing, filmmaking, martial arts for dance and theatre, modeling, and self improvement. Faculty came from the community and Hollywood and included Roscoe Lee Browne, Marie Bryant, Raymond Burr, Marge Champion, Don Mitchell, and

Raymond St. Jacques. At other times Maulana Ron Karenga, Paula Kelley, William Marshall, and Roger Mosley, among others, played significant roles in the Institute.[59]

By the mid-1970s, however, funds were drying up and the Mafundi closed its doors in 1975, when city projects and small businesses took over the building. It would subsequently reopen in 1997 complete with a coffee house to serve the community of Watts, but by the mid-1970s its time had passed, as well as that of the Watts Happening Coffee House and the Watts Writers Workshop.

With the Studio Watts and the Watts Towers Arts Center, these organizations offered an alternative conception of the arts and the relationship between the arts and the community. In them the community arts movement received its sharpest formation and perhaps its greatest organizational expression, if only for a few years, one of those bright moments when artistic vision merged with social involvement and the excitement was contagious. "It was a period where three o'clock in the morning you were still wide awake," reminisces Bobby Bradford. "[It was] just so exciting . . . what was happening. It was really good, man. We weren't making any money, but we had our jobs, so we weren't worried about it. . . . We were playing what we wanted to play. . . ."[60] According to John Outterbridge, "The energy of the political, the social, the economic, it was all around you. I mean, you were fenced in, and you had to participate." That involvement broadened the social commitment of artists, as well as shaping their aesthetic. "So I believe that that period for me is one that I can thank the artists' community for teaching me and helping to nurture language, protest attitudes, how to make comments about what I felt, because before that time I never really talked about how strong the feeling was inside to make music—and when I say to make music, I am simply saying to make art."[61] To Bradford, "The national spirit was all over the place, we were all caught up in this thing, this new black awareness about the validity of the black aesthetic on every level."[62]

This evolving consciousness encouraged the creativity of artists. It was not only a matter of providing more social and political content for their work, though this was important. For artists who were pushing at the boundaries of convention, for those whose muses drew them into new directions in the teeth of a mainstream that would not validate that work, the political focus of leaders such as Malcolm X and the challenge raised by the voices and actions of protest from people in the streets provided an inspiration, which they translated into support for their challenges to the artistic status quo. Bassist Wilber Morris remembers, "How it effected the music was the spirit of freedom, wanting more and more freedom. It was something that really had to be felt. Those were some pretty heavy times and I still draw on a lot of that energy during that time." Similarly, Bobby Bradford explains,

> And what that kind of thing does, you see, is strengthen your own resolve to keep doing what you had been doing before but every day having misgivings and ambivalent feelings about what you were doing, 'cause there were a lot of people who were saying in the period before that, "Hey man, this is not gonna work. Just do whatever you can that white people like and make as much money as you can and be happy." And a lot of people bought into that, you see. And Malcolm reminded us all, and them included, that that was a big mistake and that you don't have to do that . . . everybody who was old enough to realize what was happening, this came out in everybody's music.[63]

The Watts uprising gave rise to a cultural renaissance, to a reassertion of community values and of the role of the arts within the community, values which can be traced back through segregation to the years of slavery, but then to the traditional, communal practices of West and West Central African peoples. The return to the past was part of a deepening of a people's consciousness of their identity. In turn, that was part of a larger struggle to understand who they were in light of the uprising and to then rebuild with whatever was around, to reconstruct themselves and their community with a vision of a future arts and society beyond racism, beyond commercialism.

Lino's Pad, the first UGMA house, in 2004. (Photo by Steven Isoardi)

Horace Tapscott conduct-
ing UGMA, early to mid-
1960s. (Courtesy of the
Horace Tapscott Archive)

The Watts Happening Coffee House, c. 1967. Sign reads, "12:00 Ojenke Horace Tapscott Black Music / 3:00 Blackstone Rangers / 4:30 Super Spook Show." (Photo courtesy of the Southern California Library for Social Studies and Research)

Crowd gathers for parade on 103rd Street in Watts with Watts Happening Coffee House in background, c. 1967. (Photo courtesy of the Southern California Library for Social Studies and Research)

In concert at South Park, late 1960s. (Photo by Kamau Daáood)

In concert at South Park—a view from the stage, late 1960s. L to R: Will Connell; Arthur Blythe; unknown; Azar Lawrence, baritone sax; Abdul-Salaam Muhammad, piccolo; Ernest Straughter, flute; Al Hall, trombone; Amina Amatullah (in head scarf). (Photo by Kamau Daáood)

Horace conducting at South Park, late 1960s. (Photo by Kamau Daáood)

Arthur Blythe soloing
at South Park, late
1960s. (Photo by Kamau
Daáood)

In performance at Hancock Auditorium, University of Southern California, c. 1969. L to R: Baba Alade, bass; Wilber Morris, bass; the Voice of UGMA; Arthur Blythe, alto sax; Cerion Middleton III, tenor sax; Horace Tapscott, conductor; Ernest Straughter, flute. Projected drawing of Horace Tapscott by Michael Dett Wilcots. (Photo by Kamau Daáood)

Horace Tapscott and Will Connell at Will's house, February 1970.
(Photo by Michael Dett Wilcots)

Linda Hill's UGMAA house on 52nd Place, c. 1970. (Photo by Kamau Daáood)

"Angela Is Happening!" flyer, c. 1970. (Courtesy of Kamau Daáood)

Ojenke reading at South Park, 7 February 1971. (Photo by Michael Dett Wilcots)

The Watts Prophets. L to R: Father Amde, Otis O'Solomon, Richard Dedeaux. (Courtesy of Otis O'Solomon)

Rahsaan Roland Kirk performing in Horace Tapscott class at Riverside Community College, May 1971. Horace Tapscott, piano. (Photo by Michael Dett Wilcots)

Rahsaan Roland Kirk performing in Horace Tapscott class at Riverside Community College, May 1971. L to R: Larry Northington, alto sax; Arthur Blythe, alto sax; Will Connell, alto sax; Kirk (back to camera); Azar Lawrence, sax; Butch Morris, cornet. (Photo by Michael Dett Wilcots)

Cojoe, June 1971. (Photo by Michael Dett Wilcots)

HERBERT KEITH BAKER SCHOLARSHIP FUND

Musical In Memoriam

December 30th, 1952 to June 15th, 1970

Sunday, May 30, 1971, 4:00 P. M.

NEW HOPE BAPTIST CHURCH

(5200 South Central Avenue, Los Angeles, California)

Program cover of memorial tribute to Herbie Baker, 30 May 1971. (Courtesy of Horace Tapscott Archive)

Kufahamu doing
"Greg's Refresher
Course" at KUSC Radio,
early 1970s. (Photo by
Michael Dett Wilcots)

Azar Lawrence, alto sax, and Ray Straughter, tenor sax, at the Sun, early 1970s.
(Photo by Kamau Daáood)

Performance of *Gold Power* with the Arkestra at Foshay Junior High School, early 1970s.
Rear C to R: Cojoe, congas; Ray Straughter, tenor sax; Cerion Middleton III, tenor sax.
(Photo by Michael Dett Wilcots)

Lester Robertson, early 1970s. (Photo by Myko Clark, courtesy of the Horace Tapscott Archive)

Linda Hill with her niece, Patricia E. Hill, early 1970s. (Photo courtesy of Patricia E. Hill)

Walter Savage at South
Park, early 1970s.
(Photo by Michael Dett
Wilcots)

Kamau Daáood, early 1970s. (Courtesy of the Horace Tapscott Archive)

Leaflet for a weekend program at the Gathering, 1973. (Courtesy of Kamau Daáood)

Rufus Olivier in concert
with the Arkestra,
March 1974. (Photo by
Michael Dett Wilcots)

Aubrey Hart, mid-1970s. (Photo by Michael Dett Wilcots)

Adele Sebastian and Aubrey Hart in concert with the Arkestra in Exposition Park, mid-1970s. (Photo by Kamau Daáood)

Fuasi Abdul-Khaliq at
South Park, mid-1970s.
(Photo by Myko Clark,
courtesy of the Horace
Tapscott Archive)

Abdul-salaam
Muhammad, mid-1970s.
(Photo by Michael Dett
Wilcots)

UGMAA Foundation logo, designed by Michael Dett Wilcots, mid-1970s.
(Courtesy of Michael Dett Wilcots)

5

WARRIORS ALL

UGMA in the Middle of It

This horn is a weapon and I'm prepared to use it like that.

LESTER ROBERTSON

The first day of the insurrection, the shooting began in Will Rogers Park on 103rd Street and Central. We were further down 103rd, playing as usual out in the street, and the kids were dancing to "The Dark Tree." The police came down the street and drove around the bandstand, holding their microphone out of the car for the cats downtown to hear. They said, "Listen. This is inciting the riot. This is why the riot is happening." Then we heard the sounds of ambulances and more police cars coming into the neighborhood.[1]

UGMA had been a presence in Watts before the upheaval of 1965, but now found themselves in the middle of one of the most dramatic urban convulsions in American history. Their street-level involvement in the community, encounters with the LAPD, and anger and indignation over the social situation facing African American Los Angeles meant they would not be taken un-awares. In placing themselves and their art in the grassroots center of African American concerns and life, they also knew that they would be targeted by the police, for whom any critical black movement or organization—cultural, social, or political—was seen as a threat to the existing order. The insistent, ominous beat of "The Dark Tree" not only galvanized street dancers, as Horace Tapscott describes, but also fueled the racist imaginings of those suppos-edly committed "to protect and to serve" the people of Los Angeles.

During the next few years, as tensions continued to simmer within the community, there would be more confrontations with the police depart-ment, some on an individual basis and others involving UGMA. Horace tells of one that occurred while the band was playing at the Watts Happening Coffee House:

> The police broke in with their shotguns and told me to stop the music. I wouldn't stop. The guy in charge pulled back the hammer of his gun and yelled, "I said stop the goddamn music!" Meanwhile, they were lining up these pregnant women, who were there for a class, by one of the walls. I put my hand up in the air to stop the band. The cop put his gun back on the safety and headed out. As he walked past all the kids who were listening to the music, David Bryant, or one of the other bass players, looking right at the police, started the line from "The Dark Tree," and we all started playing again.[2]

In the aftermath of 1965, UGMA was at the center of activity on 103rd Street, as Watts became the Association's main focus. The cultural resurgence and growing politicization of the community were important turning points, reinforcing UGMA's purpose but also presenting it with more tasks, more members, and a growing circle of supporters, whose social consciousness and, in some cases, sense of self were being transformed by the times. Much of this would be expressed in the Association's music, particularly the first recording sessions (1968–1969), which codified their work in the 1960s of preserving the African American heritage, pushing the boundaries of that music, and reflecting the concerns and issues of their community.

New Recruits

UGMA's prominence in South Central L.A. and on 103rd Street attracted more artists in search of an alternative scene, of an environment that allowed for expansive artistic boundaries and participation in the evolving social consciousness of the community. The wake of the Watts uprising brought an influx of members, mostly in their twenties, many recently discharged from the military, a few already working in support of various civil rights causes, and some struggling to find their personal and musical identities while submerged in the morass of entertainment industry commercialism.

In 1950 alto saxophonist Will Connell, Jr.'s family was one of the first African American families to move into the Leimert Park district of South Central L.A. A decade later, after graduating from Dorsey High School, Will enlisted in the Air Force and spent most of his service years overseas. He was back in Los Angeles during the Watts uprising and a year later started meeting UGMA musicians. His musical tastes were different, as his studies with Central Avenue alumnus and veteran saxophone teacher Bill Green made clear.

> When I studied with Bill Green, he would try to advise everybody to be a studio musician. "You gotta do this if you want to be in the studios." I looked at him and said, "I ain't going through this shit to play no Kleenex commercials." He let me alone after that. Remember, I'm a weird combination of a very straight arrow young guy and an old salt. I've been through typhoons. I stole rifles from the air police and sold them to the Turks. I've been in Korea, closest air base to the DMZ, where you could easily have gotten killed. I still looked like a boy scout, but there was an old salt in there. After I learned the harmonic minor scale, there was no holding me, man.

His first exposure to UGMA came when he went to hear alto saxophonist Art Pepper and a few other bands at a club called Bonesville. "Horace got on the bandstand with this strange amount of grace and presence and simplicity that he had, and it was like, 'Oh, the musicians are here.' There was just something about them. It was Arthur and Lester, and Horace and David Bryant and Everett. And they had as much energy as the Coltrane quartet." Not long afterward he saw the big band play. "When I saw that band, man! It was like, 'Oh yeah, I'm glad there's some real people around. Cool.'" That UGMA served a broader purpose also appealed to Will, who was in search of something more fundamental. "I also felt a sense of community, something I could belong to. The first time I saw that band, I put my hand on one of them music stands and I served with everything I had for seven years." By 1967 Will was hard-core and remained a full-time participant until he left for New York in 1974, one of the band's key figures as a vocalist, saxophonist, and writer, responsible for copying the band book more than half a dozen times. "I was the sorcerer's apprentice."

Vietnam veteran Jimmy Hoskins (later known as Majid Shah) was already a local drumming legend when he joined UGMA. Ojenke attended Gompers Junior High School with him: "I always thought Jimmy was so out of sight, because in junior high school Miles Davis came down and gave Jimmy a gig. I don't remember where they played in town. Jimmy was like a prodigy back then on drums. He was a magician!" In a few years he would be performing with UGMA, but his intervening military experience in Vietnam and its resultant psychological consequences were enough to sidetrack a professional career. According to Ojenke, "Jimmy went into the service and I don't know if it was Vietnam or what, but whenever it was he came back, Jimmy wasn't really the same mentally. Whatever he saw over there, it must have been so horrible that it put him in a state of permanent mental jitters." Nevertheless, he was able to contribute his artistry to UGMA for many years. Will Connell remembers the drummer everyone called "the Sleeping Giant":

> He was a great drummer. His cymbal rudiment was different, sort of turned around. It was like tang-a-da-ding, tang-a-da-ding, tang-a-da-ding, tang-a-da-ding, but it swung like mad. He didn't read supposedly, but if you wrote one of his tunes, he would know where every sixteenth note was. He used to play free drum music and time in no particular pattern and some people hated it, but I loved it. The guys in the Ark used to call him "the Sleeping Giant" because he didn't know how good he was.

Percussionist E. W. Wainwright, also an Air Force veteran, arrived in Los Angeles shortly after the Watts uprising. A participant in the civil rights struggles, he had been performing in the South for the previous few years. He was the drummer on Percy Sledge's pop hit "When a Man Loves a Woman," and was a regular member of the Jazz Pioneers, which he describes as "the revolutionary band of SNCC. We all belonged to the Student Nonviolent Coordinating Committee. So we played events for them." His band traveled to Los Angeles to play at Maverick's Flats on Crenshaw Boulevard in Leimert Park. There he met Brother Percy, who told him, "If you want to play some serious music, because you guys are revolutionaries, you need to come over to Fifty-sixth and Figueroa."

The band followed him to the UGMA house, where, according to Wainwright, "they immediately embraced us. We could all play. We had just come from back east, so we were all good players. But they embraced us with serious brotherhood and that's the thing that stands out in my mind most of all about the UGMA house and Percy and the whole crew at that time." Wainwright soon fell into the routine and contributed to the house economy. "No matter where you were or where you worked, you brought food or money or something back to the UGMA house, because it was the kind of thing that we all supported. So when things looked up for me, I would bring money over. We had a rented baby grand piano and we had to keep that going, and we had to pay the house rent and keep the pot of beans going on the stove and keep the lights on."

Alto saxophonist Lattus McNeeley and trumpeter James Lee (aka Semaj) would be mainstays of the Association into the early 1970s while also fronting their own band, described by Stanley Crouch as "one of the best underground quartets of the time."[3] Will Connell remembers Lattus as a prodigious talent, "very much into the Coltrane book, the Slonimsky. He studied it obsessively, religiously, but he didn't sound like Coltrane and he had his own independent way of harmonizing everything. And he was one of the most deeply spiritual and beautiful players I've ever heard. There was no player like Lattus." His cohort, James Lee, was just as talented, a prolific writer and master trumpeter. "James could play one note for twenty minutes—he used to call it the big note—I mean James Lee could play one note for twenty minutes and make you hear everything," according to Will. "Then he would play a trumpet smear and that one note was so in your mind it was almost like hearing a bunch of harmonics, like someone had run their fingers over a harp. You would actually hear that stuff. There was no trumpet player like James Lee. Nobody. And he wrote a million tunes and they had a feeling of deep, Asian blues, but it was very melodic and out."

UGMA's increasingly high profile in the community started attracting younger players as well. Rudolph Porter, then a student at Fremont High School, was recruited to play alto and tenor saxophones, although he would subsequently have a career as a classical bassoonist. "At a young age, man, I'm around Lester Robertson, Horace, Bobby Bradford, John Carter, Harold Land. Man!"

By the time he was in his early teens, guitarist Tommy Trujillo was playing clarinet, drums, saxophones and guitar, and sitting in on jam sessions at many of the jazz clubs in South Central L.A. Before he was out of his twenties, he would play and record with saxophonist Charles Lloyd, tuba player Ray Draper, and drummer Billy Higgins. In the interval he became part of UGMA. Growing up in a predominantly white part of Los Angeles, he was discriminated against as a Mexican American, and then ostracized from the latter community because he wasn't Latino enough. "I was like a black jazz musician, you know, and a teenager with this real attitude problem, because nobody was interested in the shit I was into." Not long after Wainwright hit town, he called Tommy for a gig, and it was through Wainwright that he was introduced to UGMA. "UGMA was the most substantial of the L.A. jazz centers, the deep, artistic, Horace Tapscott center, the real black movement that was happening at the time, musically, culturally." He quickly connected with Linda Hill.

> We were together. I proposed and everything, boy, I fell in love, man. This was the baddest bitch I ever met in my motherfucking life, boy! She was a great musician. She was the matriarch. I'm sure I was not the only one, but I did propose, and I'm sure a whole lot of other moth- erfuckers proposed, too, but they weren't getting it. She was just too heavy, like Ghandi or somebody. She was a very heavy, spiritual person, one of the heaviest people that I've ever met in my life. Artistically she was very high, a highly developed musician, and just being a woman, one of the few women on the scene, and then she was not only on the scene, she was running the scene. She was living at the house, had like the center room. So, basically, I moved in the house. I was about eighteen.

Other new members included trumpeters Ike Sutton and Calvin Harvey, who had studied with Tadd Dameron, bassists Tom Williamson and Alfonse Wynn, and vocalists Vanetta, Kookie, and Black Panther leader John Hug- gins. Some artists became part of UGMA for short, but important stints in their careers. Vocalist Leon Thomas performed with the Association for four months in 1967 and told Nat Hentoff, "It was an extraordinary musical ex- perience for me. They were really into the avant-garde, into freedom-type music. And I began to hear all kinds of possibilities as I got rid of a lot of prejudices I had about the limitations of the voice. We were like a big Sun Ra family, and I learned a great deal."[4]

Linda Hill was UGMA's sole vocalist during its early years. After the Watts uprising, a chorus was formed, The Voice of UGMA. One of the first to ar- rive was Frances Haywood, soon known by the Swahili name of Aminifu and then Amina Amatullah after her conversion to Islam. Amina grew up near Compton in southern Los Angeles County and by 1966 had spent a few years on the road as a vocalist with the pop-oriented *Shindig* show. She put up with long road trips, hostile co-performers, and a relentless racism within the show and in the world around it. What she couldn't dismiss was a grow- ing artistic frustration and a concomitant dissatisfaction with her career and lifestyle. While on tour, she saw an *Ebony* magazine cover photo of the folksinger Odetta. "Here was this black woman with her hair natural. I was like, 'Oh, that's me.' Then they did another one with all these natural black women. I realized I didn't want to look a certain way. I'd been on the road trying to look like somebody I wasn't, trying to be what I wasn't, and I didn't even know that wasn't what I was being until I saw that picture. Then I said, 'Now that's who I am.'"

When she returned home, she knew she had to make a change but didn't have a direction. "I had been married. My family thinks I've totally lost my mind. They had all these hopes for me, but I don't want to do anything they want me to do. And I've always felt weird all my life. Now I'm really weird. Now I'm different and it was really not nice. It was just so painful." Amina had reached a turning point in her life. "So now I'm not singing on the road. I'm living with this guy and I've got this baby. I wanted to raise her right, but I'm just lost. So I decided that maybe I'll let her father raise her—I always kept him in her life—and I tried to kill myself. Serious—not the hit and miss thing. I took forty-five pills at one time. I wanted to make sure." Fortunately, her boyfriend returned unexpectedly to the apartment and rushed her to the hospital. "I can even remember what went on when my heart stopped beating, and that was when I knew I really was here for a purpose and that I really had to go on. Because I just kept saying, 'I don't want to die, but I just can't live like this.' We weren't even living that bad. It wasn't that. It was the fact that I wasn't doing anything I wanted to do, high all the time, not happy, and I felt so strange."

After her recovery, Amina talked to a friend, Art Sebrie, who told her he was living with some musicians at a house near 56th Street and Figueroa, and invited her to visit. "When I went there, that's when I realized there were people like me and I wasn't weird anymore. Linda told me, 'You're not weird. You're different.' She said, 'When this world is made, rows and rows of people come out the same. Every ten thousandth person: *special!*' I was like 'really?' Linda was my inspiration." Amina had found purpose at the UGMA house and soon joined Linda as a vocalist and lyricist. "The music was different and fresh, and the energy, and you were just free. Whoever you are, however you dress, however you walk, however you talk, whatever you sing, would be identified with you. So I felt no more weird. I finally had a family."

"The People's Band"—Consciousness and Politics in UGMA

UGMA was not a politically programmatic organization and consequently attracted a wide-range of beliefs and worldviews, reflecting many attitudes within the African American community. In the aftermath of the events of 1965, there was the occasional US sympathizer, and some were involved with the Nation of Islam. One member worked with a small group of militant Muslims that advocated military-style confrontations with the LAPD to combat police brutality. By 1967 UGMA was one of the two dozen organizations listed under the umbrella of the Black Congress.[5] There were also supporters of local Democratic politicians, such as City Councilman Tom Bradley; many endorsed the Black Panther Party for Self-Defense. L.A. Panther leader, John Huggins, who was shot and killed, along with Bunchy Carter, by US supporters at UCLA on January 17, 1969, sang in the Voice of UGMA. Vocalist/poet Elaine Brown, who would become the chair of the Black Panther Party in the 1970s, became closely associated with Horace and UGMA in 1967. Less than two years later, she recorded the first of two albums with UGMA backing, arranged and conducted by Horace. *Seize the Time,* with its Emory Douglas cover painting of an armed Black Panther Party member over a deep blue background, represented much of the Panther worldview and included one song, "The Meeting," that Party Chief of Staff David Hilliard designated the Panther national anthem.[6]

The identification with the Panthers was particularly strong. UGMA did a great deal of support work for the Party, perhaps more so than for any other political organization. David Bryant remembers, "We got hooked up with the Black Panthers because they were having breakfasts for the community people that didn't have anything. So we became like the musical arm of them." Horace was a regular visitor to the Panther office, which prompted the FBI to begin an investigation of him in the fall of 1970.[7] In his autobiography he tells of a performance at South Park by a musician's union band sent in place of UGMA that was stopped by some disgruntled Panthers. "Me and David Bryant went by to check it out, and then went on to our gig with the Ark at the Malcolm X Center, which was a space run by some of our supporters. After we left, two Black Panthers got on the stage with their guns and demanded to know, 'Where's the Ark?!' They shot some rounds in the air and the band broke up."[8] On a lighter note, Walter Savage recalls performing at a benefit for Panther leader Bobby Seale in a local school auditorium: "It turned out that Bobby Seale played drums with us that day and how terrible that was. He used to be a drummer, so he said. He sat in and played a little drums, and pissed everybody in the band off. It was pretty long, but it was only one number."

With nationalism on the rise, some of the members developed an exclusionary stance toward non-blacks. There were few whites living in the community and the presence of a caucasian visitor at the UGMA house could raise the level of tension. Conguero Taumbu (aka Hal Ector) remembers the day he brought a white musician, a family friend, by the house.

A couple of them got pissed off at me because it was all black. 'Taumbu, what are you doing bringing this cat over here? You're cool. You're part of the family, but we don't know this guy.' It was nationalist time. I said, 'Well, if I'm part of the family, you can trust me that I wouldn't bring nobody here unless they were cool.' But Leroy [Brooks] didn't like it. So I said, 'Okay, man, you gotta leave.' And I left, too. I said, 'No problem, I still love you guys.' And they still loved me. They hugged me, but I had to take him out of there."

By the late 1960s there would be a stronger Latino presence in the band, but during his tenure at the house, Tommy Trujillo was the only nonblack. "I remember there were a lot of people that resented that I was even there at UGMA." His commitment to the music and UGMA got him through:

I used to have my guitar and my amplifier in the back of my VW bug. I was in the ghetto in central LA, but I used to park all over and nobody ever ripped off my shit. Maybe it was because I was with UGMA. I never had no fear for nothing, nobody ever fucked with me. At that time black consciousness hadn't gotten into the black power thing yet. It was deeper, more understanding. . . . I would attract this shit because I would be the only white, non-black person and a lot of people would just come around me and start rapping, like "What the fuck you doing here?" And they would just like sound me and bounce shit off of me. I was just a teenager, and so I was wide open and I didn't give a fuck. . . . I was like all the young jazz musicians around at that time. We were just real serious about our playing and we didn't give a fuck. I just got a lot of real serious information and more understanding as to the music and culture and the way of thinking.

Political consciousness was and remained high within UGMA. "Everybody was politically aware and the music always reflected that," explains Wainwright, articulating UGMA's appeal to him. "The Panthers were very active during that time. SNCC was very active during that time. US was very active during that time. And we were at the forefront and in the middle of all of that." At the core of UGMA since its founding was a belief in the crucial role of art within the community. They performed for any person, group, or organization acting to improve the community and the black cultural tradition, regardless of political agenda. This led them to engagements at churches and mosques, schools and social centers, with nationalist and revolutionary socialist organizations, as well as with Democratic Party politicians.

From its beginnings UGMA had been supportive of activists such as H. Rap Brown, Bobby Seale, and Jayne Cortez, who had been critical of the racist status quo and had fought social injustice. They performed at rallies for Muhammad Ali after his refusal to be inducted and later played in support of Angela Davis, a communist instructor dismissed by the University of California and later targeted by the FBI. Drummer Bill Madison recalls the range of political support work: "I remember one Sunday we played South Park for the Panthers. Then we went to the other side of town and played a reception for the black Democrats, all in the same day." According to Wainwright, "We involved ourselves with anything that would speak to justice or talk about injustice. We did things in the park, we did concerts, we did free stuff, we did stuff for the homeless, take up a collection for the homeless, and fundraisers. If it was about enriching the quality of life for those people in our community, we were there, no matter what the experience was. We were the people's band, basically." In his memoir, Horace remembers,

> People were always asking us what we were.
> "Are you guys Muslims?"
> "No, we're not Muslims."
> "Are you Black Panthers?"
> "No, we're not."
> "Are you US Organization people?"
> "No."
> "Well, what are you?"
> "We're black Americans, and want to live in the American way."
> You dig?[9]

Through it all, UGMA remained focused on fostering music and culture in the community. "That was Horace's thing," Walter Savage muses. "He wanted to be community oriented. It didn't really matter who they were as long as it was something community. Of course, some of them advocated a little violence, like the Panthers and US, but that doesn't mean that we were politically affiliated." The various political currents, according to bassist Al Hines, "didn't affect the band at all. We were already there. We were preserving the arts. We were doing the same thing that they were doing, only thing was they were talking and we were playing it. That was the difference between us and them. We used to play at a great big mosque at Jefferson and Central. Anything, anywhere, we maintained our style, our approach to music, wherever we went."

The Panther support work did not reflect a full endorsement of the Party's political program. Elaine Brown concludes, "He was not aggressive and Horace didn't like some of the stuff about the Black Panther Party. He wanted people to get along more. He wanted to make peace not war, and sometimes he thought the party was too violent. That didn't deter our relationship. It just meant that we were operating somewhere differently by the time I became a full-fledged Panther." According to Arthur Blythe, "Our intentions were positive. It wasn't about the negative of race relations; it was about the positive. . . . We were just playing music and being more communally involved. It was a cultural thing; it wasn't a political thing."

UGMA in the Watts Community—From the Streets to the Stage

By the end of 1965, 103rd Street was becoming a gathering spot for artists, would-be artists of all types, and interested community members. All within a few blocks of each other, the core spaces generated an excitement and explosion of artistic activity. Though each maintained their own programs, their commitment to community arts, their proximity, and, at times, overlapping memberships fostered a great deal of interaction. David Bryant remembers, "After the insurrection there was a renaissance in Watts and everybody was performing together. It was like a big umbrella." Horace, Elaine Brown, Will Connell and others from the Watts Happening Coffee House were also regulars at the House of Respect on Beach Street. Will recalls those visits: "I loved it. It was the most beautifully manifest sense of brotherhood. The band was the band, but those poets—I loved those poets and going to hear them read. It felt like the real community. I felt more a sense of a revolution or something changing from sitting there listening to those brothers read poetry."

The Coffee House became the center of UGMA activity within Watts. It was "where all the artists got together, where you'd talk about the times, and there was lots of space for performance," according to Wilber Morris. "All kinds of things, acting, dancing, a big stage for the big band. That was exciting." All of which contributed to a palpable sense of empowerment among the members. "It was like things are getting better—revolution time. It was a new head. Let's march for this. Let's stand up and be counted here. It was about that, the spirit of correcting all the injustices."

UGMA rehearsed and performed at the Coffee House every week and in different configurations. Amina remembers singing on stage with Linda, being supported by a visiting McCoy Tyner on piano, and the connections with other artists: "This was the era when all of this connected, and Ojenke was powerful. He would do these pieces on John Coltrane. Then they had the playwrights and the Bodacious Buguerilla. They were like an impromptu workshop." Stanley Crouch produced a series of Sunday "Cultural Afternoons" there and scheduled Elaine Brown with UGMA. For Arthur Blythe, UGMA's tenure at the Coffee House was one of the high points in the organization's musical history: "Some of our best music, I thought, was made there. It was very expressional and it felt according to the time, the time being the uneasiness in the country with the Vietnam War and race relations. . . . The music took on that character to me. There was a certain sense of freedom, freedom that I hadn't experienced. It felt like freedom akin to who I was. That's what it felt like. I liked it and I wanted to do it and I enjoyed it, playing the music and being around those people."

Government War on Poverty and private foundation financing enabled the Coffee House to fund an array of cultural programs. UGMA gave music workshops, provided individual instruction, and afforded young people opportunities to sit in with the band. Drummer Wainwright was one of those working with the kids. "That's where I met Sonship [Theus]. He was a kid. He said that I launched his career. It was him and Ndugu Chancler; they'd come and just sit and watch me play. On Saturdays that was an UGMA sponsored event, just to keep young people in the music and keep them excited about the music, and teach them, hands on."

At the Coffee House many poets became part of the UGMA scene, as an important cross-fertilization developed between UGMA, the Watts Writers Workshop, and Studio Watts. On a few occasions the Association performed there with Jayne Cortez, who had been the first poet to work with UGMA backing, and soon Quincy Troupe, Ojenke, Ted Jones, and the Watts Prophets were concertizing with them. Ojenke, who started performing with UGMA by the end of 1966, remembers, "I read with them in coffee houses, parks, community centers, churches, schools. Horace liked to have poets there and all the artists. He would like to have all the artists represented, like a multi-media presentation before all that was happening. Everybody would be there—dancers, singers."

Poet Edwin Fletcher "Ted" Jones, Lena Horne's son, became a solid supporter of and participant in UGMA. According to Rudolph Porter, "He was a force. He was a poet, and he loved UGMA and he loved the music. . . . He also was on KPFK radio and he'd have UGMA on his show. He read some poetry with UGMA and he'd play what was like a little toy whistle, like a fife." Educated in Switzerland and multi-lingual, Jones combined a love of poetry and literature with a deep interest in the history of Africa and Latin America. Will recalls, "It was all informal and we used to go over there and let him teach us. He would recite poetry at our gigs and take pictures." An important supporter as performer, teacher, publicist, and photographer, Ted suffered from kidney problems and was on dialysis. He died at twenty-eight in 1970.

UGMA also collaborated on theatrical productions at the Coffee House, where Horace met actor William Marshall, then conducting acting workshops with a purpose that meshed with the Association's mission. Looking back on those times, William explains,

> I was looking for ways in which I could participate, particularly where young folk were concerned, and African American young folk in particular, since so many doors were closed. We wanted to make the effort to teach the children. I wanted to find a way to connect with them, and to see to what degree we could come together and make sense of our lives. I enjoyed working with them and trying to stimulate their interests in living richer existences.

Marshall emerged in the early 1950s playing a Haitian revolutionary, "King Dick," in the film *Lydia Bailey,* and for the rest of his life refused to perform demeaning, stereotypical roles, always bringing a strength and depth of character to his performances. His stunning stage portrayal of Shakespeare's Othello was hailed in the London *Sunday Times* as "a great new Othello . . . the best Othello of our time."[10] That deep, resonant, Shakespearean voice left an indelible impression on Stanley Crouch: "What a sound! That's another one, another one of the great sounds. Amazing, amazing, amazing voice. The two greatest sounds I've heard in the last thirty years are his and James Earl Jones. Unbelievable sound." Walter Savage remembers that Marshall was "very serious about passing on his experiences to students and younger people. He was real sincere about his art form during the sixties and real sincere about coupling it with music."

Horace and William established a firm friendship and working relationship that would last until Horace's passing. Sylvia Jarrico, William's companion of forty years, notes, "Whenever music was needed, Horace would compose it and the band would be there to perform it. Horace was William's avenue to the kind of music to express the kind of themes that were closest to him, and to which Horace never failed to respond. They just understood each other very, very quickly. There was enormous appreciation." Marshall frequently appeared with UGMA, reading the poetry of African American authors, including Sterling Brown, Countee Cullen, Langston Hughes, and Margaret Walker, and with his formally trained lyric basso voice movingly and powerfully singing spirituals, such as "Tell God." When William staged a production of *Oedipus Rex*—known to UGMAgers as "the original motherfucker"—at the

Coffee House with the setting shifted to Theban Egypt, he organized an all-black, practically all-UGMA cast, with the band providing the music. Marshall directed; Kulesa, then a resident of the UGMA house, played Oedipus. Ted Jones was another cast member, who also did the research for transposing the play to Africa and relating it to contemporary black culture.

Over the next few years there would also be collaborations on such Marshall-led projects as *King Christophe, As Adam Early in the Morning,* and *Enter Frederick Douglass.* While living in Paris during the early 1960s, Marshall and Jarrico, obtained adaptation rights from Martiniquean poet Aimé Césaire for *La Tragédie du Roi Christophe,* a play based on the life of Haitian revolutionary and subsequent ruler Henri Christophe. Translated and adapted by William and Sylvia, a full production was staged at California State University at Northridge in the spring of 1970. This was followed by performances of excerpts throughout the area—at churches, museums and assorted community organizations—which featured music written by Horace and performed by the band. One of the compositions, "Funeral," later renamed "Warriors All," a dirgelike 6/4 lament, became one of the organization's most powerful pieces. They also contributed music to William's 1973 Emmy Award–winning poetry presentation, *As Adam Early in the Morning.*

One of William's most memorable creations, later performed on PBS, was his one-man show, *Enter Frederick Douglass,* written by Sylvia. Inspired by Douglass's life and writings, especially his Fourth of July oration, and using prerecorded music by Horace and the band, Marshall performed it around the country throughout the 1970s, including a memorable July 4, 1974 evening at the Kennedy Center in Washington, DC, and into the 1980s, culminating in performances at Los Angeles's innovative Inner City Cultural Center (ICCC) during its 1983–84 season.[11]

Within Watts and South Central Los Angeles, UGMA performed wherever opportunities arose, no matter how unorthodox. At times the band would play on 103rd Street, just outside the Coffee House. One community resident gave them a flatbed truck, upon which they mounted the band, pulling up at various locales and intersections, performing a piece or two and then moving on to the next stop. "We'd just go down the street playing," David Bryant recalls.

If there was one public space that became identified with UGMA during this time, it was South Park at Fifty-first Street and Avalon, north of Watts. The Park and its bandshell figured prominently early in the Association's history, as the band would rehearse and perform there, regardless of the size of the audience. More informally, it was the sight of many UGMA family gatherings. When Watts Prophet Richard Dedeaux arrived on the scene, "South Park

seemed like Horace's place." For the Prophets it was one of the most satisfying performance spaces in the city and they performed there often with
UGMA. "Oh man, it was just like the people were conditioned for it. There
were throngs of people there all of the time. They just kept that park alive. It
kept violence down. It was no problem, no problem whatsoever there. But
that was Horace's spot. That's where they should have buried Horace. South
Park. I know his spirit is sure there." To UGMA and, undoubtedly, most of the
audience, this gathering was more than a Sunday afternoon concert in the
park. To Wilber Morris it was emblematic of the time and was a vehicle in
energizing the community:

> It was nation time, black folks getting together, trying to get our lives
> together, because we have been separated for so long. The Sixties was a
> very important time in many, many ways, man. You got to clean house.
> You know what I'm saying? You got to get the crud out, so this flower
> can grow up straight. It was about that, people discovering who they
> were. That's what the music was about, and it wasn't just a black thing.
> It was whoever listened to the music. Get your house together, because
> your house is just as messed up as mine.

The Soundtrack for 103rd Street

By the later 1960s the Association modified its name to include the many
others artists joining their ranks, becoming The Underground Musicians and
Artists Association (UGMAA). And over the span of one year, from 1968 to
1969, embarked on recording projects with Sonny Criss, the Horace Tapscott
Quintet, William Marshall, and Elaine Brown, which summed up the musical
direction of the Association by the end of the decade, reflecting its social commitment to the community and its cultural goal of preserving and contributing
to the African American artistic tradition. "Always creative, very passionate,
and it always spoke to the time," explains E. W. Wainwright of their music.

Alto saxophonist Sonny Criss, who had spent most of his teen years in
Watts and was tutored by Buddy Collette, had known Horace for some time
but in the mid-1960s started performing regularly in the community with the
band. He was especially taken by Horace's compositions and by 1968 decided
to do a record date with Prestige devoted to that material. *Sonny's Dream
(Birth of the New Cool)* was written and arranged by Horace, who conducted
the ten-piece band, featuring Criss on soprano and alto. The resulting album
revealed not only Horace's abilities as an arranger but also the range of his

compositional work over the preceding few years. "Sonny's Dream," "Ballad for Samuel" and "The Golden Pearl" displayed his lyricism and command of waltz form; "Black Apostles" (for assassinated leaders Malcolm X, Medgar Evers, and Martin Luther King, Jr.) and "Daughter of Cochise" his strong bottom sound and use of riffs and ostinati to create powerful, dark atmospheres; and in "Sandy and Niles" his adventurous harmonic and rhythmic sense.

A successful production in many ways, *Sonny's Dream* was, nevertheless, a disappointment for Horace and the band. Assuming that they were performing with Criss, Horace arrived at the studio early to find that Prestige's producer had already hired other performers. Horace was able to get an UGMAA drummer, Everett Brown, on the date but was forced to work with musicians who, although immensely talented, were unfamiliar with his music. UGMAA had been performing and rehearsing the pieces regularly with Criss and would have brought to the session a more intense, bottom-heavy, edgier sound, as characterized their subsequent recordings.[12]

One of the most important recording sessions in the history of UGMAA resulted in the album *The Giant Is Awakened.* Recorded on April 1, 1969, and subsequently issued on Bob Thiele's Flying Dutchman label, it featured a lineup of Black Arthur Blythe on alto sax (his first recording), Horace on piano, David Bryant and Walter Savage on basses, and Everett Brown, Jr. on drums, under the name of the Horace Tapscott Quintet. There were performances of three of Horace's pieces—"The Giant Is Awakened," "Niger's [*sic*] Theme" ("Nyja's Theme"), "The Dark Tree"—and Blythe's "For Fats." In the title track, Horace offered a composition originally inspired by one of the many African American folk tales of High John the Conqueror, which became an anthem for the movements of the 1960s, performances inspiring audiences to stand with their fists struck boldly skyward. "The Dark Tree" came to represent an anthem for the ages, always a part of Horace's and the band's performing repertoire. Both built on dark ostinati, surging rhythms that maintain momentum throughout the pieces freeing the harmony from a role in that responsibility, they open the musical landscape to Blythe's piercing alto, Brown's endlessly inventive polyrhythms, Bryant and Savage's atmospheric counterpoint, and Horace's intensifying dissonances.

Some of the members thought the session was not representative of the band at its best. Will Connell remembers, "That was a C minus day for those guys. Oh, man. Horace had a little raggedy car, and the car broke down trying to get to the record date. It was just one of those hellish days. And I heard them all the time. It was like a C minus day for them. They could play." Horace was disillusioned when he was excluded from the mixing process and felt that the final product gave the piano too much emphasis.[13] Nevertheless, to Stanley Crouch and some observers on the East Coast, the album offered an important new sound. According to Stanley, "Nobody was playing like Horace in New York. Michael Cuscuna said that to me a number of times. He said that when that record, *The Giant Is Awakened,* came out, if Horace and his band had come to New York, they would have really surprised everybody, because nobody in town was playing like that."

In August 1969, a few months after recording *The Giant,* UGMAA collaborated with William Marshall on a session for Capitol Records. Capitol approached Marshall with the idea of doing an album of black poetry, including Margaret Walker's "For My People." Marshall agreed to do the readings and set up a session with musical backing by the full UGMAA ensemble—band and voices, over thirty musicians strong. Walter Savage remembers *For My People* as "one of the best things up to that time that we had ever done." Will, who copied the charts for the session, was a vocalist on the date: "Horace used everything for that session. He found one brother who did harmonica. He used a full orchestra. I think that's where Arthur [Blythe] got the idea for using a cello. There was a blond woman from San Francisco who played cello. He put her and Arthur on a unison and it was just beautiful." Unfortunately, Capitol never released the album, the tapes quietly resting in an East Coast storage facility.

Elaine Brown had initially come to Los Angeles to pursue a singing career, but a growing politicization, a brief, unsuccessful initial stint in the Black Panthers, and depression combated with thorazine combined to leave her isolated and adrift. Then she took an administrative job at the Watts Happening Coffee House. With Horace's encouragement she started to sing again, frequenting the Coffee House on weekends. "Horace was the centerpiece of everything. It seems to me that I sang a song with them at some point or for him. Linda was the band singer. In my mind she was the Afro-centric Billie Holiday. That was how I thought of Linda. I think in my mind I wanted to be that person. And because Horace was so protective and nice with me, I just wanted to do stuff with Horace." Though temporarily removed from an active political role, Elaine had been composing songs based upon the people she was meeting in the community. "I was like a photographer taking pictures of these new people. Everybody was new. It wasn't just Linda. There were whole different forms of poetry. It was like the evolution of bebop. It was like being in the Harlem Renaissance. Everybody was like, 'Wow, what's happening to me?'"

By 1969 Elaine was back in the Panther fold and serving as deputy minister of information for the Southern California Chapter. A recording session, ordered by Panther Chief of Staff David Hilliard, was set for August 10. The resulting album, *Seize the Time*, arranged and conducted by Horace, featured Elaine singing her songs, accompanied on some by Horace and a ten-piece UGMAA band. Horace conducted from the piano, while Elaine played piano on a few selections. "Horace made all the musical decisions," Elaine remembers. "But where you hear any good piano, it's Horace." Stylistically, Elaine was a pop singer with gospel and classical influences, and Horace, who was moonlighting arranging for vocalists, crafted charts to support Elaine's style. It was the content of Elaine's songs that drew them together. "She wrote songs of freedom, and I loved it," Horace recalls in *Songs of the Unsung*.[14] In the liner notes, Elaine writes,

> Songs, like all art forms, are an expression of the feelings and thoughts, the desires and hopes, and so forth, of a people. They are no more than that. A song cannot change a situation, because a song does not live and breathe. People do.
>
> And so the songs in this album are a statement—by, of, and for the people. All the people. A statement to say that we, the masses of people have had a game run on us; a game that made us think that it was necessary for our survival to grab from each other, to take what we wanted as individuals from any other individuals or groups, or to exploit each other. And so, the statement is that some of us have understood that it is absolutely essential for our survival to do just the opposite. . . .
>
> This means all of us have this power. But the power only belongs to all of us, not just some or one, but all. And that was the trick. That was the thing we never understood. And that is what statement these songs make.[15]

In the Panther paper they were characterized as "the first songs of the American Revolution."[16] "Assassination" was written for Bunchy Carter and John Huggins, murdered at UCLA earlier in the year, "The Meeting" for Eldridge Cleaver, and "The Panther" for L.A. Panther leader Frank Diggs.[17] The title track, "Seize the Time," disparages political sentiment unsupported by revolutionary activism:

> You worry about liberty
> Because you've been denied.
> Well, I think that you're mistaken
> Or then, you must have lied.
> 'Cause you do not act like those who care
> You've never even fought

For the liberty you claim to lack
Or have you never thought
To Seize The Time
The time is now
Oh, Seize The Time
And you know how.

"The End of Silence" is a call to arms to achieve dignity and freedom:

Have you ever stood
In the darkness of night
Screaming silently
You're a man.
Have you ever hoped that
A time would come
When your voice could be heard
In a noon-day sun.
Have you waited so long
'Til your unheard song
Has stripped away your very soul.
Well then, believe it my friend
That this silence will end
We'll just have to get guns
And be men.

Musically, the sessions went smoothly, inspired by their common social purpose. Outside the studio doors, the LAPD was a constant presence. According to Elaine, "The joy I felt in making the music was undercut by the presence of the police, who followed us every day, who sat outside the Vault recording studio during the sessions, who stopped and delayed us going to and from the studio."[18] Nevertheless, looking back on that period and her collaboration with Horace, she recalls, "This is so emotional for me right now, remembering this period, just remembering how really pure we were, and Horace and that music. . . . That album was his as much as it was mine."

All in the Family—Life at the Second UGMA House

The increase in community activity after the 1965 uprising made the UGMA house even more of a magnet for musicians and artists, as well as for cultural and political fellow travelers. During his residency at the house, Walter Savage recalls, "There were at least twelve of us living in that house who had no place to go or didn't want to go any other place, but to be in that house. I occupied a small bedroom upstairs, and lived with the woman who I eventually married and her two kids, and also her first cousin. We all lived in the same room together." Billy Boyd occupied another bedroom, and Linda had the third, while others made do in the living room downstairs. Arthur Blythe, finding himself between apartments, was a resident in 1967. "We were just wild. It was like we were part of that hippie movement, but we were like black hippies. It was experiences with drugs, music, freedom, no responsibilities, the whole bit. But at that time it didn't seem vulgar, and the music was still the focus. That was the reason we were there. The music brought us together." Despite the usual distractions, Taumbu recalls the closeness, and political and cultural seriousness that permeated daily life at the house:

> A lot of times we'd just sit around in the living room and have conversations, philosophical and political. There was a very acute awareness of the political realities and the cultural realities. Once, we were sitting around and this guy comes up, and he has this uniform on, he says, "I'm from the light company. I've come to turn the lights off. You guys haven't paid your bill." "Well, come on in." So he comes in and looks around. "You guys can pay it now if you want to." "No, it's okay, man. Just go ahead and cut it off. No hard feelings." And then he just left, and didn't turn it off. "I'll see you guys later." And people would do that. People would bring food some times. If one of us would get a gig, most of the money would go into the house, buying food or some shit like that. . . . And it was very Afro-centric, artistic in that sense, and natural, unpretentious, and very oriented toward the unity, the one, what was best for the whole thing.

The band was growing; more members were writing. There were usually formal rehearsals for the full band on Saturdays. Because of its growing size, sections started having separate sessions as well. Linda worked the choir, the Voice of UGMA, and there were also rehearsals for the various small group configurations that sprang up. When there were no rehearsals, the music continued. Walter Savage recalls that "it was the only place in the world where you could never be alone. Nobody ever practiced, because that meant to someone else, 'Oh, I'm going to play with you.'" To Rudolph Porter, "It was a twenty-four-hour thing. Any time you'd go by there, it was music. I used to go by there at two or three in the morning with my alto and tenor, just playing and cats showing me stuff. You'd come there on a Sunday morning and there'd be maybe fifteen musicians in the living room waiting to sit in." And to Tommy Trujillo, "Everybody who was on that scene was like totally artistic. Wasn't nobody doing no 9-to-5 shit. Nobody was doing any gigs at the Ramada Inn, not even any straight gig with a jazz quartet or anything. It was like they had their own scene. It was real deep. It was formidable and it was very inspirational."

The building continued to attract not only musicians. It had the aspect of a free house or neutral zone for every "out cat" in the community or passing through. "Everybody counter-culture felt like the house was a safe place for them," according to Will Connell. As a revolving door for the cultural and political underground, it attracted its share of activists, including Stokely Carmichael and H. Rap Brown. Some members swear the phone was tapped. More militantly inclined political activists used to gather in the upstairs rooms. Will recalls, "It was like the house was a neutral space for that kind of stuff, where people with the guns and people that had the money to buy the guns would meet. It was like a safe place to do that. I remember specifically one time in Leroy's room when they were doing that. I thought these people were part of some groups, but you didn't ask questions about that."

Not surprisingly, and particularly after the uprising of 1965, the activities at the house and UGMA's visibility in the community earned them the attention of law enforcement. Most members had already accumulated a backlog of experiences with the police; simply being African American was enough to rouse LAPD suspicion and animosity. Wilber Morris remembers, "I had some personal confrontations with the police. Just a lot of harassment, you know, like, 'What's in that bag,' and I'm carrying the bass. I remember one time Arthur Blythe, Will Connell and I were up on Fifty-something street and the police came down on us. They had drawn guns and wanted to know what we had in the saxophone cases and stuff like that. And that just made things worse."

The campaign by the LAPD to criminalize black youths was driven home to Will Connell when he was arrested one evening. Wanting to score a nickel bag of pot, some friends convinced him, as the only one with an available car, to drive them. They were busted and Will found himself in jail. He'd been in the Air Force since leaving high school, and, consequently, hadn't a police record. "It was like the LAPD had a thing to give every low class black man a police record so they could restrict them from good jobs. And they were like, 'How did we miss you?' The cops said that to me, and they wouldn't put me with the rest of the guys in the holding cell until they figured it out." While frequenting local political meetings, he also witnessed police harassment.

> That place, where Angela Davis was Communications Secretary, near Jefferson and something, the cops used to park down the street and shine their brights in that place. And any black they'd beat up in that area, they'd leave him on the doorstep. They'd do it all the time.... I'll never forget there was one janitor, who said he couldn't talk about revolutionary principles, but "I can tell you how many black people were killed since the last meeting." He used to go to all the morgues to get that info. And he'd just stand up at the meetings and call the names, man. And he would go on for a long, long time.... I'm telling you, there was some shit going on in L.A.

Round-the-clock music at the house also merited the attention of the police department. Walter Savage recounts, "There weren't any serious problems with the LAPD. But at least once a week the cops came to tell us to stop playing, because we may not start playing until ten or eleven and that shit might go on until three o'clock in the morning, if nobody calls the cops. But somebody was always calling the cops; the cops were always there." Occasionally, there were some comedic or at least odd moments. Will and a number of other UGMAgers were playing late one night, when the LAPD appeared.

> There was a knock on the door. I go to the door and open it. It was two cops. One of the cops says, "Can we come in?" And I'm like—stupid me—"Well, we're smoking grass in here." I said that, and they said, "We don't care. We just want to hear the music. Can we come in?" They sat there on wooden milk crates, hat, badge, gun, everything—white cops—and listened. They came in the darkness before the dawn and they left just before it got dawn. And I remember they didn't take off their hats. I never saw them again.

Through it all, music remained the anchor that held the Association together and prevented it from dissipating into bohemian lifestylism. Horace was there only for the rehearsals, Walter remembers. "He didn't hang in that stupid shit. Most of the time a lot of that stuff didn't have a lot to do with the music. Although when it came time to do the music, everybody got out of the way." Under Horace's leadership, the music was focused and strong, according to Wainwright. "When Horace came through, it was a formal rehearsal. But when he wasn't there, it kept going. There was music there all the time. People were serious. That's what it was about." And when Horace came by for rehearsals, "It was time to learn. It was time to add some structure to what was going on. Horace had a magic about him in terms of how to deal with different dynamics, different egos, people and everything. He never had to raise his voice, not once. I don't ever remember him raising his voice or not smiling. I mean, he would say some slick stuff and you would just fall into line."

Although not captured on the early small group recordings, UGMA had a size and sound that set it apart from any other jazz ensemble, band, or orchestra. Whether in rehearsal or performance, it was not unusual to find as many as four or five percussionists, five bassists, two or three guitarists, and a phalanx of brass and woodwind players. "We had three basses, two guitars, four sets of drums, god knows how many saxophones and what have you," recalls Avotcja. "That was like a mind blower for me and he made it work. . . . One time there must have been six or seven flutes up there and he made it work." Horace added parts to existing arrangements when newcomers appeared, and in the collective free improvisations, which were part of the band approach since its inception, the veteran musicians would provide structure. Will remembers the leadership role of Lester Robertson and trumpeter Calvin Harvey:

> When we'd play "At the Crossroads," everybody would solo at once. So the saxophones would do what they would do, but Lester Robertson and Calvin would get in there and they would start stroking, like a coxswain in a boat race that calls strokes out, they would start stroking, man, making chains of rhythm to make that stuff make sense in the brass section, so we would have some real beautiful counterpoint going. . . . Man, the things they would play!

Lyrics were added to many of the pieces, usually crafted by Linda, occasionally by Amina. However, the vocalists also improvised a great deal. According to Amina, "We did a lot of things where we'd just make sounds." One vocalist might set a sound pattern and the others would join in a group improvisation.

By the end of 1968, this phase of UGMA's history came to a conclusion, when it was evicted from the second UGMA house at 56th Street and Figueroa. Will remembers, "It was a doctor's property and the doctor liked music. And we'd never pay rent. We'd talk some militant shit, and he'd back off. But he didn't really care, because he liked the music. But there was some dope problems in the building. When people in the house started breaking in and stealing some of his supplies, he called the cops on them. People with drug problems in the house started doing it." Amina arrived at the house just after the eviction. "I was gone and Linda was there with my daughter. The rest were men. I know the police came in. . . . By the baby being there, they didn't take Linda. They let her stay with the baby, but they took all the guys to jail."

Over the next few months, those members who had been resident at the UGMA house made do as best they could. Some slept on the beach, others moved in with friends. Calvin Harvey lived in an apartment building at Twenty-eighth Street and Vermont Avenue. Not long after the eviction, that building also housed Black Arthur, Linda, Amina, Kookie, Art Sebrie, and Vanetta. The second UGMA house had been an important focal space for the Association but the music continued wherever there were members. In 1966 Horace and Cecilia moved their family to 4901 Eleventh Avenue, one block from Crenshaw High School in the Leimert Park district of South Central Los Angeles and four miles west of the UGMA house. When the piano was moved in the new family residence, Horace and UGMA played on.

THE MOTHERSHIP

From UGMA/UGMAA to the Pan Afrikan
Peoples Arkestra and UGMAA

Where is your fire? I say where is your fire?
Can't you smell it coming out of our past?

SONIA SANCHEZ

Not long after the release of *Seize the Time* in 1969, the Underground Musicians and Artists Association performed with Elaine Brown at Los Angeles City College. Bassist Baba Alade was on that gig. "The Panthers came in there with drawn weapons and Elaine Brown sang that song, 'We'll have to get guns and be men' ["The End of Silence"], and I was in love. I had my bass and when I saw those shotguns—I'm young—I thought, 'The Panthers . . . Wowee!' Heroes like." The Black Panthers were at their most visible and inspirational, but after almost three years of confrontation with city, state and federal authorities, it was clear to some that an insular urban movement, which in practice did not politically mobilize the black working class and poor, but engaged in police oversight patrols, community self-defense and social work, had little chance of altering the status quo.

Tensions within the Black Congress, particularly between the Panthers and the US Organization, were exacerbated, and government and government-inspired infiltration and assaults across the country resulted in the deaths of dozens of Panthers and the incarceration of many more, including virtually the entire leadership. On December 8, 1969, the Los Angeles Police Department laid siege to the Panther headquarters at 4115 South Central Avenue and for five hours poured thousands of rounds of ammunition and tear gas into the old structure before arresting the fortified and well-armed thirteen armed Panthers inside, including Somayah Kambui (Renee "Peaches" Moore), who played autoharp and sang in the Arkestra. Everyone survived the assault.[1]

If *Seize the Time* was part of the call to arms and political consciousness of the mid- to late-1960s, the political movements spawned by that call, while failing to transform the politico-economic structure, left a heightened level of social consciousness throughout the communities. Black and pan-African consciousness was rapidly spreading by the late 1960s and early 1970s into various cultural and social organizations, as well as educational institutions throughout the country. To an extent this reflected a wider acceptance of what UGMA had espoused since 1961.

The commitment to the community and to the preservation and fostering of black art had been at the organization's core, but when first organized this placed the Association in an underground, marginal position. By the late-1960s this was no longer the case. Much of what it represented was now becoming visible on the social landscape as the search for an improved community life was embraced by many, even as the wave of revolutionary activity was subsiding. Spurred by these developments and an influx of younger recruits espousing many of these ideas, the organization expanded its involvements and started planning for a more defined structure to create, support and house their growing community arts movement.

The Pan Afrikan Peoples Arkestra and UGMAA

By 1968/1969 UGMA had become UGMAA—The Underground Musicians and Artists Association, a reflection of the varied arts now represented within the movement. Within a few years there would be further changes. In recognition of their growing visibility they soon jettisoned the subterranean designation. In 1970 the band was billed as the Community Cultural Orchestra, a name occasionally referenced in the past, and in August became the Community Cultural Arkestra. By the summer of 1971, as their activities expanded, they developed a plan for a larger organization to encompass the different areas of their work retaining the acronym UGMAA, but now designating the Union of God's Musicians and Artists Ascension. The band adopted the name that it carries to this day—the Pan Afrikan Peoples Arkestra (PAPA).

Though at this stage an expanded Union was more wish than substance, it did signify their intent to establish a more concrete organization and space for the community arts and was a summary statement of their many influences: the spirituality of many of the new members, some of whom had become Muslims, the traditional role of churches in the community, the impact of John Coltrane and pieces such as "Ascension," and the composition and purpose of the organization. In his autobiography, Horace writes,

> After a while, as we became more above ground, we started realizing what our real role was. In the beginning it was more like breaking the old mold, the old routines; just take a bulldozer and run it down. Then, we had to think about how to build it up to what we were talking about. That's when we became the Union of God's Musicians and Artists Ascension. . . .
>
> We chose the name because the black cats in my age bracket were all brought up in segregated America, which meant we spent a lot of time going to church. . . . I tried hard not to disrespect my elders, and I wanted to tear down the things they'd had to face. But I also had to have some sensitivity to what they went through in my actions. By using the "Union of God's Musicians," they understood the word *God*. They'd been hearing it all their lives. Okay, so we utilized it. "Musicians and Artists Ascension" I picked because that was the idea we had in mind, that we were going to ascend through the arts to bring about recognition and understanding of each other. We thought we had to do this as a people before we could reach out to someone else.[2]

The international dimension—Pan Afrikan—linking African Americans with Africa and the other parts of the African diaspora, meant a more explicit statement of attitudes implicit since the organization's founding, but also meant an expansion of their vision. As Horace explains, "'Pan Afrikan,' because the music would be drawn from Afrikan peoples around the world, and 'Arkestra,' building off the word *ark* and Noah using it to save different parts of the world, as told in the Bible. We would preserve the music on our Ark, the mothership, and it will be around for people to listen to and enjoy."[3] Pan African unity was an important theme internationally and was one that resonated within UGMAA. According to Will Connell, "At the time we used to think that we couldn't have any revolution until we healed the split in the African diaspora. Those were our brothers that went south and we came up here. Until we healed that, we couldn't talk about the revolution."

Originally, the organization grew by word of mouth, bohemians and musicians casually finding each other. Now it seemed that much of the community was moving in the direction they had been espousing. To Ojenke, it reflected the motion of African American society: "When they became PAPA, it was more like the political consciousness had become much more refined and focused. Black consciousness became much more intense, and black people started to really make a connection to their cultural roots. That's when they began to call themselves PAPA." With the plethora of social and cultural organizations and programs that emerged in the wake of 1965 and continued into the new decade, more of the community, especially the youth, became exposed to PAPA/UGMAA.

Their growing audience was fostered by a local radio program. From 1968 to 1971 radio station KUSC, 91.5 FM, located in the upper floors of Hancock Auditorium on the campus of the University of Southern California, offered a program called "Greg's Refresher Course," hosted by Greg Kufahamu (formerly Greg Irving, later Aman Kufahamu). After a few intense years of upheaval in the South Central areas surrounding USC, the University was looking for community outreach opportunities. Kufahamu, a graduate of Fremont High School in his early twenties with a strong interest in jazz, sound technology, and radio, approached the head of the Communications Department, Dr. Borgers, with a proposal for a radio show. Not long after, "Greg's Refresher Course" became a Sunday feature from noon until six in the evening, later switched to three hours on Saturday and three on Sunday. According to Kufahamu, "I had this spiel where I said, 'You're doing the Greg's Refresher Course. . . .' It was about not only going back trying to refresh your memory, but also to present material that we hope will inspire and refresh you to keep you striving." Controversies, including a death threat, were never far from Kufahamu because of his identification with much of the political and cultural sentiment moving through the streets of South Central L.A. "I did some daring things, playing the Last Poets' 'Niggers Are Scared of Revolution.' That's FCC stuff, which caused a problem. . . . Almost every show I played Nina Simone and I played a lot of spoken word stuff, a lot of controversial stuff."

When Elaine Brown's *Seize the Time* was released in 1969, Kufahamu featured it. "I was around Bunchy [Carter] and John [Huggins]. I was around the Panthers, the Black Congress. When this kind of material came out, it was important to me. I was on the air and it was strong. I played her stuff." At the first opportunity he arranged an interview with Elaine, who introduced him to Horace. *The Giant Is Awakened* had a profound impact on Kufahamu and it became a regular feature on the show. "That record just grabbed at me."

Hancock Auditorium also presented the Arkestra with a venue capable of broadcasting live performances and led to collaborations with artists in other fields, an important aspect of UGMAA's aesthetic. Kufahamu installed a sound system and together with graphic artist Michael Dett Wilcots formed the Universal Order of Black Expression to present concerts and various artistic productions. According to Kufahamu, "Michael Wilcots, Roho, and David Mosley, the fighter Sugarcane Mosley's uncle, were the artists. David would put posters all around. He did some of Angela [Davis], Eldridge [Cleaver], James Brown, Jackie Wilson. So they would have this art on display. The whole foyer would be filled with their art. And then there was the concert inside." Their first presentation featured the Arkestra and was followed by concerts of other local musicians, including Curtis Amy, Bobby Bradford, John Carter, and Azar Lawrence. Ticket prices were minimal, a dollar or two, or some canned goods. The Universal Order covered the costs and the money would go to the performers. Kufahamu took the canned goods to a nearby, black day-care center.

Local playwright Cecil Rhodes staged his *Gold Power, or Once Upon a Time There Lived Three Black Brothers* at the Auditorium on March 28, 1971, and incorporated the Arkestra. The play was an extended dialogue between a Maoist, a civil rights advocate, and a preacher, exploring the three different political currents dominant within the politics of the community. The Ark provided the music and in the manner of Japanese Kabuki theater, Horace integrated the band into the play. Cecil recalls, "Horace's idea from the very beginning was that we didn't need to write any music. What we'll do is assign the instruments—there were about twenty-two musicians in the Ark at that time—to the different characters. All the musicians were assigned to the three actors and it was total improvisation. After a couple of rehearsals we did it live on KUSC." Will Connell was one of the musicians: "Some of us walked around behind the actors and played like pianissimo while they talked, improvising behind them. So we were supposed to be the spirit of what they were saying."

When the Universal Order started promoting concerts at Foshay Junior High School, Michael Dett Wilcots met Horace, beginning a lifelong association. Horace had noticed his artwork and was interested in having him produce a brochure for UGMAA, one that could be used to solicit gigs. The meeting also resulted in the recognition of shared goals and a more permanent association.

> Kufahamu and I were trying to represent a broader spectrum of showcasing black arts. Some of us did spoken word or poetry, some of us did drawings, paintings, photography, and we knew other people who worked in these fields, as well as dancers and musicians. But we felt that we needed . . . a real physical, material thing, a headquarters or a building. We wanted to take it that far. So meeting Horace, we automatically had a very close relationship because we were speaking about the same things.

For Michael Dett, a recent Los Angeles transplant from Iowa via Washington, DC, it would result in a life change, as he became an UGMAA archivist, graphic artist, photographer, eventually executive director, and Horace's son-in-law, when he married Horace and Cecilia's oldest child, Renée, in 1976.

The Next Generation

Name changes, an expanding purpose, plans for a more formal organization, and collaboration with the Universal Order of Black Expression were aspects of UGMAA's new profile. Personnel were also changing. Wilber Morris and Walter Savage departed for San Francisco. Chico Roberson and Ike Williams had left the band, while John Huggins was murdered by US Organization members at UCLA in 1969. Substance abuse issues and resultant incarcerations kept some away for varying periods of time. In a tragedy that is starkly recalled by members, drummer Leroy Brooks took his life that same year. Guitarist Avotcja, who was a close friend and out of the country during Leroy's final illness, remembers him as a gentle soul: "I think he was probably too gentle for the male fantasy that somebody built up way back when, that not too many guys successfully succeed in becoming." It never fit Leroy and with Superfly on the horizon his alienation could only increase.

> We used to hang out at my place sometimes after rehearsals and we'd just lay on the floor for hours. Men and women don't do that if they're not going to bed. Leroy did it, just laying on the floor listening to music and talking about everything from the weather to what we wanted to do with our music and all that kind of stuff. I never thought of him being a nut, even when he started breaking down. I just thought that he was a hurt little boy that needed somebody. . . . He was too sensitive about everything. I mean everything hurt him. He was a walking pin

cushion, but I don't think it was because he was a psycho. I think he was just too sensitive for the times.

Despite these losses, the release of the Horace Tapscott Quintet recording and those with Elaine Brown and Sonny Criss, as well as the exposure on Kufahamu's radio program, gave the Arkestra a visibility not experienced before. Coupled with a growing performance schedule throughout the community and expanding community artistic and cultural institutions populated with members and supporters, this attracted another wave of musicians. Talented and young, they were to have a major impact on the music and the direction of the Arkestra. Among them were pianists Herbie Baker and Nate Morgan; pianist and flutist Ernest Straughter (Hamid); flutist Abdul-Salaam Muhammad (Robert Roy); saxophonists Hasan Abib Ali, Azar Lawrence, Steven Meeks, Cerion Middleton III, and Ray Straughter (Shams); trumpeters Walter Graham, Mark Lott, Butch Morris, Willie Samprite, and Kylo Turner (Kylo Kylo); trombonist Al Hall II; Robert Sims on bari horn; vibist Gary "En Medio" Saracho; bassists Baba Alade (Sherman McKinney), Richard Herrera, and Roberto Miguel Miranda; drummers John Blue, Steve Solder, David Straughter, Greg Tell, and Fritz Wise; percussionist Ernest Cojoe; poet Kamau Daáood (Luther Keyes); and, martial arts improviser Dadisi Sanyika. Unlike earlier recruiting classes, most were in their teens, many still in high school, when they first came around. Some were in their twenties and had served at least one hitch of active military duty, a background shared with many of the older members, and a few had served in Southeast Asia.

Conguero Ernest Cojoe was a Vietnam veteran when he joined the Arkestra. One of the most revered members in the Ark, Cojoe is recalled by Roberto Miranda as "a wonderful musician and a very gentle human being who had been through Vietnam and who was a true soldier and an efficient martial artist. He was not a small man, yet he wasn't really big. Yet, this cat was lethal and quiet when he needed to be in terms of his martial arts." To Abdul-Salaam Muhammad, he was an "electrifying" performer: "He played the song on his congas, and when he soloed, he had three and, man, he was so fast and the sound was unbelievable. He was one of the key personalities in the group."

His life was cut short by cancer, caused by exposure to Agent Orange while serving in Vietnam, and he died on February 13, 1973. His burial on the 20th was attended by his fellow artists, some of whom performed, including Shams (Ray Straughter):

Cojoe was just the most spiritual thing from heaven. . . . We played music while Cojoe was being put in the ground. When I started crying,

Horace came and put his arm around me. That day was everybody there. I mean everybody. Cojoe was whoooo. I mean Cojoe, man. I'm not an idol worshipper, but that's a great person. . . . Cojoe you're speaking about heart. You're speaking about something that's not even a physical body, man. This guy was deep. He would do anything you wanted to do. Help everything. If you needed anything, he wasn't scared of anything. . . . "I'll be there." That's how Cojoe was.

Kamau Daáood remembers that day:

As people began to walk away, Shams pulled out his horn. I began playing this gong, creating a drone sound, and Shams started playing this tune he had written for Cojoe. It was so beautiful and heartfelt. He got about half way through and he couldn't take any more, fell on his knees, crying. That was Cojoe's home-going. Cojoe said, "Don't stop! Take it out!" That was like a battle cry for us for a long time. "Don't stop!" Keep pushing this thing forward, keep playing, keep committed to this music and what's in it, the life that we had. "Don't stop! Take it out!" . . . That's the kind of spirit he was, a great spirit.

Cornetist/trumpeter Butch Morris was in the US Army from 1966 until August 1969, the years his brother, Wilber, was active in UGMA/UGMAA. Though serious about music since the age of fourteen, he played flugelhorn sporadically while in the military and served as a medic in Vietnam. During his periodic leaves from active duty, he got a sense of the musical activity in Los Angeles from his brother, who was also a member of an avant-garde band led by Stanley Crouch, which rehearsed for a while in the Morris family garage in Watts. "The first time I heard Arthur Blythe I was coming home on leave from Vietnam. I didn't even bother to go into the house. I went right out to the garage. I mean it was that great. I was totally knocked out by Arthur and Bobby [Bradford], and I thought I had heard a lot. . . . But that knocked me out cold. I probably didn't even talk for a whole day and a half. Hearing Arthur and Bobby play together is still one of the high points." When he was discharged from the Army, Butch returned to L.A. and enrolled at Southwest College to study prosthetics, orthotics, and physical therapy, a career path that lasted until he became involved with the Arkestra. He was introduced to Horace by his brother and Arthur. "They took me around to the UGMAA house. When I met Horace, basically he just said, 'Welcome to the band' and just gave me the music." For Butch it was a turning point in his life and from then on music became the center.

Born into a Puerto Rican family in New York City, bassist Roberto Miranda was raised in the Echo Park/Silverlake area of Los Angeles, where his family moved in 1952. In his teens, gang activity took over his life until music provided an alternative. A few years later he met Horace, Bobby Bradford, and John Carter, beginning strong musical and personal relationships that would last until the present with Bobby and until the deaths of Horace and John in the 1990s. "They picked me up early. They just heard me play one day with somebody, but basically all three of them just said, 'Hey, little brother, come here.' I had heard them play and as soon as I heard them play, I said, 'Oh, yeah. I love this music. I love this music.' And, man, these guys just loved me. They encouraged me and they gave me the freedom to play."

Among the younger recruits, Ray, Ernest, and David Straughter lived near Watts. They gained a reputation for street toughness but became musicians. By the late 1950s/early 1960s the gang presence was strong. Flutist/composer Ernest and saxophonist Shams (Ray) were nearing their teenage years when the family moved to Eighty-fifth Street in the middle of Slauson territory. Ernest remembers, "We were in a rough neighborhood. People would break in people's houses and rob them, but nobody would never try and break in our house because we were like hostile. Me and Shams would carry a bat. I used to carry a bat to school every day." Shams had even customized the bat with a deadly placement of nails. "They can try and rob everybody else, but Shams had a bat with nails in it. I said, 'Man, you been watching too much Bluto and Popeye.' . . . Never got to use it. But imagine getting hit with a bat with some nails, man. That's bad." Nevertheless, they kept their distance from the gangs. "We were musicians then. We just stuck to music. We didn't even get involved." Pianist Nate Morgan remembers them from the neighborhood. "The Straughters are a known family in Watts. You didn't mess with the Straughters. They were kind of tough. Yeah, it was safe for them to walk up and down the street with a case in their hands. Anybody else, you'd wind up seeing your horn that weekend in the pawn shop."

The Straughter brothers had become serious about music by 1967/68, and then discovered Grant's Music Center in the Midtown Shopping Center at 3306 Venice Boulevard near Third Avenue, just above the Westside. Henry Grant, a former saxophonist with Lionel Hampton's and Gerald Wilson's big bands, opened the Center early in 1965. Within months it became a magnet for black music devotees, R&B and jazz, students and professionals. He created a network of spaces covering two stories in a mall facility that offered equipment, instruments, music instruction, rehearsal rooms of varying sizes, and professional services, such as music copying and arranging. Perhaps not since the 1920s and 1930s, when musician brothers Benjamin "Reb" and Johnny Spikes operated their music center at the corner of Twelfth Street and Central Avenue, had there been such an establishment in black L.A.[4]

For the Straughters the experience at Grant's would change their lives, especially after being introduced to one of Grant's teachers, Horace Tapscott, and then attending UGMAA rehearsals there. Shams recalls the first time:

> I walk upstairs at Grant's that day on the weekend, and Horace's band was rehearsing. I'd never heard them. I never heard Horace's band before. And all the guys were up there. I was sitting in the back and Horace keeps looking at me with these funny looking eyes from way away, on the other side at the front where all the musicians are. I'm minding my own business up against the wall, just trying to see how they do it. He says, "Hey, kid. That's yours? You play tenor?"
>
> I said, "I'm just starting, about six, seven months."
>
> Billie Harris was sitting in the tenor chair, and Horace says, "Billie, I want this kid. That kid back there is going to be my new tenor player."
>
> I said, "But, I just—"
>
> "You scared?" he said. "You want to play? You want to be good? Play in my band. You'll be good. You'll know what music is."
>
> I said, "Yeah, yeah, I want to play."
>
> He said, "Well, get up here. I'm going to start you off on this." And that's how he got me in.

Ernest recalls his first experience, listening to the band rehearse "The Giant Is Awakened," and thinking, "Man, those guys are really playing what we want to play."

Shams and Ernest would play a major role in the Arkestra through their instrumental abilities, compositional contributions, and leadership. Butch Morris looks back on them as being "so talented," and "not only did Ernest write a lot, he arranged other things. He arranged things for his brother. He arranged a couple of things for me. He was really multi-talented." Ojenke retains vivid memories of Ray Straughter setting sail on his tenor saxophone, claiming he "could make the vibrations come out of his horn so powerful that if the walls of Jericho had still been standing, they would have crumbled. He was just an extraordinary horn player, so much power coming out of that little guy."

Herbie Baker was a student at Dorsey High School, Eric Dolphy's alma mater, when he encountered the Arkestra, but his passion was playing the piano and composing. At Dorsey he was a leading member of Dr. Donald Simpson's renowned Jazz Workshop, but was also leading and performing in various small groups throughout the community and southern California, as well as hanging with Horace and the Ark. He was in the studio when *The Giant Is Awakened* was recorded. His prodigious talent was evident to everyone who heard him play. Bassist Tom Williamson sat in on occasion with Herbie's band. "He was great. In my mind he was better than, say, Billy Childs at that particular point in his life. I thought the kid was going to be another Herbie [Hancock] or somebody like that."[5] Tom's impression is echoed by pianist Nate Morgan. "This boy was a genius. I'm telling you . . . this cat was already playing like a grown man that had been playing thirty years. He was there, man, and writing compositions." According to Roberto Miranda, "From the day that I met him, he was already sounding like Herbie [Hancock] or McCoy [Tyner]. He had that particular harmonic approach really together, had great chops, had great ears. His parents were nice people; they loved him. He had a firm foundation at home. He was funny; he was erudite; he was young; he was an amazing young man." Trumpeter Steve Smith, also a member of the Dorsey Jazz Workshop and later of the Arkestra, remembers Herbie as "*Incredible.* You would come to school for first period, Jazz Workshop, and Herbert Baker would be in there early. And this cat would be playing just like Herbie Hancock, sixteen years old, and you just can't believe it. He's playing away, and when he's playing a solo with his right hand, he's just singing it at the same time. Man, incredible. It was just so inspiring."

In a tragedy still felt by members of the Arkestra, Herbie Baker was killed at the age of seventeen in a car crash early on the morning of June 15, 1970. A musical collaborator and friend, Baba Alade was one of the last to be with him. "I saw him that Sunday evening, then Monday morning I woke up crying. I knew something was going on. Then I heard my mother say, 'Oh no! Honey, come here! Mr. Baker is on the phone.'" Herbie's closest friend, saxophonist Azar Lawrence, remembers that day: "He had come from one rehearsal and was going to another rehearsal, rushing." And as many others have, pays tribute to his friend: "Herbie Baker wasn't just like an old soul in a young body. He was actually the entity itself. He was like McCoy and Herbie with the experience. He played with the experience they had and everything at fourteen, fifteen, sixteen. He didn't sound like somebody trying to copy someone. He was actually *the* guy. Freddie Hubbard used him on a few things."

Saxophonist Steven Meeks, a bandmate of Herbie and Azar at Dorsey, who would subsequently play baritone sax in the Ark, recalls the following day: "I went to Jazz Workshop that morning and thought certainly that someone would have called Dr. Simpson. I got there and asked him if he heard what happened. I could tell he hadn't. I told him Herbie had died, was killed in an accident. I can't remember what happened after that, but it really devastated all of us. After that we were kind of in a stupor." Some of Herbie's compositions are in the Arkestra book, including "Prance Dance," "Little A's Chant," and *Flight 17,* a suite in three parts, which became the title piece of the first LP by the Arkestra, recorded in 1978 and dedicated to his memory.

Azar Lawrence, who would later achieve renown in bands led by Elvin Jones and McCoy Tyner, grew up in an affluent, musical family in Baldwin Hills on the western fringe of the African American community. He started early on violin and by the age of six was already performing in the USC junior orchestra. Switching to alto saxophone at eight, he quickly mastered the instrument and, when he went to Dorsey, was placed in the Jazz Workshop. By his senior year, music was his primary focus. "In the mornings I would drop my father off downtown at work, and then come by and pick up Herbie and we'd go to homeroom. Then the first period was Jazz Workshop. After that, most of the time, we'd hit the fence, ditch, and go to my house, where we had a baby grand, and play music." While at Dorsey, Azar attended an UGMAA concert at the urging of another close friend, composer/saxophonist Benny Golson's son, Reggie. "And that's how I ended up meeting Ray and Ernest Straughter and we became friends. I ended up being in the Arkestra, playing alto and standing next to the great Arthur Blythe and Will Connell. I played baritone for a period of time, too, in the Ark."

One who would not subsequently achieve musical renown, but would be an anchor in the Ark, was Cerion Middleton III, a talented young tenor saxophonist and composer from the Watts area. According to Will Connell, "He was sort of like Albert Ayler as George Coleman, that's about as close as I could come. He would start out playing very leisurely, and he would stand with one leg bent and one leg straight, like he was standing on the corner just talking to you idly. And all of a sudden he'd be playing real fast, and you never could catch it." One of his compositions, "Evenings Last Sun Rays," became an Ark staple and was arranged by Horace for the Watts Symphony. "It was like a little tone poem. He actually made the sun set the same way Schoenberg made it rise at the end of *Transfigured Night.* He just had so much facility, and where did it come from? He was out."

Nate Morgan also discovered UGMAA while still in high school. Originally from Louisiana and then settling in Watts, the Morgans were working class and also part of an extended family of preachers. From an early age Nate was devoted to the piano, and by junior high school was performing in local bands and studying with Joe Sample and Hampton Hawes. When he was sixteen, he heard "The Giant Is Awakened" broadcast over KUSC radio. "The first time I heard it, I was like, 'Damn, who is that saxophone player?' It was a different kind of a tune. It had a different kind of beat, rhythm, and everything. The composition captured you, but it was like the piercingness of that alto saxophone, that was like straight to the heart. It was a spiritual experience." Nate also heard Kufahamu announce that the band would be performing at Foshay Junior High School.

> I can remember me and my partner, Smitty, saying, "Man, we got to go." We were so excited that when we got off the bus at Exposition and Western, instead of walking around to the front of the school, we just hopped the fence and ran across the yard. We were sixteen years old. We could do that. When we got in, we heard this mad, wild alto saxophone solo and it was like, "Man, that's got to be Arthur Blythe." We go in there and this guy's killin' it, just tearing it up. And that was Will Connell. Then Arthur stepped out and played.

Nate became a regular at the concerts, determined to play in the Ark. "I could only take about two or three more concerts before I had to run up on stage. When I first introduced myself to Horace, he tells everybody that I said, 'Yeah, I'm Nate Morgan. I'm going to play with you all.' Not that I want to, but that I'm going to."

By the early 1970s, the Voice of UGMAA was reconstituted to accommodate as many as fifteen vocalists. Linda Hill was the choir director, seconded by Amina. There were also Chanima, Cynthia Hunt, Glenda, Isis, Pat K, Katu, Landern, Somayah, Vernetta, Subira and her twelve-year-old daughter, Linita, who would be the first to sing Linda Hill's "Little Africa," an Arkestra anthem. Will Connell and Abdul-Salaam Muhammad doubled as vocalists and were joined by Ali Jihad (Charles Galloway).

A few years out of Jefferson High School, Ali became friends with Abdul-Salaam, learned of Horace Tapscott, and heard *The Giant Is Awakened.* At his friend's urging, they went to the Mafundi Institute in late 1970 to hear the Quintet perform. "I was never the same again. I mean it was like 'Wow!' I had been out to jazz clubs and went to see Ahmad Jamal. He was bad and everything, but these cats were just a little different. This music was different and it was conscious." Ali had grown up in a working-class family near the Black Panther headquarters on Central Avenue and art that was "conscious" was prized. "A lot of my neighbors, cats I grew up with, politically they were Black Panthers, man. . . . I knew Geronimo Pratt. The Pratt brothers used to stay on Twenty-third and Compton." Ali followed the Arkestra to the University of California at Santa Barbara to watch them perform on a double bill with the Harold Land-Bobby Hutcherson Quintet and was sold. Not long after, the Voice was in reformation and he saw an opportunity to become involved.

Politics, Spirituality, and Music in the UGMAA Family

The newer generation was shaped by the Watts uprising, the Vietnam War, radical politics, black nationalism, and the cultural lifestylism of the late 1960s. The social consciousness they proclaimed contrasted, in some ways, with the bohemianism of the early days of UGMA. A core group of the new arrivals practiced a lifestyle that emphasized attention to diet, avoidance of hard drugs and alcohol, and a keen interest in the history and spirituality of African and African American traditions. However, this was more a matter of degree than of fundamental differences. Despite the attention given to the "generation gap" in mainstream America, there were strong bonds connecting the diverse membership of UGMAA, politically, culturally, and musically.

Having grown up during the uprisings of the mid-1960s, the newer members were politically conscious and cognizant of the government attacks on black political and cultural organizations. Nate Morgan recalls, "I was very well aware of what was going on in Chicago. I was very well aware of what was happening with Malcolm X. I was very well aware of what was going with Martin Luther King . . . that air was always in the house." Ernest Straughter became involved with the Black Panthers.

> I was focused on the music but I was hostile too. . . . That's when I joined the Black Panther Party, but not officially. I joined them, but when they started saying you got to do this, you got to go take bombs here. I said man, I don't do that. All that's okay, but I'm not going to be taking no handmade grenade anywhere. . . . I said, man, that's just getting a little bit out of hand. . . . So I quit. . . . Horace saved us. If it weren't for the Ark and having to be at rehearsal, getting pumped by William Marshall and all that stuff that was going on, I don't know what I would have turned into. I probably would have quit music and turned into a thing, man, someone that would cause somebody some harm.

Nevertheless, there still was a perception that they could be next on the FBI hit list, and members prepared for that eventuality in different ways. Ernest was packing a .22 for a while:

I was so politically engrossed with this thing that was going on, but I was a musician. I said, I'm fighting from the stage. Anything happens, I'm not part of an organization, but I'm going to fight from the stage. So I used to carry a .22 on the stage. And one day I was practicing and boom! . . . Horace went back to what he was doing. Nobody said nothing. . . . I was playing and it fell off my hip, man. I was thinking like they might come up here—Who's they? Who in the hells they? I thought they were going to eventually come while we were practicing and they're gonna take over, like the Germans, the Nazis or something, invade us and take our instruments and take us off somewhere. And Shams was making guns. He made a gadget gun, what we called a zip gun.

To Ali Jihad, the Straughters' preparations were part of the fabric of the times:

They were going through that thing of watching the Black Panther Party being disintegrated by J. Edgar Hoover. We were all watching that, because I was still getting the BPP newspaper, a weekly paper. You'd read that and you'd get mad. Politically, we saw ourselves probably being dealt with [by the FBI]. Then it came out that Horace was on the blacklist. And that made all of us more revolutionary, because we knew this was a great man here. I always thought he was, always impressed by his piano playing. But by the fact that they had labelled him, then we all felt that we were labelled. So we always knew we were a different breed, a whole 'nother flavor. That's where we were as a band, as a musical entity.

The Straughters were "prepared for the coming revolution," according to Ali and others, and their actions were a defensive reaction to brutal and repressive government policies. "We were still listening to Gil Scott Heron 'The Revolution Won't Be Televised,' The Last Poets, all these things. It was really a politically charged atmosphere in the '70s. We were just trying to be ready for whatever would come." The continual harassment by the LAPD in the community reinforced their perceptions. "The police was a real thing to make you fearful, to make you want to retaliate."

They were also immersed in the emerging black studies scene. These young people had attended Los Angeles schools in the 1950s and 1960s that featured curricula with little, if any, information on African and African American history. Unlike elders such as Horace, who had attended segregated schools in the south and been exposed to some of that history, they were without much knowledge of their ethnic past. Attending Tennessee

State University, Abdul-Salaam learned of African history for the first time. During summers back in Los Angeles, he encountered UGMAA and what he saw and heard resonated with his evolving knowledge of black history. "They were incorporating all of this in the music. The music was heavy. It was Afrocentric, as we say now. So they had a spiritual base, one that I didn't know, but I knew what they were doing and how they related to this in their compositions." Beyond the music, he was impressed by their awareness of the history. "A lot of these artists were well-read. They knew about Africa. They knew about Egypt, the pyramids. They knew about Kush and some of the very first dynamic civilizations. They knew about Mali, art."

An important source of learning for many was the Aquarian Bookstore and Spiritual Center, founded in 1941 by Dr. Alfred Ligon. By the 1960s the center was based in a storefront on Santa Barbara Avenue (now Martin Luther King Boulevard) and was the oldest, continuously operated black bookstore in Los Angeles, the only one that specialized in material dealing with Africa and African Americans. They also offered space to local organizations. One study group, the Circle of Seven under the tutelage of Ron Karenga, evolved in the fall of 1965 into the cultural nationalist US Organization.[6]

Ligon and his wife, Bernice, offered more than books. As students of metaphysics and ancient cultures, they possessed a keen interest in maintaining ancient teachings and passing them on to the next generation, offering classes in philosophy, metaphysics, religion, and black history, among other topics.[7] Dadisi Sanyika recalls, "When I got there, he was dealing with the ancient mysteries, the African mysteries, the first African universities, the ancient studies around the pyramids, the ancient sciences, meditation, altered states of consciousness, liberation of the soul—these concepts."[8] Along with Dadisi, the students included new UGMAA members Kamau Daáood, Azar Lawrence, Abdul-Salaam Muhammad, Ray and Ernest Straughter, and Michael Dett Wilcots.

While everyone was animated by a respect for their ethnic background and drawing from aspects of that past to incorporate values into their lives within the community, the greater awareness of African and African American history and culture led some to embrace African values, lifestyles, and identities, with changes in names and attire. For Horace, it was part of a person's and a people's identity, of their memory, and one could only be stronger embracing it. When working with Elaine Brown on her second album, Horace did not approve of one composition, "Can't Go Back," which represented the Black Panther critique of Afrocentric movements that turned to absorption in African culture in place of political struggle to transform the social system in the United States.

> We can't go back
> Live in the past
> Though the beauty will last
> And survive[9]

Though more often than not Horace and the Ark worked with the Panthers, Horace disagreed with this critique and asserted his view by arranging a heavy, polyrhythmic drum foundation for the piece and a conclusion with French horns sounding like elephants. Elaine remembers,

> We had a disagreement about that song. He wasn't Afrocentric in that hippy-dippy way, but was dealing with things that were African. My attitude was that we've got to deal with what's happening now . . . that we can't go back, that we have to fight now. We have to deal with the conditions that we're under now, and that going back to Africa is not going to resolve this, because it's a big global problem. This was the underlying theory of the song. So what Horace did, when I'm singing "You can't go back," he puts all these orchestrations in that are African. There are all these rhythms in there that are so purely him. You don't think I wrote that. But I just love it. So he says, "Okay. We can't go back? Fine. I'm going to put everything African in the song."

However, Horace was not interested in recreating African society nor Africans but in using that knowledge to enhance and advance the community in the present. Identity as African-derived offered access to a history and its cultural riches that could be tapped and adapted to gain understanding and to forge solutions to contemporary problems. Yet, Horace opposed the fashion of abandoning birth or slave names and adopting Arabic ones, for example.

> I questioned it, because the names they changed to were slave names in Africa from the Arabs. They took on Arabic names and their religion, Islam. It seemed they were just giving up one slave name for another, Robert for Hassan or William for Muhammad. You don't know what your ancestral name is. So if you don't know what your name is, and the only way you're hooked up with your parents is through this American name, it doesn't make sense to give it up, because then you'd be cut off from your whole family.[10]

In the mid-1970s, when saxophonist Fuasi Abdul-Khaliq changed his name, Horace refused to acknowledge it. "He was a funny cat," Fuasi recalls. "He didn't like the name changing. And he didn't wear really outrageous Pan-African clothing. He'd wear his dashiki and sometimes his hat. So he would introduce me as Ernest 'Fuasi' Roberts on saxophone. So finally I had to really tell him that my name was Fuasi, please. He finally did."

When the newer members were added to the Ark mix, a very diverse organization, reflective of the larger community, emerged. "We had some muslims in the group, some in the Nation of Islam and some were orthodox muslims," Abdul-Salaam Muhammad remembers. "Of course, you had that in the listeners. They came from every walk of life. You had Christians in the group and some that believed in the African religions." In 1972, Ray and Ernest Straughter and Abdul-Salaam joined the Nation of Islam. "So when we would play with the Arkestra, we would be out there in our suit and bowtie. And we were promoting this clean living." Poet Kamau Daáood was struck by the disparities: "You'd all meet at the UGMAA houses, but then you'd leave in your little sub-groupings. We were always the young turks. A lot of the older people had substance abuse problems. So you'd see somebody sitting up there nodding, while somebody else would be sitting over there meditating. Somebody'd be eating pork ribs and somebody over here is a strict vegetarian on the forty day fast. We had all these strange dichotomies happening." This was the scene drummer Fritz Wise encountered when he first came around at seventeen, still a student at Locke High School. "The Ark was a weird mixture of characters. You had one group that was almost winos. These were grown men doin' grown men stuff, drinking. You had another group that were these health-conscious vegetarian, religious muslims, and then you had all the mixtures and variations thereof in there."

Out of respect for each other, the music, and their common goals, they coexisted and lifestyle choices weren't forced on other members. The touch was more subtle. Abdul-Salaam notes, "The only thing that I and some of the others could do was to be examples. So that's what we tried to do." Kamau likens UGMAA to a family: "When you have a family, you have people that branch off into all different kinds of things. But when you really understand the mass family, there was more of an operational unity, for lack of a better term, that had its place in UGMAA's organization."

Underlying that unity were strong, intangible bonds that allowed the Arkestra family to smoothly absorb this array of young talent. Abdul-Salaam explains,

This was a very spiritual Arkestra, the men, the methods and the way this group of people came together. Most of these people, regardless if they had problems or whatever, had something in common, and that thing that they had in common was really a strong bond. It was greater than just the music. . . . Bands come together and try to get on the one, try to get perfection, but it was more than that. It was the rawness of it that made it really special. We never sat down; everybody stood up. Play two, three hours, and everybody would be standing up. Most bands you see, fifteen, sixteen people, and everybody is sitting down reading charts. So the music became more than just the instrumentation and the songs. It was something that was bringing us together. We were African people and we had our own sound.

To the new recruits part of that bond and sound was the Arkestra's expression of the values and politics of their time. "I can't remember playing at rallies and protests," Steve Meeks emphasizes, "but that was what the music was about. It was about all of that because of the lyrics in the songs, and it was just inherent in the music itself. It was about freedom, and our freedom and our struggle for freedom, and that's how the music was." To Ojenke, "UGMAA was at the vanguard, at the cutting edge of the African American sensibility. They were the ones who were there, seeing and expressing the trends that were affecting the black collective in this country. They were giving voice to certain imperatives that needed to be experienced at that time, and they were the only ones that were really doing that here."

Brown's second album, *Elaine Brown*, recorded and released in 1973 by Motown's Black Forum label, also featured Horace arranging and conducting the Ark. Unfortunately, and much to Horace and Elaine's chagrin, Motown over-produced, weakening the impact of the arrangements. "And the voices I hated," Elaine asserts. "I just absolutely hated that addition and I had nothing and Horace had absolutely nothing to do with that." The album was more subdued and introspective, musically and politically, than her first. Yet, it still reaffirms the importance of freedom struggles in "All the Young and Fine Men," "Until We're Free," "A Little Baby," and "We Shall Meet Again." "Jonathan" celebrates the life of young Panther Jonathan Jackson, killed while trying to free his brother, George, from a California courthouse, and "I Know Who You Are" honors an important influence:

I know who you are
I know of your pain

You've seen all your people
In shackles and chains
But you know what to do
You will make them be free
Just as you've made me[11]

Contrary to the popular perception at the time, "I Know Who You Are" was written for and about Horace and not Panther leader Huey Newton, who had ordered Brown to produce a second record. According to Elaine, "Huey always thought that this was his song. . . . But no. That song was for Horace. . . . 'You're the free man' and then I say that is the man who would make us free. He wants us to be free, free like he was, and that's really who Horace was."[12]

Newer Arkestra members were also attracted to the range of expression in the Ark's music, from free avant-gardism to African American and even West African traditions. Trumpeter Kylo Kylo was a young artist who brought a different conception of sound into the band. Roberto Miranda describes Kylo's impact on his work: "He was one of the guys who really helped me to appreciate the use of sound as a compositional tool. He would bring a box of bottles to the gig and he'd break them as part of the musical offering. If you looked at him as he was doing it, you wouldn't really understand what he was doing. But if you just closed your eyes, and just listened to what he was trying to do, it was pretty revealing." According to Fritz Wise, "When I heard Horace's music it intrigued me. It was different. Even though it had a dissonant flavor to it, I could also hear something that was very folkloric in nature, something that I couldn't really put a finger on, but I knew that his shit was important to have as part of my foundation in music."

The band book reflected this range as well, expanding to include new pieces by many members that spanned the spiritual, bebop, hard bop, avant-garde, and free stylings, including Arthur Blythe's "The Grip" and (with Stanley Crouch) "Future Sally's Time"; Everett Brown's "World Peace (With or Without People)"; Will Connell's "Inkata"; Linda Hill's "Children," "Dem Folks" and "Little Africa" (written for her grandson, Lateef); Al Hines's "People Like Us"; Roberto Miranda's "St. Michael, Servant of the Lord"; Nate Morgan's "Black Woman"; Chico Roberson's "Freedom"; Lester Robertson's "The Call" and "In Times Like These"; Guido Sinclair's "Black, Brown and Yellow"; Ernest Straughter's "Inspirations of Silence," "Masters at Work," and "I Felt Spring"; and Ray Straughter's "Elysian Park." As part of their mission to preserve African American music, they offered arrangements of spirituals and selections from older composers, such as R. Nathaniel Dett's *In the Bottoms*

Suite. More recent artists were represented with arrangements of "Lush Life" (Billy Strayhorn), "In a Sentimental Mood" (Duke Ellington), "Oleo" (Sonny Rollins), and "All Blues" (Miles Davis).

The members also saw themselves as part of the new black music movement of the 1960s and offered arrangements of works from musicians around the country. According to Michael Dett, "A lot of cats in the band and a lot of followers and other artists came out of the period of Eric Dolphy, John Coltrane, Archie Shepp. We were into that type of music, like 'Ascension'. . . . The music was way up there as far as its intensity." The band book included arrangements of Bobby Bradford's "Eye of the Storm"; Coltrane's "Cousin Mary," "Equinox," "Giant Steps," "Impressions" and "Straight Street"; Stanley Cowell's "Departure" and "Effi"; Pharoah Sanders and Leon Thomas's "The Creator Has a Master Plan"; Charles Tolliver's "On the Nile"; and many McCoy Tyner compositions, including "African Village," "Effendi," "High Priest," "Man from Tanganyika," "Mode for John," "Oriental Flower," and "Search for Peace." To many members, even the label "jazz" had become passé. "We didn't call it jazz, just black music," Steve Meeks explains. "To me it was new black music because it was similar to what Trane was doing in certain instances." To Horace they were Afro- and then African American classics.

John Coltrane, especially, offered an example of musical sophistication and independence, political consciousness and spirituality that resonated with most members. According to Abdul-Salaam, "Horace was one of those young men who stayed in the community and who wanted to create something of our own. This is one of the reasons why Coltrane was so much a part of the heart of the Arkestra, because Coltrane grew independent and he was vocal about what he wanted to do. He was a leader in the music. He was a leader in terms of spirituality." As with so many others, poet Kamau Daáood drew from the well of John Coltrane. "I was so deeply into Trane. I loved him so much and the music at that time." He celebrates Trane in his "Liberator of the Spirit."

> expanding beyond the boundaries
> blow away decay
> stale forms collide with freshness
> patterns of life
> woven sound into tapestry of meaning
> ears chewing mind food
>
> John Coltrane was a freedom fighter
> Liberator of the spirit from the shackles of form . . .

John Coltrane was a freedom fighter
Liberator of the spirit from the shackles of form . . . [13]

For vocalist Ali Jihad, his first Trane experience was life-altering:

> The first record I ever heard by him was *Kulu Se Mama* and I started
> crying. It made me cry; the first time I ever cried listening to some
> music, because it was so beautiful and I was just so overcome. When
> the record stopped playing the guy's brother looked at me and said,
> "What's wrong with you, man?" I had been touched. I think my spiri-
> tuality must have been born then, because I was always different after
> that. I knew I was growing in music, but now I felt I was also growing
> in spirituality.

Sylvia Jarrico recalls Horace and some of the musicians dropping by to
rehearse for an upcoming performance with William Marshall. "As they sat
down, I moved over to the radio, which was on the jazz station, and turned
off the radio. Horace walked out of the group, came past where I was still
standing by the radio panel, and as he passed me, he leaned over very tact-
fully, so that you could hardly see he was leaning toward me, and he said, 'We
don't turn off Coltrane.'"

The Next UGMAA Houses and the Ark in Performance

After the loss of the second house, the band was without a central location
for a few months, but the music continued with regular rehearsals in Horace's garage, as well as other residences and spaces. During the fall of 1969
Linda Hill and Will Connell moved into dwellings opposite each other on
Fifty-second Place, just a few blocks from South Park, which soon became
the center of UGMAA activity. Will's small, wooden frame house at 227 East
Fifty-Second Place was set back from the street behind a larger one. In his
front room he had a piano, bench, and a card table with two chairs, at which
he'd perform his duties as band copyist. During the week different sections
of the Ark would rehearse, with the full band coming together on Saturday
mornings. "We'd have the full Ark in there, so we'd have to tape music to
people's backs to read it."

When the Straughter brothers joined the band, their home was also used
for rehearsals. Later, when the scene was ending on Fifty-second Place during 1972, they found a house in Compton and established a collective with
Ernest Cojoe, Azar Lawrence, and others. Known as "The Sun," it became an

UGMAA performance space. "They would have free-style jam sessions down there," recalls Dadisi Sanyika. "They were really tripping off of Trane and Sun Ra, and this whole thing about cosmic consciousness. That went on for about a year or so. . . . It was the most creative and liberating time. The things we did then are still ahead of the times." The Sun also attracted artists from Watts, a short distance to the north, such as Eric Priestley, who remembers, "Me and Ojenke and a lot of the other writers used to go down there. They began to play new and innovative music."

During this heady time of social and cultural activism, the Arkestra was ubiquitous in the community. Both remembrances and the quantity of performance tapes in the Horace Tapscott Archive attest to a schedule that involved sometimes a half-dozen Arkestra performances a month and many smaller group appearances in community settings. The Arkestra, UGMAA chorus, and narrator/vocalist William Marshall performed "Spiritual Classics" at venues such as the Second Baptist Church. The program included Horace's *Suite Spirituals* ("Babylon is Falling," "Get on Board," "Steal Away," "Calvary," and "Sinner Please Don't Let This Harvest Pass"), his arrangement of "Motherless Child," and Duke Ellington's "Come Sunday." South Park continued to be a major venue for the band, whether performing at festivals held there or leading its own concerts.

Amongst the lot, there was hardly a paying gig. With an ensemble that ranged from fifteen to thirty, and then with voices, paid performances were few and far between. Yet, it never mattered to the Arkestra. They continued shaping music in their way and offering it, undiluted, to the community. If it took time for people to come around to it, then so be it. According to Ojenke, "There was no other group of artists in the black community that was doing anything like that. They performed all over the community and there was no other group that was even recognizable from that period, no group that was that consistent, that was constantly performing . . . and the community would come to hear these guys play this far-out jazz."

The band continued performing at many of the elementary, middle, and high schools in South Central. At Locke High School they celebrated "The Year of UGMAA" with the Locke Jazz Chorus. They were the closing act of a jazz festival at Jordan High School, one organized by student Jesse Sharps, later to become the Ark bandleader in the mid-1970s. Two educational institutions in particular became Arkestra venues during this time. From 1969 to mid-1970 the Arkestra performed regular Sunday concerts at Foshay Junior High School and then continued the concerts at nearby Widney High School for the Handicapped through December 1972. Frequently, the Arkestra would split the program with Bobby Bradford and John Carter's group, the Quintet or big band taking the second set. Tom Williamson, who played bass in both groups, remembers, "Sometimes there would be only ten people there, and then sometimes there were one hundred, two hundred people. Each Sunday was like a different thing. You didn't know what was going to happen. To me it didn't matter, because we went out there and played regardless. Doing the music itself was enjoyment enough for me. . . ."[14]

Memorable concerts at Widney included those with simultaneous multi-instrumentalist Rahsaan Roland Kirk, a collaborator whenever he was in town. "Before I leave here, every black kid in the neighborhood is going to be playing two horns at once," Kirk told Horace. "I'm gonna see to that. That's my role, Horace."[15] Another featured the Pan Afrikan Peoples Arkestra playing the first set, then yielding the stage to Sun Ra's Arkestra for the second. Will Connell was in the band that night: "Backstage there wasn't much room, but we were being very respectful, almost servile. 'Oh, I'm sorry, is my horn case in your way?' And they were just snarling at us. And when they played, they immediately started with three or four of them soloing at once as hard and as tough as they could. And we were like, 'Oh, we smoked 'em.' Between Arthur and Cerion and Ray Straughter, we smoked them." Also performing that night, Nate Morgan vividly remembers Sun Ra's L.A. tantrum:

> That was a nice concert until they turned the electricity off and Sun Ra got pissed off! Man, they had some janitor and he was ready to go home. He shut it down, man. I mean, Sun Ra had the dancers in the audience, and the lights, and the cellophane outfits, and the horn players; everybody was all over the auditorium. All of a sudden the sound went off and the house lights came on. They were into it and everybody had to come out of their trance. Sun Ra walked to the edge of the stage and he got to blessin' out the audience and blessin' out the school and blessin' out everybody in there. He told people about how he didn't need them, we needed him. He went off. He spoke for about ten minutes. But that was a great concert. That was one of the best concerts the Ark ever played. The Ark, man, we were up for that night.[16]

Although the music was at the core, an Ark performance was always a forum for all artists to create in the same space. Poets or "word musicians," as many preferred to be called, were encouraged, as were dancers, martial artists, and actors. Michael Dett Wilcots organized slide shows of current artwork and world events that would be projected behind the band and on the surrounding walls. Occasionally, the musicians painted their faces. According to Michael Dett, "Horace brought in more creative artists like word musicians, poets, dancers, speakers, the whistler—we had a guy that performed and all he did was whistle—oh, he was really great. Anyone who had some type of artistic skill that wanted to express themselves, Horace opened the doors for them." They even incorporated the movements of martial artist Dadisi Sanyika. "What I would do at Widney was interpretive forms, where I would use my body as an instrument. When they would improvise with their instruments, I would improvise through creative free-style martial arts form."[17]

By the late 1960s, early 1970s it was a rare performance that would pass without an offering from a word musician. Performances usually featured Kamau Daáood, Ojenke, Quincy Troupe, or the Watts Prophets, among others. Quincy recalls that his "Ode to John Coltrane," written upon Trane's death in 1967, was particularly popular with the Ark and local audiences. "Horace liked that poem. A lot of musicians liked that poem, obviously, because everybody loved Coltrane."

> But during bebop-filled avant-garde summers
> you weaved slashing thunderclaps of sound
> weaved spells of hypnotic beauty
> blew searching extensions of sublimation.
>
> Trane Trane runaway train smashing all known dimensions
> *Trane Trane runaway train smashing all known dimensions*[18]

Ojenke, one of the most influential poetic voices in the community, merged seamlessly into the larger ensemble. "So when I would blow with the Ark, I would see my stuff as part of the music also, as a musician, and not just words." Perhaps more than most, he drew not only inspiration for his poetry from Trane. "My poetry, a lot of it, was like militant and fiery. My thing was, I used to try to write like sheets of sounds, waves of images. They used to call me the John Coltrane of African American poetry. John Coltrane was actually one of my mentors in terms of articulation. That was what I was trying to simulate through words. I wanted to have that power of John Coltrane's music." In "Legacy of the Word," he writes,

> How many dead angels must fall through our blackness
> shattered bones beneath floursheim [*sic*] shoes
> How long the word has been with us
> a pearl, our flesh an oyster shell

pried open, our blood flowing through the foundations
of Wall street, stone phallus violating skys
and stars and our gods bent over open assholes.[19]

The Watts Prophets maintained a close relationship with UGMAA, and they frequently performed on each other's gigs. It was also not unusual for Horace to call them on stage, if they happened by a performance. Richard Dedeaux remembers, "Horace was such a warm guy. He'd be up there playing and see us in the audience and nod, 'come on up,' and we'd do some impromptu stuff. But in those concerts there were times when he played with us, and there were times when we played with him, and there were times when we were all in the same venue."

One of the most important word musicians in UGMAA's history, as well as that of South Central Los Angeles, has been Kamau Daáood. Growing up in a working-class family near the Leimert Park district, Kamau started writing poetry in junior high school. While attending Washington Preparatory High School, he became involved with the local drug culture but also absorbed the politics of the time. Shy and introverted, he was not inclined to activist stances, but he learned some hard political and racial realities first-hand. One night, the LAPD broke up a dance he was attending. He was beaten with a flashlight and taken to the local precinct house. "I was talking to one of the policemen and asked, 'Do you all really hate me?' 'Oh yeah, we hate you,' they said." When they arrived at the precinct house, he noticed a large pool of blood on the floor. "And the cat said, 'Oh, we're having a good time over here tonight.' That experience was eye-opening to me."

When he graduated from high school in 1968, Kamau became part of the Westside branch of the Watts Writers Workshop. "I was very angry. The sixties and seventies were very, very angry times. I was a young guy with hair all over my head, thin as can be, and just fire coming out of my mouth, just fire. They were searching times; it was crystal breaking time; stuff was being stirred up, challenged, examined. That's what a lot of my work reflected." That anger stemmed from an important realization: "When you're a young man and you really begin to understand the journey that your lineage was connected to, the story from Africa to the present day, when you really start to understand that, there is a lot of anger that rises from it, a lot of blame and a lot of focus on stuff that manifests itself as anger. It was a very, very vicious past and as young people that's what we were clued into."

Like many others, Kamau first heard of UGMAA while listening to "Greg's Refresher Course" over KUSC. As luck would have it, he then inadvertently met Kufahamu. "One day I was on Vernon Avenue hitchhiking, and there was this guy in a white Jag. I get in the car and it was Kufahamu. He gave me a flyer and I went to the concert at Foshay. That's the first time I heard the Arkestra live and Bobby Bradford. Then I became an UGMAA groupie. Wherever I heard they were playing, that's where I'd go." Not long afterward, in typical UGMAA fashion, Kamau was conscripted into the Ark during a concert at South Park.

> The band was on stage playing, and I was out in the audience. I had some of my poetry with me, and I think I was sharing it with somebody or showing somebody. Ted Jones saw me with this poetry and went over and said something to Horace. The next thing I knew, I was up on the bandstand; the Arkestra was playing John Coltrane's "Equinox" and I was reading my poetry with this Arkestra behind me. That was my introduction to the Arkestra. I was very nervous, of course, but I got through it. At that point I was drafted into the Arkestra and became a regular member.

Community Spaces and the Avant-garde

Despite the ascendancy of rock 'n' roll in the 1960s, by the early 1970s there were still a number of important jazz clubs in Los Angeles and less prominent, but nevertheless significant, local places in South Central. The Parisian Room, Shelly's Manne-Hole in Hollywood, and the Lighthouse in Hermosa Beach continued to be draws for nationally prominent jazz artists. Within the African American community there were clubs and bars, like the Tropicana Lounge, La Deuce, Marty's on the Hill, the York Club, the Sands, and Rose and Larry Gales's LB West. Somewhat unknown outside the community, these spots nevertheless featured dozens of local emerging artists, as well as some nationally renowned, including Cannonball Adderley, Gene Ammons, Hampton Hawes, Freddie Hubbard, Ahmad Jamal, the Jazz Crusaders, Yusef Lateef, Wes Montgomery, and Phineas Newborn. UGMAA members could be found at these locations, some performing, some listening, and those too young to gain admission to the bars standing on the sidewalk and leaning in to hear the sounds.

However, it was in the nonprofit, community spaces that emerged in the wake of the Sixties uprisings where UGMAA's energy was concentrated and where it flourished in an atmosphere of support for alternative cultural and musical values. Members and supporters became heavily involved in two community centers (The Gathering and the Malcolm X Center), a KCET neighborhood television show (*Doing It at the Storefront*), and a local performance space (Rudolph's Fine Art Center), all of which became extensions of UGMAA. As Kamau puts it, "If I'm over at The Gathering, then the Ark has a satellite over here."

At the instigation of its Black Student Union, California State University at Los Angeles opened a Community Relations Center in the late 1960s on Western Avenue near Forty-fifth Street, on the first floor of an old building that also housed a Masonic Temple. When the grant money ran out in June 1970, some of the students kept the Center going with their own money and labor and were joined by local artists to meet the rent and forge a collective leadership. Kamau was one of those artists: "It was a cooperative. We were dealing with male/female energy, which a lot of people would be dealing with later. It was a leaderless structure that was cyclic rather than a hierarchy. A lot of this came from our studies with Dr. Ligon at the Aquarian Bookstore." Dadisi Sanyika, one of those Cal State students, arranged performances every weekend. "So Horace and them would play. Kamau and all them would do poetry. I might do a martial arts kata. We'd show underground films. We might have a discussion. We had underground theater—the Bodacious Buguerrillas. They'd come down there and set up and create this whole environment in there."

The collective leadership took over the facility in the fall of 1970, calling it "The Gathering," and created an alternative, African-oriented school and after-school programs in music, martial arts, health and hygiene, and women's studies. The name referenced their purpose, according to Dadisi:

> The idea was that African people or black people don't know who they are and they can't travel to the Pan-African world. So we were going to gather the fragments together, so that when they came into the center, they could experience themselves in different phases of the culture, gospel stuff, rhythm and blues, jazz, the poetry, African stuff, Caribbean things. It was a whole idea of a gathering of the culture, gathering the culture together.

For many younger members, The Gathering became a second home, where they performed, socialized, taught, and brought in speakers to lecture on various topics. At the end of 1971, some members, including Ernest and Ray Straughter, Abdul-Salaam Muhammad and Dadisi Sanyika, went on fasts there. Abdul-Salaam remembers that "we would do all these cures, like we would do a grape cure. One week it would be nothing but grape juice, water and teas and stuff. We always used some kind of herbal tea. Then we went on an orange cure. I had Thanksgiving dinner and then on December the 1st, 1971, I started my fast, and I came off on January 10, 1972. I did forty days. Dadisi outdid everybody. I think he went like forty-eight days."

Though confronted with many obstacles, The Gathering lasted until 1973. Despite its cultural orientation, it was targeted by the LAPD. "We were constantly having problems with the police," recalls Kamau. "We weren't pushing any kind of military program. Basically, ours was pretty much culturally based." To government agencies, that made little difference. There were even attempts by the FBI plant at the Watts Writers Workshop, Darthard Perry, to convince them to purchase guns. Kamau was the recipient of one of those phone calls, turning Perry away with a comment about The Gathering being a cultural institution and privately wondering about his motivations.[20] What finally brought the demise of The Gathering was more prosaic. According to Dadisi, "We were operating from this whole philosophy of don't charge the people hardly anything. . . . You could come in for a dollar and see the Pan Afrikan Peoples Arkestra, two or three poets, a short film, and then for another dollar, dollar-fifty get a meal. We were coming out of the social consciousness of anti-materialism, anti-capitalism, serve the people, which was great, but there's got to be a balance."

One institution that came out of the poverty programs, became an important UGMAA space, and survived somewhat longer was the Malcolm X Center, located at 4311 South Broadway. It went through a number of directors in the late 1960s, early 1970s, one of whom was Quincy Troupe. "Kwaku Person-Lynn hired me as the director of the Malcolm X Center and I had five hundred kids in there, and Ojenke and all these people used to run workshops." Dadisi Sanyika took over the directorship from Noah Purifoy in 1972 and ran it until 1980, by which time the government jettisoned most community-based programs. "I started the annual Malcolm X picnics and we did seven of them. The idea was first of all to get kids out of the community, to experience different environments. And also, my thing was always the culture, so we used to put on concerts. Horace and the Pan Afrikan Peoples Arkestra was always one of the main acts that participated in those concerts."

When he left the Watts Writers Workshop in the early 1970s, Watts Prophet Richard Dedeaux started working at public television station KCET. He and his colleagues managed to get station support for a community-based program, produced by Sue Booker. According to Richard,

There was nothing dealing with black and brown news. So they gave us a news and public affairs show. We called it *Doing It at the Storefront.* We moved out of KCET and got a storefront building on Forty-seventh and Broadway, right down the street from the Malcolm X building. Our whole budget was so tight, like $250 a show. So what we did, we sat down and pooled all our money, and we got Horace to write us a theme song for *Doing It at the Storefront.* It's an incredible song. . . . Man, he sure made the show.

Michael Dett, who also worked on the program, remembers that UGMAA appeared frequently: "Horace was lecturing, having guests, doing live performance, and I was doing the graphics."

By the early 1970s, Ark saxophonist Rudolph Porter was in college and focusing on bassoon. Occasionally, he would sit in with a rehearsal band at Luper's Music Studio at Fiftieth Street and Crenshaw Boulevard, around the corner from Horace's home. He started teaching saxophone at the studio and soon gained the trust of the owner, who let him live there as the caretaker. After the Studio closed at seven, Rudolph opened the doors to rehearsals by the Ark and other groups.

When the school moved, Rudolph took over the lease on the building and turned it into a full-time performance space—Rudolph's Fine Art Center—that could accommodate eighty to one hundred people for Sunday afternoon jazz concerts. "John Carter and Bobby Bradford played there almost every Sunday. Harold Land played there about four or five times. Horace played there; Eddie Blackwell played there. Oliver Lake did a solo concert there. I had some hot names. And the Ark rehearsed there two or three times a week in the evening." Not an administrator, Rudolph received some timely assistance from the Burt Lancaster family: "Through Stanley Crouch and Bobby Bradford I met Susan Lancaster, who is Burt Lancaster's daughter. She helped me run it because she had a love for jazz. . . . We became good friends and she brought Burt a few times. Shook up the whole neighborhood."

Rudolph's lasted until the summer of 1976, when the property was sold. It was one of the few outlets in Los Angeles in the early 1970s for the growing jazz avant-garde and many of its younger artists. Roberto Miranda recalls, "Man, Rudolph's was the happening place. People would come from all over the city to check out the music at Rudolph's. It was one of the few places in town, where the cats who were 'guarding the avant' would come to play, man. I got that from Bobby Bradford—'guarding the avant'—I love it, man. I love it." Flutist James Newton, then attending college in Walnut and sharing a house in Pomona with Stanley Crouch and David Murray, was another performer, thanks to John Carter. "He'd say, 'Newton, why don't you come out and we'll do a whole concert of your music.' I think I was like twenty-two, and I just looked at him. I couldn't believe it. To me this guy was the greatest clarinet player in the last half of the century, just hands down to me."

Rudolph's also became a Los Angeles home to Black Music Infinity, a band of avant-gardists and UGMAA members formed by Stanley Crouch. In 1968, he had taken a teaching position at Pomona College in Claremont, California, a forty-minute drive east of Los Angeles, and his home became the band's base. Crouch remembers, "I think everybody in the band could play well except, in retrospect, me. The way I was trying to play was based on the things I heard in the very extreme school of music. You know like Sunny Murray and people like that."[21] Over the years, the band included Arthur Blythe, Bobby Bradford, saxophonist Charles Tyler, trumpeters/cornetists Walter Lowe and Butch Morris, bassists Wilber Morris, Earle Henderson, who had played and recorded with Albert Ayler, and Walter Savage, playing cello in this band. In the early seventies, they also recruited a number of students attending college in the area: flutist James Newton, saxophonist David Murray, bassist Mark Dresser and, occasionally, vocalist Diamanda Galas.

Black Music Infinity gathered together some of the finest artists in southern California, mentored a handful of important younger players, and relentlessly developed their music in performance and in marathon sessions at Crouch's house. According to Bobby Bradford, "some weekends we would just play the whole weekend. There was a woman artist [Monika Pecot] in the area who shared the house with Stanley and some others . . . who could cook this unbelievable food, man. She would put on these restaurant-sized big pots of something like gumbo. We'd play until we were just nuts and smoke weed until everybody's head was coming off, then eat, and then pass out, then wake up and play some more."[22]

In the formative stages of his career, James Newton was at a band rehearsal when Stanley walked across the street to listen and then invited James to Black Music Infinity's next session. "So I went, and that rehearsal really changed my life." Arthur Blythe and Bobby Bradford left indelible impressions.

> Arthur's sound was gigantic in the house. The sound was so huge and round and vibrant. In the lower register of the alto it sounded like a tenor, it was so big and warm. And the vibrato that he had during that time was very reminiscent of Coltrane, late Coltrane, like "Expression,"

that real kind of wide, romantic, passionate, bittersweet kind of vi-
brato. There was so much feeling in everything he played and his command of the horn was staggering. I just couldn't believe it. I had never
been around anything that intense in sound outside of church in rural
Arkansas.

And then Bobby Bradford. He was taking solos during that time that
were twenty and twenty-five minutes long, and it would be like a sculptor working, starting with marble and just chipping one thing away and
then the next, until the form is revealed and the form is flawless. And you
never knew what was going to happen next. And then boom! You hear
the chisel and then something falls off and you go, "Oh! That's where he's
going!" and it just kept evolving and evolving and evolving.[23]

While a senior in high school and visiting the Claremont Colleges early
in 1973, David Murray was taken by a family friend to hear Stanley's band
rehearse. It was his eighteenth birthday and the band made a big impression,
one of the reasons he subsequently enrolled at Pomona College. "The music
that they were playing was something that appealed to me. It was kind of far
out. It was different from what I had been playing before. I had been playing
a lot of R&B stuff, a little bit of jazz, but not so much the jazz. So it tempted
me. I wanted to participate in something like that."

The band performed occasional gigs around Los Angeles and the surrounding areas, including many of the local colleges and universities and,
of course, Rudolph's, but most of its activity was as a rehearsal band every
Saturday. It lasted until Stanley left for New York in 1975. In many ways it
was a musical extension of UGMAA, though it remained organizationally
distinct. Stanley had been close to Horace and the band in Watts and collaborated with Ark members in this band. "Stanley stayed in his own space,"
recalls Blythe, "but he communicated and related to the music that Horace
was doing and the efforts of the musicians involved."

Indeed, Horace saw it as an UGMAA-related group; he was inclined to
view all such organizations as part of a common, community totality. He
would subsequently claim some artists, such as David Murray, as part of
UGMAA, who never played with the Arkestra, but with Ark members. "David
never really played with the band," Butch Morris declares. "All the stuff I
read about David being in the Ark is bullshit. He was a kind of step-child."
And according to Murray, "I remember Butch bringing me out to one of the
rehearsals one time. I was going to meet Horace. Somehow nobody showed
up, but we were sitting out front in the car and it never happened." David did

form a close association with Arthur Blythe, whom he visited frequently, and particularly Butch Morris, beginning a long-lived musical relationship. Nevertheless, he eventually made Horace's acquaintance and claims lineage:

> Then we ran into each other a couple of times in New York, and we always talked about doing something, but we were never able to. I still felt connected and I think he claimed me anyway because I was around a lot of people that he was a guru or something to. And I wish I could be more legitimately claimed, but it just didn't work out that way. All his guys were working with me. So he claimed me anyway, and hey, I'll fall right in line too. I admired his stuff, so I guess I'm an honorary follower or whatever. I'm down with that.

The Rise and Fall of 1971–73

With the recordings of 1969, the growth of Black Student Unions in colleges and universities across the country, and the burgeoning interest in African American history and culture, UGMAA's range was expanding beyond Los Angeles. Interest in the Arkestra was strong on many college campuses, and by the summer of 1971, the band had performed in Bakersfield, Fresno, and traveled to the San Francisco Bay Area. During that summer, UGMAA also established a base in Riverside, started recording sessions for an album, and sent representatives on a cross-country tour to meet similar organizations, develop contacts, and set up Arkestra performances nationwide.

Through the intervention of George Quant, who was affiliated with the Transcendental Meditation Center in Leimert Park and who had connections with the local college scene, Horace was invited to give a music workshop at Riverside City College in June 1971. Accompanied by many of the members, he offered a class on "Black Experience in the Fine Arts." The following spring semester he was hired to present the class at the University of California at Riverside. The classes did not simply present different subject matter, but sought to transform the classrooms into an extension of the community arts movement via live music performances, poetry, student participation, and encouraging students to become involved in various community activities. In so doing they had an opportunity to articulate and develop their own purpose and worldview, pose unique challenges to students used to traditional pedagogy, offer experiences that would heighten and expand their sense of the creative process, its importance in their lives, and directly raise the question of their participation in the world around them.[24]

Various guest artists, including Rahsaan Roland Kirk, as well as slide presentations by Michael Dett Wilcots, were also part of a typical Tapscott class. Students would participate in some performances, and were also encouraged to attend events in the community and to write about them. Abdul-Salaam remembers, "We'd go out there in one or two cars, at least. The students would come in and Horace would explain what culture is, what this music is all about, and then we would actually perform. He would relate the music to Africa, to our experience."

Activities were not limited to the classrooms in Riverside. UGMAA rented a storefront in the city and soon had another functioning space, the UGMAA Fine Arts Center. Regular musical performances, as well as classes and workshops in music and other areas of the arts were the daily fare. Michael Dett and Ojenke taught photography. Vocalist Amina remembers, "We'd go to parks in Riverside. We would take the piano, every instrument we had, and everybody and their woman and their man and their babies, and we'd be out at the park with the dancers and the poets and the music."

When the class ended and funds dried up for the Riverside center in the summer of 1972, Abdul-Salaam Muhammad and Butch Morris were sent cross-country in August to spread the word about UGMAA and the Arkestra, make contacts, and line up potential stops for a national tour. According to Abdul-Salaam,

> We stopped in St. Louis and met with a cultural group there. Then we went to Chicago for a few days. We hooked up with the AACM. We got a chance to meet them. Went to New York and went to Babatunde Olatunji. He had the cultural center in Harlem. We met with him. We went to Newark, New Jersey, and met with the poet and writer, Amiri Baraka. We let them know who we were and left our material, trying to hook up this tour. . . . We went to about twenty black colleges and met either with the Black Student Unions or with the Associated Student Unions.

Armed with contacts from around the country and the prospect of a national tour, the Arkestra went back into the studio in September to finish recording an album to be titled *Flight 17*. Aside from Herbie Baker's title piece, it was to include "Why Don't You Listen?," "Dem Folks," "Children," and "Thoughts of Dar es Salaam." Unfortunately, it was not to be. Abdul-Salaam recalls:

> We're in the studio and we're doing the last night of *Flight 17* early in the morning, two or three. Two gentlemen walk in, an African American and a white gentleman in suits and ties. We're in the studio. Arthur

or Lester says, "They must be either from the mafia or the musicians' union." We don't know what's going on. We can't even hear them. We're in the studio. They're in the sound booth, the engineering booth. They're there for a minute and then they leave. So we keep going and finish. *Flight 17* is unbelievable. It's off the hook. Everybody goes home.

I talk to Horace that morning and we go over to the studio to do the editing, mixing or whatever they have to do. . . . We pull into the back and the studio has burned down. That morning it burned down—not the whole structure, but there's been a fire there and stuff has been destroyed. So here we are trying to accomplish something for the greater good, for our cause, for our independence, for the vision that Horace had, just trying to make something of the Arkestra. Now we had no tapes. Everything was squashed.

Near La Cienega and Wilshire Boulevards, the Venture Recording Studio was owned by Mickey Stephenson, who had also set up an MGM subsidiary, Venture Records. He had met Horace through trombonist/arranger/composer Melba Liston and had hired him to do some arranging for his rock and R&B artists. Horace talked him into allowing the Arkestra to use the studio. The night of the fire Mickey was out of town, but he was not surprised. "I got a call on the phone and the guy was talking to me while the studio was burning. The people in the area at the time were not happy that I was there. They voiced their opinions. One day all my windows were broke. Maybe a week later the doors were kicked in, stuff like that." UGMAA members were convinced that responsibility rested with national or local governmental agencies bent on curbing black cultural and political expression. To Abdul-Salaam, "We never got a chance to follow up on our tour. And especially those people in the colleges, they were really reaching out for something. Someone knew that. Those people controlling things knew this. . . . So it really, really hurt, but we saw the politics of the whole thing." The cause of the fire remains uncertain and speculation ranges from accident, music industry infighting, and racist neighbors, to organized crime and FBI COINTELPRO involvement. Given the widespread targeting of black movements of all types by the government, the latter was not a far-fetched assumption.

The disastrous end of the *Flight 17* project and with it the proposed national tour were a prologue to changes in the Arkestra. By the end of 1972, activity on Fifty-second Place came to an end, when Linda Hill and Will Connell left their houses, signaling another transition period for UGMAA, once again without a central space.

In the wake of the destruction of black political and cultural groups by internal dissension, financial problems, and the provocations of federal and local law enforcement, gangs reemerged in Los Angeles. Fifty-second Place fell under the control of the Crips. Conceived in 1969 in Watts, the Crips were rapidly expanding by the early 1970s. A Crip house was set up at the end of the block near Broadway, and Will felt the pressure, especially after his landlord's house was burglarized. "The Crips used to rob in the neighborhood like *Mission Impossible.* You'd have a guy case your house by walking his dog. Nobody walks a dog in the ghetto in L.A. The dog is either loose or he's in the yard." Although he was never robbed, Will was an object of Crip attention, especially after he tried to explain to his neighbors what was happening. "Then they started following me around because I was supposed to stay out of it, but they didn't rob my house. They could have taken my horn; my door was always open. After that they used to squeeze me, man. They would follow me around, and I remember one of the older men, who was in the gang, followed me into the Muslim restaurant I used to eat at, like telling me, 'Yeah, we can get you in here, nigger. You ain't safe.'"

The Voice of UGMAA also came to an end, plagued by artistic disagreements as well as pettiness and bickering. Amina remembers the impact of many of the newer vocalists:

When these voices came, they didn't know anything about UGMAA. They only knew the music they'd heard. They didn't have any cultural strength. They're into materialism. . . . But these were people who were into some substance. This was Sun Ra kind of people trying to deal with designer people in a sense. So it was always, "I want to sing the lead." "No, you can't." A lot of the words they didn't understand. They never did the "Free Angela" plays or work in Watts. They were different. What Linda and I did, there were no words. You didn't have to sit down and say "Now, sing this, this way." I would listen to her. She would listen to me. We would listen to the music, and it was on. You had to write everything for them. And then you had to re-tell them. Then if they didn't like it, they might show up late. It just was awkward.

The younger voices also had a strong interest in the musicians in the Ark, which led to other, unsettling situations, according to Amina. "When the three girls came, that's when I left, because they were all switching boyfriends, stealing each other's boyfriends, and they really had great voices. As long as Horace had me, Linda, the Ark—fine. But you start bringing in those sisters. . . . Once they got there, young women, boy, did it start to happen." Ali Jihad concurs, "I found that being in the choir there was so much conflict between those ladies. They'd be bitchin' over who didn't come to rehearsal, all the little petty stuff, and that always broke up stuff. Everything that I saw grow and flourish always got torn down by dissension. Every time." It would not be until the 1990s that Horace would form another choir.

Many artists would leave between 1973 and 1975. Guido Sinclair relocated to Chicago; E. W. Wainwright went on the road with Earl Hines and then McCoy Tyner. There were other motivations. Lattus McNeeley became involved with the Nation of Islam (NOI) and, according to Will Connell, "moved to Oklahoma, and became like a big-time rancher raising cows for *The Messenger* at that time when they tried to have their own food supplies and stores and stuff like that." Abdul-Salaam Muhammad and Ray and Ernest Straughter became more involved with the NOI. The pressures of a growing family and no income from Arkestra performances pushed James Lee into a more commercially oriented direction. Will tried to talk him into staying: "So James Lee came in with a bottle of wine, sat at the table and said, 'Let's bleed together.' 'Cause he loved me and I loved him, and he wasn't going to stay in the Ark. I remember begging James, 'How can you leave this band, man? How can you?'" Similarly, Fritz Wise married and moved away from the Ark during this period, though he would return in the 1980s and play a major role from then on. "I was trying to get involved with the so-called mainstream of music, trying to get into the whole commercial thing, trying to learn how to make a living."

The East Coast also took its cut. Arthur Blythe, Will Connell, Stanley Crouch, and Butch Morris found their ways to New York City in search of new musical challenges. For Arthur Blythe, then in his mid-thirties, "Horace was dealing with the Arkestra more. I didn't want that setting totally. I wanted some of it. I was like a stallion or a big dog. I had to get out and run. I didn't want to be sitting back, waiting until it was time to go in. It wasn't a negative. It was just a character thing with me, wanting to get in there and express myself. I just wanted to expand my thing a little more. I thought New York was the place." Will became disgruntled when the Arkestra provided the music for the film *Sweet Jesus, Preacher Man*. Although dealing with community issues that were important to Horace and UGMAA, the low budget film was not to Will's liking. "I got very upset because we played this music spiritually. We'd say it was for the uplift and this, that and the other, and now we're doing it for this cheap-ass, rip-off movie. I was really pissed off. It seemed like a travesty of all we meant and stood for, and I quit the band." For Butch Morris, his dislike of Los Angeles, coupled with the effects of a tour of duty in Vietnam, pushed him to leave. "I wasn't in the best psychological shape, coming out of the military and coming out of Vietnam. I was pretty fucked up. I mean really, I was fucked up. Then I had to get away from Los Angeles. Even my mother and my father knew that I had never liked Los Angeles."

These were potentially crippling developments, and if the Arkestra and UGMAA were to continue in the 1970s with the same level of community involvement and musical activity, as well as realize the hope of many for a stronger institutional presence, an infusion of new talent was necessary.

TO THE GREAT HOUSE

The Arkestra in the 1970s

We are a family and the music is not just something you do.
It's a way of life, and you live it and you breathe it and you are it, and you don't sell out.
You hold fast and you stay strong and play it. And you say what you have to say.
And you put it in the archives, and you write it down and you don't let anybody take it.
And you don't abuse it or destroy it. And you leave it for the children.
And that's what it's about.
And that's us: dedication.

ADELE SEBASTIAN

It was like nothing I had ever experienced.

JAMES ANDREWS

The end of the Vietnam War and the closing of many community social spaces and organizations were producing important changes within the cultural life of the African American community of Los Angeles. Much of the militancy of the earlier period had passed and debates over revolutionary political strategy diminished; many black nationalists were moving into the liberal orbit of the Democratic Party. In the late 1960s the Black Panther Party had supported the Peace and Freedom Party and the United Front Against Fascism, and then established links with the Democratic Party. In 1972, Bobby Seale ran for mayor of Oakland, California, and Elaine Brown for city council, both standing as Democrats. With less street activity, the community arts movement was relegated to the remaining local centers and educational institutions.

Faced with this shifting socio-political landscape, PAPA/UGMAA's immediate challenge was to replenish its depleted ranks and maintain its visibility and activity as one of the leading forces in the community arts movement. By the mid-1970s a reinvigorated organization emerged, fueled by a wave of new recruits that, while less bohemian in lifestyle and somewhat older than the previous group, came with a higher degree of musical training and experience, as well as a strong commitment to the Arkestra ethos and aesthetic. They formed more collective spaces, "Great Houses," which became community art centers, and actively supported new community-oriented venues that emerged during this time in Venice as well as in South Central Los Angeles. The Arkestra also became associated with the Immanuel United Church of Christ (IUCC) and its socially conscious minister, the Reverend Edgar Edwards, who offered the church as a regular performance space for more than eight years. All of this contributed to a continuing and strong community presence, renewed focus on creating music, a broader orchestral palette, and a socially more cohesive organization.

A New Arkestra Emerges

The turnover in personnel from 1973 through 1975 was the largest the organization had ever experienced. While many withdrew from an active role, some leaving for other parts of the country, a new wave of musicians arrived to replenish the ranks and take the Arkestra into its next phase. Among the new artists was a core of performers who would continue the tradition after Horace's passing in 1999 and up to the present time. With many in their twenties, this was mostly a college-educated group with a strong background in music studies, some with conservatory training, others with renowned private teachers, and a few seasoned jazz artists from Horace's generation. They included: flutists Aubrey Hart, Kafi Roberts, and Adele Sebastian; alto clarinetist Herbert Callies; reeds Fuasi Abdul-Khaliq (Ernie Roberts), Leon Amos, James Andrews, Gary Bias, Charles Chandler, Charles Fowlkes, Billie Harris, Dadisi Komolafe (Arthur Wells), Rufus Olivier, Michael "Buckwheat"

Session, Jesse Sharps, and John Williams; trumpeters Steve Smith and Jon "Mad Cap" Williams; French horn players Robert Watt and Wendell C. Williams; tuba player Ray Draper; pianists Kaeef Ali (Bob Crowley, Jr., Kaeef Razudun), Billy Childs, and Bobby West; vibist Rickey Kelly; bassists Red Callender (doubling on tuba), Marcus McLaurine, Kamonta Polk, Eugene Ruffin, and Louis Spears (doubling on cello); drummers Ishmael Balaka (Ishmael Hunter), Andre Burbage, and Ricky Simmons; percussionists "Conga" Mike Daniel and Moises Obligacion; dancer Kachina Roberts (Vicky Roberts, Pendevu Bandi); and vocalist/actor Marla Gibbs.

Multi-reed instrumentalist and ultimately Arkestra bandleader, Jesse Sharps, spent his formative years during the 1960s in Watts, a product of Jordan High School and local private teacher, Milton Hall. While still in junior high school, in 1966 he encountered the Arkestra performing on 103rd Street outside the Watts Happening Coffee House.

> This guy, Nate Morgan, came by and told us one day, "Yeah, you guys got to come up there and hear this group. There's this guy, Horace Tapscott, and they're up there playing." And we went up there and I just saw it, and that was it. I just knew that was the thing to do. You just hear it for the first time, you say that's it. I gotta do that.
>
> Oh, I remember that first day just like I'm looking at you now. I remember I walked up, you could hear these guys playing. Arthur Blythe was just standing there with his alto saxophone warming. They were standing outside. They were actually playing on 103rd Street that day. They were having the concert outside. They normally had it inside this building, but it was burnt out anyway, so it kind of made sense to just play out on the street. Ah, I'll never forget that sound, hearing him play that out shit. It was just an incredible sound, like Coltrane in the flesh. I'd listened to a few albums and heard a lot of music. And this guy was incredible, just totally incredible.

Within the year Sharps was invited to rehearsals and playing baritone sax. A busy academic schedule at Jordan and subsequent college enrollment in Ohio, where Cecil Taylor was his first teacher at Antioch College, kept him from a more active role in the Arkestra. When Jesse returned to Los Angeles in 1973, he reunited with UGMAA, playing flute at first, then soprano saxophone. After Arthur Blythe and Will Connell left for New York, he became the bandleader, a writer, arranger, and the main copyist.

Saxophonist Ernie Roberts, who took the name Fuasi Abdul-Khaliq in 1975, shared leadership responsibilities with Jesse during the mid-1970s. He grew up in a house in Watts that his father had built, began studying music at the age of seven, attended Jordan High School, and also studied privately with Milton Hall. He received a scholarship to Whitman College in Walla Walla, Washington, where, despite a discouragingly stodgy and conservative music department, he managed to survive with the support of the Black Students Union and a new faculty member, Bill Cole, the author of biographies of Miles Davis and John Coltrane.

Cole had invited a number of musicians to the campus, who were part of the newer sounds emerging in the 1960s, including Dave Burrell, Nathan Davis, Jimmy Garrison, and Sam Rivers. Garrison roomed with Fuasi and during this period he became focused on the new music. Upon graduation he returned home. Cole's parting words were, "There's a guy in Los Angeles. You should go down and look him up. A cat named Horace Tapscott, who has a group down there, the Arkestra." Early in 1973, tenor saxophone in hand, he went to the IUCC, met Horace and other Arkestra members, and sat in. "But these cats in the Arkestra were playing, man. They were playing hard and strong and with fire, and I was on fire anyway. I wanted to play really bad."

Another alumnus of the Dorsey Jazz Workshop was trumpeter Steven Smith. Although he had heard of Horace and the Arkestra, it wasn't until some years later, when he was a music major at California State University, Los Angeles, that he went to a rehearsal at Rudolph's. "That experience of seeing Horace play was just, man, it was something that I had never heard before. I was so taken by it. I had been playing music and studying long enough to know that this was a special, special experience. I knew it right away. So, I was stuck after that. They couldn't get rid of me. . . . I said, 'Yeah, this is me. I gotta do this.' And I dropped out of college."

Alto saxophonist and flutist Dadisi Komolafe started rehearsing with the Arkestra in 1974, while attending Los Angeles City College. He had graduated from Dorsey under the tutelage of Dr. Simpson. "His ears were so good he could hear a rat piss on cotton a thousand yards away. . . . So, Dr. Simpson would stop the band, the band's got fifty people in there. He would point over to one person and say, 'You're about an eighth of a tone flat.' How the fuck do you hear some shit like that? You split a tone eight ways. And out of fifty people, he'd pick out the instrument. That was some amazing shit."

Until then, life for Dadisi had been a series of shifts and struggles, from a single parent family to a mother in the penitentiary, and in and out of foster homes, juvenile centers and jail. However, listening to the music of John Coltrane, Horace Tapscott, and the Arkestra gave him a new sense of purpose and direction. After hearing Trane's *A Love Supreme*, "What I knew at that point about Trane was that he was trying to serve God and humanity through his music. So that's what I started to do at that point." Between music classes and Arkestra rehearsals and performances, he practiced whenever he could. "I was on fire. I played, meditated, drank herbal teas, listened to music very intensely, and dealt with the music about sixteen hours every day. I was a rebel and very intense. I didn't play the conventional stuff." It was a turning point in his life. "Playing with the Ark is what made me, me."

Flutist and soprano saxophonist Kafi Roberts spent his early years in Watts, but his father had moved the family out of the housing projects and into their own home just west of that area before 1965. His music studies at the new high school in Watts, Locke, were paralleled by a strong interest in martial arts. He achieved a black belt at eighteen and won world champion-ships at that level in fourteen different martial arts forms. In 1981, he founded his own style, Universal Kenpo JuJitsu, and in 2002 reached the summit, achieving a tenth-degree black belt. He is enshrined in four of the five martial arts halls of fame around the world.

After the Watts upheaval, Kafi became aware of Horace and UGMA/UGMAA, but had never thought of playing with them until the early 1970s, when he was a music student at El Camino Junior College. Hearing that Jesse Sharps was back in town and playing with the Arkestra, Kafi led a group of friends to a concert at the IUCC:

> So I took about fifteen guys from the College and, man, they just fainted. They just fell out. One of the guys said, "Man, I wonder if we could play in this band?" And that's the first time the thought ever came into my mind. . . . There were probably five or six hundred people at the con-cert that day. They brought busloads of people from UC Riverside and different universities. Man, you couldn't even hardly get over to that area. It was just crazy.

One of the group, Kamonta Polk, Kafi's brother-in-law, followed through and was playing bass in the Ark at eighteen. About one year later at Kamonta's urging, Kafi attended his first rehearsal.

Unlike the bands of earlier years, whose ranks were populated with vet-erans of the music world and the Armed Forces, many of the new members were college-trained, without military experience and steeped in the new black music of the mid-1960s avant-garde. They were complemented by the arrival of a few artists with extensive training in Western classical music. Robert Watt, assistant principal French horn of the Los Angeles Philharmonic, was hired by conductor Zubin Mehta from the New England Conservatory of Music at the age of twenty-two and arrived in Los Angeles in 1970, the only African American in the orchestra. Not long after settling into L.A., he received a message to call Horace, whom he'd never met.

I called him back and said, "Horace Tapscott, this is Bob Watt."

And he said, "The brother in the Philharmonic, huh. I bet you play that horn. We've got an Arkestra for you."

I said, "You do?"

"It's your Arkestra."

"Ark-estra?"

"Arkestra."

"Oh, Ark. Yeah. What have you got?"

"We've got a recording session for a movie soundtrack. Just show up. Bring your horn and I'll introduce you to everybody."

The Ark was recording music for the film *Sweet Jesus, Preacher Man*. When Bob arrived, he found none of the Hollywood studio players he was expecting to see.

It was an all black group. Everybody had robes on, and people were sitting around on the floor. Linda had her tambourine. I looked at them and they looked at me, and I said, "Oookay." While I was looking around, Horace said, "There ain't none of them here. This is *your* Arkestra."

"Okay."

There was this sense of "we have something here" and it was like nothing I'd ever experienced. It was just this sound; some people call it a wailing sound, but it was definitely a different world, very African feeling to it. It was a different temperament. He didn't want some things too well in tune, certain things. He wanted certain sounds and gave it this kind of something that would reach deep into you and give you this long ago, far away feeling of—ah—this is bone-shaking music; this is something special. And you could see it in his face, when he was getting the sound. "That's it. Don't worry. Feel it." And the music was such a different thing. . . . The feeling I got was "we've been waiting for you." It's like you've died and gone to heaven and they all know your name. I walked in and there was that feeling: this is where you belong and there's your seat.

Rufus Olivier would make a career with the bassoon, leaving Los Angeles in 1977, at the age of twenty-two to become second chair with the San Francisco Symphony. In 1980 he became the Principal Bassoonist with the San

Francisco Opera Orchestra and Ballet, positions he holds to this day. During his early years, the family lived across the street from Will Rogers Park in Watts but moved a few miles north before the upheaval of 1965. He attended Foshay Junior High School and Dorsey, where he became first alto saxophonist in the Jazz Workshop, while also pursuing classical studies with David Breidenthal, Principal Bassoonist with the Los Angeles Philharmonic. By the age of seventeen, Rufus was listed by conductor Zubin Mehta as a first call sub and occasionally was co-Principal Bassoon with the Philharmonic.

Then there was the Ark. During his first year at Dorsey, he unexpectedly encountered Horace.

> My parents didn't have any cars to drive me, so I had to take the bus everywhere. I was carrying an alto sax, baritone sax, bassoon, clarinet. I'll never forget walking down Western Avenue. I think I just got off the bus, and I hear this, "Hey, young blood! You with the cases! What is all that stuff?" So I tell him, and then I say "bassoon" and his eyes sort of lit up.
>
> "Bassoon? Bassoon, huh. You can play that thing?"
>
> "Yeah, I play this thing."
>
> "Come here, come here."
>
> And he took me into this warehouse right on Western and there was David Bryant and all these guys, just sitting there. I went in and he said, "This is Rufus, and he's a bass-oooon player," and he laughed. The guys were like, "Bassoon, all right!" Horace said, "Rufus, I don't want you to play saxophone. I want you to play the bassoon."
>
> I said, "Well, okay. Who are you by the way?"
>
> I didn't know who the heck they were. And I played with him all through high school.

Rufus was one of a handful of talented teenagers who were brought into the Arkestra during the 1970s. Of the hundreds of individuals who passed through UGMAA, perhaps the most treasured was flutist and vocalist Adele Sebastian, recruited at sixteen. In an organization of unique individuals, she stood out not only for her artistic merits, but perhaps more importantly for her qualities of character, her benevolence, sincerity, compassion, and ability to inspire.

Adele was born in Riverside, California, in 1957, into a musical family where everyone played an instrument and vocalized. Her mother played classical piano and sang with the Los Angeles Jubilee Singers, a touring ensemble that specialized in spirituals. In elementary school she began music studies, which emphasized Western classical training. Although her brothers listened to jazz, particularly John Coltrane, it remained outside of her musical vision until she encountered the Pan Afrikan Peoples Arkestra one Sunday afternoon at the IUCC in 1973. "I expected to see everybody in white shirts and black suits. But the whole thing was just completely different, and from that moment on my whole life was changed, my whole musical concept."[1] What Adele received that day was not simply an alternative musical approach. "They all just embraced me and I knew that this is where I wanted to be. And something about that music just turned me all the way around. It was like a culture shock, like a reflection, like seeing myself, or seeing who I was. And then I knew I was in the right space at the right time and this was it."[2]

Saxophonist Gary Bias, later to achieve acclaim in Earth, Wind and Fire, was a year younger than Adele and attended Locke High School, which boasted one of the strongest music programs in South Central, and would continue to do so under the guidance of Reggie Andrews. At eleven, Gary also became a student of Milton Hall, who had been at East L.A.'s Roosevelt High School in the 1930s. Hall embarked on a musical career not long after graduating, but his distaste for the road and the lifestyle led him back to Los Angeles, a job with the Department of Water and Power, and a strong commitment to teaching the young people in his neighborhood. Bias recalls that Mr. Hall "barely charged us anything. He was just giving himself to the community. He had an extra room in his garage and he built it, sound-proofed it as a music room. He taught for many years, taught all the woodwinds, oboe, flute, clarinet, saxophone. Just about everybody went through him." Similarly, Fuasi remembers, "When I first started, there would be a line of guys waiting for their lessons. And he would do this all day long, from nine o'clock in the morning until 9 o'clock at night. He was a great cat." Fuasi also recruited Gary, whom he met at Mr. Hall's. "He's a big name now, but I brought . . . this little fifteen-year-old guy. I said, 'Horace you got to listen to this guy.' That's how Gary got into the band, and Horace loved him right away."

An exception to the type of new member was saxophonist Michael Session, a fiery, largely self-taught performer, who would become the leader of the Pan Afrikan Peoples Arkestra on Horace's passing in 1999. Michael also grew up near Watts in the Avalon Gardens housing project, where Lester Robertson lived with his family. However, it was not until the end of his high school years that he started learning music by playing along with his radio in a park at Twenty-third Street and Second Avenue. While surfing the channels one day, he found KUSC in the middle of one of Kufahamu's broadcasts. "This cat was playing the cats that most people wouldn't play. And he was playing Horace Tapscott live at Foshay Junior High School. I'm hearing Arthur Blythe. When I turned to this station, man, it changed my whole life. It was not the commercial side of jazz. It was the real shit." Michael followed one of Kufahamu's announcements to an Arkestra performance.

> The spiritualness in the room was so dynamic and the magnetism. . . . Such a magnetism to the music that when you left there, you felt so vitalized. You just felt you could go pull down trees or something. I couldn't believe it. And the unity in there. You saw really young and really old, all playing together. It was the Ark. I never heard anything like it—and I was into jazz. But the Ark had a uniqueness that was so overwhelming and powerful to the community.

Michael made contact with the Ark in 1974, when a friend, playwright Cecil Rhodes, invited him to jam. Session reluctantly and with much trepidation agreed to go. "I somehow opened up the horn and got into it with them. Fuasi dug me and we had a nice rapport right off." Fuasi had been assigned by Horace to screen potential band members and followed up a short while later, inviting Michael to his place to play. Fuasi was looking for more than technical mastery.

> Basically, we were free; we were improvisational musicians. So the level on which we were trying to communicate was not based on a foundation of thirds, fifths, or thirteenths. We were basing it just on playing: what you have to say, how do you communicate yourself through your instrument and how do I communicate myself, and can we communicate together. That's what I was looking for, and it worked. Michael was great, man, we jumped together really fast. So I said, "Sure, man, come on in."

Social Consciousness, UCLA's L.A. Rebellion, and "Passing Through"

Those attracted to PAPA/UGMAA in the mid-1970s shared its ideals and saw it as part of the community arts and black consciousness movements, even if the sense of immediacy and the energy of the 1960s was receding. Most of the newer members had been pre-teens or in their early teens at the time of the 1965 upheaval and the subsequent years of political and cultural rebellion. Jesse Sharps remembers the heightened social and political consciousness: "You didn't have to walk around and be in the dark in those days . . . because people were just constantly pulling at you, 'Come on, brother, come in. Get off the street. Come here. Open your mind up. Wake up.' . . . You'd start reading and finding out about Malcolm X or something like that. You could never go back to sleep." Many members, like Michael Session, still identified with the lingering revolutionary sentiments.

> I was a revolutionist then. I was into black power. I hated the structure. America can kiss my ass. That was the times. And coming out of high school, there was Vietnam. The war was very unpopular. The black struggle in America was going on and had been for a while. It was a politically charged black-and-white thing. So at that time I was very revolutionary. I was like, "Yeah, hell, yeah!" And the Ark had that kind of revolutionary motif to it. It definitely depicted the struggle through the music. The vibe of what was going on was in it. The Ark is the black struggle. Everybody in it was going through all that. It wasn't no elite. It was the hard knock cats in the Ark.

While there was a high level of political awareness and an identification with the UGMAA ideal of social and cultural involvement within the community, there was less specific identification with political movements. According to Dadisi Komolafe, the music "was part of the movement that was going on, the black consciousness movement, the cultural consciousness movement, the civil rights movement and all that. We brought the music. . . . I was listening and observing and playing the music. I didn't get too involved with the political ideologies."

Instead, there was a more generalized identification with common political ideals, believed to be shared by all the groups that emerged in the 1960s and expressed in the music. In his early teens during the mid-1960s, Kafi Roberts became involved with the Black Panthers, but saw the BPP and other movements as sharing common values and goals, as did Komolafe. "When I went to US meetings they had pretty much one ideology, but it was no different from what the Panthers had, awareness and knowing your history, and pulling yourself up from the bootstraps and trying to do things for yourself. Until that faction came in that brought the dissension, it was real positive." Kachina Roberts had been involved with Maulana Ron Karenga's US Organization in the early 1970s, but the Arkestra provided her with a more encompassing approach. "It was Horace that allowed me to pull my love for jazz together and the cultural awareness that I had developed over the years and my dancing that I kind of did on my own and developed me into Pendevu. That's where I was able to really explore the avenue of art and my expression and really become who I am."

For other members without a defined political worldview, involvement with UGMAA provided a social broadening and purpose. French horn player

Wendell C. Williams was a tenth grader at Jordan High School when he joined the Ark while attending a rehearsal at his school. He remembers the Ark's impact: "It changes you for the better, because you start seeing a lot of the wrong in the world. So you contribute to try to change some of the wrong things." As a fifteen-year-old, Fuasi was one of the crowd of bystanders who witnessed the event on 116th Street that triggered the Watts upheaval of 1965. Those events brought home to him in a dramatic way the racism in the city and among the LAPD, as well as the anger within the community. It didn't lead him into an activist role then, but by the time he encountered the Arkestra, he was continuing his struggle toward a heightened social awareness. Horace and the Ark not only facilitated that but were seen as a way of expressing social consciousness.

> I was impressed because at this time I was trying to be a conscious black man, trying to be conscious of what's important for us as a people. So when I saw what was happening with UGMAA and how spiritual the sense of it was, this really turned me on. They were trying to preserve the music, to disseminate the music to the community. The vision he had made more sense to me than anything else at the time.

During the 1970s, UGMAA became involved in film projects that would express this vision and link them with an emerging generation of minority filmmakers at UCLA, recently dubbed "The L.A. Rebellion." Horace would work with a number of the young filmmakers on cinematic projects, but established a particularly close working relationship with Larry Clark, then earning a masters degree, which resulted in a cinematic statement of the UGMAA worldview in Clark's *Passing Through*, a film still featured in festivals throughout Europe, Africa, Latin America, even the United States, more than forty-five years after its first screening.

Larry Clark arrived at UCLA in 1970, having graduated from Kent State University in Ohio, where he had been president of the Black Students Union, and was admitted into the Ethnocommunications Program of the Film Department, a backdoor to admit African Americans, Asian Americans and Latinos. Among his fellow students were Charles Burnett (*My Brother's Wedding, Killer of Sheep, To Sleep with Anger, America Becoming*), Ben Caldwell (*I and I: An African Allegory, Babylon is Falling: A Visual Ritual for Peace*), Julie Dash (*Daughters of the Dust, Illusions*), Montezuma Esparza (*Only Once in a Lifetime, The Milagro Bean Field War*), Jama Fanaka (*Street Wars*), Haile Gerima (*Bush Mama, Harvest: 3,000 Years, Child of Resistance, Ashes and Embers*), Sylvia Morales (*Chicana*), Bob Nakamura (*Manzanar, Hito Hata:*

Raise the Banner, Toyo Miyatake: Infinite Shades of Gray), Eddie Wong (*Wong Sin Saang*), and Billy Woodbury (*Bless Their Little Hearts*).[3]

A combination of the political atmosphere, their segregation at the school, explorative proclivities, and a lack of funds, fostered a collective sensibility. Ben Caldwell, the founder of the KAOS Network and one of the pillars of the current Leimert Park arts scene in South Central Los Angeles, recalls their profile: "The film school was the radical part of the school at that time, because we were more involved with everything. So the school itself had us very, very watched." To carry out their projects, they supported each other's work:

> Being forced to be the "other," we ended up just playing on that. We made ourselves separate, and we organized and worked very well. And we were able to build a posse of filmmakers that were able to do all aspects of film. If Charles needed a cameraman, I could do that. If I needed a cameraman, Charles could do that. Larry could do the sound. Julie Dash could help us with this. So all of us just kind of like stirred around and helped each other. We were able to finish twenty-two to thirty films of different kinds and different sizes.[4]

Clark met Horace as he was finishing his first project, *As Above, So Below*, a film about urban guerrilla warfare, which he describes as "really a raw film. One of the professors at UCLA wanted to report me to the House Un-American Activities Committee, never mind that they had been disbanded." He was looking for someone to provide a musical score, when a friend suggested he talk to Horace, whom Larry had seen perform in the community.

> My initial goal was to talk to him and see if he knew some musicians that might be interested in scoring a student film, about fifty minutes long. He immediately, in a very nice way, began to chew me out. "What do you mean around L.A.? You have musicians right here in your community. You don't have to look outside of your community to find musicians that would like to score your film. You live in this community. You made this film in the community. Why not find musicians right here in your own community to do the film?" That was how I met Horace. I knew he was right, absolutely right.

After screening the film, Horace agreed to write the score and have the Arkestra perform it. When completed, Larry arranged a screening in South Central before a full house of seven hundred people. Set in a United States under martial law, replete with urban guerrilla uprisings, it focused on how those types of movements could be successful in a manner reminiscent of the

Tupamaro guerrillas of Uruguay during the 1960s. "It was sort of a critique of the Black Panther Party, revolutionaries who wear black jackets and black berets. You can spot them right off," according to Clark. "These were people who looked like everybody else. So that is what the film was about. And you never knew who was in and who was not in. And it's always a surprise when you found out who was in."

Not long after the conclusion of *As Above, So Below*, Larry turned his attention to another project that would eventually become his master's thesis film at UCLA, *Passing Through*. As part of his endeavor to be involved in the community, he offered a film workshop at the Performing Arts Society of Los Angeles (PASLA). Financially supported by government-sponsored endowments and located in the midst of South Central at Eighty-seventh Street and Vermont Avenue, under the leadership of Vantile Whitfield, PASLA offered theatrical training and productions to the community. While teaching his workshop, Larry met actor/director Ted Lange, then working in theater at PASLA. A veteran of L.A.'s Ebony Showcase theater and efforts to create political and integrated theatrical productions on the West Coast, Lange had also collaborated briefly with Horace on an unrealized project for a musical. Ted recalls,

[Larry] says, "I'm looking for some stories. I'm a filmmaker. I'm going to UCLA and for my project I've got to find some stories." I said, "I've got a story for you. It's about some jazz musicians. I won't tell it to you now. Be here tomorrow and I'll give you just a treatment." "Cool." I go home that night and I write the treatment. I didn't have shit. I wrote this thing called "Passing Through" and I based it on my grandfather in Oakland, who raised us, who would always talk about the earth and spirituality. He was part Indian. So I come back to Larry and I give him about three pages. He reads it and goes, "I like this. Let's write a screenplay."

After receiving a $10,000 grant from the American Film Institute in 1975, they began the film in earnest. From the start they involved Horace and the Arkestra. "He suggested that I come and listen to the music," Clark remembers, "listen to them play, go to clubs, look at the mannerisms of the musicians, etc., etc. I literally started doing a study of music and musicians, the way they talked, the way they related to each other, the whole thing." Larry developed a cast and crew through his film workshop at PASLA and his fellow students at UCLA. Charles Burnett was one of his camera operators; Julie Dash handled sound; Haile Gerima was a grip. Ben Caldwell was on the set and lent his hands, literally, to a scene with grandfather "Poppa Harris" digging in the earth. They enlisted Nathaniel Taylor, a PASLA actor, who had just won a role as Lamont's best friend in the TV sitcom *Sanford and Son*, for the lead role of the young musician, "Eddie Warmack."

For the role of Poppa Harris, Larry traveled out near the Mojave Desert to find veteran African American actor, Clarence Muse. Over the course of his career, Muse appeared in over two hundred films, five of those by Frank Capra, and was one of the founders of the Screen Actors Guild. He was a lifelong jazz fan and received writing credit with Otis and Leon René for "When It's Sleepy Time Down South," a popular tune in the 1930s when recorded by Louis Armstrong and one that became his theme song. Seemingly reluctant at first, Muse did respond to the script and agreed to participate. Later, Muse's wife told Larry that he wanted to do the role very much. "He sees the film as his curtain call," she explained to the young filmmaker.[5]

Horace directed the music and assigned Arkestra members to the different characters. Fuasi played the music for Nathaniel Taylor and Jesse Sharps played saxophone for Johnny Weathers, another of the lead actors. The final score was composed and arranged by Horace and performed by the Pan Afrikan Peoples Arkestra. A number of scenes feature musical settings and performances by members of the Arkestra as well as a few brief scenes with Horace, David Bryant, and others. Dedicated to the late young pianist Herbie Baker and many leading African American musicians, the film opens with Horace playing solo piano and then the Arkestra joining in for the intense, driving, first five minutes of Herbie Baker's *Flight 17*. Clark's idea for a musical introduction not only captures Horace and the Arkestra in strong form but sets just the tone for the film that he wanted. "When I saw it, I said, 'Oh, my god.' With the music it was just unreal. It was more than I expected. Horace's hands were moving so fast it was a blur. I mean you're shooting twenty-four frames a second and his hands are moving faster than 1/24th of a second. That opening stops everybody. People notice that this is no ordinary film you are going to see."

The script initially dealt with Ted Lange's ideas on the relationship between an older and a younger musician, but it rapidly evolved into broader sociological and political themes. As Clark and Lange moved in the world of musicians and talked at length with Horace and various UGMAA members, they crafted a story of the struggles of Warmack and his fellow musicians against an exploitive and, at times, brutal recording industry and among themselves to establish collective control of their art. Larry explains,

> I wanted the film to be about something, not just the relationship between an old musician and a young musician. . . . So I wanted it to have some kind of political content on a number of levels. One is in terms

of the struggle that black people were going through: civil rights movement, the national liberation movements. I just had to have that. We talked to Horace and we talked about the problem of distribution. That was one of the subplots in the film, this whole question of music and having control of the music and all of that.

Even the relationship between the older and the younger musician carries a strong parallel to the Arkestra ethos, the mentoring, the passing on of the tradition from generation to generation. According to Clark, "There are some double metaphors and symbols. The Poppa Harris character could be Horace. It could be the Pan Afrikan Peoples Arkestra. The Poppa Harris character symbolizes reaching a certain creative level of excellence. It could be a guide or a mentor." Lange recalls the smooth interaction between filmmakers and musicians and the consensus on the ideas underlying the film, especially the issue of artistic versus commercial control of the arts:

> What's been blatantly known for years is what was going on with the musicians and the music. . . . We all know exactly what the deal is. Nobody said, "Hey, man, that's not true." Nobody said that. Nobody said, "Come on, you think the white man did that? Get the fuck out of here." No one said that. And that's why it was so extraordinary, because everybody knew it, but nobody said it. That was the first time that it was said. Why? Because it was some little guy's student film and it wasn't distributed by Miramax.

This was the story of the Arkestra, and it was so perceived by all involved. Fuasi remembers, "We were always aspiring to record and have control over our music. We wanted to be able to preserve our music and also have a way to disseminate it, through recordings if possible, or even have a library and archive that the public could come and check out and listen to it. So this seemed to be the story of *Passing Through*. It was really the story of Horace and the Arkestra. It was like a training film for us."

Horace loved the film. When it was completed, he was at the press screening before its premiere at the Los Angeles International Film Festival in 1977. Larry recalls, "I could tell he was really pleased with it, because he kept jumping up out of his seat and doing a little dance. He was really enthused, and I was really happy about that because he had put so much work into the film." Years later, when newer Ark members visited during his final illness, Horace would put them in front of his television, slide in the cassette, and have them watch *Passing Through*.

The Sound of the Arkestra

As the dust from the migrations of the early 1970s settled, Jesse and Fuasi emerged as the Arkestra leaders whenever Horace wasn't there to lead rehearsals, though within the context of a collective with many other members, including Linda Hill, Adele Sebastian, and Michael Session in strong supporting roles. When Fuasi left in 1977, Jesse assumed sole responsibility as bandleader. In preparing the band, Sharps worked closely with Horace: "As bandleader, I was just keeping the band in order. He would tell me what songs to get ready, depending on what kind of show was coming up. We'd go over the songs or go over the scores."

Jesse's leadership style, more controlling than Horace's, fostered a cohesion that hadn't existed previously. Nate Morgan observes, "That was the most disciplined of all the Arks I'd witnessed. Usually, Jesse Sharps ran those rehearsals. We called him Sergeant Sharps and that's the way he ran the rehearsals." Kafi Roberts agrees, "*Everybody* feared Jesse. Guys were sunk down in their seats. Jesse is a fanatic, man. He told us, 'I don't have anything in life that I love as much as this music, other than my family. So you guys are going to play this stuff right.'" Despite their differences in style, Horace gave Sharps virtual carte blanche. Kafi recalls, "These guys really loved each other. Jesse's been with Horace since he was twelve years old. He was groomed for that purpose. It was perfect. Horace is our teacher and mentor and all that, but he really, really respected Jesse. And he gave him all the leverage that he needed to make the band work the way he thought. I'd seen him tell guys on several occasions, 'Talk to Jesse.'"

Under the leadership of Fuasi and Jesse, the Arkestra became musically tighter than it had ever been. The kind of esprit de corps in the band is captured by Michael Session:

> We'd practice horn lines, breathing, synchronization, and all that. We'd even take bits of lots of charts, a line from one and then a line from another chart and so on, and put a collage of lines from the book, like thirty or forty tunes, and play one line after the other, just a few bars from this tune and a few from another. We ended up creating a new tune and surprised Horace with it. The first time we told him about it, we ran it down. And I know it just blew him away. We were so into each other that we just grew to doing stuff like that. We were very hungry and young, so there were no boundaries.

James Andrews remembers the horn section adding circular breathing to their technical palate:

> That became a little thing that we all did when we played, just a natural phenomenon. We all, for the most part, circular breathed. We learned how to do that. We were all trying to get that down, incorporate that, to where it was part of our playing, the blending of the horns was the sound that we had. So, during the solos you have these guys, there's just no stopping them. They're taking it all out. We build so, so, so, so high in terms of the solo, and then you take it even higher than that. Well, it's like, these guys don't ever breathe? Well, we're circular breathing we're putting ideas on top of ideas, and got that fresh breath so that we're just taking it even further out in terms of intensity.

Music stands were soon prohibited on the bandstand and musicians were expected to have the band book memorized. James recalls, "I think we had about eighty tunes that we could play the head off of at any given time. All Horace had to do, or anybody, would be to announce what it was. And that would be from 'The Thin Line' to *Ancestral Echoes* to 'Dem Folks,' all the sweet pieces." Michael Session explains how the practice began: "I was memorizing my music so much that Horace started going around to other people's music stands and flipping their music over, making them memorize it. So then we started playing the monthly concerts without music stands." He recalls the reasoning: "Horace used to say, 'In the jungle there's no electricity, there's no paper.' Horace always said that. He wanted you to realize that you had to play from your heart and not from the paper. He used to turn the lights off at rehearsals."

Jesse Sharps considers this the most important reason for the band's tightness and not his sense of discipline: "Once everyone knows the music, you just concentrate on breathing together. If Horace makes a sign, then everyone can react to it because they can look and see what's going on. Having music stands on the stage really is not playing music. This is a different kind of thing; this kind of music you have to know it. You have to really, really know it in your heart so that you can really make some force with it."

With the influx of new members and as new charts came from the players, the sound of the band evolved as most discovered their composing voices for the first time. According to Jesse, "We started expanding, started using a full band: four trombones, various reeds, full sax section with bass clarinet, flutes, bassoon, two or three trumpets. It was fun expanded like that. Lots of percussion. Then we started doing more modern things, because the writing started to change. You got new writers. I was writing, Fuasi. We encouraged everyone." Fuasi contributed his four-part *Eternal Egypt Suite*. Horace also continued to solicit compositions. Michael Session recalls, "He was always asking, 'Did you write anything lately?' He used to tell me that writing was one of the important things, because that's something that you can leave behind." Jesse was especially prolific, penning, among others, "Clarisse," "Desert Fairy Princess," "The Goat and Ram Jam," "Macrame," "Mike's Tune," and "Peyote Song No. III," all of which were Arkestra mainstays and recorded. Michael started writing about one year after joining and stretched his conception of music:

> I called this tune "Buckwheat and Syrup," and at the bridge I had duos. If you wanted to solo, you had to have a partner to solo with. And in the arrangement I had these miscellaneous horns—like bass clarinet, oboe, french horn, bassoon. I had these instruments doing the main line in the bridge, but I had the rest of the band doing jungle sounds. I just wrote on the paper—"jungle sounds." They had to pick an animal in the jungle and these are the sounds you make, while these other guys are doing the melodic line. How did I get to thinking like this? Checking out the freedom in the Ark and the uniqueness of trying to do something totally different.

Linda turned to writing short plays for children, to which Horace contributed the music. Jesse recalls,

> For many years we would go to the elementary schools and give special concerts. Linda Hill had written these plays . . . these little stories about children mixed with African stories done her way, so the kids here could relate to the stories, *The Day the Sky Cried* and stuff like that. And they would have the kids involved in the play. They would always get some of the kids from the school and teach them the music, like a week, two weeks before we came there, and have them sing and play with us.

Horace contributed "Autumn Colors," "Ballad for Deadwood Dick," which celebrates black cowboy Nathaniel Love, and "Mothership," originally titled "Be There." Over the years "Mothership" acquired a special status in the Ark's and in Horace's immediate performing repertoire, where it was continually kept. As Horace notes in his autobiography, "The mothership was the Ark, the vessel that saves the music after the forty-day flood of commercialism."[6]

Horace also embarked on long form pieces as well. His suite *Impressions of the Ghetto* mostly builds upon some of Horace's previous compositions and is divided into six parts: "At the Crossroads," "Saturdays Mourning," "Quest for Peace," "Lumumba," "Close to Freedom," and "Listen." Jesse notes, "It's very long. It takes about forty-five, fifty minutes to play it, very intricate, a lot of parts. That was one of the best pieces." The *Drunken Mary Suite* ("Sketches of Drunken Mary," "Mary on Sunday," and "Mary at Sunset") is Horace's portrait of a poor, mostly homeless alcoholic, who was a fixture in the Houston community of his youth, sustained by the tolerance and care of those in the neighborhood. Horace's sister, Robbie, recalls, "She was the neighborhood drunk. I can see her right now, very thin and wispy and weaving. She'd sleep on your porch. You'd wake up in the morning and there was Mary." "Sketches of Drunken Mary" portrays her from Monday through Saturday, when she was drinking. On Sundays she sobered up, precariously negotiating the steps leading up to the church for Sunday service. "Mary at Sunset" evokes her last days, which ended when she burned to death in a temporary shelter.

Ancestral Echoes seems to be Horace's homage to two revered influences in his life, Duke Ellington and William Grant Still, perhaps inspired by the former's *Black, Brown and Beige* and the latter's *Afro-American Symphony*. In 1975, the Watts Community Symphony Orchestra (WCSO) commissioned Horace to compose a piano concerto as part of their preparations for the upcoming bicentennial. His most ambitious work, *Ancestral Echoes* was scored for symphony orchestra and then months later for the Ark as well, and first performed by the WCSO at the Los Angeles Music Center on 25 October 1975 with Horace as featured soloist. Divided into four parts— "Songs of Songhay," "Ancestral Echoes," "Transplantation: Songs of the New World," and "Ancestral Echoes"—it is Horace's attempt to evoke the African American experience from an African village to life in North America. "It begins in an age and city called Songhay," he explains, "where the older people and the younger people are playing in the village, unaware of what is about to happen to them, kidnapped and taken across the waters to America, and becoming slaves, and building that country. And from there it goes on to freedom."[7] Along with "Mothership" it perhaps best captures UGMAA's focus at the time. Fuasi recalls the significance of these compositions for UGMAA,

> We were all part of his mothership, and if we were to leave and go out in pods to different places in the planet, we can take what we have and plant it there and try to grow something there also. That was supposed to be our duty. *Ancestral Echoes* was talking about our ancestors,

where we come from, what we were supposed to be doing, and how we were supposed to be taking this into the future and leaving a legacy for our children.

From the Sacred to the Profane—Performing in the Community

Throughout the 1970s the Arkestra remained a strong, visible presence in the community and there was some international recognition. In 1974 Horace was invited by the International Secretary-General to join the North American delegation to the Sixth Pan African Congress in Dar es Salaam, Tanzania.[8] Unfortunately, lack of financing prevented his attending. UGMAA continued to play a role in the local schools, facilitated now by a few Ark members holding teaching positions. College gigs could be counted on each year as well as community cultural events and festivals in the local parks. Kafi remembers, "I think we played every UC or state college in California." The Arkestra continued to perform at South Park, sometimes with the support of the musicians union, Local 47, which meant a rare payday, and virtually all of their concerts were free to the community. "You know that whole time—and I never even thought about it, I think we were all just there—there wasn't any money involved at all," recalls Rufus Olivier.

Their most important venue became the Immanuel United Church of Christ, just above Watts at 1785 East Eighty-fifth Street and Holmes Avenue. Beginning in the spring of 1973, this small church would offer a stable residence for the band until 1981, when the Arkestra offered its last performance there. The minister, Reverend Edgar Edwards, was a community activist and member of the Black Congress, supporting people around his church, offering meals for children and the homeless, as well as providing sanctuary for immigrants. David Bryant remembers, "He was just a part of the community. Not too many ministers were doing that type of thing. He was broad-minded enough to allow us to do those concerts every fourth Sunday, because our music wasn't religious music particularly." The band certainly did not offer a traditional religious aspect. Steve Smith recalls the look of the Arkestra: "A lot of us would dress in dashikis and African attire, but different cats would do different things. Sometimes Jesse would show up in a college drum major's jacket with tails and jeans and a knit cap. We were a pretty wild group, but people would come and they would dig it."

The Arkestra was initially invited to perform in the upstairs multipurpose room as part of a church-sponsored community program called "The Seed." Shortly after that, the band played an Easter Sunrise Concert and then moved downstairs into the church, settling into a routine of offering a free concert on the last Sunday afternoon of each month. Yearly Easter Sunrise concerts continued as well, with the band members usually arriving shortly after midnight, setting up and performing until sunrise, when the music would reach its peak.

The small wooden structure offered a bare bones environment for the band, forced at times to bring their piano to performances. With a very high ceiling, the acoustic challenge would have deterred most other bandleaders, but it was to Horace's liking, the rawness of it, the way the sound reverberated and filled the space. According to Steve Smith, "The sound in the church I think is the wildest thing about it. The ceiling is so high and you've got all these musicians and everything is bouncing around. It would create this sound you couldn't believe, especially at the end when Horace would have everybody do their thing. Man, that was incredible."

To many members it became the Ark's most important appearance. For Michael Session, "It wasn't a pay gig, but we looked forward to that gig like it was all the money in the world. We prepared for it. And most of us, the younger unit, we were at that age where money wasn't the thing. It was to get to this music and learning and being able to perform for your community." For flutist Aubrey Hart, "These cats would be screaming so, man. I know we lit that church up every time we were there on the last Sunday. . . . That concert, last Sunday, that's what we lived for. We lived to play that."

Though not identified with organized religions, PAPA/UGMAA has always been perceived as a strongly spiritual organization by its members. According to saxophonist Billie Harris, "I never felt out of place with the music in the church, and apparently that old minister, he thought the same way. Horace was bringing music from the streets to the church and it fit." For Roberto Miranda, performing at the IUCC was one of the high points in his years of performing with the Arkestra. "I would go there to play/pray. That was one of the best experiences that I have ever had musically speaking. Christ is the core of my being and to play this music in a church, for me, was just a freeing experience. And with these people, people that I loved."

The commitment to community also meant frequent visits to youth authorities, juvenile centers, and prisons. The post-Vietnam drug explosion in Los Angeles translated into the incarceration of thousands of African Americans, and UGMAA felt a commitment to them. Dadisi Komolafe, who performed regularly with his band and with Horace in prisons, recalls, "Horace always taught us the meaning of going into prisons and hospitals, children's organizations, different types of situations where the music was needed, as opposed to just being wanted. So I took up this endeavor from Horace's teachings, never knowing that one day I might be in there myself."

The band had had its share of individuals who wrestled with addictions, and some found themselves on the inside, including Dadisi, jailed for possession of crack cocaine. "It became my nemesis for a long time. I was back and forth, back and forth. You can do well for a time, but it can bring you down in one night. You can lose everything. I'm such an obsessive type of person, obsessed with whatever I do, an extremist. So one night for me would be tragic. I'd be doing good for months and then in one night it would be gone and nobody sees me again." He served time at the California Rehabilitation Center (CRC) but was able to play and offer a music education class. Drummer Bill Madison shared experiences there: "The advantage of that was that all the musicians in California that had that particular problem were there. We had bands. We had a concert band playing stuff like *Night on Bald Mountain*. Frank Morgan and I were there. We're still best friends and the exploits of Frank and Bill will not bear the light of day."

Given the size of the Arkestra, small groups from UGMAA more often performed, but the Ark made some appearances, usually with one or more of the poets. They covered much of the penal system from the Youth Authority and Juvenile Halls (Los Pedrinas, East Lake Juvenile Center, Ventura School for Youth) to the California Institute for Women (CIW), and for Men (CIM), the federal penitentiary at Terminal Island, and occasionally places outside Southern California, like Soledad.

Those appearances posed unique opportunities and challenges, especially to the wardens. Ojenke was on many of them: "What I remember most about performing in the prisons is that after we, the poets, would perform, at a couple of prisons they would have prison riots. They had a couple of them at CRC and at Soledad, because the words or the ideas had inflamed the minds of the prisoners so much that they just bubbled over the rim." Otis O'Solomon of the Watts Prophets had similar experiences: "One time they turned the lights off. When the Watts Prophets came on—we were really hard at that time—they said, 'The show is over and you will have to leave.' That happened a couple of times." During an appearance by the Ark at the CIM, Kamau Daáood read one of his early poems, "Poem to myself and other niggers and anyone else who cares to listen," which brought an abrupt end to the concert. "It was basically a poem about all the negative things that me and other folks in that age group were involved in, and how I really needed to look at myself and break beyond that. I think it ends: 'I we ain't no niggers I we ain't no niggers

/ Help me myself yourself to be myself yourself / cause a nigger ain't shit.' After I read the poem, they told Horace that they had to stop."

To the Great House

Since the end of the UGMAA houses on Fifty-second Place, the organization had been without a substantial common space. Convinced of the need, some of the older members, including Linda Hill and Michael Dett Wilcots, joined newer arrivals Jesse Sharps and Fuasi Abdul-Khaliq to search for one. In January 1974 they found a house on West Boulevard near Sixty-third Street. Fuasi had taken a job as a probation officer, and was able to cover the rent with his salary. It was an older building, set behind a closed-down bakery. A driveway ran by the storefront, past a duplex to the house in the back. Michael Dett moved into one of the duplex units and Linda, Jesse, and Fuasi moved into the large house. Called "The Great House," it served as a rehearsal space for the band and a temporary crash pad for some of the musicians. Unfortunately, this Great House lasted only a short while. On June 6, 1974, it burned to the ground, when the old water heater ruptured and some of the drapes caught fire.

Out of the West Boulevard fire came a determination to build a stronger collective. Adele Sebastian was one of the advocates: "We loved each other and we loved the music. We said that if we're really that down, let's all hook up and live together, and eat this music and play it and work with it and really get it tight."[9] By early 1975 Jesse had located a large house—two stories with a basement and large attic—at 2412 South Western Avenue, just north of Adams Boulevard, and Fuasi again signed the rental agreement. It became the second Great House, soon to be dubbed "Quagmire Manor" by Michael Session, "The Quag" for short.

The first floor held a large front room, dining room, den, and a kitchen with a pantry; on the second floor were four bedrooms and three bathrooms. At any one time, a dozen or more people resided there, most only playing music, while a few gainfully employed covered the rent and others contributed food when needed. The largest room on the first floor, the "Concert Room," was used for performances. One of the other rooms was also large enough to serve as a rehearsal hall and two pianos were installed. Michael Session recalls, "There were so many rooms and cubby-holes. It was really laid out for the Ark. We had a room on the side of the house that was just as long as the whole house. We called it the hot dog room. It seemed like they just built a long, narrow corridor. We had beds in there. I even lived in the hot dog room at one time. . . . Man, what a house."

When UGMAA moved in, everyone worked to transform the interior, "like twenty of us, to put this house together," according to Fuasi. "We were painting, carpentering, plastering. There was an old carpet house and they would throw all their cuttings away. We would go back to their dumpster and take all this stuff and lay it down in our place, creating all these collage rugs. Everybody worked hard." Steve Smith was another resident: "We were all so excited. We're talking about a huge mansion. We rented a sanding machine, and we sanded all the floors smooth and lacquered them so we could have dance concerts. All the drapes were done in tie-die and stuff, all artistic stuff done by us. We painted every room in the entire house. I remember in my room, which was upstairs, I had a fireplace." Dancer Kachina Roberts, who moved into the attic with Fuasi—"We had the attic suite; it was so romantic"—recalls, "The brothers did a wonderful job in hooking that house up. It was beautiful. They did the floors. They sound-proofed it. It was colorful. The walls had beautiful artwork on it. It had photography. It had the history of UGMAA there."

With less street and political activities than in the sixties and fewer non-musician bohemians in residence, the focus in the house was more exclusively on the arts than in earlier ones. One of the members from the 1960s, Walter Savage, who returned briefly, found it "a little bit more serene, organized, and more focused" than the earlier houses. Despite the usual personal dramas the music provided a balm. Nate Morgan recalls, "There was always an issue going on over there of privacy, personal property, always some issue with somebody. But what I did notice was that when they rehearsed, the focus was definitely on the music and nothing else." With so many key members concentrated in one space, formal rehearsals became a daily activity. According to Jesse, "So then we rehearsed every day, seven days a week. We'd go to the park on Saturday, take the piano, and rehearse there." Michael Session even exchanged his car for a van "so we could haul the pianos and the people. Another guy did too, so we had two or three vans in the house."

As in previous houses, the music was continuous, whether or not there were formal rehearsals. "Somebody was always playing," according to Fuasi. "There was not a time that there was not music going on in that house. It was a twenty-four-hour music house." To Kachina, "Can you imagine waking up in the middle of the night, maybe to go to the bathroom, and you hear some flutes playing in one end and some congas on the other. You hear somebody singing in harmony someplace else. . . . It was beautiful." Michael recalls, "I used to come home from work and every corner of the house had somebody practicing or playing. I used to go on the roof and practice, go in the closet." For Aubrey Hart, the memories are still vivid: "Horace would rehearse, rehearse, rehearse. And then as soon as the rehearsal was over, we just hit. We hit for hours and hours right there, right there, man. So much music." Bobby West remembers,

> One time Jon [Williams] and I drove up there, and it was pretty vacant, even for early morning. So I went into the music room and started playing the piano. . . . I heard somebody start playing alto saxophone, and whoever was on this alto just came and joined in. I remember that sound and the birds outside the window. And it seemed like for a moment I was in concert with whoever it was on alto and the birds. We were like a trio, and I heard that he was taking as many cues from me as he was from the birds. I turned around and it was this gentleman by the name of Aubrey Hart, who was a flute player.

As one of the few with a regular income and one of the primary supporters of the house, Michael Session was occasionally frustrated. He captures this aspect of life at the Great House in his composition "Quagmire Manor at 5 A.M.," written early one morning after spending his printer's paycheck on food and seeing it all consumed by the residents in one day.

> We were so poor financially. I'm sure it made more than just me frustrated. I can see why cats were playing so hard. It was all they had. Our spirits were high; we had a ball, but it was a struggle. And that's why we called it the Quagmire Manor, because the quagmire is like the mucky swamp around the castle, the swamp with the alligators and rose bushes sticking you while you're trying to get to the castle. Once you got to the castle, it was heaven. And that's what the music room was. To live with each other and trying to survive was going through the Quag, but once we got to the music, we were all in heaven.

Adele Sebastian, who provided the lyrics and recorded the tune with the Arkestra, remembers, "I believe that song pretty much tells the story of what the Quag was like around five o'clock in the morning. You could find musicians somewhere in the house playing, blowing, letting it all out. And that was beautiful, too. The music was twenty-four hours a day. It was nonstop. And it was real."[10]

Now, if you've ever been to Quag at 5 A.M.
Then you must really be in tune.
Cause all the music spirits hear the call, they awaken
And they blow from room to room.[11]

With community arts centers in decline by the mid-1970s, the Great House took on more of that role, as UGMAA offered a wider range of activities. According to Adele, "We featured different artists in the community. We had a dance class going there. We had classes for the children. So it was almost like a community center."[12] Steve Smith explains, "We'd have big shows where we would get all these different groups and they would come to our house and it would be a show all night long, one group after another. Man, it was just so exciting. We might have African drummers and a dance group come in and do something. Then the Ark would play and then maybe a vocalist might come in." French horn player Bob Watt remembers the strong community reaction to those concerts: "People would just come off the street for these. 'That's my music.' Winos, street guys, would just walk in the place. It was like they were crippled and could now walk. They felt welcome by this music. They knew something about it. When we'd play in the parks, guys would come out of nowhere, like they were just being pulled to it. There was a real magical thing about it." At one of those performances, Bob took his first solo with the Arkestra:

Then that one night in the Great House we were playing a piece and I heard them start saying, "Bob Watt, Bob Watt, Bob Watt . . ."
Then Horace said, "Go up front."
I said, "Go up front?"
"Take a solo. *Ancestral Echoes.* Don't worry. Just go play!"
"Okay."
"Just do it!"
I was playing, but, man, my knees were shaking. I was so nervous. That was the challenge of the century, just to not think about it. But Horace said it would be there and it was. I heard it and I played it. Horace was like, "I told you. You played it. You played it." And they were all going, "Yeah!" Horace was just laughing, this joy because he got this classical musician to play beyond his scope. Afterward, I went to Marla [Gibbs] and said, "God, I need a drink."
She said, "No you don't, but you can have one."
"Oh, man, that was a rush."
"Yeah, yeah. I bet you don't get that at the Philharmonic."

Other musicians were drawn into the Arkestra through the Great House. Pianist Kaeef Ali, recently arrived back in Los Angeles, looked up old friend Michael Session, who brought him over. "When I walked in there, it was like this whole rush came over me, just from going in through the front door; it was like this whole vibe. . . . It was like a very, very warm type feeling of love." Inspired by the creativity in the house, "I went and I came out with 'Flashback of Time,' and that was my first arrangement. That's on our first album, *One Step Out*. Nimbus put it out. That's how it affected me." Vibes player Rickey Kelly, also back in L.A. after two tours of duty in Vietnam and studying at Los Angeles City College, was introduced to the Ark by fellow student Dadisi Komolafe. "I had never heard anything like it in my life," Rickey recalls. "I'd never seen any musicians, live, play with that intensity. To watch the Ark—I mean the whole house was filled with energy."

The band that evolved in the 1970s still had a strong bohemian element, especially among the younger artists who lived together, but seemingly without some of the distractions of earlier years. Kachina was one of four women in residence, along with Adele Sebastian, Linda Hill, and Rasheeda, and remembers, "We were just brothers and sisters. It was all about the music. We all were here for the music and truth, and most of us were on the path seeking some spiritual enlightenment as well. So we were supportive of each other. . . . For the most part, I never saw any male/female issues there."

Adele and Linda, especially, were two of the key members contributing, guiding, and supporting the Ark and UGMAA. James Andrews recalls,

> I say this about Linda, Adele, women in the band. One thing, the women in the band were first of all musicians, and there wasn't no sexism or anything like that about them. If anything, it was like they were the sisters, right, our sisters. . . . As a matter of fact, I think Linda would cold cock you, if you came out raw. She's big enough. She could do that. But you wouldn't want to mess with Linda, anything like that, and no one is gonna let you mess with her. . . .
>
> Linda was like the mother hen type. If someone needed something, or there's certain things that the guys just would not think about, it's nice to have Linda or Adele there who would think about those kinds of things that we would not be thinking about, musically, or whatever, real world stuff. It was great to have them there and the fact that musically, if Horace wasn't there, Linda would be there to play the music, the piano part, during the rehearsals. . . . And then so many of the

songs were about her or written by her. So, she was a very integral part of that. Linda was a key person in the organization.

Adele was another key person. Committing to the Ark and UGMAA in her mid-teens, she became a musical and spiritual inspiration to everyone. Saxophonist Charles Chandler attests, "Adele was such a big inspiration. She had that sound and she was kind of the glue. She just believed in us so long, so much, and in what we were doing, and she loved all of us individually. And so, that was the thing, that she just loved all of us cats individually." James Andrews concurs,

> Adele was the flower of the organization and probably because of her health issues, the fact that she was on dialysis a lot. . . . She had delicate health, but she was a ferocious player, reader. She knew a lot about how the history of the music went, how it would sound. If we were rehearsing, and it was a question of how does the piece go or something like that, she certainly would say something about it. So, she was a co-leader, that strong. If things weren't right, she could speak up, would speak up, and people would listen to her. These big burly guys were just, "Yes, ma'am," to either one of these ladies.
>
> Adele could command. She could make all these other sixteen guys jump at the pop of her fingers, if she needed to do that. And if someone were to give her some grief, she wouldn't have to even deal with that because she had backup, plenty of backup. So, it didn't get to that. The person wouldn't be around probably because of that kind of stuff. It just wasn't where we were at that time.

Marijuana continued to be a popular refreshment, but, as Michael Session remembers, "Drugs wasn't a problem in the Ark. Years before I came up that used to be the thing. I don't understand how those guys could play like that and be that way. But Horace used to say that they knew how to play it before they got that way. It taught me. I learn from other people's mistakes." The message delivered to younger players like Wendell C. Williams was to stay away from the hard stuff. "I started learning other things about how life really was, cultural things, eating good food, no pork, not eating junk. And in those days the older cats would always tell the young cats, 'Look, I don't want you doing drugs.' They would shake you and say that. 'Yes, sir.' Back then they would say, 'Even if you see someone else doing it, it's not for you.'"

Despite all the complexities that invariably came with a few dozen musicians not only trying to play, but live together, important bonds, social as well as musical, were forged that continue to the present day. There was a strong sense of UGMAA as an extended family. When Kachina Roberts became pregnant, she and Fuasi relocated to Riverside, but planned on having the baby at home with the musicians performing in another part of their apartment. The baby came one month earlier than expected. "I remember I looked up and said, 'Fuasi, the music!' And he ran and snatched the tape Horace had just recorded of *Ancestral Echoes* with the Arkestra. Of course, Kamau did the poem at the very beginning. As the music came on, Kamau started with 'From Sapphire's womb she slid,' and as he said that my daughter actually slid. I wish you could have felt what we felt. The room was just so full of our ancestors."

For Michael Session, the Great House had a profound emotional impact. "This is where I learned to say 'I love you' to another cat. I came up hard on the street, but in the Ark we learned how to say to each other, 'I love you.'" One night at the Quag, Michael realized how precious that was. Having just learned that his grandmother, someone very close to him, had died,

> I was playing "Naima" over and over. This is my funeral song that I play when there's something touching my family. The lights were off and it was totally dark in there. And cats started coming in my room one by one, while I was playing, crying. I'd hear the door open and out of the corner of my eye I'd see one guy creep in and they'd join in the tune, one by one. The next thing I knew the whole band was in the room and we were all playing "Naima," over and over and over. When we finally stopped, it was like everybody was in tune with each other, "Yeah, I feel you." That's how close we were. We were so close. It was one of the most beautiful times of my life, because I learned how to reach out to another person, a friend, and mean it. And so we grew like that. We became intertwined with each other.

The Azz Izz—The Ark's Home Away from Home

The community of Venice, straddling the coastline west of Los Angeles and south of Santa Monica, was a center of countercultural movements in southern California for many years. In the late 1960s, Venice Beach exerted a strong attraction on musicians, particularly an array of drummers, who gathered daily on the sands and boardwalk to play. Some, including Taumbu and "Conga" Mike Daniel, would encounter and jam with artists of UGMAA for the first time in Venice. When Conga Mike arrived in Los Angeles in the late 1960s,

Venice was a drum town then, right up on the boardwalk. World-class drummers were passing through. I mean it was a drum school. The Pastore brothers, they played with Billy Cobham and people like that. Taumbu. . . . There was a timbales player, who used to play with Mongo [Santamaria], who passed through. Tim Buckley's conga drummer, a guy named Carter Collins. Big Black would pass through. It was a school, for real. It wasn't a bunch of drunks. We were out there playing every day, taking acid and shooting speed, frothing at the mouth and bulging at the eyes, bleeding at the hands. Very spiritual!

By the 1970s, the area was also home to a number of important jazz venues, including the Comeback Inn and the Azz Izz Jazz Culture Center and Tea House, which became an important performance space for the Arkestra and practically another UGMAA house. The moving force behind the Azz Izz was saxophonist Billie Harris, who arrived in L.A. in the mid-1960s from St. Louis and who became a member of the Arkestra in the early 1970s. In search of a more open scene than St. Louis offered, he gravitated to Venice.

I had bought this big Helms Bakery step van and it was the beginning of hippie time. I'm digging the free spirit that all these people had, and a lot of it was going on in Venice. That's how I was drawn to it. I was making bamboo flutes, smoking a lot of reefer, drinking a lot of wine. That was the order of the day, and playing bamboo flutes. There was a lot of music, a lot of guitar playing, a lot of drumming down on Venice Beach. African drummers, Puerto Rican drummers, local drummers. I did a lot of playing with them. I went through mushrooms, peyote, through the whole scene, and I enjoyed every minute of it.

In 1970 he found a space at 1031 West Washington Boulevard (now Abbott Kinney), one block east of Main Street, not far from the beach and across the street from the Westminster Elementary School. According to Billie, "It was in a compound of buildings, the owners of which wanted a sort of artistic atmosphere. There was a potter, a picture framer, and several small, unusual restaurants. They were delighted to have someone offering jazz music in, as they called it, The Venice Place."[13] He set to work reshaping the interior.

So I started tearing walls down, every wall in the house. I just gutted it. . . . Then we went out and scavenged carpets, scavenged these big electrical spools that we used as tables, and egg cartons for sound-proofing. I built one bandstand and then built another one on the opposite side for high rise seating. Then we fired it up. We started pulling leaves off of eucalyptus trees to make tea, cooking black beans and rice, and going out and fishing on the Venice Pier, and made filet sandwiches. We just fired it up and we'd have music every night.

The Azz Izz soon became a community cultural center with music classes and workshops during the day and poetry readings and jazz performances that began around nine o'clock in the evening and lasted until daybreak. Billie established a house band, which included, over the years, André Burbage, Conga Mike, Joey Ector, Roberto Miranda, Walter Savage, Jesse Sharps, and Daáoud Woods—all UGMAA artists. Miranda, who credits Harris as an influence on his playing, remembers, "It was a small place, but it would be packed with people from all over, all over the world actually. I remember people from Europe and Japan. The Azz Izz was really important to the history of this music, like Rudolph's. If you were fortunate to know about it, you would go."

It became an important venue for the Arkestra, where the full band performed regularly and jamming was constant. Jon Williams emphasizes, "Every chance we could get, we would scuffle up gas money and we'd go out to the Azz Izz. Jazz music. Jazz music, man, I mean the greatest cats. Most of the cats, who would hang out at the Great House, would go and hang out at the Azz Izz." Rufus Olivier, then a high school student at Dorsey, recalls,

> I used to love going to the Azz Izz. There was incense burning. Then they would serve up, at some point during the night, a big old plate of red beans and rice. That was the only kind of food, and tea with that raw sugar or honey. I remember the place always being dark. One night the band was late and I was there first. So I just started playing. I just kept playing by myself, standing up there, and the people were ready for that. That's why they were there. And I played until the band showed an hour or two later. I was just standing there going for it. The band would get there, and we'd play until the sun came up, the whole Ark, just play all night. One tune could last all night with the Ark.

Also a young artist, pianist Bobby West performed there his first night out:

> When I got there, I just can't tell you. For a kid like me, I had died and went to heaven, man. When I walked in, there was just these wonderful smells, smells of exotic, Indian incenses that I had never smelled before. They permeated the air. There were three or four cats in the corner playing hand drums. Not some drunk schmucks fucking around, these were congueros over in the corner. And the smell was the very strong, but fragrant Indian incense along with high caliber cannabis. These

were different kind of people. They didn't look like anybody I'd ever hung out with. These people were free, man. These people were free.

Some of the Ark members in the Azz Izz house band also lived there for short periods of time, including Conga Mike, Roberto Miranda, Walter Savage, and Jesse Sharps. "A lot of cats were sleeping on the stage, all over the place," Billie recalls. "They'd get up, dust themselves off, and get on the bandstand. It was serious. And that's how it was able to be so musical, so constantly, 'cause cats didn't have to come from nowhere. They were there. And we were a family." Roberto had a routine: "I would take my sleeping bag, sleep next to the bandstand, and wake up in the morning, wash up and go out to the boardwalk with my bass. I'd put my hat out and play. When I got enough money in my hat, I'd buy some breakfast and I'd go eat."

By 1973, the Azz Izz was one of the main spaces to hear new sounds. Among the artists who dropped by to play on occasion were Bobby Bryant, Jr., Frank Butler, George Cables, Billy Childs, Ray Draper, Jimmy Forrest, Vinny Golia, Billy Higgins, Billy Mitchell, Frank Morgan, George Morrow, and Onaje Murray. Others, such as Art Blakey and Bobby Hutcherson, would drop by when they were in town. Billy Childs became a regular: "It was an extended family of musicians, and you'd just go there and start playing. If someone got tired from playing an instrument, you would just get up and start playing that instrument. I remember listening to Billie Harris and thinking, 'Man, this cat is bad.' He was like Charlie Parker. He was incredible." For Childs, also a regular at the Comeback Inn and some of the other small cultural centers scattered through South Central and West L.A., the scene was extraordinarily vital: "Man, it was the most alive shit that I've been through. It was how I developed. For me it was as violently turbulent as the bebop era of New York, of Fifty-second Street, of Minton's Playhouse."

By the time bassist Walter Savage returned to Los Angeles and moved into the Azz Izz on April 1, 1976, Harris was still offering music classes with the assistance of grant support, but the days of the Azz Izz were numbered. Grants were drying up. When his wife left, Harris had to care for the family on his own. Gangs were also starting to make their presence known in the area. One night Walter was forced to battle some Crips, who lived around the corner:

So those guys would come in, and any place they could walk in free, they owned, if they could get away with it. That's pretty much how gang stuff is. So they tried to take over. Two of us in the band actually got into a physical rumble. I remember this night well because of how the rumble broke up. Billie went upstairs and got his gun. While we were rolling around on the floor, he busted a cap, and when he busted that cap everybody stood up straight as a board. That's exactly what happened. Me and this guy were rolling around on the floor, and the drummer and another guy were against the wall doing it. I guess Billie was trying to stop us, but we were really going at it and I was too old for this shit already.

Harris closed the Azz Izz in 1978, but another, similar venue continued the tradition a few miles east of Venice. Onaje's Cultural Tea House, at 1414 South Redondo near Pico Boulevard, was started by vibes player Woody "Onaje" Murray. With a similar physical setup, it featured classes, workshops, speakers, and various arts' performances. Stokely Carmichael spoke there in the mid-1970s; the Arkestra performed there. One memorable day, drummer Sonship Theus gave a non-stop, twelve-hour solo performance, an event many still remember with gentle shakes of their heads. Bassist Henry Franklin was there: "Twelve hours non-stop, and he had his vibes and conga drums set up, so after he finished with the trap drums he'd play some vibes or go to the conga drums, and back and forth, non-stop for twelve hours. He did it. This was before he was on the dialysis machine though. . . . I don't know anybody else that's done that one."[14]

The impact of these small cultural centers on many artists was significant, enabling UGMAA to expand its influence and providing additional spaces to nurture noncommercial art and the next generation of musicians. Childs explains in a manner reminiscent of Buddy Collette's recollections of Central Avenue: "Onaje's and the Azz Izz and the Comeback Inn—all of those places contributed to making me the musician I am today. It had to be nurtured in an environment of tolerance and acceptance, as opposed to a combative, nervous environment. It wasn't that. You would just go in and play, and whatever you played, it was cool."

The FESTAC Fiasco

UGMAA's expansive days of the 1970s were ruptured by the collapse of the Arkestra's plan to attend the month-long, Second International World Black and African Festival of Arts and Culture (FESTAC) in Lagos, Nigeria during January–February 1977. The first festival had been held in Senegal in 1966 and the second gathering was on a larger scale. According to historian Michael Veal, "The largest Afrocentric cultural exhibition ever staged, FESTAC brought together thousands of scholars and performing artists from fifty-five countries throughout Africa and the African diaspora for one full month of concerts, dance exhibitions, poetry readings, colloquia, and dramatic presentations."[15]

A number of individuals and groups from Los Angeles were selected to exhibit and perform at the festival, including the Arkestra. In the festival program, the Ark was scheduled to perform on Friday, February 4, 1977, from eight to eleven that evening in the National Theatre Conference Hall. The band prepared to go; everyone with a job gave notice. Residents of the Great House moved their belongings to relatives' homes or put them in storage. Passports were secured and shots administered. In some cases special permission was sought from judges to appease parole officers. Bill Madison remembers, "Adele Sebastian was on dialysis at the time. The comedienne, Totie Fields, had given her a portable dialysis machine. You know, we were ready to go. I'm all shot in both arms. There was a slot on TV—I think it was Ken Jones—he taped us." For some of the members, there would be no returning; plans were made to stay in West Africa. According to Michael Session, "Half of us were planning not to come back. We were going to hide in the bushes and play our way back."

For reasons still not clear, the Arkestra never made the trip. In his autobiography, Horace suggests deliberate sabotage, emanating from Washington, DC.[16] Fuasi Abdul-Khaliq recalls, "Everybody was so hurt, really hurt. For a long time, nobody said anything. Who could you blame? We had no control over it. We never knew who to point the fingers at, so we just pointed them at someone in DC." Others attribute it to the mysterious disappearance of visas, some to the failure of a few members to have their papers in order. Many believe it was an FBI operation to sabotage the Arkestra. Michael Dett Wilcots remembers the assurances given UGMAA by one of the key people in Washington, only to be told a few days later that there were insufficient seats on a chartered plane:

Then at the last minute, the last week before we were to go, we get a phone call saying that they didn't have an airplane to come to L.A. to pick us up. They said that we could go to San Francisco, where there was an airplane. Most of the seats are taken, but there were a few seats left. Well, that meant we couldn't take the whole band, and it meant that we would have to furnish our own transportation to get to San Francisco. Well, forget that. We can't take the whole band, what are we going to do, pick out six or seven people out of this big band to go, when we had all gone and gotten our passports and stuff?

Whatever the specific reason, the effect on the Arkestra was devastating. Session recalls his first reactions: "We're supposed to take off on a Monday and we find out Saturday night we ain't going. I was so bummed out. That night I listened to John Coltrane—*Transition*—from about eight o'clock to two o'clock in the morning. I sat up in the attic and just kept playing this one record." The disappointment and anger led to the break-up of the Great House, as many UGMAAgers drifted away. Everyone left the house, except for Kaeef Ali, who lived there for another year until the building was torn down. Jesse explains, "Everybody was kind of angry. Everybody's spirit was kind of let down. We moved out of that house. Then the Ark kind of broke up for a little while as a big thing. It probably broke down to about twelve people." "It really crushed us," according to Michael Dett. "It crushed us so bad that many people got disillusioned and disappointed from that, because we had really built ourselves up for this." Musically, the Arkestra was at a peak, according to Fuasi:

> We were so ready. Everything was leading up to this point. Everybody putting the energy into, and trying to make it as tight as possible. They were the tightest moments in all the years I was there. We lived together; we were playing all the time together. We were all brothers and sisters, one family. And we didn't use charts. We knew that stuff up and down. If Horace wanted something different, all he had to do was raise his hand and we would do something different. He didn't have to say a word, just move his hands. Crescendos and decrescendos, whatever he wanted to do, or a sustained thing if he wanted to sustain a passage for four bars, he just had to give a signal. And he was continually writing, and he would continue rewriting on the spot. As the band rehearsed, he'd change things. By doing it all the time we got to know Horace's body language. I think that would have pushed us over the top. We would have been known.

The Arkestra would recover, but the disappointment over missing FESTAC lingers to the present day. Another "What if?" was missing the opportunity to perform with the originator of Afrobeat, Fela Kuti, and his Africa 70 band. Though Fela was boycotting FESTAC, during the run of the festival he was presiding nightly in his club in Lagos. Many of the performers made the pilgrimage there and, undoubtedly, so would have the Arkestra. Horace and Fela, the Ark and Africa 70 would have been an exciting match. Fuasi speculates, "It would have been perfect, a perfect marriage, but somebody also saw this obviously and didn't want that to happen, I suppose." Arkestra conguero Najite Agindotan, who grew up in Lagos and spent time with Fela Kuti in the 1970s, was at FESTAC in 1977. Not long after settling in Los Angeles in the 1980s, he hooked up with Horace and the Arkestra and the parallel with Fela was striking:

> He reminded me exactly of what Fela did, because I was always there for his rehearsals. I saw the music he would play, and sometimes it would do me like that. And I couldn't believe that I'm here feeling the same feeling. And you know what Horace told me, he told me that's the one person in his life that he always wanted to meet and never got to meet. I told him I was going to take him to Fela, but Fela died you know. O, Fela would have loved Horace. O! Fela would have loved Horace. Boy! . . . That would have been an awesome combination.

THOUGHTS OF DAR ES SALAAM

The Institutionalization of UGMAA

The promised land is over the next crest,
beyond the next battle.

CHRIS ABANI

Despite the disappointment of FESTAC and another turnover of personnel, beginning in the mid-1970s UGMAA would finally achieve institutional
stability and a concomitant expansion of its programs. This came at a time
when it was most needed in the community, as government support for the
arts and social services dwindled and many centers were closing. With the U.S.
economy in decline during the 1970s and a more conservative political leadership in power by the end of the decade, death sentences were routinely
decreed on programs not commercially viable. Nevertheless, UGMAA was
able to achieve nonprofit status and a substantial building, "the Shop," to
ground their activity and launch programs only contemplated for many
years. Despite the increasingly difficult times within much of South Central

Los Angeles, UGMAA continued to be a force for African American culture and community. One new Arkestra member, saxophonist Sabir Mateen, was given a demonstration of the organization's importance by members of a local Crips set:

> One time I was coming from rehearsal. I was alone and I had my horn with me. I was going on a bus. The Crips were coming on the bus and were getting ready to make a swoop on me, getting ready to do something to me. Then one guy said, "Hold on! Don't mess with that guy. He plays in that group around the corner." And they left me alone. There was a whole bunch of them, at least ten of them. They knew who we were. That's what I remember about how much impact the Ark had on the community.

FESTAC Aftermath

The collapse of the Arkestra's plans to travel to Lagos, Nigeria, just days before their scheduled departure in January 1977 was a blow that shook the organization to its core. During the next few months, the Arkestra performed sporadically; rehearsals were fewer. Some members drifted away or dramatically quit, while others put their energies into small groups or other pursuits.

One manifestation of the disillusionment and anger was over the issue of small bands gigging in Los Angeles. Smaller ensembles had existed within the Arkestra since the organization's inception, and many members had performed in a variety of settings with other groups as well. Dadisi Komolafe put together his Dadisi Sextet, which included Rickey Kelly, Kamonta Polk, and Jon Williams from the Ark. Rickey Kelly organized his first band with Charles Chandler. Other members—Fuasi Abdul-Khaliq, Ishmael Balaka, Kamonta Polk, Adele Sebastian, Michael Session, Steve Smith, and Bobby West—formed Acknowledgment.

In this atmosphere, however, there was a level of tension that hadn't existed before and these developments prompted an unexpected, hostile reaction from other members. "There was a meeting and people were saying, 'All the little bands in the Ark that gig outside the Ark, if you're making money, you've got to give us some of that money,'" Michael Session relates. "I said, 'What? No way.' I think it was just some egos in the band. Cats had done this before. I didn't understand this and a lot of cats didn't understand it either. This made a division in the band. All of us that were in Acknowledgment just quit the Ark."

The dispute involved mostly those who had been in the Great House. Horace and the older members did not intervene, allowing them to find their own solution. Jon Williams, who also pulled away during this period, was disillusioned: "I didn't understand how Horace could just allow these kids to screw it up, because in my opinion that's what was happening. I felt that he needed to step up a little more. As time went on, later in years, I truly understood where he was coming from. What he was actually doing was nurturing the music, because the only way that you can get this, is that you've got to live this. So he was allowing these cats to live this thing." Michael concurs, "He was letting us work it out.... Horace was like, 'Yeah, cats can't work together, they can't work together. I mean no biggie. That happens all the time. Some's out, some's out.' He had a way of just accepting. So be it."

The disappointment of FESTAC exacerbated the money issue, which was acute and was an indication of the difficult choice increasingly facing those members starting families. Fuasi, who now had a baby girl, felt the pressure. "A lot of cats are older and they've been trying to get gigs, and are having to do other jobs, and still trying to do music. After FESTAC, everybody had to try and do something else, be part of some other system to make money." Fuasi withdrew and eventually left Los Angeles, settling for a few years in Atlanta, Georgia, before moving to Germany, where he still lives, successfully pursuing a career as a jazz musician, performing internationally, recording and leading Fuasi & Ensemble.

Some of the emerging bands were avowed followers of the UGMAA ethos and sought to carry on the tradition in their own manner. Drummer E. W. Wainwright returned to Los Angeles in 1976 after playing with McCoy Tyner and spending some time in New York. In 1977, he put together the African Roots of Jazz, which tapped the UGMAA talent pool and mission. "I was fulfilling the purpose, but I wasn't doing it with Horace and UGMAA at that time. It was the same ethic and I've always been supportive of UGMAA. When I had the money, it was there." Wainwright left Los Angeles in 1980 after recording their first album and eventually settled in the San Francisco Bay Area, where he organized the African Roots of Jazz Performing Arts Academy to foster the arts in the Oakland community.

The Creative Arts Ensemble, inspired by the Art Ensemble of Chicago as well as UGMAA, was formed by pianist Kaeef Ali. The first person he approached was Horace: "I said, 'Man, I really admire what you are doing and I want to continue working with you and being one of your composers. However, I would like to form a group that would be an extension of the Pan Afrikan Peoples Arkestra.'" The Ensemble soon included Gary Bias, Aubrey Hart,

Dadisi Komolafe, Michael Session, and Majid Shah. Other members, including David Bryant, Charles Chandler, Roberto Miranda, Steve Smith, Louis Spears, and Jon Williams, performed on occasion with the group. For Kaeef, "We were derivative from Horace Tapscott and the whole UGMAA Foundation."

FESTAC aside, more typical attrition also took a toll. Rufus Olivier won a position as second bassoonist with the San Francisco Symphony. Bobby West went on the road and then settled in New Orleans for a few years. Sonny Criss, who had worked closely with Horace and many members of the Arkestra since the 1960s, was diagnosed with stomach cancer and committed suicide on November 19, 1977, the morning after appearing with the Ark at the Troubadour in Hollywood.

However, most of the original members were still on the scene—Horace, David Bryant, Linda Hill, Al Hines, and Lester Robertson. Everett Brown, Jr. divided his time between Los Angeles and Kansas City, but Ray Draper, Billie Harris, Aubrey Hart, Bill Madison, Roberto Miranda, Kafi Roberts, and Adele Sebastian were still performing, along with baritone saxophonist John Williams in between stints with Count Basie's band.

When tempers cooled, the members of Acknowledgment rejoined. Michael Session returned in December, prompted by a radio announcement of Rahsaan Roland Kirk's death. "I just sat there in despair, just mourning, thinking, because I really dug Rahsaan Roland Kirk. Then something said to me, 'Shoot, the older cats are leaving. So it's up to me to be around as many old cats as I can before they go. Horace is right around the corner. What am I doing? Shit!' 'Horace, I want to get back into the Ark.' 'Come on.' So I got back in the Ark." Through all the controversies, Jesse Sharps remained the bandleader. And despite the difficulties in the wake of FESTAC, the Ark attracted a few new members, including vocalist Jujigwa (Juan Gray), saxophonists Zeke Cooper, Amos Delone, Jr., Sabir Mateen, and Desta Walker, trumpeter Reggie Bullen, French horn player Fundi Legohn, drummers Sonship Theus and Billy Hinton, and conguero Daáoud Woods.

Originally from Philadelphia, Sabir Mateen settled in Los Angeles in the mid-1970s after Air Force service and pursued music studies at El Camino College. While growing up in Philadelphia, he had come across references to Horace and the Arkestra in the Black Panther paper and had purchased a copy of Elaine Brown's *Seize the Time*. When the opportunity arose to attend a rehearsal at the end of 1977, he accompanied a friend to watch the Ark prepare for an upcoming performance with Sonny Criss. "I said, 'Man, I'm going to join that band. I don't know how or what's going to happen, but I'm going to be playing with that band.'" A short while later, he met Kafi Roberts, also attending El Camino, who invited him to sit in at a rehearsal. "I said, 'It's cool, but, man, my reading ain't happening, because I've seen you guys.' He told me don't worry about it, 'we'll show you all that.'" Sabir was especially impressed by flutist Aubrey Hart, who became a close friend. "Aubrey shined on flute. He was the closest flute player I've met to Dolphy, more than any of them. He was fantastic. He could play saxophone very well, and piano and drums. He was like really a marvel. This cat was a genius if I've ever seen one."

The influence of Aubrey, Kafi, Horace, and the rest of the Ark soon turned Sabir's musical direction and he left college. "Their way of teaching and the way I was learning in the Ark were conflicting. It was like learning the truth after you were learning a lie. Reminds me of the song I did on *Divine Mad Love*, 'Running into the Truth after Chasing a Lie,' even though there was another meaning to that song."[1] When Jesse enlisted in the U.S. Army in 1979, Sabir succeeded him as bandleader.

French horn player Fundi Legohn had heard of the Arkestra while a student at Hamilton High School and attended a concert at the IUCC. "It was a reincarnation. In one Sunday afternoon, I got healed, musically. That sound I never forgot, and I was never the same after that. I'm still playing trumpet at that time and I was thinking, 'I have to play in this band one day. I don't know how, but, man!'" Fundi was in the music program at California State University, Los Angeles and studying French horn with Bob Watt, when he established contact with the Arkestra through Adele Sebastian, who was also enrolled at Cal State. In 1979, he attended his first rehearsal. "You walk in and open the door, and it was just notes flying all over the place, bouncing off the walls, and it was like, 'Damn, man, do I really want to go in here? These cats are bad.' You open the door and you stand there for a minute. 'Man, I don't know,' talking to myself. 'Fuck it, man, you've got to go in here. You've come this far.' But everybody was cool and welcomed me."

Drummer Sonship Theus, one of the kids watching the band at the Watts Happening Coffee House in the 1960s, didn't start playing with Horace until 1979. At the age of thirteen he was already performing at various clubs in Los Angeles and while still in high school was a founding member of an important local band, the Jazz Symphonics, along with pianist Larry Nash and bassist Roberto Miranda. During the 1970s, he performed and in some instances recorded with Hadley Caliman, Henry Franklin, Marvin Gaye, Joe Henderson, Freddie Hubbard, Bobby Hutcherson, Charles Lloyd, John McLaughlin, and McCoy Tyner.

Perhaps the youngest member in the history of the organization was Zeke Cooper, who had started studying alto saxophone with Jesse Sharps at the age of seven. Of black and white parentage, his parents had brought him from infancy to the Last Sunday of the Month concerts at the IUCC. After a few months of lessons, Jesse took him to an Ark rehearsal and not long afterward he was performing with the Arkestra. "What this little guy was doing was incredible," Jesse recalls. "He played all the melodies with us really good, and then he would take these solos, just go off, and we'd just let him play. 'Go ahead and play, Zeke.'" Horace was especially encouraging, according to Jesse. "Horace could bring the magic out, especially when they were young, because he would never say you couldn't do it. He would just say, 'C'mon. Go ahead and do it,' just push you out there. And Zeke would just want to do it."

The Foundation and the Shop—UGMAA Becomes Institutionalized

Since the 1960s, UGMAA members had wanted to establish a more formal nonprofit organization to give them a firmer base for conducting and expanding their programs, as well as to pursue grants and other forms of financial support. Not long after moving into the Great House on Western Avenue, the first step was taken when the organization was incorporated as the UGMAA Foundation on August 28, 1975.[2] Actor Marla Gibbs took the initiative: "I went to the library and found out how to do the articles of incorporation. I put our words in there. And then I met a young man named Berry Gardner, who had the ability to know how to walk all this stuff through. So we put it together, walked it through and we had it."

As the Great House took on the aspect of a community center, and with greater focus by the members on making the Foundation substantive, office space was allocated. However, given the level of artistic and social activity, this was a futile endeavor, which prompted a search for a separate office. According to Michael Dett Wilcots, "We had a desk and a telephone set up, but the traffic was not conducive for conducting business. That's putting it really mildly. Everything was going on during the day, let alone at night. So I went over to Buckingham [Road] and I found this office. Horace and I negotiated, and I think I put up the first month's rent out of my pocket." The first would turn out to be the last rent check that UGMAA would pay. Michael Dett discovered that the building was in escrow and no owner was listed in city records. When confronted, the only other tenant in the building, and seemingly the overseer, backed off and didn't attempt to collect rent. The remaining eight months of UGMAA's residency in the three-room office near Crenshaw Boulevard were rent-free.[3]

UGMAA's incorporation enabled it to pursue nonprofit status. Under Marla and Berry's direction, it was achieved and an UGMAA Board of Directors formed consisting of Horace, David Bryant, Berry Gardner, Marla Gibbs, Michael Dett Wilcots, and Jacquelyn Simpson, a Riverside recruit who relocated to Los Angeles. One of their project-planning documents reiterates UGMAA's long-standing goals: "The specific and primary purpose for which this organization is formed is to preserve Black Music of the past, present and future," which they hoped to achieve through performance and various forms of documentation. They also aimed to "bring into focus the long-rich-hidden culture of our African Ancestors and early Black Americans through the storytelling of Black Folklore, African Tales and Modern Black Literary works for all people to gain knowledge and enjoyment." To this end, they envisaged classes and workshops, particularly for those "who have no economic means for procuring training and musical guidance." The end result, in contrast to black separatist sentiment, was to "bring about and maintain a mutual respect within a multi-cultural society."[4] It was an ambitious plan and as the board met to implement and develop the purpose and structure of the organization, it became clear that Horace envisioned even more. According to Michael Dett,

> That's when we found out that Horace had in mind a massive organization, not just a group or a small business. He really wanted a large organization that would spread across the United States and influence other groups to be subsidiaries of the Foundation, which did happen. There were a couple of groups. I believe there was one in Omaha and I believe there was one in Missouri that sort of took after our standards. They were in touch with Horace. There were several groups outside of California.[5]

Michael Dett also designed the logo featuring a pyramid resting on a ship, which expressed their mission. "We envisaged a pyramid to house the many departments of the Foundation. Within the pyramid would be such things as a music department, preservation and research department, administrative department, dance department, and workshops department. The pyramid was set upon a ship, the Ark itself, that carried the Foundation. So the ship represented the theme that Horace always used: the carriers of the culture, the mothership."

With a formal office and nonprofit standing, Horace and Michael Dett went in search of funding. Over the years, they had developed a working relationship with Mary Henry at the Avalon-Carver Community Center and, along with Sonny Criss, had supported her work with periodic concerts. Through the center and with Mary's assistance, they were able to qualify for financial support through CETA, which Henry administered locally. The Comprehensive Employment Training Act (CETA), passed in 1973, consolidated previous federal job-training programs and made funds available to cities to support training in high unemployment areas. Matching funds were provided to organizations to train people in various fields, enabling hundreds of artists, for example, in Los Angeles to pursue their art.[6] UGMAA received enough money to maintain a payroll of a dozen people. Since the Foundation had no separate funds, it would receive the CETA-funded fifty percent of their projected full-time weekly salaries and the members would work only twenty hours. It enabled many of the musicians to cover life's necessities and focus primarily on their music and on developing and expanding the programs and workshops begun at the Great House.

Even at its most formal, the office at 4050 Buckingham Road was never a typical business operation and most programs were conducted at the Great House. With a handful of artists taking on the role of part-time functionaries, it soon became another UGMAA hangout. Michael Dett recalls, "Horace liked to bring people together and get them to talk. . . . So these offices were like sitting in front of a liquor store or a tearoom, or the clubhouse or the park. Horace wasn't writing any proposals with a pen and paper. He influenced and gathered the support for this to happen, but he wrote music. When he picked up a pencil, it was to write down musical notes."

The days of rent-free office space drew to a close when the property was sold in 1976. With their tenure running out, Jesse Sharps learned of a shop for sale, Wolfe's Printing, a few miles south at 8461 South Vermont Avenue. It was owned by a Reverend O. O. Wolfe from Jamaica, who occupied much of the first floor of a three-story building with his print shop and his church. At Jesse's urging, Horace and Michael Dett paid the Reverend a visit and walked away with a new business for UGMAA. Leaving a dollar as a deposit, Horace returned with Marla Gibbs a few days later, on June 5, 1976, to sign a contract for the purchase of the business for $12,000, of which $5,000 was due by the end of the month with the balance payable over the next three years in monthly installments.[7] Marla also entered into negotiations with the owners of the building, which she also purchased for $85,000 and then put to use as an UGMAA facility, with the exception of a barbershop on the first floor.

Marla had arrived in Los Angeles from Chicago via Detroit in 1969 with three children in tow. Her marriage over, she supported the family working at a United Airlines ticket counter. Her teenage daughter, Angela, became involved with the Performing Arts Society of Los Angeles (PASLA), and not long after Marla joined their beginning acting class. Upon PASLA's demise, Marla and Angela enrolled at the Mafundi Institute in Watts and worked with Roger Mosley, Raymond St. Jacques, and Nina Foch, among others, and also performed in productions at the Watts Writers Workshop Theatre. "We were around the arts constantly," Marla recalls. "I'm still working at United, getting home, and beating a path down to PASLA or Mafundi, because you came alive. I suddenly found life!"

Marla was introduced to Horace by Angela at an Arkestra performance in 1974. "I thought they were fantastic. The music was different, and I loved the piano." Soon she was singing with the Ark along with Linda Hill, Angela, and a few other vocalists, and becoming more interested in what UGMAA was trying to accomplish. "When I came on the scene, he told me about UGMAA and what they were trying to do, and that they hadn't been able to get it through. His dream was to have the dancers, the singers, the music, all one, a union of the artists and the musicians on the higher level."

In 1975 Marla won the role of the maid, Florence Johnston, on *The Jeffersons*, a TV sitcom that ran for ten years, which gave her the financial means to purchase the printing business and the building. "I was a person who believed in putting their money in. So I owned the building that housed the nonprofit and we were all one." Marla's involvement provided not only a strong material boost for the organization but also carried a validation for some members, including Roberto Miranda. "Marla Gibbs was a big influence then. She was quite a help to all of us. She was an established artist in the community and we saw that she believed in us. We saw that she was there to say, 'Go ahead, go on, you've got it. Do it.' We all respected Marla and still do. She's still there; she never left."

UGMAA quickly settled into "the Shop," as the building came to be known, and started the "P.A.P.A. Publication and Printing Center." Some of the members with a background in printing, including Michael Dett and Herbert Callies, took on printing, using CETA funds to train others (Jesse Sharps among them) in the trade. It was not something they especially enjoyed, particularly Jesse, and Michael Session, whose day job was printing, refused to have anything to do with it. "So when they got the Shop, they figured I would get in there. But for me: 'I hate it. I don't want no part of it. I'm trying to get out of it. So please don't give no printing to me.' . . . I came there to rehearse and then I left." The equipment was old, including a linotype machine, known in the industry as "hot type," which by this time was being replaced in most businesses by computers, "cold type." But the Shop enabled the organization to print their own material, including leaflets, flyers, and brochures, and it was hoped that the additional income would support their growing programs. Relying mostly on walk-in traffic, the Shop tried to meet local needs for basic printing.

The adjacent space on the first floor quickly became the rehearsal and performance space for the Arkestra, formally titled the "Dr. Samuel R. Browne Concert Hall." Michael Dett remembers, "As soon as we got in there, we began rehearsals right away. Everybody was excited." Arkestra rehearsals took place Tuesday evenings and Saturday afternoons, usually with about twenty musicians, but any time day or night someone might be practicing there. If a visiting artist was passing through, they might end up in the Shop, as was the case whenever Arthur Blythe was in town. The facility was enhanced by the addition of a sixteen-track soundboard, with microphones aplenty and sets of speakers, all procured with Marla's assistance. Michael Dett quickly turned one of the adjacent rooms into a recording studio with a glass-fronted control booth. Concerts, as well as rehearsals, were recorded and kept in Horace's growing archive. On occasion UGMAA's archivists, Michael Dett and Ali Jihad, who had purchased a van, would transport the recording equipment to various venues, such as the Last Sunday of the Month concerts at the IUCC.

The second floor was transformed into office space, classrooms, and living quarters for members temporarily in need. This became a more pressing concern after FESTAC and the closure of the Great House on Western Avenue, some members taking up residence there, including Jesse, Michael Dett, Majid Shah, and Wendell C. Williams. The office on Buckingham Road was cleaned out and the desks, file cabinets, archival material, and other office paraphernalia were transferred to the second floor. Other office necessities were scrounged from the community and from a nearby facility. Fuasi remembers, "Next door to the Shop was an old business college that had closed down, some government supported thing. Somehow Jesse found a hole in the wall and we went through it and saw all this equipment, typewriters, desks, shelving, filing cabinets. It was all dusty and dirty, so we 'borrowed' some of the stuff for our office upstairs."

The third-floor ballroom was transformed into a performance space. While the Arkestra relied upon the first-floor space to rehearse, perform, and record, this floor was used by Marla to promote a variety of concerts, dances, and theatrical productions. Her show, *Room 227*, was rehearsed and for six months performed as a play on the third floor before she sold it to television.

For the first time in its history, UGMAA now had a reliable material base from which to operate. Departments were created to offer classes, performances, and related programs in music, graphic arts, audio-visual arts, drama, dance, and creative writing. An innovative program called "Medi-Music," an idea the organization had been promoting since the mid-1960s, was developed to bring music as a therapeutic tool into nursing homes, hospitals and various health care facilities. Angela Gibbs led dance classes, while Kafi Roberts offered instruction in martial arts. Writing workshops were available, as well as classes in printing, oral tradition, and acting, which were held on Monday nights. Music classes were offered by Horace and members of the Arkestra. Hope Foye, who had sung opera professionally in Germany and Mexico, presented a class in vocalizing. Kafi recalls, "We had Isabelle Sanford, Marla Gibbs, Roxie Roker, William Marshall. We didn't just have exclusively musicians. We had actors. We had dancers. We had Paula Kelley, Rosalyn Cash, Thalmus Rasulala. And those people were part of the drama and acting wing."[8]

Horace's vision of UGMAA as an umbrella organization that housed and supported other arts-related groups was further developed when the Malcolm X Center lost most of its government funding and moved into the building on Vermont. By falling under the nonprofit status of UGMAA, the Center qualified for support from the Greater Los Angeles Community Action Agency (GLACAA). Dadisi Sanyika, the Center's director, then joined UGMAA's Board. The Malcolm X center offered African studies and martial arts classes, a dance workshop, and a pre-school program for some twenty to thirty children—"The Malcolm X Early Childhood Development Pre-school Program."[9]

It was anticipated that the printing business would economically sustain UGMAA, but other sources were sought as well. There were occasional grants, including $2,500 from the Brotherhood Crusade Black United Fund.[10] Marla organized the Friends of PAPA to sponsor and organize fundraisers. She expanded those activities into elaborate fashion shows—"Rays on the Runway"—to raise tens of thousands of dollars for the support of drug treatment centers. In an increasingly severe economic time, it was one of the few organizations that was managing to provide substantial funds for dealing with an increasingly serious community problem. At the same time, it introduced an approach that was alien to some members, who thought the world of fashion, even cutting-edge black fashion, quite removed from the political and spiritual ethos of the organization and the music.

The Shop was active twenty-four/seven. The printing business was open Monday through Saturday, but activity continued through Sunday. The last

Sunday of each month was devoted to the concert at the IUCC. Afterward everyone would meet back at the Shop to hear the tapes of the concert. According to Michael Dett, "Horace felt you had to do this. You've got to listen to what you performed right after the performance. So we would come into the Shop, I'd set up the sound system, and we'd play back the day."

Performing in and out of the Community

The Shop provided the Arkestra with a home base, but their appearances throughout the community were unabated. The Last Sunday of the Month concerts continued at the IUCC. Concerts were also offered at the Shop and at vibist Onaje Murray's Cultural Tea House. There were performances at fund-raisers for the victims of the civil war in Angola, at the First Unitarian Church, Kwanzaa events, junior high, high schools, and colleges, and in various parks throughout South Central, even at Barnsdall Park in the middle of Los Angeles. Festivals within the community continued to feature the Arkestra as well, especially the new Simon Rodia Watts Towers Jazz Festival.

Conceived by local musician Greg Bryant, Alonzo Davis, co-founder of the Brockman Gallery in Leimert Park, and the new director of the Watts Towers Arts Center, John Outterbridge, the Watts Towers Jazz Festival began with a concert on July 9, 1977. The following year it was expanded to one day at the Towers and one day in Leimert Park. Since that time, it has been staged every year, usually the last weekend in September at the Watts Towers. The Sunday jazz event has been preceded since 1981 by a Day of the Drum Festival on Saturday. Throughout the years the event has showcased the music of African American Los Angeles with tributes to Charles Mingus, Eric Dolphy, jazz mentors, women in Watts, the black composer, celebrations of jazz, rhythm and blues, and gospel music, panel sessions with artists, and visual-arts displays from and of the community. Performing artists have been drawn from the area's rich legacy, routinely including Horace Tapscott, the Arkestra, and smaller UGMAA configurations.[11]

Outterbridge sought to mold the Watts Towers Arts Center into an institution that not only conserved and celebrated the rich artistic legacy of the community but incorporated artists into center planning. "In my mind, after I knew a little about the history of the community, I said, 'We have got to do programming that embraces the history of this region, with names like Buddy Collette, Charles Mingus, Eric Dolphy, and the story that I keep hearing about Central Avenue.'" To achieve this, he sought out musicians to help program the festivals. "Giving responsibility to Buddy Collette, Johnny Otis,

Tootie Heath, Billy Higgins, and Horace Tapscott, to help you put programming together that would be meaningful, that kind of form was the most exciting thing that could be imagined." He also drafted artists to participate in other center events whenever possible, and during his almost twenty-year stewardship, UGMAA became more intimately involved with the Watts Towers. John remembers,

> When I was doing Sunday afternoon programs for small audiences, I could call on people like Horace Tapscott and the Arkestra, or a segment of the Arkestra, to come in and provide and share who they were to very sophisticated audiences who always attended the Watts Towers Arts Center, people visiting the site from many parts of the world, not just this country. Many times Horace Tapscott and the guys would be on site at the Watts Towers Arts Center and you might be hosting a busload of German visitors that would be so carried away, you couldn't drag them away from the site, Aborigines from Australia, and on and on and on.

Outside the community, gigs occasionally materialized at more traditional venues. Horace had been associated with the Troubadour since the late 1950s, and Doug Weston periodically booked the Arkestra. The Lighthouse in Hermosa Beach featured Horace and various smaller UGMAA ensembles. Concerts by the Sea in Redondo Beach, just south of Hermosa, hosted the Arkestra occasionally, their October 1976 appearance earning rare coverage in the mainstream press, fifteen years and hundreds of performances after the organization's inception, when Leonard Feather favorably reviewed the event for the *Los Angeles Times*.[12]

A few, essentially nonprofit, locations outside the community emerged in the mid-to-late 1970s that showcased the emerging avant-garde in Los Angeles and offered performing opportunities for Ark members. The Little Big Horn in Pasadena and the Century City Playhouse in West Los Angeles were small but vital incubators of musical talent whose influence is still felt today. Though the focus was primarily the music, and not necessarily a community-arts orientation, these spaces enabled artists with similar avant leanings and attitudes toward the commercial world to mutually influence each other and further their art.

Throughout the 1960s and into the 1970s, the avant-garde in Los Angeles was inspired and nurtured by Bobby Bradford, John Carter, and Horace Tapscott. "These were the three centers. . . . Period," according to Roberto Miranda. "Those three guys were always the leaders, not to say there wasn't a lot of other stuff going down; there was. But you had to go through their school." Bradford and Carter in their various ensembles and Horace with the Arkestra provided a foundation for the next generation. In addition to the various artists associated with UGMAA, there also emerged a handful of white artists, fired by the music, whose influence continues to the present day: drummer/percussionist Alex Cline, his twin brother, guitarist Nels Cline, reeds player Vinny Golia, trombonists Glen Ferris and John Rapson, pianist Wayne Peet, and bassist Eric von Essen. Although stylistically varied, their interaction with John, Bobby, and Horace exposed them to like-minded individuals in other parts of Los Angeles and gave this small, but extremely talented Los Angeles avant-garde a cohesion and focus in an otherwise fragmented cityscape.

Through his fledgling Ibedon Cultural and Performing Arts Foundation, John Carter presented its "First Annual Festival in the Performing Arts" at Studio Z, a former dancehall at 2409 Slauson Boulevard, which was owned by visual artist David Hammons and was the center of a collective of artists including, in addition to Hammons, Houston Conwill, Maren Hassinger, Senga Nengudi, and RoHo. The Festival ran for three evenings over the weekend of May 20–22, 1977, and brought together John, Bobby, Horace, Roberto, Henry Franklin, Vinny Golia, Diamanda Galas, James Newton, Azar Lawrence, as well as local bands Acknowledgment and Vous Etes Swing.

Bobby Bradford opened the Little Big Horn in Pasadena around 1974, next door to the Ice House, a popular comedy club, as a performance space for his own and alternative music in Los Angeles. It became "a lightning rod" in James Newton's words. There weren't many options for these artists. According to Bobby, "Oh, there was nothing around town where we could do anything regularly." Consequently, it was a matter of artistic survival. "I'm not the kind of guy that can sit up without doing anything and just write music and not play. If I didn't have a place to go and play, see, I would have just turned to jelly."[13] The Little Big Horn, a modest storefront with a small stage, gave Bobby the opportunity to perform whenever he wanted. He would usually play on Sunday or sometimes Friday nights, then rent the space out to other performers to fill out the weekend. Regulars included Bobby's band, John Carter's Trio, Henry Franklin, Vinny Golia, Roberto Miranda, David Murray, Onaje Murray, James Newton, Tom Williamson, and drummers Tylon Barrea and Stanley Crouch.[14]

The Century City Playhouse was a small theatre at 10508 West Pico Boulevard in West Los Angeles. In 1977 bass guitarist Lee Kaplan began staging music performances on Sunday nights with assistance from the National

Endowment for the Arts. Until the early 1980s, it would be, along with the Shop, one of the most important venues for the jazz avant-garde in Los Angeles as well as hosting musicians from around the country, including Tim Berne, Julius Hemphill, Oliver Lake, George Lewis, and David Murray (after he had relocated to New York). Horace performed there in small ensembles and with the Arkestra on a few occasions. Charlie Haden and Bobby Bradford performed as a duo. Alex Cline and Vinny Golia appeared together for the first time and made contact with other emerging musicians. For Alex, it also offered his first opportunity to play with Horace, which he did in a trio setting with Roberto Miranda. He remembers the scene:

> It was really *the* venue. . . . I played with John [Carter] there, with Marty Ehrlich, with lots of different people who would come through town. I went there every week. Sonny Simmons played there. Frank Morgan and Benny Powell played there. The first concert of the group Quartet Music was there. In fact, that was the last concert at the Century City Playhouse. . . . The Nels Cline/Eric Von Essen duo used to play there. Just all of us in one form or another.

Strictly Grassroots—Interplay and Nimbus Records

A central theme in Larry Clark's film *Passing Through* was artists' control of their work. Not long after the film's completion, efforts were made by many of Los Angeles's avant-garde to carry out their own recording projects and to organize themselves into some form of collective. Though most were short-lived, they reinforced what UGMAA preached and left an important musical legacy.

Given the interaction of this L.A. avant-garde and their shared assumptions about producing their art, there were attempts to bring the artists closer together to pool resources and coordinate activities. In an effort to create more unity, Roberto Miranda organized a meeting of those who had begun producing their own recordings, including Horace, John Carter, and Vinny Golia, but without any tangible result beyond an exchange of information. Vinny remembers that Horace's questions "were really sharp. John's questions were more about how you distribute the records, where you make them. Horace's were more to see where my heart was. It was just like he parted the waves and went to the deep part. I was the only white guy there and he wanted to see why I did what I did, why I did music." Not long after, guitarist Nels Cline was part of an effort to launch an artists' collective that would bring together the strands of the avant-garde scene:

We decided that we needed to have a collective in Los Angeles that combined all these different streams, the Crenshaw/Leimert Park stream, the John [Carter] and Bobby [Bradford] stream. John was in Culver City and Bobby was out in Altadena and they were really just kind of their own scene. We were trying to ride some of that and figure out what to do with that, and we somehow became friends with Adele Sebastian, who is the incredibly amazing and beautiful-in-every-way flute player in Horace's Arkestra at that time. . . . Adele was so charismatic and she was so gentle and she was so beautiful, everybody was just completely blown away by Adele. . . . she became instrumental in, I think, helping to try to put together an artists' collective, and she was kind of our connection to the black community.[15]

Nels and Adele were joined by Alex Cline, Vinny Golia, Lee Kaplan, and Roberto Miranda as the core group in what was to be called ONE, the Organization for Natural Expression. According to Nels, "It was going to be multi-disciplinary, but focused on improvisers and sort of jazz-related endeavors. The idea was to have concerts and workshops, and to sponsor art exhibits based on music and all that sort of thing."[16] Unfortunately, the project evaporated after the second meeting, as the core group was inundated by a variety of lawyers, assorted artists, and hangers-on, each pushing their own agenda.

The interaction among L.A.'s jazz avant-garde received its most musical manifestation in March 1982, when many gathered for the first performance of Vinny Golia's Large Ensemble at UCLA's Schoenberg Hall. Vinny's remarkable aggregation included Roberto Miranda and Rickey Kelly from the Pan Afrikan Peoples Arkestra, Bobby Bradford and John Carter, as well as Alex Cline, Wayne Peet, John Rapson, and Eric von Essen. Rounding out the band were saxophonists Tim Berne and Wynell Montgomery, trumpeter John Fumo, and trombonists Mike Vlatkovich and Doug Wintz. In the audience was Horace Tapscott, to whom Vinny dedicated one of the compositions, "The Pale Crescent." In some ways symbolic of this brief period when the L.A. avant-garde was a frequently interactive group, this performance was also a culmination. Over the next few years, this avant-garde fragmented and the level of interaction lessened, as each segment increasingly pursued their own projects in the sprawling and dispersed Los Angeles landscape.

Greater success was achieved by some of these artists in controlling the production process and issuing their own recordings. To this end, John Carter launched Ibedon Records with *Echoes from Rudolph's*, an LP of his trio with his son, Stanley, on bass and William Jeffrey on drums. James Newton issued *Flute Music* in 1977 on his Flute Music Productions label. Also in that year, Vinny Golia recorded *Spirits in Fellowship*, a quartet date featuring himself, John Carter, Roberto Miranda and Alex Cline, the first release of his Nine Winds label that continues to the present day with a catalog of over one hundred recordings, a remarkable documentation of new music in L.A. over the last four decades. In the following year, Horace and the Arkestra were recorded by two individuals, essentially fans outside the music industry, who founded Interplay and Nimbus (later renamed Nimbus West) Records to feature UGMAA artists.

Since his disappointing experiences with Prestige and Flying Dutchman in the 1960s, Horace had turned his back on the commercial recording world.[17] There were a few UGMAA-controlled sessions during the 1970s that failed to yield albums. This was partially remedied in 2020, when Bertrand Gastaut and his Dark Tree records in Paris released *Ancestral Echoes: The Covina Sessions, 1976* (DT[RS]13). However, it was not until the late 1970s that records were issued under Horace and the Arkestra's name, thanks to the intervention of Toshiyo Taenaka and Tom Albach.

In his autobiography, Horace describes Taenaka as a regular attendee at UGMAA performances while a high school student in Los Angeles, who promised to return one day from Japan and record Horace.[18] A few years later and after some business success, he fulfilled his promise by starting Interplay Records. Between 1978 and 1983, Tosh recorded sessions ranging from Horace's first solo effort, *Songs of the Unsung*, in February 1978 to small group performances, usually trio settings, including *In New York* and *Autumn Colors*. In the mid-1980s Taenaka relocated to Japan, where he continued issuing some of the recordings on CD, but without any contact with Horace, a sore point with Horace until his passing.

The most ambitious project was Nimbus Records, initiated by Tom Albach, a longtime jazz fan in Southern California and frequenter of the club scene since the 1950s. "I would go to these clubs and talk to people and this and that, and the name Tapscott used to come up." He finally had the opportunity to see and hear Horace and the Arkestra at the Century City Playhouse in 1977. "I was so taken with the music that I went up to Horace after the show." Their casual conversation led to a number of phone calls and the subsequent purchase by Tom of copies of a few tapes from Horace's archive, just for his listening pleasure.

> I was living in Santa Barbara at the time, and I used to place myself in
> a musically receptive state and then drive up into the mountains, that

beautiful coastal range of mountains surrounding Santa Barbara, and listen to these tapes. Of course, it dawned on me that I was listening to the work of a major American musical figure. I said, "Jesus Christ, something should be done about this." So, I finally got a hold of him and said, "Look, why don't we make a recording with the Arkestra."

When he popped the question, Tom had no experience with recording or the music industry. He worked as a bookie, a successful one, which gave him the financial freedom to pursue and fund this project. His interest was not completely altruistic, but served, as well, important personal needs. "One of the things that gave me impetus was that it was giving me some relief from this growing miasma of crap that I could see happening in L.A. That's probably the main reason I did it. It wasn't because I was trying to do anybody any favor. I was just giving myself some help." His reaction to the emerging conservative political climate and its effect upon the arts and media in general merged with his passion for the music:

> Well, this is what happens when great art can capture you. And I needed some stimulation, because I didn't like the artificiality and the bullshit in the southern California scene in everything. By that time it had really turned pretty rotten with all the promotional hype. When they get the people conditioned to the point where they think that the larger, the more money-making is better, is more creative, that is a real tribute to mind control. I swear to Christ it is.

What Albach heard in Horace's music gave him a purpose. "What drew me to Horace was the same thing that drew the musicians toward him, his high level of artistic activity and thinking, and his worthiness as a person. It's hard to define it any more than that. There is just something in his music. . . . Well, simply, it captured me to the point that I felt I had to do something to help the man." That something was starting Nimbus Records, "to give Horace Tapscott some more exposure than he has had. That was the original intention."[19] A key ingredient in Horace's acquiescence was Tom's agreeing to complete artistic freedom. It was never an issue because it also represented Tom's view as well, a view partially inspired by his discussions with Horace. "The more I was involved in his presence, the more I realized what a thinker he was. And also the way he dealt with people was just something to tell me that I shouldn't say anything to him at all about [the music]. Whatever he wants to record, it's fine with me. When you start telling a creative person what to do, it's going to have a deleterious effect on the end result, any way you shape it."

In spring 1978 Tom rented studio space in Hollywood at Sage and Sound and recorded the Arkestra. A short while later he brought the band into the larger United Western studio for a session with strings. Two albums resulted, the first Arkestra LP, *Flight 17*, and *The Call*. The string session proved problematic, as Horace had difficulty getting the performances he needed from the strings, struggling with the unusual intonational and rhythmic demands of his arrangements. Albach recalls, "The idea was to put out the whole album that way, but Horace got into a heated discussion or argument with the string players. He got hung up about their inability to bend notes or something." As a result, only "Breeze" on *Flight 17*, and "Nakatini Suite" and "Peyote Song No. III" on *The Call* were with strings, the rest taken from the earlier Sage and Sound session.

The last of the three Arkestra albums issued by Nimbus, the two-LP *Live at the IUCC*, was drawn from Last Sunday of the Month concerts taped between February and June 1979. To record live, Tom contacted engineer Bruce Bidlack, a childhood friend of Alex and Nels Cline, who had been recording sessions for Vinny Golia's Nine Winds label and live performances for Lee Kaplan at the Century City Playhouse. Bruce was also a supporter of the growing avant-garde scene and its communal aspect. "It was kind of a community thing, and we all had our little specialties and helped each other out, and tried to eke out a living in the process." Money was not the overriding consideration. "My whole purpose during that phase in my life was to document the music that was going on in the neighborhood."

Of the sixteen compositions represented on the four LPs, only one, "L.T.T.," is by Horace, one a standard by Cal Massey, "Nakatini Suite," and "Lift Every Voice," the Negro National Anthem by J. W. and J. R. Johnson. The other thirteen pieces are all originals by eight Arkestra members, giving a good sense of the range of writing within the band, the fruit of Horace and the other leaders' encouragement of everyone to compose in their own fashion. From the free polyphonic structure atop a bedrock eighth-note figure in Herbie Baker's *Flight 17*, reminiscent of Horace's dark ostinati, to the Latin/Caribbean-tinged "Horacio" of Roberto Miranda, the percussive, exuberant sound of Sabir Mateen's "Village Dance Revisited," and the Native American atmospherics of Jesse Sharp's "Peyote Song No. III," the music of the Arkestra celebrated not only the culture of the African American community but also reflected the broad mix of cultural influences on the West Coast.

While the recordings capture the feeling of an Ark performance, none of the musicians have felt they represent the band at its best. The post-FESTAC Arkestra did not have the tightness that characterized earlier units. Kafi

Roberts recalls, "I don't think the band that came right after that was anything comparable to the band that preceded it. . . . They made some records, good music and everything like that. No problem with that, but all the other bands had been together for so long. All the music was good and it was still the Ark, but it didn't come across the way the other bands had come across." According to Roberto,

> The Ark at its best was never really fully realized. The talent in that Ark was so profound, the breadth of musical artistry was so wide and so deep, and the problems, the obstacles that had to be overcome were so many that for me the Ark as a whole was never able to completely overcome all of the obstacles so that the entire Ark could just relax, just completely relax and just play. . . . But, man, when it happened, bro— whoa, that group was jumping, boy. I'm talking about some serious music, man.

Following *Live at the IUCC*, Tom began recording smaller groups and individuals within UGMAA. During 1980, he recorded Horace and Everett Brown in a duo album, *At the Crossroads*, and released two albums by bassist Roberto Miranda: *Raphael*, a solo bass session, and *The Creator's Musician*. The next year, he went into the studio with groups under the leadership of Gary Bias, Linda Hill, Adele Sebastian, and Horace, and issued some of Nimbus's most successful albums. Within a few months, Adele Sebastian's *Desert Fairy Princess* became the label's most popular recording. The Horace Tapscott Trio's two volume *Live at Lobero*, with Roberto Miranda on bass and Sonship Theus on drums, offers intense, explosive performances of some classic Tapscott compositions, including "The Dark Tree" and "Lino's Pad," and Roberto's "St. Michael, Servant of the Lord." According to Sonship, "'The Dark Tree'—that's a deep piece. At Lobero I had a chance to really go, just really go into that piece. He really afforded me a different way of playing, of thinking on drums. I think a little more conservatively when I play with someone like Charles Lloyd. When we did some of those ensemble things, those were the greatest times I ever had with him." With a few friends, drummer Alex Cline drove to the Lobero Theater in Santa Barbara to see the concert.

> I was excited because Sonship was back on the scene playing that stuff after his sojourn with John McLaughlin's One Truth Band and various other detours, including his own blazingly loud electric band. . . . It was just an incredibly great concert, just an amazing evening of music, not all of which made it onto those two LPs, unfortunately. The first

piece was this very long, open, free piece that was twenty minutes at least, and everyone took extended solos. And I remember that just the drum solo on that piece was mind blowing.[20]

Tom's approach to the other musicians was the same as with Horace. "When I discussed it with Adele and these people, I never told them who to hire. That's part of the respect you have to show them. Let them play what they want to play and hire who they want to hire, and, if possible, to play as much of their own music as they can and put it in their own publishing company. I've thought that with this kind of respect, you get better music, and I did." Jesse Sharps, who played on a number of Nimbus recordings and recorded an album, *Sharps and Flats*, recalls, "We had total freedom. They never told us what to play." On the eve of her recording session, Adele Sebastian told interviewer Steve Buchanan on KCRW radio: "I will be in complete command."[21] And for Gary Bias, "Yeah, I had complete control over that." Bias even retained the finished tapes. "I still have my two-inch masters from *East 101*; that was part of the deal I worked out."

Within a few years time, Nimbus Records had accumulated a collection of tapes documenting an important part of Los Angeles's music history and released a substantial number of LPs. It was the beginning of a continuing commitment on Tom Albach's part. Despite the ever-present problems of recording conditions, equipment limitations, marketing and distribution, endemic to any enterprise of this sort, the result was an important recorded documentation that would not exist without the determination of one fan. According to Dennis Moody, who engineered the small group sessions, "What I really admired about him, is that he did something for the music scene in central Los Angeles that no one else had the balls to do. No one would take the risk and record these days. He was down there finding these guys and recording all of them and I really respected that about him."

The End of an Era

Perhaps it was an omen of the tough times that lay ahead, but in July 1978 Horace suffered a cerebral aneurysm, a stroke that, in most cases then, was fatal. The effect on UGMAA was devastating. Bill Madison recalls, "I'm working for the State of California when Horace had the aneurysm. I was just like, 'This can't be happening.' He was pretty sick. When he came home, he was very frail. It was a pretty rough period." Michael Session remembers, "Man, the scariest moment of our lives, when he went down. He was such a part of us. We all prayed, meditated, played. . . . When he came out of the operation, the first thing I heard was, 'Horace is moving his fingers. All of them.' That just cooled everybody out; everyone was so happy." For Nate Morgan, "I didn't really realize how close or what this man had meant to me until that very moment. I thought, 'Oh no, we can't lose him now.' I think the hardest thing for Horace during that whole period was that then his son [Vincent] passed away of the same thing. That was the only time I can say that I've seen him where he was kind of knocked for a loop."

After Horace had returned home, Sun Ra and his Arkestra were traveling from Arizona to a gig in San Francisco and detoured to Los Angeles for an overnight visit to see Horace. Poet Ojenke met and then drove with them to Horace's home. Shortly afterward he wrote of the experience:

> Ra had heard about Tapscott's recent bout with a serious illness and wanted to pay his respects to this famous West Coast Jazz giant. . . . When we arrived at Horace Tapscott's house, even the crickets were sleeping but Horace, bright-eyed and smiling, didn't seem to mind being roused in the early morning. Watching these two jazz maestros was like seeing history in the making. The mutual respect reflected in their demeanor toward one another as the talk phased into more eased conversation.[22]

Horace was off the scene for a few months before returning to the keyboard and his community with the nonchalance that was a trademark. Roberto Miranda recalls, "While I knew that Horace had come very, very close to death, and that his recovery was something that had to be taken very, very seriously, he was so light about it that nothing ever really stopped with relationship to the Ark. . . . What he showed me was, 'Yeah, man, it's just another blues, a slow blues, you just keep the groove and keep on playing.'" By the following January, Horace was recording *In New York* with Art Davis and Roy Haynes for Interplay Records. Though he always claimed that it never affected his playing, some, including Bill Madison, noticed subtle changes: "To my ear, after that aneurysm, it seemed like his playing got crystal clear . . . everything was more articulated."

Horace's illness was only the first of many blows. By this time some members, frustrated by having to hold down full-time, non-music-related jobs and by the increasing lack of musical opportunities, enlisted in the military. Jesse Sharps and Michael Session joined the Army in 1979, and were sent to Germany. One year after Jesse and Michael left, Wendell C. Williams enlisted in the Air Force and was also stationed in Europe. Sabir Mateen left Los Angeles in 1981 and headed east, spending time in Philadelphia with his family before finally touching down in New York, where his career blossomed, now including extended stays in Italy. Kaeef Ali and Conga Mike Daniel also left for New York, while Majid Shah relocated to Chicago. Amos Delone, Jr. went to college to pursue music studies and then embarked on a teaching career in the community. Ali Jihad, Dadisi Sanyika, Steve Smith, and Michael Dett Wilcots had growing families that demanded more of their attention and steady incomes. Steve took a more commercial route. "For a long time my priority, musically, was to try to make a living. I got on that thing, 'I want to make a living playing my horn,' and that took me on a tangent. I don't regret it. It was an education and an experience. It took me around the world and opened me up as a person."

Dadisi and Michael Dett were also feeling the effects of years of around-the-clock service. Dadisi remembers, "I got burned out in the community because on minimal resources, it's like you could never get ahead. I just got burned out." Instead, "that's when I really got into the family, going to work, and dealing with my kids. I got into my martial arts and started teaching it, and teaching at the Aquarian Center." Michael Dett reached his limits after ten years of handling much of the organization's paperwork, running the CETA component, as well as building and maintaining the archive. Disagreements over how to improve the quality of the Shop, also fed some disillusionment on his part. "I had twelve people on the CETA program, and I approached them about taking ten percent [of their salaries], pooling it, and trying to purchase equipment or whatever the Foundation needs to support the Foundation so it could have some cash flow. I was turned down. Here I am getting them checks and they're hardly working, but I was turned down by everybody. So that kind of discouraged me."

The occasional substance abuse situations persisted, which caused the periodic departures of some members. Bill Madison recalls, "Ray Draper was living here. He was an excellent tuba player, composer, arranger, a triple threat guy, but Ray and I both had this affinity for euphoria. We had a rehearsal with the Ark at the Print Shop, but we had another agenda we had to attend to first, and that took us quite a while. We were late for the rehearsal and I was in no condition to play." For Billie Harris, the closure of the Azz Izz and accumulating family problems led to a withdrawal from the music scene during much of the 1980s.

Every now and then I'd pick up the instrument, but I was out of control. I was more into dealing and using. Every now and then I'd make bamboo flutes and play. I don't know if it was heartbreak hotel, trying to smother the hurt that I had felt because me and my ex-old lady broke up. And it wasn't the hurt from our break-up, it was the hurt from her abandoning our three children and my earlier little girl. So I was raising four children by myself. I always remained sober enough to make sure there was a pot on the kitchen stove, but I wasn't growing either, musically. I'd make bamboo flutes and take care of my kids, and I was dealing stuff, weed, drinking a little here and there, and staying slightly sedated throughout this whole period.

By the early 1980s UGMAA had come to a standstill. Although better positioned than most community organizations to survive, primarily through Marla Gibbs's ownership of the building that housed the Foundation, ultimately the printing business, its equipment increasingly outdated and in need of repair, proved unviable and many key members had moved on. CETA funds had been cut by the end of 1977, and finances became more precarious. Attempts to secure grants from the National Endowment for the Arts and other agencies failed. Organizational and business skills were never strong in UGMAA. It was always a situation of artists trying to be part-time businessmen, and then not very enthusiastically. Kamau Daáood recalls, "It was always like re-inventing the wheel. We were always starting from scratch. Very few of us were academically trained. Everything we did probably was really done more from the heart center than the head center."

There was an attempt to maintain the viability of the printing business. Angela Gibbs reconfigured it as Hormar Press, named for Horace and Marla, but the improvement was marginal. According to Marla, "After a while, everybody got burnt out. As we moved on with Hormar Press, my daughter got more and more ambitious, but we learned that you do not make money with stationery and business cards." After an attempt to purchase a two-color machine fell through, "my daughter then wanted out. And I said, 'Let's get right to what we want to do with the arts.' So we got rid of all the equipment, and we opened up Crossroads Arts Academy. . . ." Horace retained the UGMAA Foundation and the Arkestra continued to rehearse and occasionally concertize on the first floor, but the building was now devoted to Marla's new Crossroads Academy.

The final blow was delivered by an earthquake, which damaged the structure of the building. "They came up with this earthquake thing and everybody had to have this test," Marla remembers. "So I spent $40,000 having it tested. They estimated $250,000 [to bring it up to code]. But in the meantime

Memory Lane came up and I said, 'Well, this makes more sense.' So I let the building sit there and eventually I had to pay to tear it down. The last play we did was *Dark of the Moon*, and we left the set there." In 1981, Marla left the building, moving Crossroads to the Inner City Cultural Center,[23] and then purchased Memory Lane, a club near Leimert Park on Martin Luther King Jr. Boulevard, which she reopened in November with performances by Horace Tapscott–led small ensembles.

Also in 1981, the Reverend Edgar Edwards, minister of the IUCC, died, bringing to an end the Last Sunday of the Month concerts, the Arkestra performance cornerstone in the community since 1973. The last concert at the IUCC was held on August 30, 1981. For September 27, the concert was switched to the Shop, but that would prove to be the final Last Sunday concert, as the building was abandoned a short while later. UGMAA then lapsed as a nonprofit institution. With the offices gone, most of the leadership having moved on, and no longer any administration to speak of, the fees to maintain nonprofit status went unpaid.

The end of the Shop and the IUCC not only signaled a scaling back of UGMAA's activities within the community, but were also symptomatic of the end of much of the community arts movement in South Central Los Angeles. According to Kamau Daáood, "By the late seventies, early eighties the outlook in the community was very different. There were very few places that exhibited art or were forums for art."

Leaflet for Arkestra
concert, 1976. (Courtesy
of Kamau Daáood)

UGMAA drama class at the Shop, December 1976. (Photo by Michael Dett Wilcots)

"Eddie Warmack" (Nathaniel Taylor) and "Poppa Harris" (Clarence Muse) in *Passing Through*, 1977. (Courtesy of Larry Clark)

The Word Muscians, c. 1977. L to R: k curtis lyle, Ojenke, Quincy Troupe, Kamau Daáood. (Photo courtesy of Kamau Daáood)

Arkestra horns in performance and paint, late 1970s. L to R: Michael Session, alto sax; Jesse Sharps, soprano sax; James Andrews, tenor sax; Herbert Callies, alto clarinet; Sabir Mateen, tenor sax. (Photo by N. Osei, courtesy of the Horace Tapscott Archive)

Horace Tapscott and Cecil Taylor at The Lighthouse, Hermosa Beach, California, c. 1979. (Photo by Mark Weber)

Horace Tapscott and Arthur Blythe at the United-Western Studios on Sunset Boulevard during recording session for Linda Hill's *Lullaby for Linda*, 25 April 1980. (Photo by Mark Weber)

Nimbus recording session for Linda Hill's *Lullaby for Linda*, 25 April 1980. L to R: Tom Albach, Linda, Everett Brown, Jr., Roberto Miranda. (Photo by Mark Weber)

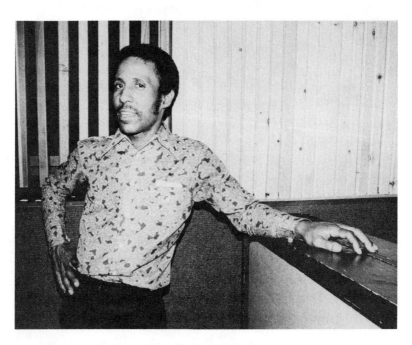

Everett Brown, Jr., 26 April 1980. (Photo by Mark Weber)

Gary Bias, alto sax,
26 April 1980. (Photo
by Mark Weber)

David Bryant, early 1980s. (Photo by Mark Weber)

Horace Tapscott Trio performing live at the Century City Playhouse, c. 1980. L to R: Horace, piano; Roberto Miranda, bass; Alex Cline, drums. (Photo by Mark Weber)

The Arkestra in performance at the IUCC, c. late 1970s/early 1980s. L to R: Horace Tapscott, piano/conductor; David Bryant, bass; Adele Sebastian, flute; Louis Spears, cello; Fritz Wise, drums; Michael Session, soprano sax; Aubrey Hart, alto sax; Sabir Mateen, tenor sax; Lester Robertson, trombone; Dadisi Komolafe, tenor sax; Herbert Callies, alto clarinet; Fundi Legohn, French horn. (Photo by Mark Weber)

Flyer for Watts Towers Jazz Festival, 1–2 July 1978. (Courtesy of Watts Towers Arts Center)

The Arkestra at the Watts Towers Jazz Festival, 7 July 1979. Featured: Zeke Cooper, alto sax, about nine years old. (Photo by Mark Weber)

Watts Towers Jazz Festival, July 1981. (Photo by Mark Weber)

The Arkestra at the Watts Towers Jazz Festival, early 1980s. L to R: Horace Tapscott, piano; Adele Sebastian, flute; Jujigwa, vocals; Herbert Callies, alto clarinet; Fundi Legohn, French horn. (Photo by Mark Weber)

Arkestra in performance at the Watts Towers Jazz Festival, early 1980s. L to R: Horace Tapscott, conducting; Al Hines, bass; Marla Gibbs, vocalist; Roberto Miranda, bass; Adele Sebastian, flute; David Bryant, bass; Ufahamu (John Walker), alto sax. (Photo courtesy of Marla Gibbs)

At the Watts Towers Jazz Festival, c. 1983. L to R: Al Hines, composer/arranger Buddy Harper, Horace Tapscott, Samuel Browne, David Bryant, Eric Priestley above David Bryant. (Photo by Mark Weber)

Horace Tapscott Trio performing live at the Lobero Theater in Santa Barbara, California, 12 November 1981. L to R: Horace, piano; Roberto Miranda, bass; Sonship Theus, drums. (Photo by Mark Weber)

Nimbus recording session for Billie Harris' *I Want Some Water*, 1983. Billie, soprano sax; Horace Tapscott, piano. (Photo by Mark Weber)

Tribute to Lester Robertson at Kabasa, 25 April 1993. L to R: Phil Ranelin, trombone; Thurman Green, trombone; Michael Session, alto sax; Tom Rawlins, trombone; unknown; Maurice Spears, bass trombone; James Andrews, tenor sax. (Photo by Michael Dett Wilcots)

An Arkestra rehearsal in Horace's garage, c. 1999. L to R: Kafi Roberts, Michael Session, Nate Morgan, Roberto Miranda, Al Hines. (Photo by Kamau Daáood)

Dwight Trible leading the Great Voice of UGMAA at the World Stage, c. 2000. L to R: Dwight, Ellen, Chini. (Photo by Jared Zagha)

Arkestra in performance at Drew Jazz Festival, 3 October 1999. L to R: Roberto Miranda, bass; David Bryant, bass; Bill Madison, percussion; Fritz Wise, drums; Michael Session, soprano sax and conductor; Conga Mike Daniel, percussion; William Roper, tuba; Taumbu, percussion; Phil Ranelin, trombone; Fundi Legohn, French horn; Rembert James, trombone; Amos Delone, baritone sax; Steve Smith, trumpet; Billie Harris (with hat), tenor sax; Danyel Romero, trumpet; Kafi Roberts, flute; Azar Lawrence, tenor sax; Jon Williams, trumpet; Charles Owens, tenor sax; Andrew Jerab, flute; Bob Givens, alto sax. Off camera, left: Nate Morgan, piano. (Photo by Tamar Lando)

Transferring the Horace Tapscott Archive to the UCLA Music Library, 2004. L to R: Michael Dett Wilcots; Stephen Davison, Music Librarian for Special Collections; Cecilia Tapscott; Gordon Theil, Head, Music and Arts Libraries; Timothy Edwards, Music Library Head of Operations; Steven Isoardi. (Photo by James Coburn, courtesy of the UGMAA Foundation)

The Arkestra and the Great Voice of UGMAA at the Jazz Bakery, Culver City, CA, 8
April 2000, "Horace Tapscott Tribute Concert." Seated front row, L to R: Kamau Daáood,
Chini Kopano, Brenda Hearns, Elesia Session, Waberi Jordan, Afifa Amatullah, Denise
Groce, Denise Tribble, Renee Fisher, Ndugo Chandler, Dwight Tribble, Amina Amatullah.
Standing back row, L to R: Robert Givens, Trevor Ware, Bill Madison, Amos Delone, Jr.,
Fundi Legohn, Nate Morgan, Rembert James, Kafi Roberts, Michael Session, William Roper,
Billy Harris, Jahid Abdullah, Danyel Romero, Steve Smith, Al Hines, Latif, Mike Daniel.
(Photo by Samir Majeed, courtesy of the UGMAA Foundation)

9

AT THE
CROSSROADS

The Ark and UGMAA in the 1980s

This is the city we've come to
all the lights are red all the poets are dead
and there are no norths

WANDA COLEMAN

The 1980s were an especially difficult time for many residents of South Central Los Angeles. African Americans were three times more likely than whites to fall below the poverty line. The continued decline of Los Angeles's blue-collar sector, rising levels of unemployment not seen since the Great Depression of the 1930s, and the concomitant rise in gang activity and the drug trade were hardships magnified by the callous indifference of a society hell-bent on conspicuous consumption and individual aggrandizement at whatever cost. By the mid-1980s, one could tune in to such prime-time television shows as the obscenely titled *Lifestyles of the Rich and Famous*. Nothing said more about the state of social relations in this country than this unself-conscious trumpeting of grotesque inequalities at a time when the poor were becoming much poorer and with fewer social nets. The Reagan Administration's "trickle down" rationale for their economic policies was a sadistic joke told by leaders and economists light-years removed from the realities of America's workers and hard city streets. For much of the African American working class in Los Angeles, discarded from the industrial sector, the 1980s took a devastating toll on the community.

The effect on UGMAA and the Arkestra was correspondingly severe. The loss of CETA funding, the Shop, nonprofit status, and the IUCC were crippling blows. And the end of easy access to public spaces, declining support for the arts, and the failure to enlist the next generation would also severely restrict the organization. Throughout its history, the Arkestra had experienced periodic waves of artists leaving but was always replenished with a fresh infusion of young, committed talent. By the early 1980s the next generation was being ground under by an oppressive socioeconomic situation, left with fewer resources within the community, and artistically moving in a different direction by reshaping the debris of postindustrial America into new art forms, such as rap. Yet, even before the spread of Hip-Hop culture among the youth of South Central Los Angeles, the economic devastation and elimination of arts and music programs within the schools and throughout the city curtailed the Arkestra's audience and potential recruits.

Los Angeles in the 1970s/1980s

Since the turn of the twentieth century, Los Angeles had attracted thousands of African Americans with the promise of blue-collar work and the opportunity to become homeowners. More than most areas of the country, it had delivered on that promise, as many people found employment in longshore, the aircraft industries, rubber factories, steel and auto plants; and one-third acquired homes. However, the absolute decline of the United States' industrial base by the late 1970s negatively affected the African American community, and the situation it faced in the 1980s was more serious than in the pre-1965 period. Not only was black L.A. shrinking as a portion of the population for the first time in the city's history, almost five percent between 1970 and 1990,[1] but by most socioeconomic indicators its standard of living had deteriorated further. Rising unemployment, decreasing residential, commercial and industrial development, the widespread elimination of social and cultural programs, and the savaging of the public school system pushed the community closer to the margins, manifested in part by burgeoning gang activity.

Overwhelmingly blue-collar by the 1960s, the community was economically devastated by the loss of jobs in heavy industry beginning in the late 1970s. By the time of the Watts upheaval of 1965, much of South Central was already experiencing double-digit unemployment. Over a decade later, as plants closed throughout the greater Los Angeles area, thousands of workers from South Central were left jobless and the numbers of unemployed soared, contributing to over thirty percent of the populace living below the poverty line, more than double the figure at the time of the 1965 uprising.[2] During the late 1970s and early 1980s, Ford's massive assembly plant and facilities owned by Bethlehem Steel, Firestone, General Electric, General Motors, Max Factor, Pabst Brewing, Uniroyal, and U.S. Steel closed. 50,000 workers lost their jobs. Even before the factory layoffs, the situation was not promising. By the mid-1970s analysts were warning that "large numbers of jobless youths with nothing to do and nowhere to turn for money will inevitably turn to more crime, first preying on blacks in their neighborhoods, and creating social tensions."[3] A few years past the mid-decade recession and unemployment for black youths still hovered at the forty percent mark, a figure that would only increase in the 1980s.[4]

Further exacerbating the situation was the passage of Proposition 13 in California in 1978 and the consequent rollback of most federal, state, and local community support programs. Proposition 13, the opening shot in the "taxpayers revolt," dramatically shrunk the state's tax base by limiting property taxes, resulting in the slashing of social services, including school funding, health clinics, and mental health facilities. By the early 1980s, the effect of the cutbacks was manifest, as public services were dramatically eroded or eliminated throughout inner-city areas. Hospitals and drug treatment centers closed and patients were thrown out on the streets. Support for cultural and social organizations evaporated. "The bloom was off the California dream," writes Joe Domanick, "and what had once been among the finest public service and social welfare systems in the country was about to shrivel up. Once the proud leader of the nation in the funding for education, California would fall from second in state spending per student to forty-eighth."[5] Schools were understaffed, in disrepair, and lacking even basic textbooks for students. Horace recalls in his autobiography: "I live across the street from Crenshaw High School. It was a first-rate school when they built it. Starting a few years ago, they didn't have enough books for the kids. How did that happen? I couldn't believe it. My granddaughter, Raisha, came up to me after her first day and said, 'They don't have any books, papa.'"[6]

The subsequent upsurge in the economy of Southern California during the 1980s, driven by trade throughout the Pacific Rim and the financial centers of downtown Los Angeles, had little impact on the black community. Not only was much of the black proletariat no longer needed, but little of this economy found its way into South Central L.A. At its best, residential, commercial and industrial development occurred only half as much as it did in any other area of Los Angeles. Urban scholar Eugene Grigsby notes "how little investment has been directed toward the Black community. Black communities are not only losing their population base, they are also not benefiting from the tremendous economic prosperity enjoyed by the region as a whole."[7]

With little chance of employment—meaningful or otherwise—and few support services, thousands of inner-city youths reverted to gang activity. As the political upheavals of the 1960s and the community's social awakening had drawn many young people away from the gangs, now many of the next generation saw gangs as the only viable option in their lives. Former Black Panther leader Elaine Brown recalls that "in the late 1960s and early 1970s, during the time the Black Panther Party existed in southern California, there was *no* gang activity in Los Angeles. Once the party chapter was effectively wiped out or driven underground, rather typical neighborhood gang rivalries were renewed."[8] The Crips and their rivals, the Bloods, a loose coalition of groups in areas around Crip territory, grew into dominating street forces in L.A. and then around the country. As one Watts teenager put it, "The only groups we know about is the gangs—Cuzz [Crip] and Blood. This is all Cuzz territory. Right across the street there, that's Blood."[9]

Organized by Raymond Lee Washington and Stanley "Tookie" Williams, the Crips emergence coincided with the government's attacks on black political and cultural organizations, the influx of drugs into the community, and the return of many soldiers from Southeast Asia, who had acquired addictions while on active duty. By 1972, they and the Bloods were rapidly spreading through South Central, and conflicts with the LAPD were escalating. Bassoonist Rufus Olivier spent his teen years learning his instruments in the midst of this escalating conflict:

There was literally shooting every night. And this was in our new neighborhood that was supposed to be better. It got so bad that I would practice underneath the windows with the lights off at night, and I would hear the shootings the whole time. But what really turned me, what really affected me and stuck in my head, was when they started using the helicopters. I'll never forget. I was lying in bed, taking a nap.

It was dusk. I'll never forget being awakened and this incredible light outside my window. I woke up, totally afraid, and heard this noise. I looked out and there was this thing, this huge thing above the house, with a light that they were able to shine over two city blocks to make it look like daylight. I'll never forget that. That was the beginning of the end, as far as I'm concerned. It just became an encampment. . . . I remember practicing scales and hearing police running up and down the street. I could hear the boots, and see them running up and down the street with rifles, and you would hear shootings. I would just keep playing. I wouldn't stop. I'd turn the light out and sit down behind the piano and book case, thinking that if something happens I'd be pretty safe, but I wouldn't stop.

It was the sudden arrival of large quantities of "rock" or "crack" cocaine on the streets in the early 1980s that would turn parts of South Central Los Angeles and Compton into war zones. According to Elaine Brown, "these south-central Los Angeles neighborhood gangs—primarily the Crips, eventually the Bloods, and their various subsets—became embroiled in increasingly violent conflicts over distribution of crack cocaine. Before that time, poor blacks did not use cocaine, as it was either too expensive or unavailable."[10] Consequently, writes Domanick, "It was they, the Bloods and the Crips, who owned the eighties in L.A., not the LAPD."[11]

As the community deteriorated, Horace continually reiterated that the influx of guns and drugs was being orchestrated from outside. It was a charge he was to repeat later in his memoir. "It's horrible and it's been put upon—the dope first, now the guns—by the establishment, by those in power, by those lawmakers who are running things."[12] On the streets of South Central, this was common knowledge, and CIA was said to stand for "Cocaine Importing Agency." It was not until 1996, when the *San Jose Mercury News* ran a three-part series in their April 18–20 editions, that evidence to support Horace's claim was publicly revealed. Research by journalist Gary Webb and other staff members clearly placed the onus for South Central's crack epidemic of the 1980s at the doorsteps of the CIA and Ronald Reagan's government in Washington.

While crack had existed since the mid-1970s and had appeared in small quantities in the community by 1980, in 1982 the trickle turned into a torrent, unleashed by Nicaraguan drug dealers working in the United States under the protection of the federal government to raise money for the Fuerza Democratica Nicaraguense (FDN)—the "Contra" army formed by the CIA to battle the victorious Sandinista revolutionaries in Nicaragua. At one point El Salvadoran Air Force planes were shuttling tons of cocaine from the growing fields of Colombia to a U.S. Air Force base in Texas, where the shipments were routed to Nicaraguan Contra agents in Florida and California and then to their distributors in the black communities. By 1984, some one hundred kilos a week were being sold to the Crips and Bloods, who controlled the streets. Through their Nicaraguan connection and intermediaries, the gangs were also sold a range of weaponry and communications devices, including Uzi submachine guns and Colt AR-15 assault rifles.[13]

The Contra war was not a military success for the United States, but the drug dealers—former wealthy landowners, businessmen, and supporters of the ousted dictator, Anastasio Somoza—emerged relatively unscathed in the 1990s to live comfortably in a more conservative Nicaragua, partly off the largesse of the American taxpayer. No one in the United States government was held accountable. Their contacts in South Central, however, faced life prison sentences, while the community was left with years of nightmarish violence and a more forbidding and stark social landscape. "Crack cocaine had fostered a 'gangsta' culture and become the primary economy of black America," writes Brown. "In that cancerous decade or so, the use and distribution of crack cocaine in the black communities of America had come to destroy the lives of millions of black people and their children, as it would their children's children."[14]

The Crisis of the Community Arts

The situation facing the Arkestra and UGMAA in 1982 was another manifestation of the desperate times experienced by many in the community. UGMAA was moribund and the Arkestra was without a central space for the first time since its inception, when Linda Hill's home off Central Avenue became the first UGMA house. For two decades a series of houses served as living quarters, rehearsal spaces, occasional concert halls, and social gathering places. They were support systems for artists, mediums of cultural and social exchange, and they fostered an attitude of artistic creation by and for the community. They housed the future of the Arkestra, usually the younger artists without many outside commitments and personal obligations, those willing and able to push into the background the more material concerns of everyday life to pursue their art and lives as community artists.

With the deterioration of the community's social infrastructure and the eradication of cultural centers and music programs in many schools, there were fewer opportunities to perform in the community. The Arkestra's use of public spaces had been at the core of its work since its inception and now that area was dramatically contracting. As historian Robin D. G. Kelley observes, "Black working-class communities in Los Angeles were turned into war zones during the mid-to-late 1980s. Police helicopters, complex electronic surveillance, even small tanks armed with battering rams became part of this increasingly militarized urban landscape."[15] The use of public spaces became increasingly precarious, extending even to residents' front doors. "But as the streets become increasingly dangerous, or are perceived to be so, more and more young children are confined indoors, limited to backyards. . . . For inner city families, the threat of drive-bys has turned porches and front doors, which once spilled out onto sidewalks and streets as extensions of play areas, into fortified entrances with iron 'screen' doors that lock from the inside."[16]

With fewer opportunities to perform in the community and the decline of music programs in the schools, the pool of young artists that the Arkestra had tapped in the past dried up. For the first time in its history, the band was without the next generation. One of the few avenues open to young artists was the Wind College at 2801 La Cienega Avenue, opened in 1983 by clarinetist John Carter, bassist Red Callender, flutist James Newton, and saxophonist Charles Owens, which offered instruction on most instruments to students from six to fifty, with the majority in their late teens and early twenties. Despite their best efforts, the school did not survive the Eighties.[17]

Mortality and illness also depleted the Arkestra. On November 1, 1982, tuba player Ray Draper was murdered on the streets of Harlem, while visiting family in New York City.[18] Between 1983 and 1992, the Arkestra lost four of its staunchest members: Everett Brown, Jr., Linda Hill, Lester Robertson and Adele Sebastian. Long-time drummer Everett Brown resettled in Kansas City, Missouri, in the mid-1980s, as Parkinson's disease impaired his physical abilities. Trombonist Lester Robertson, performing less frequently, died in 1992.

Perhaps more than anyone else, Linda Hill was affected by the loss of a central space for UGMAA. Since the early 1960s, she had been the Ark matriarch and was usually one of, if not the central figure in the various houses. The loss of that space and the changing climate throughout society affected her deeply and was a contributing factor in her escalating addiction. Her son, Leland, relates, "She's playing, but this is the period when her addiction was getting the best of her. They didn't have a central pad then, and at that period she started doing real bad. Then she was diagnosed with cancer. I don't think she took treatments. She didn't believe in it. She just didn't want to go out like that; she would rather just play it out." Linda died in July 1987 with only a few friends in attendance. For some, like Jesse Sharps, Linda's passing typified a growing callousness that seemed to be taking over Los Angeles. "It seemed about that time around L.A. people stopped caring about each other a lot. In the old days the Ark had a big network and that never would have happened."

Another tragic moment in the history of the Ark was the death of Adele Sebastian on September 30, 1983, at the age of twenty-six from a lupus-induced kidney ailment. Adele became sick in June 1973 about the time she joined the Arkestra. In addition to her various musical and cultural involvements, she worked with Dr. Randall Maxey and the staff at the Research Foundation for Ethnic Related Disease, authoring a manual for dialysis patients titled *Living with Hemodialysis, The Most Important Run*, and during her remaining years served as a counselor to patients.[19]

From her arrival on the scene until her death, she was one of the central figures in UGMAA and one of the most beloved. Fundi Legohn recalls the steadying influence she had over the members: "Even while going through all of that, Adele had a way with all of us knuckleheads getting out of line. Adele was soft-spoken. She just floated, man. Her playing was just sublime. She had a way with herself that when the knuckleheads would get out of line, she would speak and cool everything out." And to Fuasi,

> You got thirty cats and they're all big guys, and they're all rough and had done all this stuff, and she's in the middle, her little flower self. She was like a real flower, a beautiful blossom, in a briar patch so to speak. So Jesse wrote this tune called "Desert Fairy Princess." . . . She really showed us an inner strength that all of us were trying to strive for, but that she had mastered. . . . I mean everybody fell in love with her, and not just for sexual reasons, but just for the love that she had. She was such a special person, who came into the midst of us, and everybody, no matter what you were about or how hard you were, even if you were a killer, you melted, just melted.

When Kafi Roberts joined the Ark, Adele was the section leader for the flutes and insisted that everyone know the music. "Adele stayed on my case. 'Now, if you don't learn this music, you can't play in the band. I'm the section leader, so I'm telling you what to do.'" The respect they developed for each other turned into a strong bond:

> It was kind of like a knife in the heart when she passed. Boy, I took that real hard. She was just like one of my own biological sisters to me. The thing that sticks out the most about Adele is that she was just full of

love and very compassionate, very outgoing. She would give you the shirt off her back. The only thing that I ever knew to upset her was the music not being played right or not being presented right, but I never heard her say anything negative about anybody or have any negative thoughts. She was just real positive. She lived for the Ark; that was her life. To see someone get up off their sick bed and do certain things, and never make excuses for her illness, and always just put out 110%—I'll always have just undying respect and love for her.

Adele's commitment was graphically demonstrated at a concert just a few days after a serious illness. Kachina Roberts tells,

One time, I believe she had a heart attack and she was out for two days or so. When she woke up, there was a nurse there and she said, "Give me my horn." So the nurse gave her the horn and she sat up. She said, "What day is it?" She told her it was Saturday or something like that. She said, "What time is it? I have a concert." They were like, "Adele, you can't go to a concert. You just had a heart attack." Adele wouldn't hear of that at all. She made that hospital get a van and a nurse and they brought her to the concert. She sat in a wheelchair and she played. When it was time for her solo, she stood up and she played her solo. When the concert was over, she got back in the wheelchair and went back to the hospital. That's what Adele was like. She was just an incredible, incredible person.

To this day, recollections of Adele invariably bring an awkward pause, a nervous clearing of the throat, and usually a few tears to the eyes of Ark members. To Rufus Olivier,

Oh—she was—oh. I was in love. Her—ah—she was just—When I see her in my mind's eye, I see an incredibly warm smile. She was one of the warmest human beings I've ever known. I was in love with her. When she played her flute, that personality was in there, that sound came rolling out like that. How do you meet somebody that has no angst or hatred towards anybody? You got that feeling when she was in the room, even when she was struggling with the kidneys. She was just a walking, talking piece of love.

And for Jon Williams, still moved by his close relationship with Adele,

We were due to get married. I would take off my job every other day, make sure she got to the hospital. She had lupus and went through hell.

I wanted to love her and take care of her. And she knew that, and she saw all of the juice I was putting into her well-being, and she just kind of backed off of me. And she told me why, too. It was basically due to the fact that she knew she didn't have that much longer to live. And she didn't want to put me through that kind of thing. That's what I'm talking about, right there, man. . . . [A while later] I was blessed to meet my wife, Loretta, and we had two beautiful kids. I'll never forget where I was when my wife came to me and said, "Jon, Adele is dead." [long pause, cries] That was deep, man. What was even more deep was that it was my wife that told me, and that she had enough respect for me and Adele, because she knew how much I loved Adele. Deep, man, deep. Ain't nothing but jazz music. Ain't nothing but jazz music.

With the additional loss of these veteran members, the Arkestra ceased being the kind of everyday force within the community that it had been. "Wasn't no Ark in the Eighties," pianist Nate Morgan remembers. "The Ark was on hold for a while, really up until the Nineties. [Horace] might have pulled together one or two large ensemble concerts that were grant funded or something, but basically he was just dealing with solo piano and smaller groups, trios, quintets." Word musician Kamau Daáood recalls, "We'd still do things at the Watts Towers. We were still the community's Arkestra. When gatherings were called, they still looked for us to supply the music, but the community in general had changed."

Keeping the Motion in Troubled Times

While not tapping into the youth base as the Arkestra had done in previous decades, there were some new recruits and veterans who returned to contribute. UGMAA archivists Michael Dett Wilcots and Ali Jihad returned when Horace asked them to record a month-long engagement in 1982 at Memory Lane, the club taken over by Marla Gibbs. Jesse Sharps returned in the mid-1980s from service with the U.S. Army in Europe. Thurman Green, who had been an occasional participant in the second UGMA house during the later 1960s, took Lester Robertson's place as the main trombonist in the ensembles. Roberto Miranda recalls, "What a player, man, subtle, like leaves on a tree. You don't realize how special this cat was." Multi-reed instrumentalist Charles Owens had grown up in San Diego, a contemporary of Arthur Blythe. He settled in Los Angeles in 1970, but it was not until August 1982, that he got a call from Horace to play at Memory Lane, beginning an association that would last until Horace's death in 1999. Saxophonist Ufahamu John Walker performed with the Ark in the early 1980s, and bassists Jeff Littleton came around in 1988, as did Trevor Ware, when he began his association with Horace and the Arkestra during a West Coast tour in Horace's quartet.

Nigerian conguero Najite Agindotan of the Efere griot family grew up in Lagos and was an avid follower and sometime performer with Fela Kuti. He left Nigeria after FESTAC in 1977, disillusioned by the military government's attack on Fela at his compound, the Kalakuta Republic, in Lagos. "It was because they had just bombed Fela's house. They did all kinds of terrible things to him. They killed that whole nourishing vibe, that atmosphere of awesome, rich, spiritual consciousness."[20] In 1978, Najite traveled to the United States, settling in Los Angeles by 1980. He quickly established himself and during the mid-1980s was invited to perform at the Watts Towers Jazz Festival by John Outterbridge. The Arkestra was also on the program, and Horace's affinity for Fela Kuti and his music drew him to Najite, who recalls that first meeting:

> I got off stage and everybody shook my hands. Then I met this guy with a hat, thin-looking, tall. He walked to me and I held out my hand to shake his, but he just grabbed me and it was such a strong hold. Nobody had ever held me like that before, until that day. He held me tight and said, "You are my brother. You are my brother." I said, "Okay, okay, my brother, okay." I didn't know exactly who he was. Maybe he was one of those crazy guys. Then he pulled me back and said, "You are my brother." I said, "I know, I know. Okay, okay." Then he walked away. Later that night, I heard his big band on the stage. I saw this guy and I said, "Oh shit! This is why this man held me like that!" I saw Fela through him. Yes, I saw a lot of things come together for me. I said, "Okay, that is why this guy said I was his brother." So after, I went to him and I said, "Yes, you're my brother." He said, "I want you to play with me sometime." Finally, I think it was . . . at the Kabasa, that was the first time we really played together with the whole band. It was beautiful. From then on I would play pretty regularly with Horace.

Just before Fela's passing in 1997, Najite sang to Horace some of the instrumental lines from Fela's "Why Black Man Dey Suffer" with his brief lyrics. Horace then composed "Fela Fela" in his honor, one of his last compositions. "I told Horace about the music and Fela. I then sang the horn line in those words. He sat on the piano and took the horn line I put to song to a different height. He blew my mind." Horace performed the piece only four times before passing, and only once with the Arkestra in a concert at the Los Angeles

County Museum of Art on July 24, 1998. Its first release came in 2019, when Bertrand Gastaut's Paris-based Dark Tree records produced *Why Don't You Listen?*, an excellent CD of that concert.

The Arkestra remained a presence, even if its nonmusical activities had lapsed and members spent much of their time performing in smaller groups. Major cultural events within the African American community, such as the Watts Towers Jazz Festival, usually featured the Ark, and there were still college and prison gigs. When there was a community event, the Ark was usually there and, when needed, rehearsals continued in Horace's garage, high school music rooms, and whatever other community spaces could be arranged. French horn player Fundi Legohn was now heading the music program at Jefferson High School and facilitated the Arkestra's rehearsing and occasional performances there.

> We had a few rehearsals over there for little gigs coming up. . . . There's just so much emotion and love in that music, man, that you want the next day to be another rehearsal, another gig, and they were so few and far between, that for me that was pretty depressing because that was my life. Even though we weren't playing it regularly, I would hum melodies every day from Ark compositions, man. That was my lifeflow. And then being at Jeff I had the feeling that I was upholding the legacy of Sam Browne, letting the kids know what came before them here. And the music that I selected for them to play, we would play the tunes and I would introduce them to the music and let them know what Central Avenue was all about in the day. So I had a proud group of kids, even though it was primarily Latino. I taught the culture and how our cultures have come together. We had blacks and browns fighting each other and my thing was turning that around.

However the form of the Arkestra and UGMAA might change, no matter how dramatic the personnel swings might be, their lives were being community artists and they would continue living those lives, regardless of circumstances or the size of the band. According to Roberto Miranda, "The music stayed alive. Horace kept us all together as often as he could in a large ensemble." Outside the Arkestra, small group performances proliferated, as various ensembles of UGMAA artists continued to combine and recombine, performing in community-based as well as the more traditional venues. If the Arkestra had lost some of its cohesion, the smaller units became tighter. Roberto notes, "So it seemed that Horace kept us all together in small groups. . . . We would hire each other and stay together in smaller groups, and then come together whenever Horace would call us for the Ark."

The post-Shop era was inaugurated when Marla Gibbs took over and opened Marla's Memory Lane in November 1981, just east of Leimert Park, with a Horace-led small group. The following August, Horace returned to lead an ensemble for the entire month. Among the musicians performing were saxophonist Charles Owens, trumpeter Oscar Brashear, trombonist George Bohanon, Melvin Moore on trumpet and five string violin, Louis Spears on cello, bassist Roberto Miranda, and drummer Sonship Theus. For Sonship, those nights at Marla's may have represented his best work with Horace: "Man, he had a gift for playing piano. I've never heard anybody play like that. We did some Ark things, but we did things in ensembles that were just some phenomenal things. . . . That was some of the most powerful playing I've ever heard him do, where he got a chance to really stretch." Charles Owens was similarly impressed. "We just created something. You could write for trumpet or violin. You could write for violin and cello. . . . It was just a great gig, and one hell of a band." Sonship, in particular, made a big impression: "The power, his foot speed, his hand speed, and the feeling that he got, just a powerful, great drummer. He was right up there with Tony Williams, as far as I was concerned. It's the power, the groove, the feeling and the taste, and knowing how to fill phrases and still be right there. And he'd make you play. You had to. You'd be dead in your behind. That's what impressed me about him, and then his dedication. He was a pure jazz musician, a pure spirit."

Over the next few years Horace also teamed up with other local musicians. At the Comeback Inn in Venice, he performed in trios with Roberto Miranda and James Newton, and on other occasions with bassist Charlie Haden and drummer Albert "Tootie" Heath. He performed in loft concerts at the Brantner Design Studio in downtown Los Angeles and at the newly opened Catalina's Bar and Grill in Hollywood. There would be duo sessions with pianist Nate Morgan in Santa Barbara and at the Jazz Bakery in Culver City, and also with Mal Waldron in Santa Barbara. In April 1984, he appeared in a trio setting at the Wadsworth Theater in West Los Angeles with Charlie Haden and drummer Billy Higgins.

Although Arkestra performances and community activity declined dramatically during the 1980s, the series of recordings that began in the late 1970s for Interplay and Nimbus Records introduced the Arkestra and many of its members to national and international audiences. Distribution for both labels was limited, but interest in Horace and the Ark was growing nevertheless, and performing opportunities outside the West Coast were emerging, particularly in Europe. To deal with these possibilities Horace sought managerial assistance. Later in 1982, a young writer and sometime booking agent, David Keller, wrote a cover piece for the *L.A. Reader* on Horace. David had more than a nodding acquaintance with Horace, who approved of the piece, telling him, "They always just play all the sensationalist stuff, but, man, you nailed it." A little while later he asked David to represent him, and Horace now had an agent for the first time in his career. While still remaining rooted in his community, Horace was starting to explore more of the landscape of the professional jazz artist.

In his new role, Keller met Nimbus Records owner Tom Albach. At Tom's suggestion they proceeded to organize a "World Piano Summit" for February 17, 1984, at the Wilshire Ebell Theatre in Los Angeles, featuring Andrew Hill, Randy Weston, and Horace in an evening of solo performances. On the eve of the concert, Tom explained his purpose and selection criteria to Don Snowden of the *Los Angeles Times:* "The men were selected because of a contribution they've made to music. . . . They've never lowered their standards and become stooges for the record companies by playing junk. They refused to do it, and that's why they've gone into such eclipse."[21] The concert was a success, and Keller remembers, "That's a beautiful hall, and everybody sort of in the scene in L.A. said, 'Jeez, you did an incredible job!'" Vinny Golia was one of those present. "Horace played first and he made that place like a church. It was deep. He hit the first chords and all of a sudden it was like going into this thing, into the tunnel of Horace. You were going to be there for a while. Then Andrew Hill came, and his thing was really abstract. Randy Weston played third and he just swung the crap out of the place. It was a really wonderful night of piano music."[22]

Gigs followed up and down the West Coast at various clubs and on university campuses, some assisted by grants from the California Arts Council. Koncepts Gallery in Oakland, Kuumbwa in Santa Cruz, and the Bach Dynamite and Dancing Society in Half Moon Bay, California, were populated by Tapscott enthusiasts. By the mid-1980s David was booking Horace and his ensembles throughout North America. Engagements followed in Vancouver (a duo with Steve Lacy) and Ottawa, Canada, in Dallas, sponsored by the Afro-American Artists Alliance and the Dallas Museum of Art, in Boston at the Willow Club, in New York at the Jazz Center, and in Washington, DC, at various spaces including the One Step Down.

In 1991 David finally arranged a date at the Village Vanguard in New York City. "Max [Gordon] had passed and Lorraine booked Horace. I just pestered and pestered and pestered, until she said yes." Stanley Crouch, who had been in New York since 1975, recalls, "When he came to play at the Village Vanguard, he shocked these piano players in New York. They didn't know he could play that much. I mean, he was serious. And he was playing for real. When he came to New York, he let them know something. He was playing his originals and he was playing standards. I mean, he was smoking on all of them."

Horace-led small groups also appeared in Europe. He played Verona, Italy in June 1980 followed by solo tours over the next few years organized by Tom Albach. By 1983, European trips became a staple of his yearly schedule. For David Keller, it was an easy sell. "It's so much better than here. It was really going well. That basically continues almost every year." Performing solo and in groups that ranged from duos to octets, Horace and various UGMAAgers performed in Austria, Belgium, Finland, France, Germany, Italy, Switzerland, and The Netherlands. In 1983 a Horace-led quartet of Dadisi Komolafe, Roberto Miranda, and Everett Brown (in one of his last appearances) performed at the Willisau and Karlsruhe Jazz Festivals. As one of the most eloquent and searing improvisers in the Arkestra, Dadisi impressed European audiences, was offered a number of other gigs, and remained for a while in Europe to play after the rest of the band returned home. Vinny Golia, at Willisau with his own band, recalls, "So Dadisi's playing. Horace gets up from the piano and he stands right in back of him, going, 'Play! Play! Yeah! Play! Go!' He was just on this cat like glue. 'Yeah! More!' Just whipping him into this frenzy thing. He was gonna get every ounce out of him. It was amazing. It was unbelievable." The next stop was at Karlsruhe and Vinny was asked to play with Horace for the first time.

> We played one tune of Horace's, which I think was "Sketches of Drunken Mary," and the other one was Roberto's tune, "St. Michael." Man, it got to this one place where it was just up there. It was really cool. It was like, "Whoa!" So I got the Horace bug. I wanted to play with him all the time. I'm telling you, it was like having this big fire under your ass and there was no way to escape. It was deep. And Everett, man, he put this thing in there. As soon as he hit the cymbal, it was like the air changed.

Horace's traveling also brought him in contact with other artists, including Cecil Taylor at Willisau. Jesse Sharps and Michael Session, then resident in Germany, drove to see Horace, as well as festival headliner Taylor. Jesse remembers it as "the most incredible concert I've ever seen."

So they came and asked Cecil when he wanted to play. Did he want to play last? He said, "No, no, no, no. I'm not playing last. Horace got his quintet here. I'm not going up against his quintet. You let Horace play last. I'll play next to last." So we got in the wings and Cecil came out. Whew! I've seen him play a lot of times, but he came out and did something I'd never seen him do. He crawled inside the piano with his whole body. He got up in the grand piano and got inside of it with his hands and legs, and started scratching and kicking at it, and just going whap, whap, whap, whap-whap-whap. Oh man, fantastic sounds. . . .

So he was finished and then I was just talking to Cecil and said, "You ever hear Horace play?" He said, "I've never heard Horace, never heard any of his recordings. I've just heard of him." So we were just standing there, when Horace started. We didn't move the whole concert, and Cecil was really into it. After it was over, he said, "Man, Horace is one of my favorite piano players."

Other highlights included an appearance by the "Horace Tapscott Arkestra," an octet that appeared at the 1987 Verona Jazz Festival and offered the bottom-heavy instrumentation of a typical Arkestra lineup, including David Bryant and Roberto on basses, Fritz Wise and Donald Dean on drums, along with Arthur Blythe, Gary Bias, Thurman Green, and Horace. In 1988 Horace gave a solo recital at Berlin's Philharmonic Hall.

For over forty years Hans Falb has directed the Konfrontationen avant jazz festival in Nickelsdorf, Austria, presenting some of the finest musicians in the world. During the 1980s, particularly, he invited many musicians from the Los Angeles scene. On July 10, 1987, Konfrontationen featured the "Together Again Band." It included the three leading figures in the Los Angeles avant-garde jazz movement of the 1960s and 1970s—Bobby Bradford, John Carter, and Horace Tapscott—and some of their closest collaborators, Arthur Blythe, Roberto Miranda, and Donald Dean. The band also performed two days earlier on July 8 at the Gaststätte Waldsee in Freiburg, West Germany. The members of the sextet had performed with each other in different configurations for some twenty-five years, but these were their only appearances together in one band on the same stage. The Together Again Band performed and Horace Tapscott played solo as well. John Carter was also to play in a trio with pianist Cecil Taylor and drummer Andrew Cyrille. According to festival director Hans Falb, this trio was expanded to a quintet when Cecil Taylor asked violinist Leroy Jenkins and Roberto Miranda to join the group.[23] This produced one of Roberto's most challenging and inspiring performances, and one of his best stories:

> I've got a great Cecil Taylor story for you. When I met Cecil Taylor I was on tour with Horace Tapscott. Maybe I had met him before. We were in Nickelsdorf, Austria. It was John Carter, Horace Tapscott, Donald Dean, and me. Horace's band was going to play one evening and Cecil played solo piano. And then the next evening Horace played solo piano and Cecil's band played.
>
> After the concert the first night we're all just hanging out, and Cecil and I start talking. So he says, "Miranda, I want you to play with my band tomorrow night." I said, "Yeah, well, I'd do that for free. Beautiful, man. I'm at your service." . . . It was [Leroy Jenkins] and John Carter and Andrew Cyrille and Cecil and me.
>
> I made the mistake of getting dressed up in a three-piece suit. We're outside. It's a warm day. About 45 minutes into the first tune, I'm soaking wet. I'm just soaked, and I'm really, really, tired. My whole body is saying, "Ahhhh!!" And I prayed. "Lord, I'm really, really tired. I've played everything that I know how to play. And I really need some help."
>
> Now when the band was first setting up, I asked Cecil, "I've got a pretty good ear, I trust my ear. But if it's okay with you, I'd like to set up close to your left hand so that maybe every once in a while I could just check over." And he said, "Yeah, sure man, no problem." I said, "Cool." So I set close to Cecil's left hand.
>
> Cecil played the entire concert like this [covering his left side]. So now I'm soaking wet, I'm really tired, and I just finished making this prayer to the Lord, man. And by the way Cecil had never looked up at any point. He was just "rrrrrrrr." All of a sudden these notes started moving through me. These big, beautiful, fat notes. And it was the only time in the entire concert Cecil looked up at me, and goes, "Yeahhh-hhhh." And then he goes back. I will never forget that as long as I live. That was an amazing experience, just amazing.

Recorded Work in the 1980s

Recordings of UGMAA artists continued primarily through Tom Albach's Nimbus Records, until he left for Amsterdam in 1989 for a six-year sojourn. Tom recorded Horace's monumental solo sessions and various small group ensembles, some led by Horace and others by various UGMAA musicians.

The solo sessions were recorded at the Lobero Theater in Santa Barbara, California. Opened for the first time in 1873 and rebuilt in 1924, its stage has supported a coterie of piano masters from Vladimir Horowitz and Sergei Rachmaninoff to Dave Brubeck and Herbie Hancock. Over a three-year period from 1982 to 1985, Horace recorded twenty-six hours of solo piano for Nimbus, which has released, as of 2022, eleven volumes, comprising approximately nine hours of that music. Albach broached the idea for the first solo session with Horace at UCLA in March 1982, during the initial performance of Vinny Golia's Large Ensemble.

> Afterwards, outside, we were milling around and saying hello to whomever, and he seemed really depressed. Horace was the type of person that socially, if he was really depressed, he would try to conceal it from you. But he didn't even bother trying to conceal it with me. I don't know what it was, but it must have had some reference to the inability to get his own Arkestra played. Anyway, I said, "Look. You like that piano at Santa Barbara in the Lobero Theater. Why don't we do a solo piano recording there?" He said, "Alright."

The sessions were done late in the evening with only Horace, Tom, and engineer Dennis Moody present. According to Dennis, "Horace would play for hours and we recorded all of it. We just let the tape roll and then ask to take a break; put another tape back on and then play some more." Tom took a seat in the rear of the theater. "We turned all the lights out, and I went and sat in the back row. There was one real dim overhead light, but he could barely see the color of the keys. I sat in the back of the thing and I felt like a potentate. The fix that he gave me, it just made everything so crystal clear about where we missed the road, where a paradise could be, if we had taken that road. That kind of a state, man, it's just so enriching that you can't describe it." From then on, he was sold on Horace's solo work, which became his principal focus.

> I listen to his solo playing. If I can get off with that fifteen years later at seventy-five years of age, I know fucking well that I'm listening to the greatest goddamn interpreter of the waltz that this country has ever produced. That's what I'm listening to, because I am a critical son-of-a-bitch, and the waltz is the strongest form of music on earth and this man recognized it. The only guy that I compare him with is Prokofiev. That's where I put Horace with his expansive folk themes and his love of the waltz.

UGMAA ensembles were recorded as well. Dadisi Komolafe's work in Horace's small groups and as leader of his own bands convinced Tom to record him. The result was one of Nimbus's most powerful records, *Hassan's Walk*, which featured Dadisi on alto sax and flute, supported by pianist Eric Tillman, vibist Rickey Kelly, Roberto Miranda and Sonship Theus. Dadisi also appeared on Rickey Kelly's album, *Limited Stops Only*, recorded at the same time. Saxophonist Billie Harris led a quintet with Horace, David Bryant, Everett Brown, and Daáoud Woods for his *I Want Some Water*. The label also documented the work of two other exceptional L.A. pianists, Curtis Clark and Nate Morgan, during the 1980s. Clark had taken up residence in Amsterdam during the mid-1980s, but Albach managed to record five albums in California and in Europe: the solo *Deep Sea Diver*, and leading small groups in *Phantasmagoria* (with Roberto Miranda and Sonship Theus), *Amsterdam Sunshine, Letter to South Africa*, and *Live at the Bimhuis*. Nate Morgan's three albums as a leader—*Journey into Nigretia, Live in Santa Barbara*, and *Retribution, Reparation*—display not only fine ensemble playing and Nate's impressive command of the keyboard, reflecting the influences of both Horace and McCoy Tyner, but also showcase his talent as an exceptional composer. Other ensembles were recorded, including a sextet session led by Jesse Sharps and a trio date with Kafi Roberts on soprano saxophone, Aubrey Hart on flute, and Horace on piano, the latter not released until 2021 on Nimbus West Records as *Tapscott + Winds*.

Not long after Tom left for Amsterdam in 1989, another recording opportunity arose, when live sessions were recorded at Catalina's Bar and Grill in Los Angeles by Hat Art Records. Horace was put in a quartet with his longtime local friend and sometime collaborator, clarinetist John Carter, but UGMAA artists were ignored by the record company in filling out the band. Instead, bassist Cecil McBee and drummer Andrew Cyrille were flown in. Recorded over five nights, from December 14–18, 1989, two CDs were issued under the titles *The Dark Tree I* and *II*. While McBee and Cyrille were kindred spirits—Cyrille would continue his association with Horace afterward in some East Coast gigs and European recording sessions with French saxophonist Nelli Pouget—they were not then familiar with the music of Horace and other UGMAA artists, which was the focus of each night's performance. Kafi Roberts, who attended the rehearsals, relates,

> To sit in rehearsals with Horace and see those guys struggle with that music, I thought, "Man, I'm really privileged to be associated with Horace." They literally had to stop rehearsals and say, "Wait a minute,

Horace, you have to explain this stuff." And there were some things that Andrew Cyrille really, really struggled with. I've been listening to Andrew Cyrille since I was a kid. He's was one of the greatest drummers ever, man. And Andrew said, "Horace, man, you're telling me to play two, and you want me to play five and seven. How many meters is this?" Horace said, "There's a couple more. I'll let you know when we get to it." That really, really impressed me. These are the greatest musicians in the world. For them to come in and have the time that they had with this music, I said, "Man, maybe I do know how to play." The Ark is really a unique band.

The pairing with John Carter was unusual as well. While both were explorers of the harmonic and rhythmic boundaries, John's spare, pointillistic note selection and phrasing contrasted with Horace's cascading single-note runs, massive clusters and pounding percussiveness, particularly in ostinato-driven pieces like "The Dark Tree." It was precisely this contrast, however, that made for exciting music. Vinny Golia believes John was pushed into new territory:

> John's really good, but Horace plays so much that you have to go over it. You can't go in it. It's kind of hard to wiggle your way through it. With the saxophone it's a little more powerful. The clarinet is like a filigree instrument. But that being said, it's really nice to hear them play together. It's one of my favorites. I think it pushes John to an area where he's not used to being, because he had gone away from the piano for such a long time. Then he's back with somebody that powerful. It's just amazing. I was there and I know John was having trouble, but that trouble was him being pushed beyond his place.

A Gathering in Leimert Park

While *The Dark Tree I* and *II* represented an artistic triumph for Horace and his stature was rising internationally, he never relinquished his role as a community artist. When not on the road, he remained in his community and more often than not was a presence on the streets and in the few small clubs and spaces remaining. His performances at Catalina's Bar and Grill featured compositions by Thurman Green, Roberto Miranda, Nate Morgan, and Michael Session that were not included on the two *Dark Tree* CDs. He had also broached the subject to a few people during the 1980s of again expanding Arkestra and UGMAA activities and had asked Nate Morgan to start reorganizing the band book. By the late 1980s Horace thought it was time to move the Arkestra forward again. Despite the savagery of the social landscape, or perhaps because of it, it was a sentiment in support of community arts that was shared by others, who gathered in the Leimert Park district of South Central during the 1980s.

Leimert Park has served as a cultural gathering place since African Americans moved into the community in substantial numbers in the 1960s. Originating in the 1920s as a planned development by Walter H. Leimert some six miles southwest of downtown Los Angeles, it was home to working- and middle-class white families until the Watts upheaval of 1965 provided the final push in a white flight begun in the 1950s. The centerpiece of the community is a small park at Forty-third Place and Crenshaw Boulevard, designed by the Olmstead Firm, who also crafted New York's Central Park. A number of streets radiate from the park, one of which, north-running Degnan Boulevard, contains a block of small shops between Forty-third Place and Forty-third Street. With this "I"-shaped formation at the center, the area became home to the community arts movement in the 1990s, a conscious carrier of a tradition stretching back to 103rd Street in Watts in the 1960s and to Central Avenue before that.[24]

In the wake of the fires of 1965 and the unrest of the mid-1960s, the first art space in Leimert was opened in 1967 by brothers and artists Alonzo and Dale Davis at 4334 Degnan Boulevard. Art students in their early twenties and active in the civil rights movement, they were confronted with a lack of opportunity for black artists. Dale recalls, "One of [Alonzo's] finest teachers . . . said, 'What are you going to do when you leave? After you have this arts degree, what are you going to do?' Basically the suggestion was 'I think you better get a teaching credential because you won't have a place to show.'"[25] The Brockman Gallery, christened with their mother's maiden name, was the first in Los Angeles devoted to the work of African American artists.

They not only established an outlet for artists, including John Biggers, Gloria Bohanon, Nathaniel Bustion, Elizabeth Catlett, Dan Concholar, Houston Conwill, Kinshasha Holman Conwill, Mark Greenfield, David Hammons, Suzanne Jackson, John Outterbridge, Noah Purifoy, John Riddle, Betye Saar, Ruth Waddy, Timothy Washington, and Charles White, but also exhibited Chicano artists, as well as Japanese-American and some European Americans. For the next twenty years they served artists and community and were the foundation for other artistic enterprises in the area. The gallery offered classes and workshops in the visual arts and expanded to include adjoining storefronts, offering spaces for rent to working artists. In 1973, they organized

Brockman Productions to produce larger artistic events in the area, such as festivals in the park that would bring together musicians, visual artists, poets, and the community. The Brockman Gallery would remain a Leimert Park institution until its closing in 1990.[26]

Just as the crack epidemic was taking over in South Central, drummer Carl Burnett began ARTWORKS 4, a small performance space around the corner from the Brockman Gallery at 3436 West Forty-third Street, in 1982. The space opened with a live radio broadcast of a performance by Billy Higgins and his band. There were appearances by the George Coleman Quartet and Burnett's quintet performed most weekends with Chuck Manning on saxophones and a group of UGMAA musicians—Jon Williams, trumpet, Bobby West, piano, and Christy Smith, bass. Carl also performed regularly with Horace during the 1980s and they used the space to rehearse as well.[27]

Though Carl had intended nothing more than an occasional music and poetry performance venue, he responded to the growing interest from the community and expanded the programs to deal with emerging needs. "Everything just kind of developed. In dealing with it different things would come up. . . . So, I said, 'Well, okay, let's try it and see what happens.' So we began to advertise and people showed up." A weekly vocal workshop was started by Cynthia Utterbach, Phyllis Battle, and Dee Dee McNeil, which would also feature artists such as Ernie Andrews. Vocalist Dwight Trible, soon to be recruited by Horace to play a major role in the Pan Afrikan Peoples Arkestra, attended the workshop and also sat in with Carl's quintet on weekends. "We got involved with doing some one and two act plays; started creating workshops for musicians and singers and poets," Carl recalls. "We had a women's discussion group, a book club on women writers. . . . I got a few of them to come and talk."

ARTWORKS 4 also had a men's discussion group that Carl felt "was really enlightening. There was not many situations where men had the opportunity to come together and discuss things in life. . . . We would discuss everything from sex to nationalism, anything you could think of we dealt with." And as rap was starting to gain a national presence in the early 1980s, there were sessions at ARTWORKS 4. "We presented some of the first young rap artists who came and performed. At one point we had about one hundred—almost two hundred young people, man, inside and outside—because we had rap artists, you know, expressing themselves and dealing with things from a beginning perspective, because it was new. But we dealt with it from a positive aspect. And, man, there were so many young people, and we had kids from almost every high school in Los Angeles that sent some group that they had over to perform."[28]

Other individuals, also interested in developing a community arts scene, were moving into the area. Ben Caldwell, a graduate of UCLA's film program in the 1970s, who had worked on *Passing Through* and was a former professor at Howard University, returned to the community in Los Angeles, worked with Brockman Gallery and ARTWORKS 4, and in 1984 opened a space called the KAOS Network at the corner of Forty-third Place and Leimert Boulevard, a few doors east of Degnan and across from the park. Ben established KAOS as a training facility for people in the community interested in the technical aspects of filmmaking and sound production, but he quickly opened the doors to those interested in pursuing other arts. KAOS became an artists' studio, classroom, production center, poetry space, and through the internet, a connection with other community spaces throughout L.A., the Caribbean, and Africa.

Brian Breye moved his Museum in Black onto Degnan Boulevard during this time, offering West African art and artifacts, as well as a stunning collection of historic racist memorabilia. Marla Gibbs continued to put the benefits of her acting career to community use, purchasing the Vision Theater on Forty-third Place and a nearby space on Degnan that became the new home for her Crossroads Arts Academy. Laura Hendrix opened Gallery Plus, exhibiting the work of local artists. Visual artist Ramsess set up his studio in 1982 in one of the Brockman storefronts, and was soon contributing to the scene by creating mosaics for the area, including one of Paul Robeson, which presided over Degnan. Hunched over his table of tiles day and night, at times working on the sidewalk, he offered a strong, everyday artistic presence in the community.

Nevertheless, by 1989, as the Davis brothers were winding down the Brockman Gallery and Carl Burnett was closing ARTWORKS 4, it seemed that Leimert's best years as a community arts center had passed and that the appearance of two new spaces, The World Stage Performance Gallery and 5th Street Dick's Coffee Company, would make little difference. Poet Kamau Daáood was determined to make an attempt at keeping the community arts alive and on June 1, 1989, rented one of the small Brockman spaces at 4344 Degnan, opening the World Stage to house rehearsals, performances, and arts classes. Kamau removed the small stage platform and seats from Carl's place and dragged them around the corner. When he opened the Stage, he ordered three keys. He kept one for himself and gave the others to Billy Higgins and Horace Tapscott, who would be at the core of this movement. Jazz performances were offered on the weekends, and during the week a variety of workshops were available to the community in the tradition of ARTWORKS 4. But his inspiration reached back to the community aesthetic he had absorbed twenty years earlier in the community arts movement that had arisen in the wake of 1965 and from being a member of UGMAA.

> The work that I have been engaged in is very much an outgrowth of the values that I learned in the Arkestra. Horace would always say that our work was contributive rather than competitive. It was things like that. In Leimert Park it's the difference between developing poets and guiding poets in the direction of understanding stories, understanding the voices around them, the role of taking these voices and giving them back to people in a way that they can see themselves, rather than going in and setting up a slam and gearing it towards making money.

A few years later in April 1992, Richard Fulton opened a coffee house, 5th Street Dick's Coffee Company, on Forty-third Place, a few doors west of KAOS, and around the corner from the World Stage. Richard was a Vietnam veteran, but alcohol abuse had rendered him homeless, a transient resident of Fifth Street in downtown Los Angeles's Skid Row for six years. By the late 1980s, he was in recovery, pursuing his carpentry skills, and contemplating his future. For Richard it was merely a matter of focusing on his passions. "The three things I love to do most in the world is sit on my ass, drink coffee and listen to jazz." It was a short step to the idea of a jazz coffeehouse serving the community. "Music tends to make a community have rhythm. Once you get rhythm, you can get harmony. And that's the heartbeat of the community. So you take jazz music and you play it loud enough and you play it long enough, in the environment, what happens is that people come together. Because the music is the thing that makes everything gel. It's alive."[29] He set about renovating the small storefront across the street from Leimert Park.

Despite these new beginnings, it seemed the area would not recover from the loss of the Brockman Gallery and ARTWORKS 4. Both had been highly visible in and out of the community, and had offered a wide range of programs that integrated the arts with community life. Vocalist Dwight Trible remembers,

> I would go by and there would never be anything going on. Kamau used to call my house: "Dwight, we're having a thing down there tonight," just calling anybody who would come. One night we went by there and they were having some kind of jam session. Hardly anybody was there; nothing was going on. Don [Muhammad] said, "Hey, man, when are you going to come and do a gig down here?" I said, "Oh, we'll do something." But really in my mind I was thinking, "Man, ain't nothing happening down here."

Dwight's attention was elsewhere. He had hooked up with Jon Williams and Bobby West and regularly took bands into a nearby club, Jazz Etc., behind the Crenshaw Mall. He and his wife, Denise, did return to the World Stage, however, one evening to hear Jon and Michael Session play. It was at this event in the early 1990s that he heard Horace perform for the first time.

> Michael asked Horace would he come and play. Horace got up there and played something a cappella. And when he started playing, it was so intense. It was too much for my senses to handle. I had never heard anybody play like this before. I said, "Man, who is this genius that we've got in this neighborhood?" And then I wondered, "How does he stand hisself? How is he able to handle all of this emotion that he has within him?" Because it seemed that if I had all of this going on inside of me, it would be difficult for me to sit still. It's just too much. When he got finished, I was exhausted. That just stuck in my mind, this man with all of this great emotion, living in this community.

Dwight finally relented and over the next two years performed a few times at the World Stage, despite the lack of an audience.

> When we would play, hardly anybody would be in the audience. Richard had just opened up 5th Street Dick's, but I mean *nobody* was there. The whole street was dark. We used to tell everybody on the break to go around there and buy some coffee or tea from Richard. We'd go around there and I'd talk to Richard. And he'd be telling me all these big, grand ideas that he had about music being upstairs and he'd show us all. But in my mind I was thinking, "I feel sorry for you because I'm afraid this place is not going to make it and you're going to be closed in about a month from now."

In less than a month's time, the events of April 1992 would transform the African American community and much of Los Angeles in ways similar to 1965, again bringing the community arts movement and the Pan Afrikan Peoples Arkestra into more prominent roles. With the hope of eventually offering live jazz performances, Richard opened 5th Street Dick's shortly before the end of April 1992. Within a few days some of his first customers would be members of the U.S. military occupying South Central.

THE HERO'S LAST DANCE

The '90s Resurgence

i want to wipe the bull's-eyes
off the backs
of your children

KAMAU DAÁOOD

Unlike the struggles of the mid-to-late 1960s, the uprising that shook Los Angeles in April 1992 was a multiracial reaction to accumulating social and economic inequalities and injustices. In South Central, the previous fifteen years had witnessed the further impoverishment of the community and elimination of much of its arts movement. Even so, there was less talk of revolution and more of simply making gains through self-help. Though initiated earlier, the uprising saw the spread of a truce between the Crips and the Bloods, which led to their issuance of a proposal to rebuild much of the infrastructure of South Central and to make it more capitalistically viable.[1] It was a far cry from the days of political activism and at least verbal commitment to the ideals of revolution that swept through the community in the

1960s, but after the flatness of the 1980s, to paraphrase Marx, even small hills appeared to be mountains.

While the uprising did little to alter the economic status quo, it did to some extent lift the torpid social atmosphere of the 1980s and galvanized the community's artists. The Leimert Park arts scene had been struggling to survive, upheld by a core of committed artists and small merchants, many of whom had participated in the Watts Renaissance of the 1960s, some with strong memories of Central Avenue. After April 1992 it became the heart of a rejuvenated community arts movement. For the scattered members of the Pan Afrikan Peoples Arkestra, some of whom had started coalescing and broaching plans for a more dynamic community presence in the 1990s, it was catalytic. As the arts movement emerged in Leimert Park, Horace and his UGMAA artists, once again, were in the middle of it, asserting the importance of community and its griots.

Class and Racial Conflict in Los Angeles—The 1992 Upheaval

While the Watts upheaval of 1965 may have shocked much of white America, it came as no surprise to most residents of inner-city communities and to anyone listening to what some artists and activists had been proclaiming for the previous few years. By the late 1980s much of the black community was struggling, not to improve upon its situation of twenty-five years earlier but merely to return to that level. Unlike the early 1960s, however, there was no one of the stature of James Baldwin to warn about the coming fire. There were no Malcolm Xs nor Martin Luther King Jr.'s articulating the plight of the oppressed to a national audience. But there were voices for those willing to listen. One of the few art forms expressing social consciousness, even if minimal compared to the 1960s and 1970s, was rap music. As Kamau Daáood describes, "It wasn't really until the late '80s and '90s, with the whole youth movement and HipHop culture, that a folk or people-based culture began to rise, that wasn't being stimulated by marketing wizards."

From Melle Mel's "The Message" to Run-DMC's "It's Like That," followed by the more politically focused work of Public Enemy and Boogie Down Productions, MCs called attention to the worsening conditions in America's inner-city areas. The seriousness of the situation was reflected most sharply in gangsta rap, which emerged from the streets of South Central Los Angeles in 1986 and 1987. With its glorification of lumpen street mentality and confrontationist attitude to the police, it served as a lightning rod for the political establishment throughout the country to justify greater police budgets, attacks on civil liberties, more severe jail sentences, and a dramatic expansion of the prison system as solutions to the country's ills.

What also emerged from the raps of Ice-T, Niggaz with Attitude (NWA), and others was an expression of the continued impoverishment of these communities in Los Angeles, their brutalization by an unrestrained police department, and the seething anger that was building. Ice-T's "Escape from the Killing Fields" portrays South Central as an impoverished land deformed by an oppressive economic system.[2] While NWA's "Fuck Tha Police" challenges the LAPD as simply a larger gang to combat.[3] Confirmation from an unlikely source came from retired LAPD Deputy Chief Louis Reiter, who was charged with investigating police abuse, when, in 1981, he observed that officers "have developed the philosophy that everybody who is black is a bad guy and the only way to (police the community) is to be a hard-driving street army, to show them who is boss. And as a consequence, their tactics are terrible most of the time, and the shootings we get show that the tactics are terrible most of the time because they are running it like (police) are king of the street."[4]

The growing movement for police reform in the late 1970s, in response to an unprecedented wave of LAPD killings, fifteen inflicted by the notorious choke-hold, was short-circuited by the early 1980s as the crack influx exacerbated turf battles between the Crips and the Bloods. By the late 1980s, there were more than three hundred gang-related killings per year, more than half the national total.[5] Under Chief Daryl Gates, one of former Chief Parker's protégés, the issue of reform was easily brushed aside and the use of violence by the Police Department continued unrestrained with the nodding acquiescence of most establishment liberals. "So just as it looked as if the LAPD would, in the early '80s, become less brutal," writes Joe Domanick, "South-Central succumbed to malign neglect and the cops were then told to take care of it."[6]

The violence escalated. "People were being shot or choked to death," relates Domanick, "for wielding such items as a liquor decanter, wallets, sunglasses, gloves, a hairbrush, a silver bracelet, a typewriter, a belt, a key chain, even a bathrobe."[7] Commenting on the Christopher Commission investigation of the upheaval, John Gregory Dunne writes, "Compared with officers in the other five largest US cities, LAPD cops killed or wounded the greatest number of civilians, adjusted to the size of the police force."[8] Officers involved were rarely found to be out-of-line, let alone prosecuted. According to a *Daily News* investigation, "Since 1985, LAPD officers have been involved in 387 shootings—153 of them fatal, police records show. None of the officers was criminally charged, district attorney records show." During that same period internal investigations led Gates to discipline thirty-five officers for injuring or killing people needlessly, which usually meant a suspension of anywhere from three to 129 days. Only two were dismissed.[9] A *Los Angeles Times* series in 1982 posed the following after the brutalization of another innocent man, Udell Carroll: "But to disillusioned blacks inclined to doubt the police side of any story, the question becomes: Why is the police version always right and the version told by the Udell Carrolls always wrong?"[10]

The filmed attack by the LAPD on Rodney King of March 3, 1991, revealed to an international audience that the Udell Carrolls were right and provided a graphic demonstration of what had become standard practice vis-à-vis the black community. Rather than respond to this grotesque assault, people waited for justice to be dispensed by the legal system. Novelist Chester Himes's observation of the Watts uprising is again apt: "We are a very patient people."[11] The subsequent acquittal on April 29, 1992, of the four police officers charged galvanized people throughout Los Angeles from Watts to the San Fernando Valley, from East L.A. to Hollywood—blacks, whites, and Latinos—to take to the streets.

The killing of fifteen-year-old Latasha Harlins the previous March by a Korean store-owner who suspected the teen of stealing a container of orange juice, and the owner's subsequent sentencing to five years probation, had already inflamed feelings throughout the black community. The Rodney King verdict was the final provocation, shattering faith in a legal system seen by many as the last peaceful opportunity for justice. Over three days a multiracial explosion of class and racial anger shook Los Angeles, as thirty-eight died, almost 4,000 buildings were torched, and one-half billion dollars of damage inflicted throughout the city.

Though as politically limited and unfocused as the Watts uprising, unlike 1965 this was a black, white, and Latino protest, even if inchoate, against the systematic impoverishment of much of the population during the Reagan years, of looting at the top, such as the savings and loan scandals, and of the continuing officially sanctioned police abuse. Not long after the upheaval, the *New York Times* editorialized, "The fires of Los Angeles cast harsh new light on the way America writes off places, urban wastelands that are more patrolled than policed. Even worse, America writes off people—another generation of young black men."[12] It was typical of first reactions that they were focused on African Americans, although the event transcended the black community. Nevertheless, the events of April also made starkly clear that Los Angeles had discarded an entire community.

The Community Arts Movement in Leimert Park

In the Leimert Park district of South Central, as the fires raged nearby, merchants and artists gathered in front of their small shops and performance spaces along the 4300 block of Degnan Boulevard, just east of Crenshaw Boulevard, to provide mutual assistance and support. The threat of fire forced Brian Breye, the proprietor of the Museum in Black, with the assistance of some artists and shop-owners, to move his inventory of African art and slave-era artifacts across the street. He and others along the block stood guard over the next few days to protect their spaces and to assert their value to anyone bent on destruction. According to Richard Fulton, "That's how Leimert Park came together. That's how Leimert Park became Leimert Park because of '92. Because everybody stayed to protect their property and things and we all got to know each other and we all became a community right then and there. . . . That's what pulled us together, that's what bonded us. . . . It just lit up this area."[13]

Similar to Watts almost thirty years earlier, the Leimert Park scene changed dramatically within weeks of the upheaval, as the streets, shops, and performance spaces filled with people. Dwight Trible witnessed the transformation:

> All of a sudden things started happening there. The next thing you know, I went around to Richard's place one day and the whole street was just full. It seemed like it happened overnight. It was just full. Then Richard started having music. I think he started on Sundays. Then he got bolder and started having it on Friday, Saturday, Sunday. Then he was having music seven days a week. The whole street was just really lit up. Then people started bringing more shops there and stuff like that started opening up. It was just a very beautiful, beautiful time.

For many people of varied political consciousness and persuasions, the community arts scene, its performers and griots, once again became a means of personal and social exploration in dealing with the events and ramifications of April 1992. It brought people out and brought them together, and by 1993 the Leimert Park community arts scene was ascendant. At night there were as many as four or five spaces within one and a half blocks offering live music. Peaceful, crowded sidewalks gave rise to continuous conversations with friends, acquaintances, and, just as often, strangers. Artists of many different styles and genres, community residents, fans and supporters from throughout Los Angeles mingled on the streets and in the spaces. The World Stage offered weekend jazz performances and during the week there were jam sessions, poetry, drum, and vocal workshops. 5th Street Dick's hosted jazz performances most nights, featuring seasoned professionals as well as neophytes, and usually lasting until four or five in the morning. Richard also placed tables and chairs on the sidewalk, creating a common area for conversationalists, chess players, and kibitzers.

On Thursday nights, beginning in 1994, Ben Caldwell's KAOS Network became home to Project Blowed, a successor to the rap nights at the Good Life Café with a wide-ranging collective of hip-hop artists from members of the Freestyle Fellowship and Jurassic 5 to break dancers and local rappers. Rejecting gangstaism and the commercialization of the music, some were crafting their styles for the first time, while others were seasoned veterans. Aceyalone, one of the Fellowship, seizes the mic:

> Five thousand boomin' watts
> KAOS Network state of the art
> Audio-video, filming and editing
> Capoeira and meditation, computers and tele-beams
> At the workshop, every Thursday night
> Where we give the new definition to opening a mic
> I hope you all don't mistake glitter for gold
> While we doin' it and puttin' it down
> At the Project Blowed[14]

To complete the range of secular African American music represented in Leimert Park, Laura Mae Gross relocated her blues club, Babe's and Ricky's Inn, from Central Avenue to a space next to KAOS in 1997. Lady Walquer Vereen and Pat Taylor created a Dance Collective, offering African American stylings, as well as West African dance. Earl Underwood's Leimert Park Art Gallery opened, featuring the work of West African as well as local artists, while Kongo Square (later Zambezi Bazaar) offered jewelry, sculptures, books, and records.

In the midst were Horace and members of the Arkestra. Nate Morgan ran jam sessions at 5th Street Dick's for a few years. Horace performed there and in various ensembles at the World Stage and on the streets and presided over the festivities in Leimert Park every New Year's Eve. Drummer Donald Dean recalls, "No matter what he was doing, he would always play New Year's Eve there. And there was no money involved in these things, not very much anyway. Horace is that kind of guy. I would do it mainly because of Horace. Just playing with him and being with him, that's what made it special." To Michael

Session, "Leimert Park is now the home of the Ark because of the World Stage, 5th Street Dick's and Horace's house is just a few blocks away. All the creative juices have been concentrated from the hood in this little area."

In terms of its ethos and the aesthetics of the individuals involved, this burgeoning arts scene drew from the legacy of Watts in the 1960s and Central Avenue before 1950, even if it lacked the dimensions of its predecessors. For poet Ojenke, one of the major figures within the Watts Writers Workshop, there are parallels as well as striking differences. "What we have today in Leimert Park is probably the hub of the cultural/artistic thing for the black community here in Los Angeles now, but it in no way compares to the amplitude and just the force that was existing during that time." For bassist David Bryant, a veteran of the Central Avenue scene, Leimert Park was growing in old and fertile soil. "We all have the same idea. It's all a part of the same movement. The Ark is part of that. 5th Street Dick's, the other places, are all sort of interconnected. Yeah, we're part of the renaissance. It's not the organization as it was, but it's the same idea. I know how Central Avenue was and it's moving in the same direction." To others, such as the griot and poet laureate of Leimert Park, Kamau Daáood, the roots and inspiration are deep in the heritage of African Americans:

> my heart is a djembe drum
> played upon by the dark hands
> of a fifth street cappuccino
> my invisible turban is an angelic saxophone solo
> the sidewalk is hardened mud cloth
> massaging the soul of my feet
> i do West African dance steps
> reflecting the sun off my Stacey Adams shoes
> i stand on the o.g. corner
> tell old school stories with a bebop tongue
> to the hip hop future
> i see new rainbows in their eyes
> as we stand in puddles of melted chains[15]

The Post-1992 Arkestra Resurgence

Since the late 1980s Horace had been planning to reenergize the Pan Afrikan Peoples Arkestra and UGMAA. He and Michael Dett Wilcots prepared lists of creative objectives and priorities during 1988 and 1989, including plans for reopening a print shop and for a variety of concerts and jazz-related media programs.[16] Horace had earlier told saxophonist Yaakov Levy (Joshua Spiegelman, Joshua Natural Sound): "I'm gonna start a young cats Ark and I'd like you to be in it."[17] Though most would be unrealized, they testify to a renewed vigor. Pianist Nate Morgan recalls, "I can remember around '88 Horace mentions that he wants to start doing some things with the Ark again, wants to start rehearsing, that there's a possibility of some things coming up."

There seemed to be growing interest from other members as well. Saxophonist Michael Session returned from Germany at the end of 1987 and a few months later was in the studio recording his first CD as leader, 'N Session, featuring Horace and other UGMAA musicians, including Henry Franklin, Nate Morgan, Steve Smith, Sonship Theus, and Jon Williams. Michael was back and anxious to play, a sentiment shared by others.

Trumpeter Steve Smith, who'd been off the scene for a while, raising his family and working for Xerox and as a professional musician, was coaxed back by Michael for the date and was soon playing with the Arkestra on a regular basis.

> I'm sitting at home one day and the phone rings and it's Michael Session. He's back in town. He says, "Look, I'm getting ready to cut this album. I want you to play on it." I said, "Look, man, I really appreciate it, but I haven't really been playing that kind of music. Get me on the next one. I really appreciate it." He said okay and hung up. Then the phone rang right back. "No, man! You're playing on my album. That's bullshit!" I said, "Okay, man, okay." That was it. I was back in the Ark then.

Jesse Sharps, also back from Europe, resumed his role as bandleader and organized rehearsals and performances at Kabasa, a performance space on Fifty-fourth Street just east of Crenshaw Boulevard and a few blocks south of Leimert Park Village. Opened in 1989 by hand drummer Jai Jae Johnson, the Kabasa Drum and Arts Studio was a collective of visual artists, musicians and poets, offering weekly performances and floor to ceiling displays of original artwork by such artists as Charles Dickson, Melvino Garratti, Milton Poole, and Teresa Tolliver. According to Jai Jae,

> I still think it's very important to try to create other waterholes, because the music has to live, but you have to have some place to play the music inside of the village where you live. And there has to be an ambience to it that will allow the spirit to come out and flow and show itself.

Sometimes you get places but it don't have the energy to it. Cats go in there and play and do their thing, but it's about something else, money, but you don't really get spirit. It's really hard to create a space where you can nurture spirit. That's what Kabasa was and that's why I named the space Kabasa. Kabasa is named after the *ka,* the *ba* and the *sa* from Egypt. The *ka* is the soul. The *ba* is the double image of that. And the *sa* is the papyrus lifesaver that you would put around you, when you traveled across the Nile. So we were soul savers. That's what Kabasa meant to me.

Jai Jae was inspired by the Arkestra performances at the IUCC in the 1970s, even using church pews in his studio, and Kabasa also provided living spaces in its upstairs loft for some UGMAA members, including Jesse Sharps, Taumbu, and Dadisi Komolafe, until its sudden end by an electrical fire in 1995. Not long after its opening, Jesse moved in and contacted Horace about the Arkestra: "Called Horace and he said, 'Great idea.' Anything to start it back would be fine with him. We gave one big concert and it was a big hit at the Kabasa."

In the wake of the '92 upheaval, new avenues were explored. Horace and San Francisco–based pianist Jon Jang, founder and leader of the Pan Asian Arkestra from 1988 to 1994, discussed organizing a musical response to the events. Jon recalls,

> We were responding to the riots after the Rodney King verdict, and part of it was that we were dissatisfied with Peter Ueberoth and this whole rebuilding of Los Angeles. We didn't want them to rebuild it so that it could become a problem again. It was more a need to re-create Los Angeles. These ideas were that I and some of the members of the Pan Asian Arkestra would come down and we would perform and collaborate with Horace in his community. And then he would come up with some of his members, and it would be this kind of exchange.

Although the collaboration with the Pan Asian Arkestra never materialized, it was another fillip, and Horace set about establishing a more regular schedule for the Pan Afrikan Peoples Arkestra. Horace also asked Nate "to come over and get the charts together, get all the music put in the right folders and that kind of stuff. And then it was about '92, '93, he actually started trying to rehearse some more." Not long afterward, the Ark was selected to conclude 1993's Los Angeles Festival, a month-long, citywide celebration of the arts. On the final day, Sunday September 19, Degnan Boulevard and Forty-third Place were closed off to traffic and a large bandstand erected in front of the park. The daylong arts celebration, which included performances by Dwight Trible's band Oasis and Taumbu's International Ensemble, was brought to a close with a performance of Horace's most ambitious work, *Ancestral Echoes*, which had not been performed in its entirety since 1977 with the Watts Symphony. The thirty-five-member aggregation brought the Festival to a rousing close with a stunning, ninety-minute performance of the work.

The Arkestra that mounted the stage that day under Horace's direction was mostly a veteran group, but it also included some new artists who would be involved through the 1990s, some up to the present time. In important ways, however, it was a different, evolved band. According to Kamau Daáood,

> The Ark had really become seasoned within the eyes of the community, even a larger community than that which it pulled its energies from, as *the* representative of this movement to continue the work of black musicians and black artists. It just solidified as that in the '90s. When you think of Los Angeles and you think of this kind of energy, then this is where you go to get it. This is who will represent it. All of the artists that were youngsters were now mature artists, mature people with histories that they had built, sometimes outside of the Ark, but had also contributed their lives to this collective energy.

Although Jesse Sharps moved back to Germany after the uprising, there were some new and returning faces. Conguero Taumbu relocated to L.A. two weeks after the spring upheaval and immediately rejoined Horace and the Ark. Among the new faces was Horace's granddaughter, flutist Raisha Wilcots, who had been studying with Central Avenue alumnus Bill Green, and his son-in-law, drummer Darryl Moore (JMD). Bobby Bryant, Jr. performed on alto saxophone. Multi-reed instrumentalist Vinny Golia realized a long-held dream and joined the Arkestra for the L.A. Festival performance playing bass clarinet, the first white musician to appear in the Ark. The death in 1992 of bassist and tuba player Red Callender, who had performed and recorded with the Arkestra since the 1970s, prompted Horace to invite William Roper to join in 1993. In his late thirties at the time, Bill had grown up in the community, just north of Leimert Park, and had been playing tuba since junior high school, performing in symphony orchestras, and studying at the Cleveland Institute of Music and Carnegie-Mellon University. He was active in Los Angeles new-music circles in the 1980s, performing with Vinny Golia, John Rapson, and pianist Glenn Horiuchi, among others, but had never heard of Horace. Roper elaborates:

I've been a classical musician for most of my life, but I improvise the way I improvise. I don't improvise as a 'jazz musician' in the limitations of jazz. I'm not really a jazz improviser, but I'm an improviser. To some extent that explains my not having heard of Horace, but I still find that quite strange. . . . One day I got home, turned on my machine and there was this message that said, "Roper, this is Horace. I need you, man." Well, I didn't know who Horace was and that was kind of an out message. I called him and that was our beginning. That's the beginning of my life with Horace.

Though lacking much of the brashness of twenty years prior that led them to set up in parks, streets, and on the backs of trucks, taking art to the community by whatever means necessary, the Ark was reasserting its presence and purpose. Community events loomed larger in the post-1992 period and it was called upon to perform more often. It continued to play the Watts Towers Jazz Festivals, as it had since the Festival's inception in 1977, but also participated in other annual events, including the Kwanzaa celebration, the African Marketplace, and the Leimert Park Jazz Festival, inaugurated in 1995 by promoter Diana Wimbish. There would be performances at festivals and concerts organized by the Artists Network of Refuse and Resist! to protest police brutality and at rallies in support of Geronimo Pratt, the former Panther leader unjustly convicted of murder in 1972 and imprisoned until his release in 1997. Also in 1997 the Arkestra performed for the reopening of the Mafundi Institute and Watts Coffee House on 103rd Street, over twenty years after they had closed.

In 1993 David Keller, Horace's manager for the previous ten years, relocated to the Seattle area and was succeeded by Corinne Hunter, an acquaintance of Tom Albach in Santa Barbara, who continued to book Horace and small groups in Europe but sought opportunities for the Arkestra as well. The band performed that year at the 15th Annual Chicago Jazz Festival with a formidable saxophone section: Arthur Blythe, alto; Teddy Edwards, tenor; and Michael Session, baritone. With Horace on piano, the band also included trumpeter Oscar Brashear, trombonist Thurman Green, Roberto Miranda on bass, and drummer Fritz Wise. According to one reviewer, it "provided the weekend's finest moments. The band surged in powerful waves, propelled by a driving swing."[18]

In early June 1995 the Ark, seventeen pieces strong, flew to Germany to perform at the Moers Jazz Festival, its first trip outside the United States. Jesse Sharps and Arthur Blythe joined the band at Moers. Along with Horace,

Arthur, and Jesse were saxophonists Charles Owens and Michael Session, trumpeter Steve Smith, trombonist Thurman Green, Fundi Legohn on French horn, William Roper on tuba, pianist Nate Morgan, bassists David Bryant and Roberto Miranda, drummers Sonship Theus and Fritz Wise, and vocalist Dwight Trible. In the hour-and-a-half set on June 3, they performed Ark classics: "The Black Apostles," "Motherless Child," "Dem Folks," "Ballad for Deadwood Dick," and "Little Africa," which was becoming Horace's closing number. The performance was a triumph and for many of the members the reception was a vindication of their work and Horace's, as well as a partial fulfillment of the promise of international recognition that FESTAC was in 1977. Nate Morgan recalls,

> But the beautiful thing was that was the first time I saw people rush to hear Horace's music. When they opened the doors, it was like first come, first serve on the seating, and the people ran to the front of the stage—young people, old people, kids, men, women, they all just ran to the end of the stage. You would have thought some rock band was coming on. . . . It held about 5,000 people and they all rushed up in there, and they were on top of him, who he was. They knew. They weren't faking interest; it was genuine.

For Nate, it was a poignant moment, one "that really brought tears to my eyes, because in all the years that I've been dealing with Horace, I'd never seen him get the respect in L.A. that I know he deserved."

Especially after Germany, there was renewed energy surrounding the Arkestra. Rehearsals became a weekly routine, occurring on the first three Saturdays of each month in Horace's garage. Not only were performances becoming more frequent, both within the community and without, but more members were returning, some new recruits arriving, a few recording opportunities arose, and Horace also thought it was the right time to reconstitute the choir as "The Great Voice of UGMAA." In Dwight Trible, he had not only found an extraordinary vocal talent with an exceptional instrument, but also someone with the musical authority and organizational skills to lead the voices. Without any formal training, he had developed one of the most expressive and powerful vocal instruments in jazz with an operatic range, a blues- and spirituals-drenched sensibility, and a fluid improvisational free spirit.

Dwight had arrived in Los Angeles from Cincinnati in 1978, joined by his wife, Denise, a few years later, and settled into Watts. As Leimert Park reemerged and Dwight became an integral part of the burgeoning community arts scene, Horace was watching. Dwight recalls, "One day out of the clear blue sky Horace called and said, 'Dwight, I got a song that I want you to sing for me.' I said, 'Oh, man, okay.' . . . And we started having rehearsals maybe once or twice a week with just me and him working on this material." By the time of the Moers Festival appearance, Dwight had been performing with Horace for almost two years, and during this time, Horace talked about restarting the choir. "He would talk to me about this choir off and on and I would say, 'Hey, man, whenever you want to do it, just let me know.'" Not long after Moers, Dwight received the call:

> One day—it was on a Friday—he called me up: "Dwight, call the voices together. Tomorrow we're going to have a rehearsal." [laughter] I couldn't tell him no. So I called all the people that I thought would be interested and told them to show up tomorrow. He had the Arkestra and everybody over there on Saturday. I think we had about two or three rehearsals with the band on Saturdays. . . . Then we started working on Monday nights and it became such a beautiful thing. People just knew that on Monday nights we had choir rehearsal.

At full strength The Great Voice of UGMAA added another two dozen members to the growing organization. They included returning members such as Amina Amatullah, one of the first voices in the 1960s, and Ali Jihad, but also newcomers Afifa Amatullah, Nikia Billingslea, Norma Carey, Dante Chambers, Alaah Deen, Renee Fisher, Denise Groce, Brenda Hearn, Waberi Jordan, Chini Kopano-Roberts, Ndugu "Jingles," Torre Reese, Maria Rose, Elesia Session, Bernice Taylor, Denise Tribble, and Carolyn Whitaker. From this point on, they would be an integral part of Arkestra performances.

There were also new and returning instrumentalists in the mid-1990s. Danyel Romero, a resident of the second UGMA house before 1965, returned to the trumpet section. Among the new faces was multi-reed instrumentalist Phil Vieux and saxophonist/flutist Yaakov Levy. Yaakov was a product of the San Fernando Valley and a graduate of North Hollywood High School, who had been playing tenor since the age of twelve. When he met Horace in 1980, he was a twenty-one-year-old under the spell of John Coltrane and performing wherever he could, not infrequently on the streets of Los Angeles. In *Songs of the Unsung* Horace recalls seeing him in front of the Music Center, a favorite haunt because the tips were good, playing all the Coltrane he could.[19] By day, Yaakov was involved in the Watts community working with and performing at the Westminster Neighborhood Association and the Golden Age Adult Day Care Center. The opportunity to play with Horace came in May 1984 at St. Elmo Village in Los Angeles, where Yaakov was performing with artists from Alice Coltrane's ashram. After a few years of asking, "Hey, Mr. Tapscott, any sitting in today?" he got the nod from Horace: "Yeah, maybe, stick around." On stage performing Coltrane's "Equinox" in D minor,

> There was this absolutely wonderful and remarkable sense of being supported. This very warm sense and non-verbal communication that was very clear, that said that "you are free to go wherever you want to go and to do whatever you want to do. I got you covered. I'm here. I'm supporting you. I'm with you. Just let your soul be free; don't have any limits or bounds." It was almost like an empowering, strengthening feeling, absolutely incredible. I've played with some great pianists and nobody ever had that particular quality. . . . So we played "Equinox." I remember at one point I was playing a low B on the tenor and something said, "Go play the low B flat." I thought, "Well wait a minute. Is that gonna work?" And the feeling was like, "No, just go on and slide into it." I slid down into it, and he played a change. . . . I was like wow! He was right there with me, almost like holding my hand or like dancing together. That was wonderful.

Over the next ten years, Yaakov would play with Horace on many occasions, but it was not until 1997 that Horace invited him into the Arkestra, playing his first Ark gig at the Wadsworth Theater in West Los Angeles. That performance was, in part, a memorial for trombonist Thurman Green, who had just died. The Ark opened with Horace's "Thoughts of Dar es Salaam" and when it came to Thurman's solo, the ensemble played through the chorus, leaving the solo space and a single chair on stage open for their departed comrade.

Another new face was trombonist Phil Ranelin, an advocate of community arts for almost thirty years, who started performing with Horace in the early 1990s. He had been in Los Angeles since 1979 but had met Horace earlier in Detroit, where Phil had settled in 1968. By 1970, he was working in the Detroit community arts movement with trumpeter Marcus Belgrave and teaching music at the Metropolitan Arts Complex, a government-funded program for the community. Phil also cofounded the community-based Tribe with saxophonist Wendell Harrison. When he relocated to Los Angeles, he organized his own band, performed off and on with Freddie Hubbard, and established contact with Horace. "I played with Horace out in Watts at the jazz festival, but he had his trombone section. Thurman and Lester had been there forever. So I would talk to him occasionally. It was around the time that Lester passed that he called me and said, 'Phillip, I need you. I need you to start getting some of these youngsters together.' I was never really a permanent member until after Thurman passed."

Two recording opportunities also arose, one successfully concluded, the other commercially unrealized until almost thirty years later. Don Snowden, who for many years covered the local jazz scene for the *Los Angeles Times*, decided to use some of a recent inheritance to record Horace in a manner that would do justice to him and the other artists. Roberto Miranda recalls, "Don said, 'I'm going to record this. This is just too beautiful, man.' Like Tom Albach did, he put his money where his ears were." Over the next few months he would spare no expense, paying everyone above union scale, and ultimately spending some $35,000 on a number of live and studio recordings. With Horace's approval, Don brought Horace's former manager, David Keller, to Los Angeles to produce the sessions.

David arranged to record Horace's Sextet on December 19–20, 1995, at Catalina's Bar and Grill in Hollywood. The band included Michael Session, Thurman Green, Roberto Miranda, Fritz Wise, and Dwight Trible. Engineer Wayne Peet recorded both nights and sixty-eight minutes were chosen for release, including "The Ballad of Deadwood Dick," "Motherless Child," "Breakfast at Bongo's," "Close to Freedom," and "Little Africa." This was followed on December 21–23 and then March 7, 1996, with Horace-led sextet, septet, and octet sessions at Sage and Sound Recording Studio in Hollywood. The Catalina's band was expanded to include cornetist Bobby Bradford, tuba player Bill Roper, and Phil Vieux on bass clarinet.

The plan was to issue two CDs, one of live material to be titled *Legacies for Our Grandchildren*, and another of studio recordings, *Songs for the Unsung*. William Claxton was brought in to photograph one of the studio sessions. Unfortunately, neither was picked up by a commercial record label. While artistically satisfying, the experience merely served to reinforce David Keller's initial decision to leave the music business. "The frustrating part, and part of the reason I decided to get out of the business, was you'd get people, who would say, 'Yeah, this is a nice tape, but I think it would sound a lot better if he had a New York rhythm section.' After you do an excellent job, you get to the next level and there's some little squeak-type character who thinks he knows more than the artist and it doesn't get released. So I just had to step back from it."

However, Don and David have been working with Bertrand Gastaut of Dark Tree records to finally make this material available. The live sessions were released on CD in the spring of 2022, to be followed by the studio CD, being worked on as of this writing.

Not long after the Snowden sessions, Horace was contacted by New York–based Arabesque Records, who offered him a three-disc contract to record with East Coast lineups. In 1996 the first CD, *Aiee! The Phantom*, was issued featuring compositions by Horace, Jesse Sharps, and Ernest Straughter, performed by Horace, trumpeter Marcus Belgrave, alto saxophonist Abraham Burton, bassist Reggie Workman, and drummer Andrew Cyrille. One year later *Thoughts of Dar es Salaam* appeared, a studio session with bassist Ray Drummond and drummer Billy Hart. Horace would not live to realize the third disc, and he was hoping for an Arkestra studio session as the next project.

There were also recording sessions with the Watts Prophets and the Freestyle Fellowship, one of the most important rap groups to emerge in the 1990s and one that has steadfastly displayed a firm commitment to the community. Horace's relationship with the Prophets stretched back to the late 1960s and continued into the 1990s. In the spring of 1993, the Prophets brought Don Cherry and Horace together to perform with them at the Ivar Theater under the auspices of C. Bernard Jackson's Inner City Cultural Center. A few years later Prophet Richard Dedeaux arranged a performance at the Terminal Island Federal Penitentiary for the Prophets and Horace.

> My son was in the pen at the time, and that's mainly why I talked everyone into doing the show, because I wanted to see my son and at the same time entertain him. The day we got there, they had put him in lockdown. It was so disappointing. But Horace, man, he burnt those keyboards up. It was so funny when we went in there, because everybody knew somebody in there. Somebody called out Horace's name. . . . There was some guy Horace hadn't seen in years.

When the Watts Prophets recorded their 1996 CD *When the '90s Came*, Horace was asked to play on "breed what you need." Otis O'Solomon recalls, "Horace played so beautiful these people were really shocked. It's a beautiful cut." The Prophets continued to work within the community and were soon organizing the Los Angeles Hip Hop Poetry Choir to "share the beauty of the spoken word, the power of a confident pen, and the value of a vibrant culture." Workshops in the community followed, designed to "serve widely diverse ethnicities, but we have discovered that the roots of rap and the griot tradition of rhythmic storytelling is a legacy of every culture."[20]

Horace appreciated the emerging rap scene and saw the range of African American music along a continuum of common shared experience. This was reflected in his own compositions, most explicitly in pieces like *Ancestral Echoes*, but also in his assessment of contemporary musics. Fr. Amde of the

Watts Prophets credits Horace with first impressing him with the importance of rap: "Horace was the first one to let me see what rap was, and he always said rap music was blues. 'It's the blues of today. That's why they're not listening to the old blues. They're doing their own blues.'" In his late night wanderings, Horace would occasionally drop into Project Blowed in Leimert Park to check out the new sounds, and he recorded with the Freestyle Fellowship. In the early 1990s, at the first session for what would become the Fellowship's 1993 Island Records CD, *Innercity Griots*, he played on "Hot," a recording finally released in 2000 on *Project Blowed*. Another cut with Horace from the same session, "Danger," appeared on Mikah 9's *Timetable* in 2001.

Horace's Final Days

1998 was to be a full year for Horace and the Arkestra. Leimert Park was vibrant and there was a growing demand for the music outside the community as well, throughout North America and particularly in Europe. Horace started planning for an Arkestra performance as his third CD release for Arabesque. Locally, there would be performances throughout Leimert Park, at Catalina's Bar and Grill, the Jazz Bakery, the Los Angeles County Museum of Art, and Museum of Contemporary Art, all venues that had featured his ensembles during the 1990s, as well as the various community festivals. In March, he was back in Northern Europe with bassist Roberto Miranda in a series of duo performances, with more scheduled for 1999, and perhaps another trip by the full Arkestra.

Horace had started the process of putting together an autobiography during his sixty-third birthday celebration on April 6, 1997, at the Shabazz Restaurant in Leimert Park. By the summer of 1998, *Songs of the Unsung: The Musical and Social Journey of Horace Tapscott* was nearing completion. The previous four years he had been a member of the editorial board and contributed a chapter to the book released in March 1998 by the University of California Press, *Central Avenue Sounds: Jazz in Los Angeles*, documenting one of the most important influences in Horace's life. Throughout the spring and summer, there were signings and events with Horace enthusiastically attending every one.

Over the Memorial Day weekend, May 23–24, Horace was the featured performer/composer at the Seventeenth Asian American Jazz Festival, held at the Asian Art Museum in San Francisco's Golden Gate Park. Horace and Jon Jang had enjoyed a close relationship for many years, and this gave them the opportunity to realize a long-held dream of working together. Horace was commissioned to write a new piece for the occasion and his *Two Shades of Soul* became the focal point for the weekend, which was inaugurated with an extended panel discussion featuring Horace and pianist/composer Jang.

The Saturday and Sunday evening performances began with solo presentations by Horace and Jon, followed by a set with the Jon Jang Quintet, including the premiere of *Two Shades of Soul*, conducted by Horace. According to the Festival's artistic director, bassist Mark Izu, "Horace Tapscott's composition explores the profound links between the development of Asian American jazz and its African American heritage. Both Horace and Jon Jang creatively draw upon the influences of culture and politics as ways to build cross-cultural communication."[21] The quintet included Chinese erhu virtuoso Chen Jiebing. An ancient, two-stringed Chinese instrument, the erhu provided Horace with a wider compositional palette, and in one of the weekend's many highlights he performed Jon's "Two Flowers on a Stem" in an exquisitely beautiful duet with Chen.

Planning was also moving forward on reestablishing UGMAA as a nonprofit organization, and there was the prospect of a substantial grant from the National Endowment for the Arts to be administered through the Watts Towers Arts Center. The grant would support performances within the community by the Arkestra and the Great Voice of UGMAA, small ensembles, and Horace's composing, and serve to relaunch UGMAA.

Yet, there were also disturbing signs that all was not well. By early 1998, it was clear that the grant from the National Endowment for the Arts would not materialize. Michael Dett Wilcots, his son-in-law, thought the effect on Horace was devastating.

> The shot at this $100,000 was kind of like his last stab at trying to do something for the Foundation, for UGMAA, to keep our original story together, our original programs and projects that we wanted to develop, to make this happen. We're all getting much older. His reaction of losing that grant, I mean facially I just saw the energy leave him. It was the first time that I saw him saddened, hurt, really upset about that situation to the point that I began to see his health change. . . . He seemed to physically have been damaged by that. He began to always be cold, could never get warm. He began to have trouble with his circulation.

Nimbus West's Tom Albach sensed a growing disillusionment with the political state of the country: "I hate to admit this, but at times I get into a state where I think that Horace was ready to go, that he couldn't stand the fucking horror of all this. And it's going to get so much worse. Listen, man, I wouldn't be surprised if we had martial law in the next four years. I'm fucking serious. I think there is that much dissatisfaction and unrest in this country and these people are that unaccommodating."

While performing with Roberto Miranda in Northern Europe in March 1998, Horace's right leg started bothering him. When he returned home, he was told to stay off his feet for a couple of weeks and walked with the assistance of a cane for a few months. Nevertheless, he continued performing and by summer seemed back in form. On July 24, he led the Arkestra and the Great Voice of UGMAA in a concert at the Los Angeles County Museum of Art, which was taped by MediaOne TV personality Annya Bell and engineered by Wayne Peet for later broadcast. Much of the concert was released on CD and LP in 2019 by Dark Tree records—*Why Don't You Listen? Live at LACMA, 1998*. Wayne recalls, "It was such a great concert. The choir was great and Dwight is just a fantastic singer. I loved hearing him with Horace. Him with Horace was a great combination and Dwight is such a great vocal improviser. There are a lot of vocalists around, most of whom shouldn't be allowed, and the rest are good, but Dwight is just at a level of scat singing and improvising that there are only a few of in the history of jazz."

Horace's next gig was August 11–16 at Iridium in New York City with his Arabesque recording trio of Ray Drummond and Billy Hart. That was to be followed on August 18 with a solo performance at Lincoln Center. As the plane made its final descent into New York, Horace awoke to find that he couldn't move his lower right arm. In Manhattan, friends were called and doctors consulted. A preliminary diagnosis was that Horace was suffering from a form of palsy. He decided to cancel the solo performance at Lincoln Center, but played the entire Iridium engagement using only his left hand. For those who witnessed any of Horace's performances, it was a remarkable experience, the stuff of jazz lore. Pianist Randy Weston, who always made a point of catching Horace in performance, recalls, "He played the whole set with his one left hand and you closed your eyes and you'd never know it was one hand. I never knew Horace was that great myself."[22] According to Stanley Crouch, also in attendance, "That last gig he played, when his right hand stopped working—one of the most amazing things I ever saw. The way he played, I couldn't believe it, man. *Stunning*. He was something—Horace Tapscott."

When Horace returned home in mid-August, the round of medical examinations continued and he was diagnosed again with a palsy that might take months to overcome. Rehearsals continued and Horace tried to play. Michael

Dett recalls, "He was in pain, but he used to tell me, 'Once I hit that first note, the pain's forgotten.' The music just took over. But as soon as he got up and walked off stage, it would hit him, and each time it would hit him heavier." On Tuesday evening, September 8, he performed with his sextet for a conference of educators at the Los Angeles County Museum of Art. Playing mostly with his left hand, he used the middle finger of his inert right hand to spear single notes and his elbow to pound clusters. It was the last time he would play the piano publicly. On September 13, with his right arm in a sling, he conducted a performance of the Pan Afrikan Peoples Arkestra to conclude the annual Leimert Park Jazz Festival. Charles Owens recalls, "He couldn't raise his right arm before the gig. When the Ark got to playing, he could raise his right arm. It's amazing what the music did to him and what he could do with music. . . . Shit, it comes out and he starts directing."

At a Monday rehearsal of the Great Voice of UGMAA, other remedies were tried. Amina Amatullah recalls,

> When he told us, every one of those sisters, one at a time, went up to him and whatever their remedy was—some held his hand and prayed—he sat there and he let each one do whatever it was. And I watched and I knew, because he never would have let that happen. He let everybody touch him and do whatever it was they were going to do. We still rehearsed. Then one night we came to rehearsal and he played. He played "Isle of Celia," and he just played it and played it and played it. When he finished, he turned around and told all of us, "That's it. You'll never hear me again. That's the last time I'll play." And he didn't say another word.

Not long afterward, during one of his late-night rambles, he visited Amina.

> He came by my place once again and it took him maybe five minutes to get up those stairs. He sat down and said, "Can I just sit here for a minute with my eyes closed." So he laid back for maybe five or ten minutes. I rubbed his arm and he said, "Baby, you know I saw the mothership. So I wanted to come by here. I want you to know." He stayed maybe a couple of hours that night. He laid down and I played some CDs and he went to sleep I guess. Then he got up and I helped him put his coat on. Then he left. I knew he was very, very ill.

On Sunday afternoon, October 25, while at home watching television, Horace suffered a seizure and was rushed to Kaiser Hospital in Los Angeles. Tests revealed that he had lung cancer, which had metastasized into brain tumors. He was given six months to live. Eschewing further treatments, Horace returned home a few days later to be with his family, his UGMAA members, and his community, still maintaining that characteristic quiet dignity and calm. Recalling the experience of the aneurysm in 1978, he told his sister, Robbie, "Well, I was given twenty years." Close friend Marla Gibbs remembers visiting: "It was just time for him to make his transition and he understood it, and he accepted it. He said, 'I'm just trying to be accepting.'" To Charles Owens, he was wry: "Not long after coming back from New York, he tickled me. He said, 'You know Charlie, I just started making some decent money, doing my thing, now I got to get cancer. Ain't that a bitch.' He was never drug about it. He just said, 'Ain't that a bitch.'" Phil Ranelin recalls, "I've never seen anyone die with any more courage or dignity with an illness of that magnitude. That says a lot about the man. It's not only the way he lived, but also the way he got out of here."

During the following months, Cecilia drove him through the neighborhood. He was unable to stand in his front yard and greet his neighbors—a Tapscott ritual—but many friends and admirers drove by tapping out phrases from Horace's compositions on their car horns as they passed. He met and talked over the phone with dozens of friends, artists, and well-wishers from around the world. Roberto Miranda recalls their last meeting, "I asked him, 'What is the one lesson that you've learned that you can tell me right now, that if there were a million people looking, what would you say?' And he just said, 'Keep it simple.'" The future of the music, the Arkestra, and UGMAA were important concerns and he consulted with everyone involved to lay plans for their continuation. According to Michael Dett,

> He also invited and asked for certain people to be called over that were a part of the band and the Foundation, and during some of the conversations he would give assignments. He was still telling people what to do, all the way to the end. He wanted to keep this going. He passed on to me to preserve the music, keep the music available for the band, work with some people [on unfinished business]. He also wanted the business end and the administration end of the Foundation to exist so that it could negotiate these type of business matters on an official basis. . . . So he gave me that role also, to support the family and to support the Foundation, and "Michael, don't go commercial with the music. I know there has to be a way for this to be provided for monetarily, just don't make it commercial."

Nate Morgan remembers his meeting:

At that point he was just kind of giving everybody orders. He was like, "I want you to do this. I want you to do that." And he made me promise that I was going to do some arrangements of some of my music for the Ark. There were a couple of compositions I had written that he really liked. "Retribution, Reparation"—he really liked that piece and he wanted me to arrange that. I'm still working on it. The "UGMAAger" piece that I wrote. He didn't get to hear "Tapscottian Waltz." I was really thinking in terms of his writing when I wrote that.

Fundi Legohn also received his marching orders: "Before Horace left he told me some things that I had to do: keep the music right, write some music, make sure the music stays on. I dream about that from time to time. I don't want Horace coming up, snatching me, and saying, 'Man, you're not doing what you're supposed to do.'" For those more recent arrivals in the Arkestra, it was necessary that they sit in Horace's television room and watch Larry Clark's film *Passing Through*. When I arrived one day, Dwight Trible was settled in, watching the film at Horace's urging.

Horace's autobiography was completed and plans were made for documenting the history of the Arkestra and UGMAA. Horace set up the first interviews, which were conducted in his television room, while he rested. When Father Amde of the Watts Prophets visited for the last time, "Horace told me that he wanted me to speak at his funeral, but he told me he didn't want me to talk about him. I said, 'Well, what you want me to say?' He said, 'Tell them what a wonderful wife I had.'"

While Horace celebrated the New Year watching movies and boxing matches with his family and a few friends, raising a glass of champagne at midnight, plans were moving ahead for a tribute honoring him featuring a performance by an enlarged Arkestra. Rehearsals took place and by concensus saxophonist Michael Session emerged as the person who should take over leadership of the Ark. This triggered a memory for Michael of one day in the 1970s at the Great House.

> I'm up in my room practicing. There's a knock on the door and Horace comes in. He's got a very serious look on his face. He said, "Man, I had a talk with the spirits last night." I said, "Oh." He said, "Yeah, the direction of the Ark depends on you." I was like, "Oh yeah?" He turned around and left. I kind of thought he was tripping or something, but I didn't trip on it. I just turned around and kept on playing. And it really left my mind. Didn't trip on it for years. . . . Then when he died. Whew! . . . Then it really hits me: Horace twenty-five years ago.

Kamau Daáood had just written his magnificent ode to Horace, "Papa, the Lean Griot," and appeared with Kafi Roberts on Stevie Wonder's radio station, KGFJ, to promote the concert.

One of the things I was going to do was read this poem to Horace Tapscott as part of the promo. I didn't know it, but they had actually hooked up by telephone with Horace that morning. Me and Kafi talked a little bit about the concert. . . . Then the dj asked him what he wanted to be remembered for. Horace said that we carried the story forward, that it would be here for people to receive whenever they needed it, that he was here to be a part of that process. "While I was here, that's what I did. I made sure that the story would be here and would be available for those who needed it." After Horace finished the interview, I had the opportunity to read the poem, which I had just finished, to Horace over the phone. He got a chance to hear the poem.

Scheduled for Sunday, February 28, at the large auditorium of Washington Preparatory High School, Horace was to be brought by limousine to an afternoon of music by dozens of artists that would culminate in a performance by the Arkestra. Horace passed just before midnight on Saturday, February 27, 1999.

The next day more than a thousand people gathered at Washington Prep. Among the music luminaries were George Bohanon, Bobby Bradford, Clora Bryant, David Ornette Cherry, Billy Childs, Dr. Art Davis, Teddy Edwards, Billy Higgins, Pharoah Sanders, and Gerald Wilson. The long program was brought to a close by a performance of the largest version of the Pan Afrikan Peoples Arkestra ever assembled. Drummer Fritz Wise was on stage: "You had all these cats coming in and wanting to play. You didn't want to say no, because it was coming from the heart. It was no ego thing. 'I just want to be on stage.' They all just wanted to express their gratitude to Horace." Under a large banner reading "Horace Tapscott / A Man of the People," more than fifty musicians, spanning the forty-year history of the Arkestra, filled the stage and then followed the lead of conductor Michael Session into the first piece, "Lino's Pad." Jon Williams recalls,

I can't tell you what we played. There was so many of us that were there that day, and I'll never forget when they said that Horace had passed. We found out as we were getting ready to play the concert. I remember getting weak at the knees and crying, and I remember pandemonium. Nobody knew what to do. Then I remember that peace and that calm that took over as we decided to start playing. Then I kind of remember just viewing this from another level, like a dream. It was just so beautiful, the way people came together and played.

Charles Owens remembers that day as musically one of his finest.

> The best playing I ever did with the Ark was the Tribute Concert, the day after he died. And Nate Morgan played some of the best piano I've ever heard him play that day. I get kind of choked up when I think about it now. And his grandson played the drums, played the hell out of the drums. He was touching people all through life. I loved the man, that's what I did. When we played with the Ark at the Jazz Bakery [one year later on Horace's birthday], Roberto Miranda did the prayer and toward the end of it, he was almost crying and I was almost crying. We could see how much Roberto really loved the guy. He stopped just in time before we all couldn't play.

During the next week, while hand drummers paid tribute outside, hundreds visited the Harrison Ross Mortuary on Crenshaw Boulevard, just a few blocks from Horace's home. French horn player Bob Watt was one: "I remember going to view Horace's body and thinking that this is where he'd want to be, in his community, right here, right where it all happened. And there he was. That was a sad moment for me. But I sat there and thought that here was someone who added a dimension to my life and to many lives, someone who broadened us all."

On Saturday, March 6, Horace's funeral was held at the Brookins Community A.M.E. church, a short distance from his home, and that afternoon he was buried at Roosevelt Park Cemetery in Gardena. "The men had a hard time," Amina relates. "A bunch didn't even go to the funeral, because they couldn't. They wouldn't let it go." Father Amde and the Watts Prophets, along with their band, including pianist Nate Morgan, were on tour and unable to attend the services. Nate recalls, "That was hard. I was literally breaking down on the airplane." In Father Amde's absence, his wife, Shirley Hamilton, read Horace's words about Cecilia. "I want the world to know what a queenly, grand lady she has always been with me, my soul mate."[23]

The day of the funeral the Watts Prophets were at Texas Tech University in Lubbock. As they walked on stage, Otis O'Solomon stepped forward:

> "In Los Angeles there is a great musician by the name of Horace Tapscott and they're having his funeral today. And he's been a great mentor to the Watts Prophets and to all the members of this band. If we had

been in town, we would have been there. We didn't have the opportunity because we made this commitment many months ago to be here. I'm sure Horace would have wanted us to do that. Some of you may have heard of him and some of you may have not, but he was an outstanding musician. If you will be kind enough just to allow us to take a minute of silence in acknowledgment of this great community musician, it would mean a lot to us." It got so quiet and it felt really good.

Horace had wished for more success within and for his community and struggled to achieve that. But he had already realized an important part of his dream with the founding of the Underground Musicians Association in the early 1960s, surrounding himself with a creative community in South Central Los Angeles. In so achieving his return home almost at the beginning of his artistic career, he devoted most of his life to deepening and sharing that homeland. Consequently, Horace left with few regrets, content with his accomplishments and aware that they would loom larger after his passing. To the end, he was open and explorative, approaching life as he had throughout his sixty-four years. Charles Owens recalls his last conversation with Horace: "I said, 'Horace, it must be really a drag to die.' He said, 'You haven't been dead, so how would you know? It might be cool.'"

AIEE! THE PHANTOM

Horace Tapscott

i am Horace Tapscott
my fingers are dancing grassroots
i do not fit into form, i create form
my ears are radar charting the whispers of my ancestors
i seek the divinity in outcasts, the richness of rebels

KAMAU DAÁOOD

Eulogizing Horace at the postfuneral repast in Leimert Park, Kamau Daáood asked the assembled mourners, "A great tree has fallen. What will hold up the sky in its place?" Horace's passing left a void in the African American community and its arts world. For almost forty years, undeterred by whatever problems arose within the community, he was a continual artistic presence, who created and guided the Pan Afrikan Peoples Arkestra and UGMAA, performing before thousands and attracting hundreds of artists to support a movement focused on their community in which the only certainties were great music, passing on a rich tradition, and few financial rewards. Without fanfare or thought of personal material advantage, he immersed himself in its life confident that he could contribute something of value, gaining satisfaction from the myriad personal, artistic, and social connections he forged with those around him. As he concludes his autobiography, "I found my part to play and I fit in, just my part and not as so-and-so fit in, or as Coltrane did it. At the end I want to be able to say, to show, that I lived in the community and I appreciated it, that I wanted to keep it up and I wanted to be a part of it, because I loved people and I learned to love life."[1]

In an increasingly market-driven society dominated by selfish individualism, Horace's achievement is all the more remarkable, while simultaneously raising a number of intriguing questions. During its brief residency at the Shop in the late 1970s the UGMAA Foundation issued a brochure of some two-dozen pages outlining the purpose, personalities, and programs of the organization. As executive director, Horace was portrayed in coat and tie, seated at a desk in front of a paneled wall, pen in hand, and hunched over a stack of papers.[2] It is a most uncharacteristic image. One can only imagine the photographer's skill in somehow maneuvering Horace into such a traditional pose of institutional leadership. Yet, if this role was so out of character, then how did the Arkestra survive over a period of almost forty years without a dominating leader or leadership and lacking strong organizational structures? How did Horace keep it together and replenished, when there was rarely any money involved? Why were artists continually attracted to it and willing to make the necessary sacrifices to be part of this movement? The answers lie in aspects of his character and lifestyle choices, in the quality of his musical art as composer, pianist, and bandleader, and, most importantly, in the role he forged and the example his life set as a community artist, exemplifying an ethos and aesthetic that resonated throughout his community.

The Man

The success of the Pan Afrikan Peoples Arkestra can be partly attributed to certain aspects of Horace's character, especially his charisma, "cool" demeanor, integrity, enduring loyalty to those around him, and to his lifestyle choices, which embraced both elements of bohemianism and a commitment to family. These are not the sum total of Horace and in many respects he was all too human, as some of his lifestyle choices reveal. But the combination of these characteristics was potent and gave him a revered status within his organizations and throughout much of his community.

One of the words most frequently used by UGMAA members to characterize Horace's appeal is "charisma." There is no other word adequate to the task. "The men loved him. The women loved him," notes Marla Gibbs. "He definitely had it. He definitely did. That smile!" Arthur Blythe concurs, "He had that charisma. He could get support from the musicians. He had a way of getting it without it having to be about economics." During his tenure in the second UGMA house of the 1960s, Tommy Trujillo saw Horace at rehearsals a few days each week. "He was like this big godfather of the movement. Everybody respected Horace, and he just had this presence and this aura. This was when he was young and he was like bad. He was just a heavy motherfucker. And everybody was, 'Hey, whatever you need, Horace. You need us to blow up the fuckin' City Hall?' It's a good thing he was just a musician." And to Danyel Romero, "He was a magnet, what can I say. Everybody came. . . . He made things happen in the unseen world. He made something out of nothing and that's godly. That's what it's all about. We all have that potential, but I've never known anybody like Horace." Among the players who arrived in the 1970s, Fuasi Abdul-Khaliq notes, "He stood so tall and looked like he was ten feet tall. When he walked into a room, he commanded such a presence, everybody was like, 'Hush. Horace is here.'"

Feeding this charisma was the manner in which he related to those around him, his integrity and his refusal to speak badly of anyone, which was strongly felt by members through the years. According to his sister, Robbie, "One of the things that impressed me most about Horace, even as he was a little boy, was that he would not say derogatory things about anybody. He always found something good to say." He usually professed to be the lucky one in another artist's company. According to Najite, "He told me that he was lucky to play with me. For somebody of that great caliber to feel lucky that he's playing with me, imagine how that makes me feel. Man, if there was anything I could do—I would have given a life, you know." Friends and musicians also speak of his integrity and selflessness. According to Arthur Blythe, "I might not agree with some of his conclusions, but he would be genuine. I've never known him to be false." Reggie Andrews, former director of the Locke High School music program and an heir to the tradition of Samuel Browne, agrees, "Basically, he was committed to the spirit of the music and what music does to culture, what it does to community. He was genuinely concerned about those things. . . . He was real. There was game involved in Horace. There was no fronting or posturing for the wrong reasons."

His unmistakable "cool" (again, no other word for it) demeanor was another compelling trait. Horace talks in his memoir of his temper and his struggle to master it. Indeed, he could be intimidating and there was never any doubt about his resolve. According to Fuasi, "He stuck to his word and he was a strong person; didn't take no shit from nobody, and would throw down. I mean physically throw down with anybody. And everybody knew it. He was a tough cat."

However, within the realm of the Arkestra and UGMAA, there is scant evidence of him ever becoming angry. He personified "cool" in its original connotation, defined by Amiri Baraka as being "calm, even unimpressed, by what horror the world might daily propose."[3] According to E. W. Wainwright, "I'm telling you, man, I can't remember Horace ever raising his voice, but everybody stayed in check. He kept everybody in check. He'd raise that one eyebrow and tell you what to do and what was happening, man, and you did it. And the smile, what a smile! You know, he had the gift." Jesse Sharps, the Ark's disciplinarian bandleader, found himself in a situation that would have provoked an angry reaction in most people:

> One time we had a job at the Watts Towers and we forgot something. He told me to take his car and get it. I went over there and some guy pulled out of a driveway and just crashed and totaled the car out— Horace's favorite car, his Chrysler. What tripped me out was when I finally got there, he said, "Are you all right? Nothing happened to you?" He never asked me about the car. He never said, "Is it totaled? How is it?" He just kept saying, "Are you sure you're ok? Do we need to take you to the doctor? I'll pay for it. You okay?"

"He got that keyboard smile, that's what I call it," offers Watts Prophet Richard Dedeaux. "Man, when he flashed those ivories, he just sucked you right in. I never heard him yell. I never heard the guy yell, just always talked at a very calm pace, low key." For Michael Session, who would succeed Horace as leader of the Arkestra, and other members, it was more than just an attitude, rather a deeply spiritual quality:

> Many people are chosen, but few are touched. Horace was one that was touched. He was an angel-like person on the planet. I even sit up and think about him now. The way he was with everybody. You would think he was so beautiful to you, but he was that way to everybody. I can't ever remember a time he was pissed or frowning. He was always so open and warm and smiling. You'd know some things troubled him, but he never showed it.

Michael was touring Europe in the late 1980s as part of a Horace-led quartet. After a few performances, the bass player's complaints about the rhythm section escalated and he asked that a friend of his replace the drummer. Michael watched as the bassist confronted Horace:

> Horace just sat in his seat and listened to the cat. Then he calmly said, "Hey, I understand. You're not getting along with the drummer? I understand; some cats just can't click. If you don't want to play, you don't have to play. We'll find another bass player or we'll play without one." I mean it was like no sweat. Me, or anybody else, it would have been like confusion in the band. Horace just sat there. No problem. "You can go. I'll work it out." He just smoothed that right over. I never forgot it. My boy stayed; you can believe he stayed. He didn't make him feel alienated, nothing. Everybody was still cool, no problem. He had a way of cooling everybody out, just making everybody feel special and loved.

Horace's support of his drummer without antagonizing the bassist attested to his deep loyalty to those around him. The social bonds in the Arkestra, UGMAA, and among his friends overrode narrowly musical concerns. Not long after Rufus Olivier joined the Arkestra in the early 1970s, he was participating in a recording session for *Sweet Jesus, Preacher Man* under the critical eye of the producer, who was not pleased to have a high school student at the session. "The guy literally stood behind and over me, watching me play the music. I'll never forget, something happened, and he stopped it, saying, 'This kid missed a note' or something. Then Horace said, 'No, he was exactly right. You misread it.' Then silence, and the guy just left and went back in the booth." At the beginning of his collaboration with the Arkestra, actor/director Ted Lange questioned Horace about the condition of one of the musicians.

> There was one guy who was a big heroin addict in the Arkestra. Sometimes he couldn't see straight, but he would show up for the rehearsals. He would get his shit together for the music. I said, "Horace, this guy is fucking out of it, man." He'd say, "Don't worry. He'll be all right. Look he's got problems, but he's a great musician. He knows how to make music. I'll worry about the musicians. You just worry about the play and the actors." And I said, "You got it."

Horace's friendships were many and strong, and each person felt special because of that bond. Bob Watt enjoyed the casual encounters: "We'd run into each other at times and just start laughing. Not hello, how you doing, slap hands, but just start laughing, just glee and joy that we ran into each other, such a special, unique feeling." While Vinny Golia was leading his

Large Ensemble at Hop Singh's in Marina del Rey, California, to celebrate his fortieth birthday, Horace and Cecilia walked into the club. "During intermission, Horace came up and played 'Happy Birthday' and took it out. Man! But the coolest thing was they sat with my mom and dad, who had come out. It was like old home week. I was almost crying. It was just amazing." Bobby West recalls, "Here is a guy, who simply loved people. The last eight years I've been doing a lot of traveling, and, no matter what, Horace would take an interest in what I'm doing, where I'm going, how am I faring. He never told me, but I always knew that he was proud of me." Amina Amatullah captures this quality: "He had so much caring, and he had so much love in him, that everybody got individual love and attention. Even if we were all in the same room together, you could feel that individual thing."

While these characteristics explain many of the close personal relationships that provided much of the social cement within the Arkestra over the years, Horace's lifestyle choices also fostered his larger-than-life persona. His life embraced two dramatically different, seemingly incompatible paths. He lived as a bohemian, serving his muse and reveling in his artistic freedom, as well as indulging in the excesses of a rootless artist. Yet he was also a dedicated family man, bearing the responsibilities of a husband and father, and advocating the importance of family. Though his life was not without problems and, at times, discord, managing both roles successfully contributed to Horace's stature.

As much as anyone could, Horace followed his own drummer, regardless of artistic boundaries and social conventions. Poet and novelist Eric Priestley saw him as a true bohemian, "somebody that draws a line in the sand and says, 'My time is my time, and I'm going to spend it being who I am. I'm going to spend it doing my art.' There are very few people who can do that, who actually draw that line because it's real difficult. Horace lived like that." According to Stanley Crouch,

> He was a totally original person. I've never met anybody like him. You couldn't think, "Oh, he's like so and so." He didn't remind me of anyone. He had his own sense of humor; he had his own carriage. He was always the same way from when I first met him to the end. He was clean and he had fun, too; he had a lot of fun. He was also amazing in that way. He was really a special person, a very dignified guy, very down to earth, extremely intelligent, and very proud, but not in an obnoxious manner, very great pride, but it was a soulful kind of pride.

Horace's bohemianism included aspects of his life lived outside of social conventions, involving varied relationships with women, a lifelong penchant for marijuana, and many sleepless nights and late-night wanderings around South Central Los Angeles. In many ways he was elusive, recalling tricksters, rambling musicians, and other such figures from African American folklore. In 1996 Arabesque Recordings released Horace's CD *Aiee! The Phantom*. The title track, based on a piece Horace composed in the early 1970s for the film *Sweet Jesus, Preacher Man*, was a reference to an image that had come to be associated with him, a reflection of his bohemian, underground reputation and his penchant for late-night ramblings, his sudden visits to friends and music venues, and abrupt disappearances. "He'd just appear out of nowhere, talk for a while, and then he'd be gone, just gone someplace," Charles Owens recalls. Frequently, he would go days without sleep and was liable to turn up at any time, day or night, signaling friends by tapping out the beginning of "The Dark Tree" on his car horn. According to Donald Dean, "At night time, he'd come by my house and 'beep beep beep beep-beep beep.' He'd want to take a ride. And we'd go around to everybody's house, talk a little, and then go on—the Phantom." Arranger and copyist Marion Sherrill placed a lamp in his study and turned it on to signal Horace whenever he was up late. Choir member Amina remembers those nights when "the phantom would call," a low voice at the other end asking,

"What you doing? You gonna be around?"
"No, I'm gonna be a square."
"Well, I'm gonna be a square, too, baby. I be there at ten."
"Okay." . . .
It would never be for a long time, because he didn't stay any-where long. And it would always be when the moon was full, around midnight, for years. I'd look up and see the moon, and say, "Oh, the phantom will probably be here." Sure enough the phone would ring— "What you smokin', baby?"—and he'd come by. Maybe he'd just been at Leimert Park or Catalina's and he'd put in the tape and we'd listen to it.

While he eschewed hard drugs and alcohol, Horace indulged in his favor-ite herb, marijuana, which he smoked religiously. He enjoyed telling the story of Louis Armstrong and Lionel Hampton turning him on as a young man in Hamp's band in Las Vegas, and of Armstrong's extolling the medicinal benefits of weed. "I've been smoking reefer since I came out of the womb, and I'm gonna smoke reefer all the way to the tomb" was an Armstrong mantra that Horace repeated to the end of his life.[4] When supplies ran low, there were urgent phone calls. According to Donald Dean, "That was one of his favorite things; he had to have it all the time. He'd call you up no matter what time, three or four in the morning, 'May Day! May Day!'" A stick was always at the ready. Not long after earning his private pilot's license, Bob Watt received a call from Horace asking to be taken up. Soon he was taxiing down the runway with Horace and two other Ark members settled into the passenger seats of a small plane.

> I pushed the power in and as we go down the runway, I say, "This is it. You ready?"
>
> Horace said, "I'm ready."
>
> I rotate and as soon as we get the nose off, I hear [inhaling sound]. You can imagine in such a small space and he's passing it around. I look and I say, "Oh shit! What are you doing?"
>
> "I always wanted to do that. I couldn't do it in a jet, but this is private. This is all right, isn't it?"
>
> I said, "It's private and it's much smaller than a jet. And we're all going to get high together."
>
> He said, "You, too?"
>
> "Yes, no shit."
>
> "Oh—You ever flown?" [referring to getting high]
>
> "No! Now you did it. Now we can all experience what it's like to fly high, even me, and I ain't never done it!"
>
> "You gonna be all right, Bob? What do you think?"
>
> "I don't know. I can't tell. I've never experienced this. I feel okay." The plane was full of smoke. . . .
>
> It was something and I thought "only Horace."

Horace's relationships with women also took him considerably outside of social convention. During the family's early years in Los Angeles, his sister, Robbie, recalls, "All the gals were crazy about Horace. I could never get to use the phone because they were always calling Horace." Wendell Lee Black, one of Horace's earliest friends in Los Angeles, marvels, "The girls were after him. They were after Tap. . . . And all these girls would bring him food. I don't know what it was, but they'd feed him. Everybody wanted to take care of Tap." As an adult, the combination of his personality, bohemianism, and artistry proved irresistible to many women and Horace indulged. He recounted the affairs that resulted in children in his memoir, but it was an ongoing aspect of his lifestyle. Donald Dean rolls his eyes: "I got stories to tell you, but they're mostly x-rated. And a lot of women loved him. Boy—whew—I knew all the mothers of his kids, and watched his back on many occasions. I mean—whew—he'd come down here and slap me upside the head: 'Doubles, don't say nothing!' He was a character." And through it all, Horace emerged relatively unscathed. Jon Williams concludes, "You know a guy is true blue, when women can't get mad at you."

The bohemian phantom was also committed, however, to his family, one of the reasons he decided against a mainstream career in jazz, and another, final reason for his appeal to those around him. Growing up in a mostly female household, Horace claimed a particular appreciation for women. "He spoke often of his mother and his grandmother," according to Amina Amatullah, "and of the compassion that he felt from them and the strength he got from them as women. When a man can connect to women's strength and women pain and women everything, and then hold it without it being a threat, hold it in very, very high esteem, this makes for a very compassionate person." Eric Priestley explains that even in his talks with local gang members, Horace held out the importance of family and heritage: "He didn't appreciate the gangs and the violence. He didn't like that at all. These guys would ask him where he was from and he would say, 'I'm from Robert out of Mary.' He was a beautiful cat."

While in junior high school, Horace met Cecilia Payne, who would become his wife on July 5, 1953, shortly after he enlisted in the Air Force. A few months later, their first child, Renée, was born. At the age of nineteen Horace became a family man and for the rest of his life shouldered his responsibilities for them, while they provided unwavering support for his career. Donald Dean remembers, "His wife knew him well and stuck by him. I don't know a woman in the world that stuck by a man as much as Cecilia stuck by him. And he loved her very much. There was no way in the world he would ever leave her." Elaine Brown muses, "This one had to be like a saint. She deserves everything, because he would never have been able to maintain a life. . . . I loved Horace. I don't mean that I would have liked to marry Horace, because who in the hell could live with Horace? That's why I said this woman deserves a medal. . . . It's like living with Mozart or something. Who the hell could live with these people? You have to be a saint."

The Composer

If Horace's personal qualities provided essential cement for the Arkestra, it was the sound of the Ark that drew artists and audiences and inspired many to become part of this movement. His authority rested on compelling talent as a composer, pianist, and bandleader. His musical corpus contains work that is technically sophisticated and challenging, and that captures aspects of African American life and history, celebrates the legacy of African culture, while simultaneously disclosing the universal aspects of these experiences. In combining these elements in his work, he offered to hundreds of artists an irresistible opportunity to participate in the celebration of their culture, to gain a deeper sense of self and of community, and to share their history with an international audience.

Some of the more unorthodox and appealing aspects of Horace's compositions stemmed from his attempt to capture the sounds, images, and feelings of his community. Just as Noah Purifoy, John Outterbridge, and other assemblage artists created masterpieces from found objects, many of Horace's complex rhythmic patterns were drawn from the motions and emotions of the community, from the cadences in his environment. As he observes in his autobiography, "I might see somebody walking and think what time is that. Every day, you see different patterns and rhythms going on, and it's just paying attention to what's around you."[5] He concludes, "Every time I write something, it's about what I've been a part of or seen. If the community changes, then so goes the music. That's just the way it is. I can write about red roses on a bush like everyone else, because we have them here. But it's where those red roses are growing that is really what my music is about."[6] Noticing a different pattern in an individual's gait or the complex rhythms of a group sauntering down a street could lead to a composition in unusual and sometimes rapidly changing meters. Otis O'Solomon observes, "Horace heard music everywhere. Everything was music, the raindrops, the footsteps, everything. 'Did you hear that?' And then he'd go and play it." Horace's relationship to his community was organic. "That's all I write about, is my neighborhood, consciously or unconsciously. That's what I play about. It's not a thing I ever work on, it's just what I do."[7]

Consequently, the music is raw, a rawness that reflects the streets. According to Adele Sebastian, "The value Horace brought to me was the importance of that preservation of our music, keep playing the music and keep it in its raw, natural state."[8] To Fundi Legohn, "That's Horace's style. The hood is raw and this music is coming from the hood." Billie Harris sees the complexity of every day life: "Horace's music is more like life is. It's full of changes. It's full of different moods and timings. It's closer to how we are, to how we live. You can set up a lifestyle to go smoothly a certain way, but you didn't bank on a headache coming up or a storm. All of those things be in his music! That's the only way I can explain it. He was writing life."

The harmonic and rhythmic complexities in his compositions pose challenges to even the most proficient reader. According to vocalist Dwight Trible,

"They always went somewhere you weren't expecting them to go. . . . Even if you did the same material, it was still different. Nothing was ever, ever the same. Even if the guys played it the same, once Horace started playing, it always took you someplace else." On the vocal lines, choir member Denise Tribble reflects, "I can understand why in the past a lot of the choirs didn't really try to do some of those harmonies. They're difficult. The harmonies that he has in the songs are so close. It's not four-part harmony like a barbershop quartet, where it's so easy to hear. Sometimes altos are singing as high as the sopranos and the two notes are just a shade different. It's really difficult to sing."

Time had to be spent gaining a feel for the flow of a piece. In some instances, Horace withheld the scores, instead teaching from the piano as the band and choir vocalized the music, a method used by composers like Charles Mingus, known for his difficult charts. Fritz Wise reflects, "I'm convinced more and more, I don't care how good you're supposed to be, you just can't come in and play that stuff. . . . When I'm listening to somebody else, I can tell that they don't have a handle or a clue as to what it is, or how they should be going about doing that stuff, because they use real conventional approaches toward it. And that shit ain't conventional. You have to come with an open mind."

The sense of community and environment, as well as African American and African tradition and folklore, permeates Horace's writing. Robbie started noticing how special his music was by the 1960s: "Floyd Dixon is a low-down blues man, but it was Floyd who began talking about how great Horace was. I then began to take notice." It was during the 1960s that she became aware of "the blackness, even though his music has always had a kind of universality. If you know some of the chord progressions, I could hear sounds of blackness." To non–African American members, the feel was unmistakable. According to Yaakov Levy, "The sense of warmth, of the continuity of history, of what the African American spiritual is about, the sense of history in terms of African American history, the sense of community, of support, of a moving forward, of an evolution with a great sense of love and respect, nurturing—man, all that was in his playing. Whenever I played with him, my sense of that was much more clear and much more pervasive and wide."

Aside from his focus on African themes in pieces such as "Lumumba," "Thoughts of Dar Es Salaam," and *Ancestral Echoes*, the freedom, range and expansiveness of Horace's music are in many ways also an expression of African culture. James Newton hears the African elements,

Not only in the polyrhythms that he would use in his grooves, the modes that he would use in the structuring of the songs. When he would use the title Pan Afrikan, that was a very apropos title for him in the sense that he was ahead of the loop, in the sense that he was putting together music of many different elements of the African diaspora long before people had that kind of knowledge. It just wasn't Sun Ra of the West Coast. It's very different and very unique, and it reflected his leadership and his vision.

According to Bob Watt, the more varied and communal aspect of music in African cultures is especially manifest in Horace's conception of an artistic experience, giving it a powerful emotional force.

Western culture thinks that everything has to be thought, and that which is thought is high art and more technical. In eastern culture and African thought there is a connection, mind and body in a universal context, instead of this separation and hierarchy. There is so much of a sense of feeling. Horace understood black people and how black people could lock into that, which I think is a wonderful thing as a human trait, to have this feeling, to be able to feel together and have this whole thing together. Luckily, this is not lost, because western thought believes you have to think everything out in order to do it, that you can't trust the feeling, and that the best way to make sure that you're feeling is to think. It sounds almost insane.

Much of the African feeling came from a large and firm bottom sound, a constant in Horace's writing. From his earliest years he was drawn to the sound of drums. "Since I was a kid, I've had that feeling—expectant, ominous—about drums, and I've built a lot of tunes off that drumbeat."[9] It was not unusual to have an Arkestra performance with two or three drummers, as many as three or four congueros, two to five bassists, and a tuba. Horace wanted to feel the ground move. One can only imagine the result if he had been able to realize his dream of amassing a large Arkestra for a performance in the Grand Canyon. As he told Michael Dett Wilcots, "I just want to hear that sound. I just want to hear it." Founder and leader of the Large Ensemble, Vinny Golia was strongly influenced by this aspect of Horace's art.

I saw him at the Lighthouse with three basses once. I never could fathom why he was doing that. Then when I started writing for the large group, the first thing I added was a tuba, then another bass. It became pretty bottom-heavy. It's indicative of listening to those people who really like bottom stuff. Mingus is one guy and Horace is the other guy. So I always felt a great affinity to that, because he has that really dark, left-hand thing, which is like mystical, like a mystic thing from Egypt. It is remarkable. And that's how you identify him, almost immediately.

In pieces such as "The Giant Is Awakened," "The Dark Tree," "Thoughts of Dar Es Salaam," and "To the Great House," the drums, basses and/or low brass carry an ostinato that anchors the compositions. Nate Morgan observes, "Horace's writing, man, he could be as deep as anybody could ever want to go, like in 'Thoughts of Dar es-Salaam,' which is a solemn piece. You have this ostinato rhythm going on underneath that never changes, but then you've got a million things going on top of it that just evolves and evolves and evolves." Even when dealing with older material, such as favored tunes from the bop era, Horace found a way to heavily root the composition, while still exploring unique harmonic extensions. According to Vinny,

The first time I went to see him in the church [IUCC] with the Arkestra, the bottom of it really stuck out, like a real underpinning, foundation-wise, especially with [baritone saxophonist] John Williams, who played with Basie. His anchoring was really something, almost like the pivot, so that even the basses could move around. He always had a guy like Roberto [Miranda] moving around, but he always had this pivot. His music moves like that, in big slabs and I really like that.

The other thing about it is that I liked the melodies. When he played bop things at these breakneck tempos, like "Oleo," these things almost went against the left-hand thing. So you have to open them up. It's too dark on the bottom, so you need to open the tune up for it to really stretch out. If you have too much density in the bottom, then something has to give because the notes aren't clear. So he found a way to extend them, but he didn't extend them up. He seemed to extend them down. So in order to do that, you have to open that tune up more in some manner. And he found a way to do that with those kinds of tunes, rhythm-change tunes and stuff like that.

Horace's melodies have a similarly ominous feel, reinforced occasionally by lower-pitched instruments carrying the melodic line, as with the tuba and basses in his arrangement of the spiritual "Motherless Child." Jesse Sharps remembers, "I hear a lot of Monk in there, a lot of everything with these melodies, just strange, but they fit and they're real dark, haunting." Horace's unorthodox instrumentation initially posed problems for Will Connell, the

Ark's copyist in the late 1960s, early 1970s, but it soon alerted him to broader arranging possibilities:

> Normally when you set up a page, like with a regular symphony, you have the flute, oboe, clarinet, bassoon, then you have the horns and then the violins. With a jazz score you'd probably put the tuba at the bottom, because it's the lowest instrument. But with Horace, the tuba might have the melody. Then it would be funny to look all the way down the page for the lead. So I evolved a way of writing where I'd always put the lead on top, whoever had it, then whoever had the second melody. . . . That taught me a lot of the fluidity of instruments and broke me out of that stereotypical way of looking at and handling instruments, because Horace's handling of instruments is totally free.

Horace routinely adjusted arrangements as the Arkestra's personnel changed. Butch Morris, who developed an improvisational approach to conducting known as "conduction," drew some of his ideas from Horace's handling of shifting ensembles. "I think he can challenge anybody else's right to be a great composer, but I think he was a great ensemble player, and that's the way he wrote, like a great ensemble player. He was a great accompanist, too. He knew how to accompany people and support them. And I think that's what I learned most from Horace. How to create an ensemble construction that can help support the composition itself."[10] As the personnel of the Arkestra changed, the sound reflected those changes, giving the band a rejuvenating freshness. Rufus Olivier muses,

> I do new music all the time, and the music we were playing back then was just as good or better than the stuff that's coming out now. It's just amazing. Horace was so far ahead that I'm almost spoiled, because the [San Francisco] Opera has been commissioning a lot of new work. Last year we did a new work and Andre Previn did the score. To my ear, the score was old. It was just old, but it shouldn't be. This year [2000] we did a production of *Dead Man Walking*. It was a total hit, but the music was old again. . . . [None of this] is as new as the Ark was. It was fresh; it was new; it was experimental.

Even those steeped in earlier musical styles found much to admire. Wilber Morris recalls, "Benny Harris used to love him, little Benny Harris, who wrote 'Ornithology.' We were very good friends . . . and I used to take him over to listen to the UGMAA band all the time. Now here's a staunch bebopper that loved this music as it was tending toward the outside. He used to say,

'Oh, it feels good.'" For many artists, performing with Horace created that special feeling. Fr. Amde recalls,

> I have never—and the Watts Prophets have been with some of the greatest musicians in the world, in fact we were making an album with Bob Marley when he died, Quincy Jones, we did things with him—but I've never went to heaven except with Horace. I would take off and be in the music. There was something in Horace that came out in his music, but it was Horace. There was nothing like doing poetry with that Arkestra when Horace was there, and I was doing it in my early years in South Park, in Watts. There was nothing like it. Believe me, nothing like Horace Tapscott, and I do mean that I would get on a music ship to heaven. It was very different. Never, never, ever have I got that feeling elsewhere.

The Pianist

Horace's first instrument was the piano and in the early 1960s it became his sole instrument, as dental problems forced him to put aside the trombone. Having studied with Samuel Browne and then Lloyd Reese, Horace possessed a solid technical foundation but also manifested an adventurous spirit that grew as he matured as a player and came to characterize his unique pianistic voice.

The impact of his performing was dramatic. Whenever Horace appeared in public spaces, crowds would gather. As the concert progressed, more and more people would stop and stare, riveted by Horace's playing. Bob Watt recalls one such event:

> I remember Horace played something and in such a way that it was "spoken." And when he finished somebody in the audience went, "God! Oh!" He couldn't help it. Horace stated it so well it just spoke to you. I have seen him just mesmerize people with solo piano. That was always the thing I enjoyed the most, listening to him sit down and play solo. Ah! It was a type of detail that was just indescribable. If God is in the detail, then there was the touch of God there. It would just reach you, music strong enough to cut through all the stuff that's happening today, all the lies. It was just so profound.

Those who were on the bandstand with Horace were similarly impressed. Roberto Miranda recalls, "Horace Tapscott was a technician of superb sophistication. This cat had rhythmic independence that would blow away most drummers. He had not only an intuitive sense of how music works, but a very educated sense of musical theory." His command of the keyboard was such that even recalcitrant instruments posed little challenge. Pianist Wayne Peet recalls one such piano at System M in Long Beach, California:

> That piano got worse and worse to the point where there were notes missing right around middle C, which is right where you're playing a lot. That's one of the biggest drags in the world. It just throws you, and you have to work around it and think about working around it. I've seen him play that same piano that I've played and had a ton of notes missing, and you would have never known those notes were missing. He knew where they were and worked around it. That's a whole other technique, and he'd still make them sound amazing.

Even in developing his technique, Horace was unorthodox. Will Connell recalls, "Horace once told me that he didn't think he could really use his left hand at the piano, if he didn't use it in his life. So Horace went through days when he would use his left hand for everything. He'd brush his teeth with his left hand; he'd drive with his left hand; he'd open doors with his left hand. Oh, Horace, man!" As Thelonious Monk evolved an unorthodox playing style that suited his music, much the same could be said with Horace, who shaped his approach to achieve the sounds he wanted, rather than sacrificing sound and vision on the altar of formal piano technique. According to Bobby West,

> Papa could go into cascades of sounds and arpeggios that could be considered Debussy-like, but a classical pianist who would actually play Debussy would probably not use the same kind of fingering that Papa used. His approach to playing the piano was as unique as the sounds you heard come from it. . . . He did what he needed to do with his hands and fingers to create those great sound sculptures that he was able to do in a way that nobody else could.

Horace never had a structured practice regimen, but played continually, wherever and whenever possible. In this sense he was always in the moment and the boundaries that exist for many artists, between practice and performance, formal and informal venues, simply were not there for Horace, who lived and played with the same level of intensity and commitment. As an artist twenty-four/seven, simply being on a stage did not alter his approach. He was spontaneous and expected his fellow artists to be the same, prepared to honestly express themselves at any moment, in any context. Kamau Daáood remembers,

> Musically, I've been in spaces and heard music come from him that basically seems physically impossible and the energy would be so high that everyone in the room would be at the edge of screaming, just from the awesomeness of what would be happening at a given moment. I've literally walked over to the piano afterward and seen Horace's blood on the piano from his fingers, where he gave that much. And no matter where we were or what the occasion was, he could tap into this spirit, and give all and then some to a given moment. Whether there would be five people in the audience, or whether it would be some little rinky-dink program, poorly organized with a bad piano, he approached it like he was approaching the most high in prayer, with that kind of seriousness.

As much as anyone could, Horace lived in the moment, constantly working out new ideas, new voicings, abandoning old approaches, and challenging himself and all those around him. According to Vinny Golia, "You get to a point when you're playing with him, where he can go back and bring more stuff up, and you've got to dig. He's like a bottomless pit, and you've just got to keep coming up with stuff." Every performance was a new exploration for Donald Dean. "I'd go to a gig thinking we were going to play it one way, and at the gig, he'd—you know? Whew! I just don't know how he did it. I always thought it was because of his extremely long fingers that he would think of all these different voices." To James Newton, "His playing was at times very percussive and at other times very rhapsodic. There was a real sense of discovery every time you heard this man play. It wasn't like somebody you'd go to hear play and say, 'Oh yeah, there's that lick I've heard before.' It wasn't lick driven at all. It was compositionally driven and spiritually driven, emotionally driven. It was compelling." According to Charles Owens, "You have to be honest first; you have to know the horn. Then you have to trust your feelings and not be trying to impress anybody. You're just following the spirit. That's when the best things happen, and Horace did that all the time, *every time.*"

His stylistic and technical range made it difficult to pigeonhole Horace, and truly placed him beyond category, as he drew from the music and ideas of many periods and cultures, harmonizing them into persuasive musical expressions. According to Bobby West, Horace incorporated "the entire history of the black experience in one single performance. By that I mean you could hear everything from field hollers to tin roof church revivals, to the earliest origins of the blues, to stride piano and back to church again, but this time to a sanctified church, which is a little bit different. And he will always throw hints of Duke Ellington. Duke is never far away from anything Horace has ever done." From African percussiveness and polyrhythms to minor blues and vamps, dense bebop extensions, sparse dissonances, and chromatic runs, the music's full range was present. Though at times introspective, particularly in his solo sessions, and frequently dark, his music was open and broad in an orchestral sense. In Horace's playing one heard not just the piano, but an orchestra.

His playing was also characterized by an organic quality that blended "inside" and "outside" elements in a coherent unity, rendering the distinction irrelevant. According to Sonship, "I can't even describe how Horace plays. It's almost surreal. I don't know what it is. I've never heard anybody play like that. It reminded me somewhat of the avant-garde thing, but Horace's playing was powerful and rhythmic, and it was musical also." To James Newton, Horace "had the ability to have that kind of range where sometimes the playing was not only either inside or outside, but both at the same time. The only two people I've heard do this, to where they're playing changes in the left hand and playing out in the right, are Horace and Don Pullen." In Wayne Peet's judgment,

> His outside stuff was always very organic to the music. It was never some pasted on kind of thing, like "now we're going to be free form." It was just very developmental to the point where he could play a Parker tune or some straight ahead tune, and play in clusters and play in textures, and it wouldn't seem like "What's he doing that for?" It would be very developmental, and then he'd come back. That was influential, the fact that it was very organic to what was going on, just developing into these thicker textures.

Seeing Horace at the piano was an unforgettable experience. He admired the great Western classical pianist Vladimir Horowitz for the way he embraced a piano and just "played the motherfucker."[11] So it was with Horace, exploring the expressive features of the piano, using everything from strings to keys, pedals to wood. His long arms, spread to their full extension, seized a piano, seemingly enveloping the instrument, and then standing, his lanky frame craned forward, extending into the instrument's inner workings to play upon the strings and wood. He might play a melody on the strings or simply relish the sounds of microtones and glissandi.

His approach could be exquisitely gentle and lyrical, but also full of thunder, stretching the physical limits of the piano, drawing as much as possible from the instrument, keeping the pedals depressed to alter or sustain the sound and pounding every emotion from the keys. It was not unusual for the force of his playing to raise the piano off the floor, and there were instances of keys flying from the keyboard. At Horace's sixty-third birthday party at the Shabazz Restaurant in Leimert Park, pianist Rose Gales's band took a break. When Rose saw Horace moving toward her electric keyboard, resting lightly on aluminum supports, she dashed toward the instrument, imploring Horace to go easy on it. Fundi Legohn recalls, "Soft-spoken as he was, but just such a driving force, man. I've heard of people breaking piano strings and playing hard, but seeing somebody do it . . . and on a good piano . . . and just playing with emotion, from somber and sweet, lush and pretty and sublime, to forceful and passionate, all energy and anger in the music, the full spectrum—an unmistakable sound. You know it's Horace. A giant. A giant."

The Bandleader

Given Horace's musical talents and personal charisma, he would have been able to maintain a loyal cadre of artists to perform his work, a group committed solely to furthering his artistic vision, had that been his preference. That he never seems to have entertained such a course reflects how deeply engrained was his attitude toward his fellow artists and the creation of community art. This was exemplified in his role as the leader of the Pan Afrikan Peoples Arkestra, in a pedagogic, organizing, and performing style that elicited, encouraged and celebrated artistic achievement in all those around him.

The Arkestra was open to anyone in the community with the desire and commitment to learn and play, and over the course of forty years some three hundred artists became part of the ensemble. Horace did have certain criteria and he would never put a musician in a position they couldn't handle. Involvement was not necessarily based on the level of one's musical development or experience, but rather on the person's core. Kaeef Ali emphasizes that Horace wanted "to see what was in a person, and if they were sincere with what they wanted to do with their music. It wasn't just about his music. Who else is like that?" Similarly to Phil Ranelin, "The emotion and the spirit are the main essence of it. He looked into people's heart, their spirit, and not just their musical ability." Ernest Straughter recalls his early experiences rehearsing with the band:

He would just say, "Do it again. Do it again. Don't worry about it. Sounds okay." Then he'd turn his back on it. Horace was putting up with some crap because we were out of key. We were just bad. But he gave us the inspiration. . . . Yeah, we were playing out of key, but that wasn't what Horace was after. . . . It's the soul and the essence of what they call in Indian music the raga, the spirit music, the music of the soul. Everybody has it. The composers that write it in Germany, they may call it classic, give it any name you want, it's coming from inside. That's what it is. You can't keep doing something like that and not get paid, get kicked around, and not love it. You just can't. And it's not just in the black culture. It's everywhere, wherever you do it. In our case, here in the black culture, it came from Horace. He's the godfather that put it down out here.

Given the sincerity, Horace was nonjudgmental in dealing with a wide range of personalities. Gary Bias remembers, "It was a situation where he was at the helm, but he had a very open attitude, and it seems like he really had an appreciation for whatever your efforts were. Whether you were playing well or not, the fact that you were there and involved seemed as though that was enough for him." Just before recording *The Giant Is Awakened,* an uncertain Walter Savage approached Horace. "At the last minute I told him, 'I don't want to do this. I don't want to mess this thing up.' He said, 'Aw, don't worry. You can't mess it up. All you can do is add to it.'"

Whatever level of expertise one possessed on entering, Horace sought to develop that, challenging his fellow artists to reach further. Bob Watt remembers Horace once saying,

"I know it's out of your range, but that's where we have to go, because there's nowhere else to go. So why not? Why can't we go there?"
I said, "Wow, that's high."
"Yeah, but that's where we have to go."
"Okay." That was very liberating.

Sonship Theus recalls, "It's different than the way I would think when I play with Charles Lloyd, than when I play with Freddie Hubbard. His thing challenged you to the end of it, the end of your wits as far as creativity." As with others, for Sonship every performance became an exploration: "I enjoyed the most stretching with him as an adventurer. As far as you wanted to go, he would say, 'Okay, come on. You want to go a little further? Yeah, I can go there.' He'd take you to the fullest of what you could go to. I really appreciated that about him. If nothing else, I appreciated that *the most.* Some of those times I'll never forget them in my life. That powerful, that powerful."

One of Horace's techniques involved turning off all the lights and playing in darkness. Bassist Al Hines was present on one such occasion: "The first time was at Eight-fourth and Vermont [the Shop], just Sonship, Horace and myself. Horace turned all the lights off, and we played one tune for one hour and fifteen minutes. We couldn't even see each other. It was just so beautiful and so spiritual." Horace continually pushed guitarist Avotcja to stretch for new sounds.

> I have very small hands and because of that people said I could never do certain things. . . . So, he forced me, since I liked some sounds and I just figured I couldn't do certain things I wanted to do. . . . And then he would force me to get those sounds that I actually wanted, like 13th chords, which were my favorite, and find different ways of fingering so that I could get them, even though my hands were too small. I'm really grateful to him. He pushed you to think all the time. And as soon as you thought you got one thing, he was going to push you in another direction. . . .
>
> And he always sort of knew what would make a person go a little bit further. . . . Well, I think Horace, his band, his Arkestra was sort of put together based on the sounds that he knew that he could get out of it. Not so much of what we already knew we had or other people thought we had or what have you, but what he knew we had, sometimes when we didn't know we had. And for me it was like he was putting together a puzzle from the places we could go, rather than where we were going already.

For Avotcja there was no going back: "[Horace] was the thing that charges the battery that makes the car run. He turned the motor on. . . . Whatever was speaking through him, I'm grateful that I had a chance to walk that way, because he sure opened my mind to a lot of things and it'll never be shut again."

As well as stretching for new sounds, Horace encouraged everyone in the Arkestra to compose their own music and the band book reflected the variety of musical voices. The Arkestra Nimbus recordings contain contributions from eight other members. This was not only a matter of fostering the development of individual artists, but also was essential to Horace's idea of expressing, preserving and passing on the culture of the community, something which could not be accomplished by any one artist.

According to Abdul-Salaam Muhammad, Horace's constant refrain was, "What are you hearing? Write!" Fuasi Abdul-Khaliq recalls the effect of Horace's encouragement upon the members:

> One time he had a huge chest. He called it the treasure chest, because you open that sucker up, man, and there was so much music—scores, scores, scores—all over from everybody from the beginning, when it was called the Underground Musicians Association. So everybody was like, "Yeah, man, I want my chart to go in there." Everybody's writing and throwing their chart into the treasure chest to be a part of the archive. That's what we wanted to do. And then he would play it. We'd play everybody's chart and everybody had something to say. So in that sense he was an even greater icon than Sun Ra. He was really preserving the music and not just his music, his way, but our music, our way. It was the community's way.

Whether composing, arranging or performing, Horace encouraged self-discovery. Arthur Blythe recalls the freedom he felt when he first came around: "One of the main experiences with Horace that helped me focus was that I had the opportunity to be free playing with him. If I had played with some other people, there would have been some restrictions and would have hampered my growth." It wasn't a requirement that one play free jazz, but that one play freely, whatever one's stylistic preference. Encouraging individual expression, exploration and honesty in artistic statement, was a sine qua non under Horace's leadership. Fuasi explains that "it was like whatever you have to say, however you want to say it, however you can do it, if you have to squeak, honk, blow, play arpeggios, or whatever, just get it out, say it." According to Charles Owens, "I could play with the Ark and do anything I could possibly imagine, and the stuff I couldn't even imagine that I could imagine. That's what it was about, an experimental place where you could really stretch to the limit and not have to feel guilty when you walked off the bandstand. That's where Horace was coming from."

No matter how different the music became, or what the reaction might be, Horace relentlessly encouraged every player without imposing a particular style. James Andrews explains,

> One thing I appreciate from him is that Horace never told me what to play, how to play it, unless it was a composition that he had written, that he did. It was something he was after. But he never told any of us what to play, how to play. Don't play that. That doesn't sound good.

He'd never do that. Once, I think, he picked you, chose you, that you were in his organization, he left it up to you. . . . I never got any criticism from him except for one time. And that's because I wasn't playing the music as was written one time and he lit into me. But other than that, he never had a negative thing to say about what you were doing. As a matter of fact, he bolstered you. He supported you in what you're trying to do.

For Sabir Mateen, this approach contained a life lesson as well. "I learned, basically, life, which is music, and he showed us how to be ourselves and how to really reach the boundaries, go to the limit, not be afraid of anything, just do what we do and what we believe in, and stick to what we believe in, and just do it."

Along with composing, Horace encouraged everyone to solo as a vehicle of personal, musical exploration and expression. Rarely were compositions performed under ten minutes because of the number and length of solos. According to Edwin Pleasant, "When he gave you a solo, he wanted you to play, whatever came out of your head. He wanted it to come through that horn, or drum, or piano, or bass. He didn't try and tell you what or how. He'd just say, 'Play. This is your solo, play. You got thirty-two bars. You got it.'" Billie Harris recalls, "He was an excellent leader because he knew how to pull out of you what was in you, rather than have you lean on him to carry you through your musical experience. He would nurture you, but as soon as you stood on the edge of the nest, he would push you off and make you try your wings. . . . He did that to me . . . almost every time. He knew what kind of hang-up I had, but he wouldn't buy it." Fuasi remembers the first solo he took with the Arkestra, on "Lino's Pad" at the IUCC one month after he joined:

I was playing and whatever I was playing wasn't working, but Horace didn't care. He was like, "Play!" I thought I was finishing my solo and he jumped up and said, "Play! Play!" I kept going and, man, I must have taken one hundred choruses before he let me sit down. . . . I think he was trying to get me to forget my inhibitions, my fears, and just to play what you have to say, say what you want to play. And he was going to make me stay up there until I said what I wanted to say, until I had worked through my fears and inhibitions. By the time I was finished playing, I had released whatever I had to release. He had already foresaw this and he knew that's what I needed. After that, there was nothing to be afraid of.

Horace's search for authentic expression also was manifested in the way he put bands and performances together, frequently a spontaneous response to each situation, shaped by the mood and scene. Artists were never sure what was going to be performed, nor when they might be called upon. "Horace would rehearse maybe three or four tunes to perform for the event," Fritz Wise explains, "and then get to the event and do something totally different, do one tune. He did that on several occasions." He had a knack for picking those pieces that fit the mood and temper of the time and place. "You'd never know what he was going to do," states Donald Dean. "You had to be ready. And the response from the people was just tremendous. It seemed like he had a feel for what the people wanted. He could really excite a crowd. I've seen times that they would be just screaming and hollering."

There was also uncertainty of who might be performing on any particular day. Donald remembers, "You never knew what Horace was going to do. I'd come, set up my drums, and maybe two, three other drummers would come up. Or he'd have five and six bass players, two piano players, tubas. Horace would always come up with something different and he made it work." Choir member Amina Amatullah recalls, "The Voice wasn't always on the program. You were always ready and would go to the concert, but Horace was the only one who knew if you were going to perform that day." Similarly, no one knew ahead of time who would be soloing or when. They had to be prepared when Horace pointed at them. Fundi Legohn notes, "It really tripped me out, how when it was your turn to play a solo, Horace would be playing, burning, and he'd just look up at you, just a little. If you missed it, he wouldn't say anything, but later he'd say something like, 'Why didn't you play?'"

The dancers and poets or word musicians also had to be ready when Horace nodded. Since they didn't know what pieces the Arkestra would be playing, most poets brought a sheaf of pieces to choose from or improvised. According to Kamau Daáood, "At any given time, and most times without warning, he would call me up to read. So it wasn't like 'we've got a concert this Sunday and we're gonna do this piece and I want you to read this piece.' It was more like a soloist. That sharpened me. Every time something was played, I immediately had to think what would fit with this, what would work with this, in case I got called." From Horace's standpoint, you were always an artist and should be ready to contribute, when the mood dictated. It was a part of everyday life, not something apart.

There were also times when Horace might pull someone up on stage from the audience to perform with the band. James Andrews recalls one memorable performance by the Ark of Fuasi Abdul-Khaliq's *Eternal Egypt Suite* at the Pomona Fairgrounds:

> Fuasi's writing was just grandiose. He wrote in the Horace tradition. All the horns, and all of us had our parts. There would be counterpoint, all that rhythmic counterpoint to all that. The band was just hitting the song—da da da-da da da-da-da. Then Horace beckons this guy on the stage, this elderly black gentleman. He had on a little tattered suit and this little hat and his harmonica. And he starts wailing the blues, while we're playing *Eternal Egypt,* right in the middle of what we're doing.
>
> Then Horace kind of looked at us and gave us a little smile. He's up there conducting. We were just flabbergasted. We were just like, Yes! And we're in the middle of one of our most written pieces, one of those really hard pieces to play with all the different parts. But this guy is just wailing the blues. He could have been doing some Mississippi Delta blues or something like that. He was playing against us, a counterpoint thing, and Horace just made that happen. I don't know what it was sounding like out there, but up on the stage it was something else.

Horace alternately occupied the piano chair, conducted, or danced around the bandstand as the music moved him. Over the years, he evolved an informal approach to conducting using hand signals, gestures, and body movements that enabled him to restructure compositions in the middle of performances or to direct group improvisations. French horn player Wendell C. Williams recalls, "We'd play avant-garde and he could direct that and just take it up and out. We'd sound like birds all of a sudden. We didn't rehearse that; he'd just direct it. He'd stick his hands up in the air, and we knew to take it out. He'd wiggle his fingers, and we'd start sounding like rain. We knew what he meant. We knew the hand signals." Butch Morris explains, "Horace had certain signs and everybody knew what those signs were just from having been in his band and playing with him. Those signs were sort of intuitive."[12]

Rehearsals under Horace were never routine, and there was little separating them from gigs. According to Fundi Legohn, "Once he sat down, it was like a concert, man, even in rehearsal. Gone! Count it off—gone! I had never been with cats sweating so profusely soloing." Rehearsals concluded whenever Horace and the band felt it was time to stop. According to Edwin Pleasant, "We'd rehearse and rehearse and rehearse, and never grumble about how long we've been rehearsing. Anybody else's band we'd be saying, 'Man, when are we going to end? We've been rehearsing for three hours already." Not with Horace. I never heard anybody complain about how long his rehearsals were, or how long we'd been playing one tune." Sometimes rehearsals would pass without any music being played. With Horace there was no separation between performance, rehearsal, and socializing with musicians. They all fed the same process. William Roper, a stickler for times and structure, recalls,

> I remember one rehearsal, we didn't play anything. There was the waiting for people to show up. The joints came out; that's going around, but I'm not smoking that. Then whatever the time was that the rehearsal was supposed to go until, three o'clock or whatever, I said to Horace, "Okay, Horace, I got to go."
> "Alright, Rope. We didn't play, did we?"
> "No, we didn't play."
> "Sometimes those are the best rehearsals."
> And that's true. That's the time to get to know Horace and the band.

The spirit of the band and its music grew out of the close personal relationships within the Ark, bonds forged outside the rehearsal room and performance stage. On many occasions Horace would just sit with people and converse. "We'd have these great meetings in the back room of his house," according to Fuasi Abdul-Khaliq. "That was the room where we would do our thing. We'd smoke, and talk, and listen to tapes of what we just did." Ali Jihad learned of the early music history of African American Los Angeles from conversations with Horace: "I knew nothing about the history of Central Avenue, until I talked to Horace myself. We'd sit there and he'd get to talking. He was a talker, always conversation." At times he would round people up, according to Michael Dett Wilcots, day or night:

> Sometimes, very early in the morning, he would come by my house and say, "Get up!" I'd come outside and there would be a couple of carloads of other people he had got up, and we would go to a park, like La Tijera, and sit on the side. Now what? "Well, we just gonna talk." He hadn't been to sleep, but he would always gather all of his comrades, and talk about any and everything in the world. It was that closeness and that caring that made us work, made us do our craft with no pay, because there wasn't no pay, but it really made the music flourish and it also preserved what he was trying to preserve.

The Community Artist

The family man, committed to his wife and an everyday presence in the lives of his children, and the bohemian, who single-mindedly pursued his art, indulged his appetites, and drove the streets at night visiting his extended family of artists, were reconciled in the community artist, which provided Horace with a merged aesthetic and ethos. By inextricably tying his family with his fellow artists and the community at large, he evolved an ethic of community activism and cultural practice that would focus his artistic and social energy, and provide a unifying force in his life.

To Horace, the community was an extension of the family. Kamau Daáood recalls, "Horace taught me so much and made the connection about family and the community, and how they're really both the same, how they're really supposed to be the same." Perhaps what exemplifies this most is what Horace once told Kafi Roberts: "'Man, I don't get comfortable playing until I hear a baby cry.' He was saying that he likes the family venue, and he knows that when you hear a baby cry, that's the perfect setting. He told me his fondest memories were always when the kids were part of it." Horace always encouraged that involvement, no matter the setting. "Whenever Horace walked into a room," Dadisi Komolafe relates, "if there was a child there, he would acknowledge the child before he would acknowledge anybody else, whether he knew the child or not. He'd make eye contact and he'd go up, 'Heeey!' He loved children, loved children." Denise Tribble tells of a performance Horace and Dwight gave at an elementary school: "Horace got up off the piano and started skipping around the room and all the little kids were following behind him. He always had a special thing with children."

For many members, Horace was a brother or surrogate father as well as a peer. To Azar Lawrence, "Horace was a very beautiful, big brother kind of image, very guiding. His calling was to shape us young people." Shunned by his family because of his involvement with UGMAA, Fuasi Abdul-Khaliq came to rely on Horace for familial, emotional support as well. "I kind of replaced my father with him, because in my eyes he was everything I needed, not only as a big brother, but as a father figure." Similarly, Denise Tribble recalls, "When he passed, it was as if my father had passed and I felt more about him than I did my own dad." For Kafi Roberts, "It was like he didn't touch me; he touched my whole family. My wife, my kids, that's their Papa. Horace had a real deep and profound and lasting effect, not just on the guys in the band, but Nate [Morgan]'s kids. That's their grandpapa, and the same with my kids. It went past that boundary of just playing the music."

Being part of this community family meant being a resident, someone who not only performs there but who is an every day presence on the streets, in the stores, interacting with those around. To understand, influence, and become part of the community meant being there, in good times and bad. Horace explains in his memoir:

> That's one real convincing way for a youngster to take note of someone, is if they see them all the time. That person might be known throughout the United States or all over the world, but in this neighborhood they're one of the people, one of the community. And that's how kids, young folks, gain confidence. "If you want to teach me something, now I can listen to you, because I believe you. I believe you, because you're here." They won't say, "Oh, well, he's going to Beverly Hills. He ain't thinking about us now." So we were where it was important to be. If you're really thinking of trying to help the community, you can't just jump into it. You have to really figure it out and it's not easy.[13]

Watts Prophet Otis O'Solomon draws deeply from this teaching: "The arts belong to the people, and they need to see art in their community; not just the people on TV, the people who are famous and such, but people who they see every day, on a daily basis." And there Horace remained until the end of his life. "Horace never wanted to move from that area," Elaine Brown explains. "The Crips could come; the Crips could go. He didn't care."

During the bad times, Horace was always there, from performing in prisons to offering a shoulder in times of tragedy. When Bill Madison's wife died, at his daughter's request Horace performed Stevie Wonder's "Ribbon in the Sky" at the services. Bill remembers: "I told Horace, 'It seems that whenever tragedy strikes me, you're always around and I appreciate that.' And that was one of the things I told him . . . the week before he passed. 'You've always been there; you had faith in me. You were willing to go along with me and trust me and help me grow, when a lot of people were not. And that's worth more than life to me.'" In the 1990s gang violence brutally intruded on Steve Smith's family, when his nineteen-year-old son was shot and paralyzed in a drive-by shooting:

> When something like that happens, you just have no idea the depression or the pain that you can feel, even more so than if something had happened to yourself, but you just find a way to go on. Especially in the first days, it's real hard. I've always played music to help myself feel better, to heal, be around that healing energy. I was playing with

Michael [Session]'s band, and we were rehearsing at the World Stage. And I remember Horace walking in—he had heard—walked straight up to me and hugged me. He had just come up there to do that. Then he walked out and left.

Kamau Daáood and his family went through the torment of having a young son diagnosed with a brain tumor and then undergoing five surgeries. "We were blessed because he ended up playing football at Westchester High School, but an eight-year-old, finding a brain tumor, all this kind of stuff, me and my wife living at the hospital for over a month. There were several times when I would go to Horace and just break, and be crying and talk to him. He'd be there for us. You know when you love somebody so much—[cries]—I guess that said it, man."

As a community leader and artist, Horace was less concerned with the requirements of particular styles and more with music as a vehicle for transmitting African American culture. According to Bobby West,

> With him it was less about the technological wizardry of a McCoy Tyner. It was less the recital hall brilliance and beauty of a Bill Evans. It had less to do with the technical wizardry of somebody like Oscar [Peterson], where it's chorus after chorus. No. Papa's approach was that his music was going to encapture and his music was always going to exemplify his cause. And his cause was struggle. It was always that. That's the reason that he lived the life he lived. If he could have changed up his style, he certainly possessed the skill, the technical ability to play any kind of piano for any kind of person. No, Papa's thing was, "This is my gift from God, but this is also my shield and my sword to carve into everyone's consciousness what is going on with the black experience."

In so doing, he became an exemplar of that experience, reflecting the social and cultural forces of his time and providing a voice for those forces, awakened and unleashed within the community that, in part, came together as UGMA and then the Pan Afrikan Peoples Arkestra. "Horace Tapscott was ahead of his time. He never got caught in the bullshit. He couldn't be bought. He did it his way, all the way, forever," eulogizes Tommy Trujillo. "He was like the Muhammad Ali of that scene. He lasted a long time and he inspired these motherfuckers and all these people in L.A. and in the world who knew about him. Anybody that was a part of that scene was heavy. I don't care what they say. You had to be heavy even to be hanging out. Maybe you didn't play, but you had to have that consciousness."

He was the inspirer, instigator, creative center, and facilitator through his quiet example and the force of his consciousness and music. To Jesse Sharps, "Like Kamau said, he made being a community musician respectable.... You've got to really believe in that, and that was his thing. He made it; he conceived it; got it started; got it rolling, and he never wanted it to end." Danyel Romero puts it succinctly: "Once we start helping people, like Horace helped others, that's when the true blessings come, that's when you can blow the notes and play the phrases that Horace could play." Ultimately, that's where his legacy lies. According to Kamau Daáood,

> I think that Horace's impact on the community is that of a leader, a natural leader, one that arises from the people and takes on the responsibilities of leadership unflinchingly. That's a rare quality, to be able to bring people together in that way and to hold people together, to where your power is based not necessarily in an organizing skill or from some source of force, but power that basically is generated from people believing in the vision that your being radiates. Horace's being represented something that was very, very old, ancient perhaps, this spirit of connectedness, a wholesome spirit of connectedness. And that's what the music did. It connected us together. It connected the players of the music together. The music connected the community together.

THE BLACK APOSTLES

The Arkestra/UGMAA Ethos/Aesthetic:
Music, Artists, and Community

But it's beautiful to love the world
with eyes
that have not yet
been born.
And splendid
to know yourself victorious
when all around you
it's all still so cold,
so dark.

OTTO RENÉ CASTILLO

A Nigerian proverb cautions, "One tree cannot make a forest."[1] Neither did one individual make the Pan Afrikan Peoples Arkestra and the Union of God's Musicians and Artists Ascension. Hundreds of artists came together around Horace Tapscott's vision of a collective, community-based arts movement. During a forty-year period they developed that vision into an ethos of community involvement and an aesthetic rooted in African American social life incorporating aspects of West African cultural tradition and looking beyond the commercially driven values of contemporary society to a richer, more cooperative cultural life.

Evolving through their everyday practice as community artists, they offered neither treatises nor manifestoes, but the straightforward example of lives animated by this purpose, leaving their imprint on the myriad individuals and community they embraced. The Arkestra and UGMAA demonstrated the essential role of the arts within the community, the importance of collective artistic endeavor, the wide range of artistic talent within a community, and how a collective movement brings out that talent within individuals, allowing it to flourish and develop. As such their most important contribution was not a product or a commodity, though their recorded and compositional legacy is significant, but a process of cultural production and development within and for their community.

An Alternative Aesthetic: "Ain't no more stars, every living ass this time"

The Arkestra's commitment to artistic integrity and the environment which nurtured it sublimated individual values. In rejecting personal aggrandizement as the primary motivation, they offered individual growth within the context of collective achievement in the belief that this was necessary for the uplift of the community and each artist within it. Kamau Daáood recalls, "Everybody was constantly helping everybody else. The main thing was getting the music right. There weren't a lot of egos being thrown around. The work was really what was important. We really felt we had something that people needed." Will Connell explains,

> I used to say then that I'm a live coal from the center of the fire, whose name and form have been burnt out eons ago. We felt that the thing was to have no ego. We used to say, "Ain't no more stars, every living ass this time." That was one of the things the Ark was about, like Africans for whom there was no such thing as an artist separate from the tribe. The tribe made art in unity, as one thing. That's what the Ark was about. That's why I was there.

Capitalist culture constructs society as composed of self-seeking atoms and posits an opposition between the individual and the group, one in which individuality is only smothered within a larger entity. However, the UGMAA collective brought out and encouraged individuality in hundreds of artists.

According to Dadisi Sanyika, "The experience of the music dealt with releasing the creative potential that each and every one of us has, that we have something to give to the world." Sabir Mateen, who walked away from a college music program after joining the Ark, remembers,

> They gave me the opportunity to know who I am. No school could do that, because the schools don't teach you the spiritual side of music. They don't teach you how to look within yourself to find yourself musically. This is what the Ark did for me, one thing out of many. On the physical side, they taught me how to read music, how to be a composer, [but also] how to be contributive and not compete. You always get that competitive feeling in you. Everybody has an ego, but it's how you control that ego. Can you use that ego to better yourself, or to harm others and destroy yourself? It's the same thing with music. How are you going to use it? That's the spirituality part.

Instead of a competitive belief in only a few surviving to take a limited number of seats at the top, the Ark allowed for an expanding number. "Their souls were so warm," Rufus Olivier recalls. "There was never even a hint whose solo was better than his. Everybody was allowed to be who they were. I was a greenhorn. I was allowed to be a greenhorn. Nobody made fun of me at all. . . . No one tried to be like someone else. Everyone was allowed to be themselves. I was allowed to learn. I was allowed to be great."

Whether in rehearsal or in performance, at whatever level of musical experience, the Ark aesthetic required self-expression. Adele Sebastian recalls her first, reluctant solo with the Arkestra: "I knew nothing about improvisation, and they would always try and get me to play. 'C'mon, baby, play a solo.' I was only about sixteen and scared to death, and here was this band with all these heavy cats. I knew nothing straight out of high school. Finally, I got the Arkestra initiation, where everybody walked off stage and left me by myself. It was beautiful though, and I learned to stretch out."[2] As new members appeared, scores were expanded to accommodate. Since the Ark never appeared in rigid sections, there was always room on the bandstand. Never a chair in sight, aside from the piano bench and drum seats, the band formed a loose, standing semicircle, which fostered a raw, street-level quality to the music. If this meant a loss of more narrow musical values, it was justified by a more accurate conveyance of the sound and look, which its audience would recognize as "our band."

A competition to see who would survive could have easily happened. There was a wide range of talent within the Arkestra and a core of exceptional artists. However, the attitude was always one of mutual support. The cutting contest, sharpening your skills at the expense of other musicians, akin to a shoot-out in the old West and sometimes consciously made so by musicians and critics, was held to be counterproductive. "Our music is contributive, rather than competitive" was a constant refrain, a slogan displayed on the Nimbus Arkestra records. According to Fuasi Abdul-Khaliq, "The thing in [Horace's] concept was not to damage anybody, but to enhance everything, to build everything up, whatever it takes. If somebody looks slow, then you show him how to read." To Dadisi Komolafe, "Cats used to try and cut each other up, but with the Arkestra it was never that type of thing. It was always uplifting each other, and when we played, we played together. He never taught us about cutting and stuff like that." Zero-sum games, where one's advantage would necessarily entail someone else's loss, were alien to the Arkestra. Michael Session recalls, "Horace always said, 'No one can play better than you, but you.' That's always stuck in my head. 'You can do anything with anybody and be as strong as anyone else, because you are.' He had a way of saying things that really strengthened you, whether you knew it or not."

Not surprisingly, the sounds of the members were unique and individual. Gary Bias recalls, "There was a mixture of guys there. Some of the guys were kind of out, and some of them weren't. I think mainly what everybody had in common was a love for the music and a need for an outlet to be able to express musically. In that situation there was so much improvisation. It was a situation where the barriers that existed in a lot of other places didn't exist." Roberto Miranda is fond of saying that a true improviser is someone "simply playing the song his spirit is singing," and this was expected of each member, regardless of stylistic preference or level of technical development, regardless of the artistic boundaries then current. Edwin Pleasant recalls Roberto's embrace of this aesthetic,

> I'll never forget Roberto playing a solo and instead of playing on this side of the bridge, Roberto reached out and played below the bridge, which was all right because he was getting sounds. He'd just be playing, bowing the string below the bridge, and he might say, "Ahhh!" and then he'd go back and play some more. Then he might tap on the side of the bass and yell again, before going back. Well, whose band do you know is going to let you go through all that madness? But with Horace, it was all right. "Play, man, play! Whatever hits you, play it!"

This encouragement influenced people in other areas to be innovative as well. For Dadisi Sanyika, a martial artist and community organizer, "it just facilitated people, in the audience or on the stage, to be creative. That's really the essence of what it's all about.... Everybody has an instrument. At the time I was an organizer, and I was saying, 'Organization is my instrument.' So I just started organizing."

Shaped by and emerging from the area, the artists learned to express their visions to the community in an ongoing dialectic, each performance and composition a summary of the current status of that dialogue, of the ongoing conversation on their lives as members of the community. In so doing, they preserved the history and helped shape the community by offering art that was a reflection of its evolution, its values and torments, virtues and problems. In this, the purpose of the Ark was crystallized, as Kamau explains:

> In the music is the emotional history of a people, and it's a language that is higher than a verbal language, because it has a way of communicating through feeling and connecting people through feeling in ways that language can't, and it cuts directly to the place it needs to go. I think the unity that people seek is in the music, that it has the elements that give us the common understanding that we need to work together and to do things outside of the music together.... That was our mission, to bring the people together and try to make them understand.

Consequently, Horace felt that the arts were not the possession of individual artists. Being a community artist meant receiving inspiration from the world around you, processing that information and those feelings, and expressing it to your community with your bandmates. Otis O'Solomon recalls, "He stressed that the arts belong to the community, to the people in the community, and although not all the people in the community were musicians and artists, the artists had to represent them." At most performances Horace would announce, "This is your music" or "This is your Arkestra." Speaking at a memorial service for Horace at New York City's Knitting Factory in June 1999, Will Connell recalled that rather than identify a composition to the audience, Horace would sometimes simply say, "This is one more you wrote through us."[3]

Without reservation or dilution, the Arkestra presented its work, which ran the gamut from free-form improvisation to folk songs and spirituals, in some cases suggesting the history of African American music in one composition. Occasionally, one piece might last through a set, with long, searching, and searing solos. As cutting-edge as it often was, there was never an artistic leveling to cater to an audience. It was vital to respond as a participant in the communal life and to present that response with integrity. If the organization was to fulfill its mission of raising the community through the arts, it could not be a compromised art. According to Kufahamu, "Emotions and feelings come through in that music. Hearing 'Warriors All,' you know what the underlying emotion is. This is some kind of reality we have to deal with, and you should deal with it, if you're going to be living in the real world. So in that sense, it gave the community another sense of who they were and what they were capable of becoming."

"Respectable and Noble Work"—A Community Ethos

The example of Horace's abandonment of the commercial world to be a community artist animated the organization from its inception. Butch Morris recalls, "Wherever we went, whether it was for two dollars, gas money, or whatever the money was, that [community ethos] was paramount in everybody's mind. In many ways that's why the band still exists." According to Steve Smith, "Can you imagine Horace did all that with no money? In terms of keeping a band together? We were not paid. Why do you have this commitment from people like Charles Owens and so forth? You gotta have that other side, or you just lose everything, just a bunch of notes. You'll be playing the exact same music and it just won't have the same effect." And to Dadisi Sanyika,

> For certain events the Peoples Arkestra was there. You could count on them being there, not based upon money or none of that kind of stuff, and that's like the highest level of humanity. The experience of that is the most powerful thing. The music is there and it's great, but what's driving it? It was the goodness of it, the love. That's what the whole UGMAA experience really embodied, man, that everybody had this love and this energy of creative exchange.

Joining the Pan Afrikan Peoples Arkestra meant participating in a collective dedicated to improving the community and oneself through art. It was not simply a question of "giving back" in grateful acknowledgment of early, shaping influences but a deeper engagement with those sources, a participation in a complex and nuanced, lifelong dialectic as a member of the community and as an artist. According to Kafi Roberts, "The Ark is an institution within the community. It gives the community something to look toward, to take from, to add to, and to be a part of. We don't separate ourselves from the community, because we come from the community. We are part of the community and we are servants of the community." Sabir Mateen recalls performing in South Central: "Believe me, it's such a beautiful feeling, a great,

great feeling. It's hard to explain. It's that good, like coming home and seeing your family that you haven't seen in years. It's almost like that. That's the kind of feeling I would get every time I played the church or the Watts Towers or Vernon Park, or any of those places."

For most artists, a commitment to non-commercial goals usually means exclusion from the traditional performance spaces and economy and a search for other forms of cultural production. Most such efforts during the post–World War II period involved attempts by musicians to control the usual milieus of commercial performance, viz record production, distribution, and venues. The Arkestra developed a broader focus on alternative cultural production by removing it from any commercial context, one aspect of which was searching out public performance spaces where people gathered, such as schools, parks, street corners, and community centers. "They won't give us work?" Edwin Pleasant asks rhetorically. "We'll make our own work."[4] None of these spaces would provide economic benefits, but performing there would have a decisive impact on the area's culture and on the children who would be exposed to the arts. Amina recalls, "We started doing concerts in parks that were free. We did them in community centers. The community needed everything we had to give, and the only stage or auditorium we had was churches, school gymnasiums, and parks. Horace would always make it free for the attending community, and we sang the music of the people and it grew."[5]

Aside from finding spaces to perform, they also inspired and recruited artists from the community. The arts were seen as an essential good that did not have to be imported. All that was required to produce art was within their area and within every individual. Horace believed art or creativity was an inherent aspect of a person, and the more that aspect was encouraged and drawn out of people, as performers, supporters, or appreciators, the more a community would prosper. Those who had the particular focus to be artists represented a pool in the community to be tapped. Roberto Miranda explains, "What he was saying was, 'You have artists right here in your community. You don't need to go to New York. You don't need to go to Europe. You got artists right here in L.A. Love them; play their work; respect them; study with them; teach them.' . . . He didn't need to go anywhere else to find high art. It doesn't get any higher than it is here."

By pulling artists from their area, constantly presenting art as part of everyday life, addressing political and social issues in their art, as well as undertaking such tasks as distributing food and offering classes, they became a social support for and cultural bearers of their community, preserving and developing its heritage. Kamau Daáood explains, "Community artist is really a very meaningful concept to me. I've often said that to live and work in a community and be known for the work that you do in that community, is respectable and noble work. And this is the concept that basically I learned in the Arkestra." To Father Amde of the Watts Prophets, influenced by the immediate examples of Horace, Billy Higgins, and Don Cherry, that vocation is a high calling, in many ways reminiscent of the traditional West African griots:

> It's one of the most important things to a community because artists give a community definition, and a community artist has a great responsibility and that is to breed others like him or her, and that's what these artists did. They nourished and took care of the young artists of the community. They exposed them to art at its finest and it was free. They weren't always reaching for a dollar or trying to tell you to get in the background. That wasn't where they were at. A community artist is very, very important to the development of culture, and he's the keeper of the tradition, the culture and history of a community. And that's what all of those guys were.

In this sense the community artists and arts provide a cultural and spiritual sustenance, essential to the success of any community. Members perceived, embraced, and contributed to a spiritual quality in the music that was both personal and community-based. Michael Session explains, "The Ark is not a commercial band. It's a spiritual band. I've seen other big bands, a lot of big bands, and the Ark is totally different. It has ghetto music. You don't hear big bands play this kind of music. . . . It has a community, street flavor, but it's not a raggedy sound. . . . It was tight, but it was loose. It wasn't conforming. It had so much life and spontaneity to it. It's hard to describe, but once you see and hear it, you feel it."

For Steve Smith that commitment distinguishes the Arkestra: "What makes it special is the spiritual aspect, and that's doing things for the community. That's the basis of what makes it powerful. So no matter how much you're trying to practice now and figure things out, until you get that kind of feeling and commitment and get together on it, you don't have that guiding force pulling you forward." According to artist John Outterbridge, "How do you keep the wings and the directives in music being not just about sound, but about spirit? [Horace] was very much into that, and about the power of a relationship to your belief vessels. His music did all of that, and it made you know that it's not a horn alone that you're blowing, or it's not a bass that you're picking, but that's a spirit thing that you're with at the moment, and know that." Hand drummer Jai Jae Johnson elaborates, "When Horace played, people would be reborn. Their souls would be redeemed or saved somehow because the music reconnected them and brought them back to a certain consciousness that was lacking in their life. And that's what was so important about Horace. His music was medicinal; had a medicinal quality on it that would heal, and people would come for that."

As a crystallization of the values UGMAA and the Arkestra embodied, the music was the organization's purest expression of its community ethos, and despite ongoing problems—economic survival, drug issues, family matters, different generational and political perspectives—it was the music that acted as the cement. Its creation and performance exuded an energy that celebrated UGMAA's spirit and touched everyone involved, generating a collective consciousness that more than anything else was responsible for the cohesion and duration of the band.

Trombonist Lester Robertson, who was present at the creation in 1961, penned a composition in 1969, "The Call," which celebrates the commitment made by many of the artists, who speak not simply of joining a band, but of being "called" to the purpose and mission of UGMAA and the Arkestra. Michael Dett Wilcots recalls, "One time, in one of the Great Houses, everybody was sitting around and everybody had a story of 'The Call.' Everybody had a story of how they were attracted to Horace and the music before they heard Horace and the music. That meant that it is something greater than ourselves." Michael Session felt the pull the first time he saw Horace and the Arkestra: "Like the time he said, 'You young cats gotta go through here before you go anywhere else. This is your Ark.' Once you hear the call . . . the day he said it, I heard him so loud and clear that I started striving for that. He let us know this was our band."

Whenever anyone left the Ark, they never lost their place. It remained theirs for life, open to them whenever they wished to return. According to Al Hines, "Through it all, all the people I've played with, and groups that I've been involved with, UGMAA was with me. I could always be with UGMAA when I wanted to. When I left UGMAA to go on a gig, I'd come back to UGMAA." Amos Delone, Jr., who had been teaching music at the John Burroughs Middle School, was at the tribute to Horace the day after his passing, when "they asked me to play because all the former members were performing. I saw a lot of people I hadn't seen in years and years. Michael [Session] and Steve [Smith] told me that I'm still a member, so if I want to come back. . . . I've been practicing with them since." Sabir Mateen left Los Angeles in 1981 and after a brief stay in Philadelphia relocated to New York City. "The first gig I played in New York was with Kaeef [Ali]. I ran into all these people who used to play in the Ark from all these different periods. I met Wilber [Morris]; met Butch [Morris]. I met Will [Connell]. Me, Will and Wilber play a lot together now. . . . The Ark vibe never dies. Like I said in an interview, 'You're in UGMAA. You're never out.'"

Passing It On

If their work within the community was to have any long-term import, members recognized the imperative of transmitting it to succeeding generations. "'Pass it on.' Those were [Horace's] famous words. You gotta pass it on. If you don't pass it on, you didn't really have it, or you won't have it long," Jesse Sharps explains. The music was to be preserved as an aspect of community identity, passed on to future generations, not as a commodity but as a process of artistic expression and an inextricable part of community life. These attitudes were clearly and consciously reflected in the way artists were recruited from the community and in the manner that music was encouraged and passed on within the Ark.

Mentoring was multifaceted, involving formal and informal classes, individual and group tutoring, on-the-job training, constant give-and-take between the members, and being thrown into the deep end. Avotcja recalls, "People used to hear and say all the time, 'Each one, teach one,' but it's like a cliche. In [Horace's] thing it wasn't. Everybody who was there, it was their responsibility to teach you. It was your responsibility to teach somebody else." Learning, developing technical skills were important, and members devoted hours of practice to improving their technique. At times Horace gave informal classes in music theory at his home on Monday nights. Rufus Olivier attended those sessions: "He would use the piano and would explain the leading tones and how to use certain notes in solos, and no note is really a wrong note. It's just how you play with it, like Monk did; turn a mistake into a masterpiece." Similarly, Lester Robertson offered insights into harmony at the keyboard. Steve Smith was one of his students:

> [H]e would sit down at the piano and he had this way of voicing chords where his hands would be so stretched and the chords would be so long that it would just be incredible listening to his concept of chord progressions and things. He was really deep into that. A lot of that was so advanced to me, musically, even though I'd been studying for a long time. And here again, he wasn't the type of guy that would sit down and say, "Well, look, this is an E-flat major 7. That's what we were playing

on. . . ." No, it never went down like that. You just would look over his shoulder.

Horace and Lester's informality was one more aspect of the Ark approach that reflected a more traditional West African orientation of learning by immersion. When Gary Bias first came around, "There was always this very open-armed attitude in the Ark. If you were a musician and you had a desire to play, that pretty much was all it took for you to be accepted. They just kind of took you in. It was not so much a setting where somebody is sitting down with you and tutoring you. You just kind of went in there and hung out, and once the music starts, the music more or less spoke for itself." For Michael Session, without any formal musical training, this approach, at first disconcerting, soon fueled his fire:

> Nobody ever said a word. If you asked a question, they'd be glad to answer and they'd tell you these answers that would freak me out. I'd be saying, "Well, how do you play?"
> Lester would grab you: "Grrrrr, stand over there in the corner. Practice. Practice."
> "What do you practice?"
> "Put the horn in your mouth. Play."
> "How do you play all this shit, man?"
> "It's all a growing thing. You live and you play."
> They'd give you these kind of answers. I'm looking for the formula. Tell me the shortcut, because the shit they played, it just knocked you on the floor. How do you get to that? But they were telling me exactly what you do.

At Michael's first rehearsal with the Ark:

> We get to the rehearsal and they pass out the music. I was like "Oh, shit." They started reading. I was still on the first two measures, when they were down half the page. Going that fast, it was all like Chinese to me, but no one ever said a word. After they read it down, Horace said, "Yeah, okay. Let's go over it again." But nobody said nothin' to me. I was sitting there waiting for somebody to go off on me, like "What's the matter with you?!" But nobody said a word. . . . And that just blew me away, man. It was like I didn't mess up. Nobody gave me any looks, nothing negative, and Horace with his big smile and hugs. . . . Afterwards, it was cool. I asked if I could take the music home. So I took it home and memorized it.

Guided by the patient hands of their elders, this was treated as an evolving, lifelong process and not something that could be acquired through a regimen of formal classes. As was the case in Duke Ellington's band and other great ensembles, there was always more to an arrangement than what was on the paper.[6] Roberto Miranda recalls one of his early rehearsals with the Ark:

> I remember something happened where all of the cats in the band played this lick together. I mean it was tight. Oh! It was like, "Yeah, man!" It was like a football team executing a play perfectly. It was beautiful, but I thought that they read the chart wrong. It didn't matter to me that everybody played it together. I had the audacity to say, "Man, that's wrong, isn't it?" . . . I remember it was either Arthur Blythe or Horace Tapscott—I'm paraphrasing now, I don't remember the exact words—but it was something like, "Oh, you mean we all made the same mistake at the same time?" It was just like Bruce Lee laying a right cross on me, but doing it with a really soft glove. I said, "Oh, okay, let me just shut up." Nobody ever said anything after that, man. I guess they were being merciful. Maybe they thought, "Here's this little brother on the path. I've been there. I remember when I was there. Let me just have a little mercy on him." . . . It taught me a lot. They treated me wisely. That's what happened. That's it. They treated me wisely.

Most who joined the Arkestra had already acquired some musical training, but the approach carried into their classes with children and people learning music for the first time. Prior to any theoretical training or even introduction to an instrument, the first task was to encourage musical expression in any way that was natural, through vocalizing, clapping, pounding on floors or walls, seizing whatever was nearby to create sound, whatever assisted its coming out. Only when they felt comfortable spontaneously expressing musical ideas and feelings were they ready for an introduction to fundamentals, theory, and an instrument. In his memoir, Horace describes this approach in UGMAA's music classes with children:

> We would try to identify those children who might not be good readers first off, but could really hear music. Then we'd hone them to the point where they would be playing without knowing what they were doing. After that, we'd put them in a course on reading music. We didn't want to lock them up from the top, starting them off with the paper and notes. They weren't ready for censorship, and we wanted them to be as open as possible to sounds. We'd have them playing with each other,

putting things together, humming out a phrase, all long before they reason.[7]

A few months before the Shop opened, Horace explained to *Billboard* magazine that "we teach them to hear music first. The youngsters sit around and listen to our orchestra play. Immediately after we conclude, we have them try to play what they heard." Their musicality was addressed before introducing any music formalities, and even then different approaches to playing instruments were recognized:

> If an individual has an unorthodox way of playing an instrument, the instructor immediately attempts to correct it. This more often than not turns youngsters off. They begin to feel that they are in school with strict rules. And it's no longer fun to them. Our way is not to change the position of their fingers or the way they choose to hold an instrument, but to teach them how to play the instrument in a way that is comfortable for them.[8]

Trying to get past inhibitions and encrusted ideas, cutting through layers of acquired rules, and pushing spontaneous musical expression and self-exploration were goals of Ark pedagogy. "I play like the kind of person I am," Horace once told an interviewer.[9] In so encouraging musicians, the Ark was pushing artists toward self-realization as artists and people. His or her sound should be a personal statement, part of an ongoing exploration of their humanity and the world around them. Rufus Olivier remembers being instructed by Linda Hill: "She said, 'Don't play, unless you have something to say. Don't even blow. Don't just play for playing's sake. Unless you're saying something, don't even start.'" Fuasi Abdul-Khaliq recalls David Bryant's advice: "You should always play like it's the last day of your life. You're not promised tomorrow." Musicians were inspired to learn and play purposefully, and finding music all around them, training their ears to hear and play a wide range of sounds. Billie Harris, in a manner reminiscent of Eric Dolphy, even took musical instruction from birds:

> I end up playing with birds, until they diss me, and they always diss you, because you can't keep up with them, because they're so *bad*. Birds—whoosh, man! I make bamboo flutes and I love to trip with what the birds say. I've tripped with a mockingbird. Whenever the mockingbird took off, I'd get in there. Early in the morning, just before daybreak, everything he would say, I would say it just like him. Then one time he hit two notes with one breath. It was harmonics I'd never heard. It

wasn't even a dissonant. It wasn't a third. I don't know what it was. It may have been three notes coming out of his vocal chords, and he made them descend together. He said, "Man, try this." I cursed him out and I meant it, too. I took my horn and went on in the house.

Life lessons also became an important aspect of Ark pedagogy. The elders not only performed in the community but lived and worked there and spent as much time discussing life with their younger members as the intricacies of the music. Rufus Olivier explains,

> All these guys taught you how to be outside the instrument. You weren't a walking, talking bassoon. You are a human being who enjoys life and who also plays an instrument. Now in my [San Francisco Opera] orchestra we're getting an influx of people who are so into their instrument that nothing else matters and there's a difference. You can hear it. So they taught you how to be, how to have a life, and how to incorporate your life into your art. Life is art. To Horace it didn't matter what kind of piano it was. It didn't matter if your reed was good or bad. They played past the instrument. It wasn't about "I need a good instrument to play good." It was about "I can make music on a washboard"—that's what it was about—"because I have music in me."

Life issues were fundamental in shaping the artist, in determining his or her approach to the music, in inspiring compositions, shaping technique, and affecting the role that the Arkestra would play. Fuasi Abdul-Khaliq remembers Linda Hill counseling Adele Sebastian: "Adele came in so young, sixteen years old, and was learning about womanhood, the whole thing. Linda was trying to tutor her, like 'You come with me Adele, I'll show you the ropes, every one of them.' And there was nothing she hadn't seen." According to Michael Session, "Horace would bring up girl friends, going with 'em, breaking up with 'em. I'm going, how does this relate to music? He'd say, 'All these life things relate to music. Just live and play. All this will evolve in your playing.'" For Rufus, merely observing the elder musicians in their everyday lives contained a powerful lesson about the nature of music:

> The older guys were so normal. If you saw these guys at a bus stop, they were just guys at a bus stop. And you learned that, too. Music is in you. You don't have to show it when you walk down the street. You don't have to wear it on your shirtsleeves. It's in there and no one can take it from you. No matter what anybody said to you or did, you knew who you were. They instilled a certain amount of the real ego, not the

false ego—real pride. You are what you are and you know it, and that's all that counts.

The elders exercised authority by virtue of their musical talents as well as their commitment to the culture and community. They never controlled by fiat and never had formal rules or a cultic leader or organization. Jon Williams explains, "It's about us. It's about we. And I realize that's the reason Horace didn't come with the firm hand. He didn't come with the disciplinarian kind of attitude, and he didn't conduct the Arkestra on that level. He allowed the band to conduct themselves." Their values, passions, purpose, and decency attracted individuals and drew them to collaborate over four decades. Rufus first encountered them as a high school freshman: "I was green, man, I was so green, and I was around these guys that were *so* hip. And whatever they went through—and you knew they had these experiences—they were all extreme gentlemen, which was really cool. They were very, very nice to me, and very polite, and I got the feeling they liked me, even though I was a nerd. They liked you and they liked you being there."

The Universality of PAPA and UGMAA

The Arkestra arose to meet the needs of African American artists and their community, and their focus was and has always been explicitly African American. However, in addressing the artistic and social concerns of their community, and in the manner of their doing so, PAPA and UGMAA have offered an experience that is also universal, reflecting not only more traditional cultures but also addressing needs in the most developed centers of the modern world. To artists like Yaakov Levy, the music, while most directly reflecting African American tradition, achieved universality:

> [Horace] had this ability and a gift to transmit this music that's at once both very particular to African Americans' experience and also very universal to human experience. One of my favorite words in terms of talking about life or music, whether it's Trane or Horace, is its redemptive quality. There is this profound redemptive quality that takes the grit of human experience and molds it into something beautiful and uplifting, rejuvenating and revitalizing. It's a tremendous thing.... I mean I'm a professional musician, man. I played in big bands. I played a lot of music in my life. I ain't never done anything like this. It's a combination of many factors. It's the music that Horace wrote, it's the feeling and the spirit that he wrote it with, it's the people who are playing it,

and it's the whole historical continuity that everyone brings to it, the historical experience, the vision. Man, it's a lot.

Early on, the Ark attracted Latino artists as well, a recognition of both a shared position (geographically and socially) within a racist society and common musical interests. In its early years there were no white artists contributing. Probably only a handful in segregated Los Angeles were even aware of UGMA, although some, including saxophonist Art Pepper, jammed occasionally at the UGMA house. This situation changed in the 1970s as some of the young Euro American and Jewish avant-garde musicians in L.A. emerged under the tutelage of, or were influenced by Bobby Bradford, John Carter, and Horace Tapscott. Alex and Nels Cline, Vinny Golia, Yaakov Levy, and Wayne Peet, among others, were not only regulars at concerts throughout South Central but by the late 1970s or early 1980s were performing in various small groups with and around Bobby, John, and Horace. Scheduled to play for the first time with Horace and Roberto Miranda at the Century City Playhouse, Alex recalls their first rehearsal: "I was kind of nervous because I knew this guy was really into helping his people out and who the hell am I? At that point I was twenty-three or four, this long-haired, blond guy. If he has trepidations, I'm going to understand. But he got right down to business. He was extremely amiable; he seemed completely happy with what was happening."

When Vinny Golia settled in Los Angeles in the mid-1970s and became part of the avant-garde scene, they were "always polite and respectful to some white kid, who had a horn and could play in a couple of keys, and they were just like it was the greatest thing ever. They treated you with so much respect, it's like why would you not want to be a part of that family of people? And why wouldn't you want to contribute to that scene in any way you could?"[10] He recalls playing with Horace: "I don't know what Horace saw in me, but it was a big thing for me. I felt that now my path was the right path. Having Horace be so gracious and open to me, and bringing me into his family—'Come over to the house'—and not only him, but his wife being so nice to me, and then befriending my parents and doing all of this stuff . . . that's an honor. I feel pretty blessed."

Performing with the Arkestra, however, was another issue and another purpose, demanding an everyday involvement with and focus on the needs of the African American community. Horace explained to one interviewer in 1986: "We're in a black neighborhood, and it's just that black musicians don't have many chances as the white musicians."[11] Yaakov Levy asked Adele Sebastian in the early 1980s if she thought he'd get a chance to play in the Ark:

"She said, 'No. Horace probably won't let you play in the Ark, but he might let you play with one of the smaller groups.' When she said that, I was kind of drugged." Yet, Yaakov appreciated the situation: "I knew all the cats in it. I felt we all shared this love for the music and what it means. It was frustrating for me for a long time, but I also respected where Horace was coming from and what it meant to black people in Los Angeles, in terms of the movement, if you will." Other musicians share that understanding. Alex observes, "Part of it was that Horace felt a real responsibility to the African American musicians in the community, and part of it is just that these are cats he'd played with for years and was comfortable with." Similarly, to Wayne Peet,

> It always came across that his concentration was [on the black community], rather than that he was against anything else. Going down to South Central and looking at the Arkestra, there was never any kind of weird attitude, like "What are these white people doing here" or whatever. There was never any kind of weird feeling about my being there. It gave me, as a white player, that much more respect for what was going on, rather than a really hard-ass kind of attitude in terms of defending black music or whatever. He was always very accepting of me and very supportive of me as a piano player, which was very inspirational. I mean, he came to my wedding, when I got married in '87, and I didn't really know him that well at that time. That was a great honor. The way he walked that line between really coming down and supporting the black side of the art, and yet not just cutting off from white players, was a really wise way to pull it off.

The Arkestra did not represent simply a reflex reaction to a white-dominated society and culture. It was not in that sense a subculture formed in negation but rather one which drew a purpose and direction from its own history and community. Bill Madison explains, "We were coming from a black perspective, and a lot of that had to do with being who you are and where you are in the situation that you're in, not to the exclusion of anything else, or to put anything else down, but that this needs to be uplifted and brought out, and this is the way we're going to try to do this." To Quincy Troupe,

> They were very, very proud of being African Americans, and of this culture and history. It wasn't that they were racist, they were just proud of being black persons, and I found that very refreshing. They were a counterpoint and a counterweight to people like Ron Karenga and the nationalists, because they were into being black and a lot of people hated

whitey. I never did hate white folks. I thought that they had fucked up, which I would tell them. I didn't mind telling them they had fucked up. But I had lived in Europe and I knew that every white person wasn't bad. . . . So I never bought into that and neither did they. They were proud of being black and I could really deal with where they were coming from.

Beginning in the 1990s, perhaps reacting to the experience of the multicultural upheaval that occurred in Los Angeles in the spring of 1992, Horace took steps to connect the Arkestra with others outside the African American community. There were the discussions with Jon Jang about performances with the Pan Asian Arkestra, and other artists started appearing with the Ark: Vinny Golia in 1993 and Yaakov Levy in 1997.[12]

The Ark's influence did and continues to extend beyond the confines of its community, encompassing a diverse audience aware of its contributions. Horace's example influenced Jon Jang's founding the Pan Asian Arkestra. "I was inspired by what Horace Tapscott symbolized, that music is contributive and that it's an important part of the communities, and that it helps build the communities." One of Jon's regrets is that "Horace did not live long enough for me to help find a way to get him to China."[13] In contemporary Los Angeles the example continues to be potent. The nonprofit Silverlake Conservatory of Music in Los Angeles was started in 2001 by Red Hot Chili Peppers bassist Flea not long after he had read Horace's autobiography. "[H]e wanted to do something for his community that he came up in. And when I read that book I was, like, 'Fuck it! I'm doing it, no matter what!'"[14]

In East Los Angeles, guitarist Quetzal Flores preaches and practices community arts with his group, Quetzal, one of the most important bands to emerge from Los Angeles during the 1990s. Combining urban and traditional sounds from Stevie Wonder, Chaka Khan, and Miles Davis to Gilberto Gil, Quetzal has expanded their contacts to link up with the growing El Movimiento Jaranero in Veracruz, Mexico. According to Flores, strongly influenced by Horace's autobiography, "His life, the way he was committed to building community through art, through music, through culture, through telling history, is an example and model to any artist who seeks an alternative."[15] Painter and muralist José Ramirez, whose works grace many public spaces in East Los Angeles and who collaborates with Quetzal in multimedia presentations, is resolutely committed to being a community artist, in part inspired by the story of Horace and the Ark:

His philosophy toward the role and responsibility of the community artist is a validation to us in a world where most art has been removed from everyday life and put on a pedestal where only the elite can view, comment and understand art. The spirit of Horace lives in the hearts of the progressive HipHop poets, artists, muralists, writers and musicians of Los Angeles, who understand the power of art and are struggling to redefine its place in our community.[16]

To many UGMAAgers the universality of their endeavor is evident. According to Sabir Mateen, "This thing of community, I would take it to an expanded level where the whole planet is the community instead of us taking it to one area of people." E. W. Wainwright, who continued the tradition in Oakland, California through his African Roots of Jazz, stresses, "Not only are we keeping the culture alive and teaching music and different forms of performing art, but we are actually building character and we are building bridges between different races and cultures. I know it's a cliché—'Music is the universal language'—but it comes alive in the people." To Roberto Miranda, UGMAA now carries a universal message:

> While Horace loved the community that he was from and needed to address certain injustices that were leveled at that community, and needed to let the young people know that there was a place that they could come to and learn, and be loved and be nurtured, and have an orchestra ready to play their works, he also loved humanity in general. I think that in a sense there is a misconception that UGMAA is only for a select group, which happens to live in a particular part of town, which is a shade darker than most human beings. Not true. From what I have learned not only from Horace, but from his wife Cecilia as well, UGMAA is in a sense like following God's plan. . . . It's about respect, and it's about treating people a particular way and about being an artist. For me it's a very Christian concept. In a sense, there's only one way in and that way is love. Then once you get in, you create.

And to Yaakov Levy, this universality is experienced in the common elements of the different traditions that have shaped his life:

> To be involved with this particular music, and inspired by John Coltrane, and be able to play with Alice Coltrane, and to be able to play with and be around Horace Tapscott, to me it's really remarkable that this is the way that's been given to me to reach into my tradition. So there's a unity within it that I'm still learning about, and that has to do both with the exodus from Egypt and Harriett Tubman. And I'm still learning about it, and it's quite a journey.

Conclusion

The Arkestra and UGMAA did not emerge as an auxiliary of the political struggles of the 1960s but from the general social situation facing African Americans in postwar America. The ability to transform society was beyond them. They never directly addressed the question of political power as an organization and viewpoints were diverse. According to Kamau Daáood, "There wasn't a lot of that in the Ark. Basically, we were artists first." As a movement whose origins rested in part in a rejection of a racist and commercial society, it did have a political aspect and some held strong views. "Horace believed in making the music stay true, stay true to the people, and to belong to the people," Kachina Roberts explains. "And his refusal to compromise and commercialize is probably one of the most political statements a person can make."

The vision of an alternative future was always there, and from that vision came an expansion of the field of artistic expression. They offered the opportunity to hundreds of artists to give voice to concerns, aspirations, dreams, complaints and outrage, undeterred and undistracted by the need to satisfy the commercial world. In so doing, it presented an offering to our multicultural society, not a vehicle of separation. Members saw themselves as griots, as deckhands on a mothership called the Arkestra, preserving, carrying, and developing their culture and also offering something of value to the larger world community. Adele Sebastian explains,

> I have been blessed with the gift of music. It was presented and taught to me by several musical Griots. A Griot is a cultural historian whose mission is to preserve and pass on his/her knowledge to current and future generations. I consider myself a Griot. It is an honor as well as a great responsibility. Music reaches all kinds of people in all walks of life. It is music that communicates the message when there are no words. Therefore, it is important that my music be truthful, spiritually motivated, and meaningful.[17]

Operating in a capitalist society, the Arkestra continually ran up against the boundaries of that hostile system, subject to the economic vagaries, social dysfunction, and destructive forces at play that tear at the fabric of communities, nations, and a world, exacerbated by the marginalization of African Americans in disproportionate numbers. Many of the difficulties the organization experienced, from the personal to the communal levels, can be traced to the contradiction of attempting to foster noncommercial values in the midst of the capitalist citadel, particularly in such a monument to un-restrained commercialism as Los Angeles. Michael Dett Wilcots observes, "The hard knocks of this school is that the school is in the public streets. You don't have a building and campus that [surrounds] you and almost protects you from any outside forces. This is an open campus, the UGMAA Foundation and Horace. So while you're in class, everything else is going on at the same time. There's no security."

Short of a revolutionary transformation, the task faced by the Arkestra and UGMAA remains almost Sisyphian, as it most certainly is from an individual standpoint. As Theodore Adorno observes, "No artist is able to overcome, through his own individual resources, the contradiction of enchained art within an enchained society. The most which he can hope to accomplish is the contradiction of such a society through emancipated art, and even in this attempt he might well be the victim of despair."[18]

However, from a collective standpoint, more is possible. Though society's transformation was beyond them, in collectively responding to their own needs—personal and artistic—and the needs of their community, they provided a vital energy, a demonstration and process of emancipated art to their community, improved their quality of life, and pointed toward a future beyond commercialism that is of international validity. As André Breton, Diego Rivera, and Leon Trotsky wrote, "True art, which is not content to play variations on ready-made models but rather insists on expressing the inner needs of man and of mankind in its time—true art is unable *not* to be revolutionary, *not* to aspire to a complete and radical reconstruction of society."[19]

Eschewing the commercial path, they did limit their impact in the marketplace and faced severe financial constraints. Yet, they also found alternative means to become artists of integrity and not simply to reach people but to establish connections with them. By forming a collective, sinking roots within their community and orienting toward it, they also avoided an alienation from society that the individual artist feels when a position is taken in opposition to dominant social values. In so doing, the Arkestra never fell victim to despair. In forging artistic and cultural values that embraced their past and rejected a racist, commercial society, they successfully offered an alternative process of cultural creation that even adds flesh to Trotsky's international vision: "The essence of the new culture will be not an aristocratic one for a privileged minority, but a mass culture, a universal and popular one."[20]

EPILOGUE

The Post-Horace Pan Afrikan Peoples Arkestra

Now the Ark is needed more than ever.

MICHAEL SESSION

This oral history concludes at the turn of the century, but the movement continues to this day. It has not been without difficulties and challenges, but has also experienced a great deal of energy, new faces and voices, continued community support, and the reaffirmation of the Arkestra/UGMAA ethos/ aesthetic. Through the ups and downs of its history, in good times and bad, the constant has always been that politico-cultural commitment and spirit, that consciousness bonding members throughout. As saxophonist Sabir Mateen so succinctly put it, "You're in UGMAA. You're never out."

Horace Tapscott's passing in 1999 gave urgency to the tasks of the entire organization. Although everyone worked collectively, Horace had always been the rudder that steered the Ark, who provided guidance, inspiration, and support in many ways, musically, socially, politically, and personally. The absence of his leadership, as well as the lack of an institutional structure to provide continuity, raised the key question of how to move forward. Horace had discussed with many UGMAAgers during his final weeks what had to be done and the responsibilities of each individual, but that fell short of creating an organizational structure.

UGMAA was renewed as a nonprofit in December 2000 with Michael Dett Wilcots as Executive Director and a start was made to create structural elements. A Board was reconstituted which included bassists David Bryant and Al Hines, founding members of the organization in 1961. Administrative officers were Horace's wife Cecilia Tapscott as CEO, her daughter Renée as treasurer, as well as choir veteran Amina Amatullah, Brenda Hearn, Denise Groce, Ali Jihad, my partner Jeannette Lindsay, and myself. Michael Dett set up an UGMAA headquarters and website, organized meetings on Wednesday evenings, planned various activities and events, hosted repasts for those involved in the Arkestra and UGMAA, and briefly issued a monthly PAPA@ UGMAA *Newsletter*. In his opening address to UGMAA members, Michael Dett wrote, "We are a performing Pan-African/American musical and artistic organization, that preserves the music of Horace Tapscott, as well as the works of the many members and associates of his Arkestra. Our objective for this new millennium is to perform musically and artistically to a worldwide audience, and to document and preserve the programs, performances, projects, and artistic expressions related to our history."[1]

Planning also moved ahead on projects to preserve, develop and circulate the music. The Horace Tapscott/UGMAA Archive, consisting of some 250–300 compositions, 650–700 tape recordings dating back to 1960, and a few boxes of ephemera, was kept in Horace's garage/studio and was catalogued in 2001–2. In 2003 it was then donated by the Tapscott family to the Music Library Special Collections at UCLA, later reorganized into the Performing Arts Special Collections. The first of what was hoped would be a series of band books was created using Horace's six tentet charts for the Sonny Criss album *Sonny's Dream—Birth of the New Cool*. The plan was to circulate copies of the spiral-bound scores to music programs in the community, and then to sell the rest to raise funds for the next book of music from Horace and the Ark. Trumpeter Steven Smith and multi-instrumentalist Jesse Sharps organized and digitized much of the sheet music, greatly assisting its preservation and future use.

Unfortunately, much of this energy dissipated within a few years, as the lack of structure took its toll. The nonprofit status lapsed; only two issues of the newsletter appeared during November and December 2000; and, although fifty copies of the first band book were created, they were not widely circulated. That would be the only effort to make the sheet music more accessible within the community, aside from sharing charts when requested by interested musicians.

These difficulties were among the growing challenges community artists faced in the new century with the continued reactionary political climate and declining social consciousness, as well as lack of support for the arts. Horace's passing was the first in a series that would damage the arts scene in Leimert Park Village. Earl Underwood, owner of the Leimert Park Art Gallery passed away in 1999, Richard Fulton of 5th Street Dick's in 2000, then drummer Billy Higgins in 2001, and drummer/instrument maker Juno Lewis in 2002, a staunch presence in the streets and clubs. At the same time rents were increasing and driving artists and small merchants away. Gentrification was coming to Leimert Park. The incredible vibe of the post-1992 era was dissipating and many people, who had been regulars in the Village, were no longer seen. The World Stage, KAOS Network, and a few other spaces continued, but the challenges were manifest.

Nevertheless, under saxophonist Michael Session the Arkestra moved forward. Rehearsals continued as members committed to carry on the work. Though not as frequent, there were performances throughout the community and elsewhere in Los Angeles: at benefits, in clubs, and at jazz festivals. Tribute concerts were held in honor of Horace Tapscott over the years, initially at the Jazz Bakery in Culver City, but subsequently at the First Sweet Home Baptist Church and California State University at Dominguez Hills.

New faces appeared in the Arkestra including AACM veteran flutist and vocalist Maia; saxophonists Tracy Caldwell, Randal Fisher, Ralph Gibson, Bob Givens, Mercedes Smith, and Kamasi Washington; trumpeters Rafeeq Abdul-Wahab and Richard Grant; trombonists Rembert James and Isaac Smith; pianists Jamael Dean, the grandson of Arkestra drummer Donald Dean, and Austin Peralta; bassists Latif and Nick Rosen; and drummers Don Littleton, Derf Reklaw, and Mekala Session, Michael's son. Bands were also assembled by Ark veteran Jesse Sharps—The Gathering—and conguero/radio personality Carlos Nino—To Build An Ark—that incorporated core groups of Arkestra members and carried on the aesthetic of the Arkestra in performances and recordings. Filmmaker Tom Paige documented The Gathering's day-long recording session of 10 October 2005 in his film *The Gathering—Leimert Park: Roots & Branches of Los Angeles Jazz*.

Compared to earlier years, appearances and performances in public spaces were fewer and too far between. The period also witnessed the passing of important members, some of whom had continued to be involved with the Arkestra, including Afifa Amatullah, Amina Amatullah, Arthur Blythe, Everett Brown, Jr., David Bryant, Will Connell, "Conga" Mike Daniel, Billie Harris, Al Hines, Ali Jihad, Bill Madison, William Marshall, Nate Morgan, Butch and Wilber Morris, Edwin Pleasant, Rudolph Porter, Derf Reklaw, Dadisi Sanyika, Guido Sinclair, Steve Smith, Sonship Theus, Taumbu, Raisha Wilcots, Jon "Madcap" Williams, and Tom Williamson.

However, by the mid-teens there were new winds blowing. Although many spaces had gone out of existence in Leimert Park, new ones emerged, including Eso Won Books, the Hot and Cool Café, Haroun Café, The Barbara Morrison Performing Arts Center, and Fernando Pullum's Community Art Center. The World Stage, now under the dynamic leadership of vocalist Dwight Trible, moved across the street to a larger space with an excellent sound system, while Ben Caldwell's KAOS Network continued to be an anchor within the community. And through the artistry of a number of African American artists, Leimert Park was becoming known internationally.

The years 2015–17 would bring unprecedented attention to the arts in the black community, when some local artists achieved international recognition and offered credit to their community and roots in Leimert Park. In 2015 Kamasi Washington's 3-CD *The Epic* was released to tremendous success, and by the end of the year he and his fellow musicians in the West Coast Get Down were touring internationally. That same year rapper Kendrick Lamar's *To Pimp a Butterfly* dropped, again to phenomenal success. Then in 2017 the U.S. Pavilion at the Venice Biennale, the largest and most important visual arts presentation in the world, was given over that year in toto to Mark Bradford. Fast becoming the most in-demand visual artist in the world, Bradford had spent some of his early years in Leimert Park and in his mother's hair salon there. Simultaneously, Bradford created a foundation, Art + Practice, with partners Allan DiCastro and Eileen Harris Norton, that would quickly buy property and create studios and exhibition spaces in Leimert Park in the hope of creating an international art center.

The ground was starting to shift and it was palpable. In 2017 Michael Session's son, drummer Mekala Session, in his early twenties and a recent graduate of the California Institute of the Arts, took over leadership of the Pan Afrikan Peoples Arkestra. In a couple of years he recruited a cadre of young musicians, more than at any time since the 1970s, who brought a new energy to the music, blending with the OGs in the band. Newer participants have included: saxophonists Devin Daniels, Aaron Shaw, Rickey Washington, and Tony White; clarinetist Angel Bat Dawid; trumpeters Camerahn

Alforque, Johnny Chais, Yaseen El-Magharbel, Emile Martinez, Nolan Shaheed, Sara Sithi-Amnuai, Tatiana Tate, and Chris Williams; trombonists Masai Marcelin and Zekkereya El-Magharbel; oboist Riyan El-Mergharbel; bassoonist Yousef El-Magharbel; French horn player Malik Taylor; tuba, bass, and baritone saxist Corbin Jones; pianists Diego Gaeta, Brian Hargrove, and Jesse Justice; bassists Chris Palmer, Lawrence Shaw, and Gina Ramirez; percussionist Ahmad Rezon; vocalist Sharada Shashidhar, and vocalist/choir leader Jimetta Rose with The Voices of Creation.

With his cohort pianist Jesse Justice helping carry the administrative and promotional side, and with pianist/composer Jamael Dean, Mekala Session has the Ark concertizing in various settings and growing. They also started The Village recording label to produce music from the archives, from the current Arkestra, and other community artists. At the same time Bertrand Gastaut's Paris-based Dark Tree records has started issuing recorded and live performances from the Tapscott Archive, and Nimbus West records, now under the guidance of sound engineer Matt Whitehurst upon Tom Albach's passing, has carried on with producing previously unreleased recordings and reissues.

Regular Ark performances have followed at the World Stage in Leimert Park, Zebulon and other spaces in Los Angeles. The Arkestra was chosen to highlight the annual New Year's Eve Countdown Concert at Grand Park in downtown Los Angeles on 31 December 2019, a citywide visibility never before experienced. Not long after in October 2020, a one-hour documentary film, "The New West Coast Sound," premiered on KCET public television. A project of director Sandrine Orabona and producer Anke Thommen for KCET's "Artbound" series, it focused on Mekala and the Arkestra, its current motion and its history. In July 2021 it was awarded an L.A. area Emmy.

Even though UGMAA is institutionally moribund, the spirit is alive and the Ark is moving forward with renewed energy and commitment. According to veteran saxophonist James Andrews, "The fact is to realize that the Ark, the music, was a living breathing organism. It was something that outreached. We did things other than music for the community. . . . So, we can't let that disappear and go by the wayside. People need to know about this organism that lived and breathed at that particular time. It continues." Whatever the future holds, it is certain that the great gift of hundreds of artists—musicians, poets, dancers, actors, martial artists—technicians, and supporters remains to inspire people throughout the world to a more just and richer life than contemporary society is capable of delivering. To echo the battlecry of Arkestra conguero Cojoe, "Don't stop! Take it out!"

A VIEW FROM THE BOTTOM

The Music of Horace Tapscott and the Pan

Afrikan Peoples Arkestra

Roberto Miranda

The analysis you are about to read is that of a bassist/composer/love-to-be *conguero*, who played music with Horace Tapscott for over thirty years. He, Bobby Bradford and John Carter taught what this music is all about. I say "this music" because different people have different names for it. My wife, Deborah, pretty much pegged it when she said, "I don't care what you call it as long as it touches me." Duke's famous quote, "There are only two kinds of music, good music and the other kind," also gets to what I really mean when I say "this music."

Horace's music swung hard. By that I mean his music breathed; it always had life. The time signature didn't matter. If his music changed time signature or meter, it didn't matter. If it sped up, slowed down, or stopped and started, it didn't matter. If it was slow, medium or fast, it didn't matter. It always swung. I remember playing with the Ark or the small groups in situations where the music was totally free of any preimposed structure whatsoever, and the band would be swingin' so hard my heart would almost burst with joy. This was one of many ways in which Horace followed the example of Duke Ellington. In a harmonic sense, except for the free/avant-garde playing/arranging, I don't believe you will find anything in Horace's music that you would not find in the music of Duke Ellington.

It is important to study the masters from a technical aspect, so that we can learn how to utilize the same tools, techniques and insights to create our own art. But whatever I write about the technical aspect of the music is not the quintessence of why Horace was a great artist. He was great because God allowed him to bring life to the music, allowed him to imbue the performances with his love. And Horace did that very thing that he was allowed to do with every ounce of his being. I believe that's what made him great.

THE SOUND OF THE ARKESTRA

Billy Higgins once said, "The swing is in the sound." Kenny Burrell punctuated that by saying, "Sometimes it's all about the sound." Horace had his own sound, and because of the striving of the musicians in the Ark to achieve that, the Ark had its own sound. Duke's orchestra didn't sound like Duke just because of Duke. Johnny Hodges, Russell Procope, Cat Anderson, Stuff Smith and all of Duke's friends were a big part of that sound. Each of these musicians developed an identifiable sound of their own. They lent that sound to Duke's orchestra.

It's the same thing in the Ark. Steve Smith and Michael Session each have their own sound, and together they sound like no other two horns. Lester Robertson had his own sound. When [bassists] Henry Franklin, David Bryant, Louie Spears, Al Hines, Trevor Ware, Jeff Littleton and I all got together, it sounded like a rumblin' river looking for the sea. When David Murray, James Newton, Bobby Bradford, Arthur Blythe, and Edwin Pleasant got together, the sound was incredible! The Ark sound was rich, dark, deep, luscious, joyful and painful. It was the blues. It was full of tears and babies' laughter. It was a longing sound. It longed for heaven and still waters. Horace heard all of this. He heard it as a soloist and as an arranger/composer.

After listening to Horace's music with Bobby Bradford, we talked about the fact that Horace's music was not "nice." It wasn't a tight, clean big band sound. That is not to say that the music was in any way sloppy; it was relaxed and loose. It was tight in the sense that the band swung and kept the structure or the character of the piece. The musicians were not asked to blend in the same way a studio band blends. Each musician in Duke's band had a completely different sound. He never did anything to take away from that individuality. Horace was the same way, not looking for a sameness in the different sections. We were asked to blend only in the sense that we would accommodate the particular piece. We were never asked to have all the players in the section sound the same. There was a sound, which was a result of all the band's parts, which could never have been achieved with a sameness in each section.

I have heard on several different occasions how musicians, standing in close proximity to Duke's band, would be reading the music and asking themselves, "How is he getting that sound? I'm reading this music and it shouldn't sound like that!" My point is that it is not just the notes that the composer writes. As James Newton said during a recent conversation, "The notes don't define the music. They are a means to an end." It is also the way each of the musicians interprets the music. Now that is a very obvious reality, but when you take into consideration the fact that Duke and Horace knew who they were writing for and went for a group/section sound on purpose, it takes on a whole new meaning. It means that these composers not only knew the sound of each individual musician, they knew how the musicians, not the instruments, sounded together.

With Horace the process was further complicated by the range of experience in the Arkestra. It was, to quote James Newton again, "miraculous" how he dealt with a wide range of proficiency levels in the Ark. This is certainly nothing new. Mentors have been sitting side by side with students throughout history. But in this case we are talking about some people in the Ark who were great readers and soloists sitting next to some who couldn't read at all! That is completely different from a professional violinist sitting next to a student who is taking private lessons and reading music in various student ensembles. In some instances in the Ark, over a period of years that student matured into a great musician, who had mastered the technique of reading and the arts of interpretation and soloing. Michael Session is an example of that process. In Michael's case, as in many others in this music, he already had a pretty good idea of what soloing was all about when he first came in. He had a great ear and, from the beginning, was well on his way toward developing his own sound. Horace heard that sound.

Duke and Horace also knew how to take the sound of each individual player and use it to get a particular color or feeling. Bobby Bradford talks about how Duke would use Cootie Williams when he wanted that sound or flavor. Horace would do the same thing with Michael Session or Arthur Blythe, who in James Newton's opinion, influenced everybody in Los Angeles. James went on to state that in African American music it is very rare today to find young musicians with their own sound. When James and I were growing up, we were encouraged from the very beginning to find our own sound. During rehearsals with our teachers we were constantly urged to search for that special sound that expressed who we were. In fact, we were criticized if we didn't have an individual sound. This was of paramount importance.

Composers like Duke and Horace, Mingus and Monk were looking for that. They could call any musician they wanted. All they had to do was pick up the musicians' union directory. But they didn't want just the voice of the instrument, they wanted the voice of the person. Theirs were not bands of "readers," where the chart is everything. They wanted something beyond the notes. They wanted the life of the player expressed in the music.

ORCHESTRATION

While Duke wrote for a large ensemble, Horace always approached the Ark as though it were a small group. Whether it was five or thirty musicians, whether the music was modal or based on changes, it was the same approach. One of the compositional techniques used was stratification of the timbre. Another way to say this is that he layered the sound colors. It wasn't just a matter of stacking the horns to outline the chord. It was using William Roper, Thurman Green, Steve Smith, Jesse Sharps, Michael Session, and Arthur Blythe to get particular sound colors. Tuba, trombone, trumpet, tenor and two altos are going to get a particular sound. But, Roper, Thurman, Steve, Jesse, Michael, and Arthur are going to get something totally different.

As was stated earlier, many times the notes written are a means to an end. The "head" or main melody is used as a starting point, as well as a point of reference throughout the piece. Duke used this material at the beginning of a piece in the same way many western classical musicians used it and often referred to it throughout his longer pieces. A perfect example is *Black, Brown and Beige,* where Duke used the theme of what became "Come Sunday" throughout the piece. Horace did this, but not as consistently as other composers. In his music, more often than not, the head was the take off point for the soloist. After that the musical statements were usually different materials than those used on the head, and those materials were used to propel the soloist to greater heights and depths.

Other techniques Horace used were the "vamp" and the "riff." The vamp, or recurring rhythm section figure, was used as support for the soloist or as wind-down time after the solo. Much of Horace's music was vamp oriented. We are often tempted to think of a vamp as being in common time. In Horace's case the vamp could be in four, five, six, seven, eleven or thirteen. It could even be in any combination of those in the same piece. "Ballad for Deadwood Dick" by Horace and "Voices from the Bottoms" by Thurman Green are good examples of that.

Another technique Horace used was the "riff," a recurring figure in the horns, played in unison or harmonized. It was used to propel the soloist and to create motion in the ensemble. Oftentimes, as in "Better Git Hit In Your Soul" by Charles Mingus, several riffs were used simultaneously. Duke, Mingus, and Horace all used this technique. Bobby Bradford points to the subdivisions often employed by composers. An example is Duke's "Mood Indigo," played by three of the musicians in the orchestra. In Horace's introduction to "Motherless Child" at the Arkestra concert of June 1995 in Moers, Germany, we hear the use of the subdivision and the "round" by the saxophone section made up of Arthur Blythe, Charles Owens, Jesse Sharps and Michael Session. Children often do the round with a song like "Row Row Your Boat." Horace incorporated it in this instance in a rubato form. He gave each musician artistic license to interpret the melody how he wanted, and by the end of the intro we are listening to a saxophone quartet's marvelous improvisation on the theme.

This technique, which Bobby Bradford calls an "incantatory intro," was often a part of Horace's music. It may be in or out of time; it might be with the whole group playing in a "call and response" style; or, it might be with a rhythm section vamp and an intro/solo horn before the actual statement of the head. It can take any of several forms, but its function is that of an introduction or a prelude to the piece. Because it is often of a musical quality that can be easily identified as having its roots in the Christian church as experienced by African Americans, it can be perceived and is often played as a prayer. Ergo, the name "incantatory."

Finally, although the human voice can obviously be a musical instrument, Horace often treated the voice as part of the Arkestra, not just a lead instrument singing words, but integral to the band, lending its "voice" to the color of the composition at any given point during the piece.

This is just a superficial look at Horace's arranging. It would not surprise me that during the course of a deeper study certain techniques might come to light as being specifically "Tapscottian" or belonging to a small group of arrangers. But as a whole, as I mentioned earlier, most of the techniques can be found in a study of the tradition of the great African American composers and arrangers.

Personnel frequently fluctuated throughout the Arkestra's history, and the orchestration changed just as consistently. When new artists joined the band, Horace seemed to deal with this in several different ways. First, they might be given a part written earlier for their specific instrument. Second, they might double a part with another player written for their specific instrument. Third, they might be given a part written in their key, but for another instrument. If the new player was a soprano saxophonist, he or she might be given a trumpet or B flat clarinet part. (This accents Horace's treatment of the large ensemble as though it was a small group.) Fourth, Horace might sing or play a part for them to immediately memorize. This part might or might not be written down at some point, but it was definitely something Horace and the player remembered every time that composition was played. And, fifth, at some point Horace might hand that player a part written specifically for him or her. Often it would have his or her name written on the top of the page.

Depending on how long a person was with the Ark, he or she might settle on one part or float between several parts for a specific tune. The great bassist Richard Davis has spoken about how Thad Jones sometimes gave him the score rather than a specific part to read. He would be asked to pick a part, roam, or make something up based on the score. This may sound unorganized, but it wasn't. Think of it this way. An artist is painting the changing color of leaves on a tree during a particular season. Each leaf changes color at different times and speeds so that there are, simultaneously, many colors on the tree ranging from different greens to oranges, browns and reds. In nature these colors exist on the tree at different places at different times. Horace wanted to remain true to the nature of the tree. Once a tune was set with regard to the options available to a player, one could say the tune had its "character," although Horace was always open to change.

One of the things I found particularly admirable about Horace was that a player was always free to submit a part he might hear at a place in the composition, and if Horace liked it, he would keep it in the piece. It was as if he was telling the player, "Yeah! This is *our* arkestra! I might have written that same part. Let's keep it in."

HARMONIC AND MELODIC CONCEPTS

Harmonically speaking, Horace most often would create tonal, modal or free compositions on which to solo, but he always used and encouraged the use of Tertial (thirds and sixths), Quartal (fourths and fifths), and cluster (seconds and sevenths) harmonies. Although I personally never saw an actual twelve tone or serial composition by Horace, he certainly incorporated twelve tone structure into his soloing regularly and effortlessly.

I asked James Newton if there was anything about Horace's music that he really wanted to impress upon those truly interested. His immediate comment was, "Clusters, clusters, clusters!" (This is a way of voicing the notes in the chord/sound close together in seconds and sevenths rather than thirds and sixths or fourths and fifths.) James expressed the intriguing proposition that if an orchestrator were to transcribe clusters to a large ensemble or full orchestra in the way Horace used them in his solo playing, the effect would be worth the work many times over. He also brought out the fact that historically, starting with Horace and going backward in time through Monk to Duke, we see that Duke was the first "Jazz" musician to use clusters in the way they were employed by all three composers.

Horace also delved into and encouraged the use of microtonality. As a pianist he would sometimes get inside the piano and isolate certain strings. The piano is tuned in such a way that there are three strings for each note. One is slightly flat, one is right on, and one is slightly sharp. Horace would sometimes pick one or the other, or he would bend all three or any combination thereof.

A musician in the Ark had to be ready to play through some serious changes at any given point in time. Horace was famous for ripping through "Giant Steps," "Cherokee," "Close to Freedom," "I Got Rhythm" chord changes or any other set of changes at breakneck speed on the bandstand. This he would do without counting it off, all the while smiling that great smile of his. The rest of the band would then join him at the top of the form and proceed to have a great time.

I'll address Horace's melodic concept by relating an experience I had with Horace, when he was teaching at the University of California at Riverside. If memory serves me correctly, Arthur Blythe, John Blue, and I went out there to join Horace in playing for his class. At one point when the band was playing hard, we all stopped for a moment. This was unplanned and out of the blue. We just stopped. At that precise instant a bird that was either outside of an open window or had flown inside the high roofed building sang out clearly and distinctly for all to hear. That is as close as I can get to Horace's melodic concept. It was like a bird in a tree.

THE IMPROVISING PIANIST

Horace's soloing and solo piano work, on the other hand, stands in a very unique place. Horace was a master improviser. One way to express the definition of a master improviser is the following: A master improviser is a person who can play what they hear instantaneously. The music exists inside of you first. You "hear" it in your being. I call it "the song your spirit sings." Your job as an improviser is to be true to the music within you.

How does one do that? First, you need to correctly identify the intervals (the space between the notes) and how long each note and silence lasts. This is what musicians call "ear training." In other words, you need to know what it is you are hearing. Secondly, the musician needs to have trained his body to respond to the music he hears inside and the analysis his brain has made by playing the notes he hears at the time his brain sends the signal. That is why we train our bodies with practice. All of this happens faster than a nanosecond. An improviser at his best has no idea of what he is going to hear ahead of time, but when he hears it, he must be completely committed to playing that and nothing else.

Horace was a master at this. Besides his concept of rhythm as a composer, his literal mastery of the piano, and his ambidexterity and rhythmic independence, his soloing was a strong point in his music. As a soloist, Horace's use of melodic and harmonic inventiveness, chromaticism, polytonality, rhythm, dynamics, and sheer pianistic ability was not only creative, it was astounding. His left hand was incredibly strong. You always knew where one was; he made sure of that. It was like stride piano in changing time signatures. His left hand would hold down the rhythmic structure in a relaxed authority that was a combination of inspiration and mathematical precision. However, it was in no way robotic. He would be varying voicing, doing different kinds of melodic phrasing, and basically improvising with his left hand at the same time that he would be holding down the rhythmic structure! If that wasn't enough, he would be playing improvisations with his right hand that were truly genius! His right hand seemed totally free. We would be playing this exacting tune, sometimes at a very fast tempo with all these time and harmonic changes that had to happen like clockwork, and his right hand would be like a bird flying above it all. He'd be dippin' and divin', climbin', and soarin'. It was beautiful. He'd be smilin' that smile of his, just burnin' so hard, and then he'd look at me and laugh. All I could do was laugh with him and play as hard as I could. I know of no pianist that played more creatively than Horace.

RHYTHM

The last thing about Horace's music I wish to bring to the reader's attention is his sense of rhythm as a composer and pianist. Horace not only had no difficulty in playing many odd time signatures, he excelled in odd time signatures. I remember many times experiencing a feeling of absolute astonishment at how hard this man was able to swing in 5, 7, 11 or 13. In his "Ballad for Deadwood Dick," Horace constructed a piece of six bars of 5/4, three bars of 6/8, two bars of 5/4 and four bars of 4/4. The rhythmic structure of "Dee

Bee's Dance" is two bars of 4/4, one bar of 6/4, two bars of 4/4, and one bar of 5/4. The bridge section is eight bars of 4/4. The opening statement of "Lino's Pad" is seven bars of 7/4, one bar of 8/4, four bars of 7/4, one bar of 8/4, and four bars of 4/4. During the solos the structure is five bars of 7/4 and four bars of 4/4. "Mothership" opens with fourteen bars of 7/4, two bars of 6/8, one bar of 3/4, one bar of 5/4 (the 3/4 and 5/4 bars are repeated), and four bars of 7/4. The soloing is in 7/4. Horace never stopped swinging when he played this music. He blew through those time changes like the wind blows through the trees.

Conclusion

There are two things that stay with me to this day. One is Horace's combination of ambidexterity, concentration and flat-out creative genius. The other is the way in which Horace would support other players. He would be there for his people. He was there all the time on the bandstand. When it came time for you to solo, he laid it down for you. During the performances of the odd time signature pieces, as well as everything else we played, he was like a rock you could dance on. He inspired the other players to support in the same way. When a player soloed in the Ark, it was like everybody else was saying, "Go ahead, we got you surrounded. You're safe." Musically speaking, Horace always made me feel like he was saying, "I got your back. Be who you are, that's why you're here. I love you."

In essence, we are talking about an incredibly creative talent. He concentrated on the music of his community and broadened that concentration to artists of like mind. He was a teacher. He understood his art form and he was uncompromising in its execution. He is missed. I, for one, thank God for creating him and allowing me to spend the time I did with him.

NOTES

PREFACE TO THE SECOND EDITION

1 Horace Tapscott, *Songs of the Unsung: The Musical and Social Journey of Horace Tapscott*, ed. Steven Isoardi (Durham, NC: Duke University Press, 2001).
2 Don Snowden, "Horace Tapscott at the Lighthouse," *Los Angeles Times*, 17 November 1979, sec. II: 11.
3 William Marshall and Sylvia Jarrico, interview by Steven Isoardi, 8 April 1999.
4 Clora Bryant et al., eds., *Central Avenue Sounds: Jazz in Los Angeles* (Berkeley: University of California Press, 1998).

CHAPTER 1: ANCESTRAL ECHOES

EPIGRAPH: Langston Hughes, "The Negro Speaks of Rivers," in *The Collected Poems of Langston Hughes*, ed. Arnold Rampersad and David Roessel (New York: Alfred A. Knopf, 1995), 23.

1 Tapscott, *Songs of the Unsung*, 79–81.
2 James R. Grossman, "A Chance to Make Good: 1900–1929," in *To Make Our World Anew: A History of African Americans*, ed. Robin D. G. Kelley and Earl Lewis (Oxford: Oxford University Press, 2000), 375.
3 Grossman, 375–77.
4 Tapscott, *Songs of the Unsung*, 4.
5 D. T. Niane, *Sundiata: an epic of old Mali*, trans. G.D. Pickett (Essex: Longman, 1965), 60.
6 See LeRoi Jones (Amiri Baraka), *Blues People: Negro Music in White America* (New York: William Morrow, 1963), 27; Ruth Finnegan, *Oral Literature in Africa* (Oxford: Oxford University Press, 1970), 272–84; K. Maurice Jones, *Say It Loud! The Story of Rap Music* (Brookfield, CT: The Millbrook Press, 1994), 17–24; Cheryl L. Keyes, *Rap Music and Street Consciousness* (Urbana: University of

Illinois Press, 2002), 17–38; Paul Oliver, *Savannah Syncopators: African Retentions in the Blues* (New York: Stein and Day Publishers, 1970), 43–52; and David Toop, *Rap Attack 2: African Rap to Global Hip Hop* (London: Serpent's Tail, 1991), 29–34.

7 Recent postcolonial critiques of earlier cultural analyses have also raised the issue of individual uniqueness. See Kofi Agawu, *Representing African Music: Postcolonial Notes, Queries, Positions* (New York: Routledge, 2003); and Paulla A. Ebron, *Performing Africa* (Princeton: Princeton University Press, 2002).

8 J. H. Kwabena Nketia, "The Musician in Akan Society," in Warren L. d'Azevedo, ed., *The Traditional Artist in African Societies* (Bloomington: Indiana University Press, 1973), 82.

9 James Fernandez, "The Exposition and Imposition of Order: Artistic Expression in Fang Culture," in d'Azevedo, ed., *The Traditional Artist*, 217.

10 Henry John Drewal and John Pemberton III with Roland Abiodun, *Yoruba: Nine Centuries of African Art and Thought*, ed. Allen Wardell (New York: The Center for African Art in association with Harry N. Abrams, Inc., 1989), 230–31.

11 Herbert M. Cole and Chike C. Aniakor, *Igbo Arts: Community and Cosmos* (Los Angeles: UCLA Museum of Cultural History, 1984), 83–110; Drewal, Pemberton and Abiodun, "The Yoruba World," in Drewal and Pemberton, with Abiodun, *Yoruba*, 14–26; Jean Laude, *The Arts of Black Africa*, trans. Jean Decock (Berkeley: University of California Press, 1971), 101–36; Laure Meyer, *African Forms: Art and Rituals* (New York: Assouline, 2001), 120; and Nketia, "Musician in Akan Society," 80–82.

12 Meyer, *African Forms*, 120. See also Miles Mark Fisher, *Negro Slave Songs in the United States* (New York: The Citadel Press, 1963), 5–10; and Eileen Southern, *The Music of Black Americans*, 3rd ed. (New York: W.W. Norton, 1997), 4–8.

13 William Bascom, *African Art in Cultural Perspective: An Introduction* (New York: W. W. Norton & Company, 1973), 86.

14 Oliver, *Savannah Syncopators*, 28–36.

15 Cole and Aniakor, *Igbo Arts*, 224.

16 Fred Warren, *The Music of Africa: An Introduction* (Englewood Cliffs, NJ: Prentice-Hall, Inc., 1970), 21–22.

17 Cole and Aniakor, *Igbo Arts*, 224.

18 David W. Ames, "A Sociocultural View of Hausa Musical Activity," in *The Traditional Artist*, 152–53.

19 Nketia, "The Musician in Akan Society," 87. See also enthnomusicologist Roger Vetter's description in the accompanying booklet to *Rhythms of Life, Songs of Wisdom: Akan Music from Ghana, West Africa* (Smithsonian/Folkways Recordings, compact disc, SF CD 40463), 7–8.

20 Niane, *Sundiata*, 17.

21 Thomas Hale, *Griots and Griottes: Masters of Words and Music* (Bloomington: Indiana University Press, 1998), 18–58. See also Michael T. Coolen, "Senegambian Influences on Afro-American Musical Culture," *Black Music Research*

Journal 11:1 (Spring, 1991): 8–9; Ebron, *Performing Africa*, 16–19; and Patrick R. McNaughton, *The Mande Blacksmiths: Knowledge, Power, and Art in West Africa* (Bloomington: Indiana University Press, 1988), 6–7.

22 Hale, *Griots and Griottes*, 16. Emphasis his. On the griot's verbal and musical art, see 114–71; and Oliver, *Savannah Syncopators*, 43–52.

23 Wande Abimbola, "Preface," in Drewal and Pemberton, with Abiodun, *Yoruba*, 11.

24 Quoted in Drewal and Pemberton, with Abiodun, *Yoruba*, 234. See also *Yoruba*, 42; and Rowland Abiodun, Henry J. Drewal, and John Pemberton III, eds., *The Yoruba Artist: New Theoretical Perspectives on African Arts* (Washington: Smithsonian Institution Press, 1994), 113–14.

25 Chinua Achebe, "Foreword: The Igbo World and Its Art," in Cole and Aniakor, *Igbo Arts*, ix.

26 Drewal and Pemberton, with Abiodun, *Yoruba*, 26.

27 Achebe in Cole and Aniakor, *Igbo Arts*, ix.

28 Ames, "Sociocultural View of Hausa Musical Activity," 152. See also 145.

29 Suzanne Preston Blier, *The Royal Arts of Africa: The Majesty of Form* (New York: Harry N. Abrams, Inc., 1998), 38. Michele Coquet also speaks of many kingdoms characterized by "an artistic quest for originality, which was encouraged by the sovereigns themselves." See her *African Royal Court Art*, trans. Jane Marie Todd (Chicago: University of Chicago Press, 1998), xi.

30 See Bernard de Grunne, *The Birth of Art in Africa: Nok Statuary in Nigeria* (Luxembourg: Adam Biro, 1998).

31 On the tribal groupings maintained in some areas, see Douglas Brent Chambers, "'He Gwine Sing He Country': Africans, Afro-Virginians, and the Development of Slave Culture in the Virginia, 1690–1810," vol. I (Ph.D. diss., University of Virginia, 1996), 4–9, 37–39, 59, 308–10. On the importance of kinship networks, see Chambers, 334–35; and Peter Wood, "Strange New Land: 1619–1776," in *To Make Our World Anew*, 85.

32 Lawrence W. Levine, *Black Culture and Black Consciousness: Afro-American Folk Thought from Slavery to Freedom* (Oxford: Oxford University Press, 1977), 80. See also John W. Blassingame, *The Slave Community: Plantation Life in the Antebellum South*, rev. ed. (New York: Oxford University Press, 1979), 31–36, 109, 147–48; and Deborah Gray White, "Let My People Go: 1804–1860," in *To Make Our World Anew*, 190.

33 Blassingame, *The Slave Community*, 39–41, 109–14, 127–34; Chambers, "He Gwine Sing," 356–95; Levine, *Black Culture and Black Consciousness*, 81–135; and White, "Let My People Go," 181–82.

34 Southern, *Music of Black Americans*, 166. See also 156–204.

35 Levine, *Black Culture and Black Consciousness*, 30.

36 Chambers, "He Gwine Sing," 364.

37 Wood, "Strange New Land," 85–86. See also Blassingame, *The Slave Community*, 22–23; and Levine, *Black Culture and Black Consciousness*, 5–16.

38 Southern, *Music of Black Americans*, 201.

39 Southern has presented many persuasive examples. During the colonial period, slave festivals, such as 'Lection Day and Pinkster Day, occurred yearly in
northern locales. Large audiences "watched the black celebrants sing African
songs, strum banjos, and dance to the music of drums constructed by drawing
skins over the ends of hollow logs" (55). During the antebellum period hundreds
would gather in New Orleans' Congo Square, reflecting the influence and
number of slaves brought from the Congo in the 1800s (137). Similarly, shouts
carried African influences into the nineteenth century. "Here were the same
ring formations, the loud chanting, the shuffling movements, the intense
concentration of the participants, and the gradual build-up of the performance
to a wild and frenzied state" (183). See also Samuel A. Floyd, Jr., *The Power of
Black Music: Interpreting Its History from Africa to the United States*
(New York: Oxford University Press, 1995), 38, 42–45; and Robert Farris
Thompson, "Kongo Influences on African-American Artistic Culture," in
Africanisms in American Culture, ed. Joseph E. Holloway (Bloomington: Indiana
University Press, 1990), 149–50.

40 Levine, *Black Culture and Black Consciousness*, 89.

41 John Hope Franklin and Alfred A. Moss, Jr., From *Slavery to Freedom: A History
of African Americans*, 8th ed. (New York: Alfred A. Knopf, 2000), 177; Gross-
man, "A Chance to Make Good," 368–69; Earl Lewis, *In Their Own Interests:
Race, Class, and Power in Twentieth-Century Norfolk, Virginia* (Berkeley:
University of California Press, 1991), 24–25; and Southern, *Music of Black
Americans*, 70–71.

42 W. E. B. Du Bois, *The Souls of Black Folk* (New York: Dover Publications, Inc.,
1994), 117.

43 Noralee Frankel, "Breaking the Chains: 1860–1880," in *To Make Our World
Anew*, 278. Also Franklin and Moss, *From Slavery to Freedom*, 313–15; Grossman, "A Chance to Make Good," 367–68; and Lewis, *In Their Own Interests*, 23,
70–72.

44 A detailed consideration of the emergence of black popular music is in Lynn
Abbott and Doug Seroff, *Out of Sight: The Rise of African American Popular
Music, 1889–1895* (Jackson, MS: University Press of Mississippi, 2002).

45 Southern, *Music of Black Americans*, 259–60.

46 Levine, *Black Culture and Black Consciousness*, 222. Also Jones, *Blues People*,
65–67.

47 Levine, 237. Emphasis his.

48 Levine, 239. In the performances of bluesmen and the divas of the 1920s,
Earl Lewis (*In Their Own Interests*) calls attention to the communal role and
its roots in African tradition: "Through the blues, [Mamie] Smith and her
counterparts became more than troubadours. They furnished a running
digest of blacks' integration into the rapidly changing industrial economy. In
some ways, the songsters became contemporary equivalents of West African
griots, preserving and recalling for the audience the triumphs and travails of a
people" (100).

49 See Lowell Dwight Dickerson, "Central Avenue Meets Hollywood: The Amalgamation of the Black and White Musicians' Unions in Los Angeles" (Ph.D. diss., University of California, Los Angeles, 1998), 125–28; and George Seltzer, *Music Matters: The Performer and the American Federation of Musicians* (Metuchen, NJ: The Scarecrow Press, Inc., 1989), 109.

50 In retrospect a few veterans of the Los Angeles amalgamation movement have told me that they should have opposed segregated locals by admitting white musicians into Local 767, which some young, white jazz musicians had asked to join. On the struggle in Los Angeles to eliminate segregated Locals, see Bryant, et al., eds., *Central Avenue Sounds: Jazz in Los Angeles* (Berkeley: University of California Press, 1998); Buddy Collette with Steven Isoardi, *Jazz Generations: A Life in American Music and Society* (London: Continuum, 2000), 110–20; and Dickerson, "Central Avenue Meets Hollywood." For a brief overview of the history of African Americans in the American Federation of Musicians, see Seltzer, *Music Matters*, 108–14. On the experience of Chicago Local 10–208, see Clark Halker, "A History of Local 208 and the Struggle for Racial Equality in the American Federation of Musicians," *Black Music Research Journal* 8, no. 2 (Fall, 1988): 207–23.

51 Brian Priestley, *Mingus: A Critical Biography* (New York: Da Capo Press, Inc., 1982), 46–47; and Gene Santoro, *Myself When I Am Real: The Life and Music of Charles Mingus* (Oxford: Oxford University Press, 2000), 97.

52 Noal Cohen and Michael Fitzgerald, *Rat Race Blues: The Musical Life of Gigi Gryce* (Berkeley: Berkeley Hill Books, 2002), 165–71.

53 Quoted in Robert Levin, "The Jazz Composers Guild: An Assertion of Dignity," *Down Beat*, 6 May 1965, 17.

54 Levin, 18.

55 John Litweiler, *The Freedom Principle: Jazz after 1958* (New York: Da Capo Press, Inc., 1984), 138–39; John Szwed, *Space Is the Place: The Lives and Times of Sun Ra* (New York: Pantheon Books, 1997), 205–07; and Valerie Wilmer, *As Serious as Your Life: John Coltrane and Beyond* (London: Serpent's Tail, 1992), 213–15.

56 See Szwed, *Space Is the Place*, 94–95, for myriad names of Sun Ra's organization.

57 Graham Lock, *Blutopia: Visions of the Future and Revisions of the Past in the Work of Sun Ra, Duke Ellington, and Anthony Braxton* (Durham, NC: Duke University Press, 1999), 13–43.

58 David G. Such, *Avant-Garde Jazz Musicians Performing "Out There"* (Iowa City: University of Iowa Press, 1993), 118.

59 Quoted in Wilmer, *As Serious as Your Life*, 76.

60 Quoted in Wilmer, 77.

61 Ekkehard Jost, *Free Jazz* (New York: Da Capo Press, 1994), 180–99; Litweiler, *Freedom Principle*, 138–49; and Szwed, *Space Is the Place*, 93–196.

62 Szwed, *Space Is the Place*, 210–12.

63 *Sun Ra: A Joyful Noise*, prod. and dir. Robert Mugge, 60 min., Rhapsody Films, 1986, videocassette.

64 Quoted in Wilmer, *As Serious as Your Life*, 119. Emphasis theirs.

65 Ronald M. Radano, *New Musical Figurations: Anthony Braxton's Cultural Critique* (Chicago: The University of Chicago Press, 1993), 99.

66 John Litweiler, "AACM at 30: A Chicago Free Jazz Survey," *Coda Magazine* 267 (May/June 1996): 10.

67 Anthony Braxton, *Tri-Axium Writings I* (n.p.: Synthesis Music, 1985), 416–34; Jost, *Free Jazz*, 163–79; Robert Levin, "The Third World: Anthony Braxton and the Third Generation," *Jazz & Pop* 9, no. 10 (October 1970): 12–14; Litweiler, "AACM at 30," 10–13; Litweiler, *Freedom Principle*, 172–86; Kai Muni, "AACM: Continuing the Tradition," *Be-bop & Beyond* 4, no. 2 (March/April 1986): 8–12; Eric Porter, *What Is This Thing Called Jazz? African American Musicians as Artists, Critics, and Activists* (Berkeley: University of California Press, 2002), 210–14; Radano, *New Musical Figurations*, 77–92; and Wilmer, *As Serious as Your Life*, 112–19.

68 George Lipsitz, "Like a Weed in a Vacant Lot: The Black Artists Group in St. Louis," paper revised February 1999, 3. An earlier version appeared in Sue-Ellen Case, Philip Brett, and Susan Leigh Foster, eds., *Decomposition: Post-Disciplinary Performance* (Bloomington: Indiana University Press, 2000).

69 Lipsitz, 4. Also Braxton, *Tri-Axium Writings I*, 434–38; Litweiler, *Freedom Principle*, 186–89; and Wilmer, *As Serious as Your Life*, 222.

70 Arnold Jay Smith, "Billy Taylor and Dave Bailey: Magnetizing the Arts," *Down Beat*, 1 December 1977, 14–15; and Wilmer, *As Serious as Your Life*, 218–19.

71 Porter, *What Is This Thing Called Jazz*? 215. See also 215–39; and Peter Keepnews, "What is the CBAE?" *Down Beat*, 28 February 1974, 10.

72 Quoted in *Message from the Tribe—An Anthology of Tribe Records: 1972–1977*, Universal Sound, compact disc, US CD 5, 1996.

73 *The Time Is Now!* Hefty Records, compact disc, Hefty32. See also Phil Ranelin, interview by Steven Isoardi, 6 August 2001; "Wendell Harrison, Phil Ranelin and Tribe," *JazzTimes*, September 2001, 34–37; and *Message from the Tribe*.

74 Braxton, *Tri-Axium Writings I*, 441.

CHAPTER 2: BALLAD FOR SAMUEL

EPIGRAPH: Arna Bontemps, *Black Thunder* (Boston: Beacon Press, 1968), 83.

1 Quoted in Lonnie G. Bunch III, "A Past Not Necessarily Prologue: The Afro-American in Los Angeles Since 1900," in *20th Century Los Angeles: Power, Promotion, and Social Conflict*, ed. Norman M. Klein and Martin J. Schiesl (Claremont, CA: Regina Books, 1990), 101.

2 Quoted in *Vernon-Central Revisited: A Capsule History* (Washington, D.C.: A NeighborWorks Publication, 1989), 10.

3 Clora Bryant, et al., eds., *Central Avenue Sounds: Jazz in Los Angeles* (Berkeley: University of California Press, 1998), 205; Bunch, 115–16; and "Pickets Store, Gets Arrested but Released," *California Eagle*, 26 January 1934, 1.

4 Bunch, "A Past Not Necessarily Prologue," 110–12; and *Vernon-Central Revisited*, 7–8, 22–27.

5 Bryant, et al., eds., *Central Avenue Sounds*, 215–16.

6 Samuel Rodney Browne oral history in Bette Yarbrough Cox, *Central Avenue—Its Rise and Fall (1890–c.1955) including the Musical Renaissance of Black Los Angeles* (Los Angeles: BEEM Publications, 1996), 107.

7 Cox. See also Frank Morgan, interview by Steven Isoardi, UCLA Center for Oral History Research, 1996, 17–18.

8 Cox, 108.

9 Burt A. Folkart, "S.R. Browne, Pioneer Black Teacher, Dies," *Los Angeles Times*, 20 November 1991, B8.

10 Pan Afrikan Peoples Arkestra, *Flight 17*, Nimbus West Records, compact disc, NS 135 C.

11 Quoted in William Overend, "A Black Teacher Recalls Another Era," *Los Angeles Times*, 14 September 1979, IV:12.

12 Horace Tapscott, *Songs of the Unsung: The Musical and Social Journey of Horace Tapscott*, ed. Steven Isoardi (Durham, NC: Duke University Press, 2001), 33–34.

13 Bryant, et al., eds., *Central Avenue Sounds*, 209–10; and Cox, 7–22.

14 Arna Bontemps and Jack Conroy, *Anyplace But Here* (New York: Hill and Wang, 1966), 252.

15 Floyd Levin, *Classic Jazz: A Personal View of the Music and the Musicians* (Berkeley: University of California Press, 2000), 30.

16 Phil Pastras, *Dead Man Blues: Jelly Roll Morton Way Out West* (Berkeley: University of California Press, 2001), 81.

17 Bryant, et al., eds., *Central Avenue Sounds*, 256–57, 358–59; and Cox, *Central Avenue*, 46–47. On the life and career of Alma Hightower, see Vi Redd, interview by Steven Isoardi, UCLA Center for Oral History Research, 2004.

18 Bryant, et al., eds., *Central Avenue Sounds*, 378–79; Buddy Collette with Steven Isoardi, *Jazz Generations: A Life in American Music and Society* (London: Continuum, 2000), 81–82; and Lora Rosner, "Billy Higgins: Making the Music One," *Modern Drummer* 16 (February 1992): 29.

19 Joe Darensbourg as told to Peter Vacher, *Jazz Odyssey: The Autobiography of Joe Darensbourg* (Baton Rouge, LA: Louisiana State University Press, 1988), 67.

20 Tapscott, *Songs of the Unsung*, 29.

21 Tapscott, 27.

22 See LeRoi Jones (Amiri Baraka), *Blues People: Negro Music in White America* (New York: William Morrow, 1963), 149–55.

23 Collette with Isoardi, *Jazz Generations*, 71.

24 See Floyd Levin, "Kid Ory's Legendary Nordskog/Sunshine Recordings," *Jazz Journal International* 46:7 (July, 1993): 6–10; and Floyd Levin, "The Spikes Brothers—A Los Angeles Saga," *Jazz Journal* 4:12 (December, 1951): 12–14.

25 Leroy E. Hurte, *The Magic of Music: An Autobiography* (Apple Valley, CA: Bronze-Lyric Publishing Company, 1997), 10–12; and Leroy Hurte, interview by Steven Isoardi, UCLA Center for Oral History Research, 1997, 36–46.

26 Jim Dawson, *Nervous Man Nervous: Big Jay McNeely and the Rise of the Honking Tenor Sax!* (Milford, NH: Big Nickel Publications, 1994), 35–37; and Arnold Shaw, *Honkers and Shouters: The Golden Years of Rhythm and Blues* (New York: Macmillan Publishing Company, 1978), 152–55.

27 "Copy received at Copyright Office," 14 August 1944, No. 387789, fax from Leroy Hurte; and, Hurte interview, UCLA, 43–48. The original 78 rpm recording of "I Wonder" on Bronze Records is very rare and was not reissued until 1999, when Rhino Records released *Central Avenue Sounds: Jazz in Los Angeles (1921–1956)*.

28 On the origins and early years of R&B in Los Angeles, see Joseph Bihari, interview by Steven Isoardi, UCLA Center for Oral History Research, 1997, 24–154; Bryant, et al., eds., *Central Avenue Sounds*; Dawson, *Nervous Man Nervous*; Ralph Eastman, "Central Avenue Blues: The Making of Los Angeles Rhythm and Blues, 1942–1947," *Black Music Research Journal* 9:1 (Spring, 1989): 19–33; Willie R. Collins, "California Rhythm and Blues Recordings, 1942–1972: A Diversity of Styles," in *California Soul: Music of African Americans in the West*, ed. Jacqueline Cogdell DjeDje and Eddie S. Meadows (Berkeley: University of California Press, 1998), 213–43; Johnny Otis, *Upside Your Head! Rhythm and Blues on Central Avenue* (Hanover: Wesleyan University Press, 1993); and Shaw, *Honkers and Shouters*, 89–272.

29 Bryant, et al., eds., *Central Avenue Sounds*, 333–36; and "Former Lunceford Trumpeter in Rehearsal with New Swing Band," *California Eagle*, 12 October 1944, 12.

30 Bryant, et al., eds., *Central Avenue Sounds*, 335.

31 Quoted in Raymond Horricks, *The Importance of Being Eric Dolphy* (Tunbridge Wells, Great Britain: D J Costello Publishers, 1989), 19.

32 Tapscott, *Songs of the Unsung*, 27–30.

33 Tapscott, 30.

34 Bryant, et al., eds., *Central Avenue Sounds*, 336.

35 Bryant, et al., 336.

36 Ted Gioia, *West Coast Jazz: Modern Jazz in California 1945–1960* (New York: Oxford University Press, 1992), 14.

37 Bryant, et al., eds., *Central Avenue Sounds*, 185, 221–22, 351, 354; Collette with Isoardi, *Jazz Generations*, 62–63; Gioia, *West Coast Jazz*, 9–15; Robert Gordon, *Jazz West Coast: The Los Angeles Jazz Scene of the 1950s* (London: Quartet Books, 1986), 23–26; and Ken Poston, "Bebop Invades the West," in *Central Avenue Sounds* (Rhino Entertainment Company), 46–57.

38 Gioia, *West Coast Jazz*, 336. See also Brian Priestley, *Mingus: A Critical Biography* (New York: Da Capo Press, 1983), 27, 35, 39–40.

39 Bryant, et al., eds., *Central Avenue Sounds*, 129–30; Collette with Isoardi, *Jazz Generations*, 67–72; Gioia, *West Coast Jazz*, 337–39; Priestley, *Mingus*, 29–30; and Gene Santoro, *Myself When I Am Real: The Life and Music of Charles Mingus* (New York: Oxford University Press, 2000), 69–71.

40 Anthony Ortega, interview by Steven Isoardi, UCLA Center for Oral History Research, 1997, 71.

41   See Horricks, *The Importance of Being Eric Dolphy*, 21; and *Last Date: Eric Dolphy*, prod. Marian Brouwer and dir. Hans Hylkema, 92 min., Rhapsody Films Inc., 1991, videocassette.

42   Clifford Solomon, interview by Steven Isoardi, UCLA Center for Oral History Research, 2000, 114.

43   Collette with Isoardi, *Jazz Generations*, 87.

44   Buddy Collette, liner notes, *Man of Many Parts*, Contemporary, compact disc, OJCCD-239-2.

45   Collette, 165–67. Although performed on a few occasions, Buddy's twelve-tone blues has yet to be recorded.

46   Tapscott, *Songs of the Unsung*, 36.

47   Tapscott, 26.

48   Tapscott, 24–26; and Grace M., "African American Musical Traditions in Los Angeles: Ethnographic Portraits of Four Musicians" (master's thesis, UCLA, 1996), 80–81. On Still's years in L.A., see Catherine Parsons Smith, *William Grant Still: A Study in Contradictions* (Berkeley: University of California Press, 2000), 69–93.

49   Collette with Isoardi, *Jazz Generations*, 47. On Reese's pedagogy, also see Gioia, *West Coast Jazz*, 40. On his work with a beginning student, see Ortega, UCLA interview, 21–29, 116–18, 189–90. The importance of Reese in Mingus' development has been documented, unlike other aspects of the bassist/composer's early years. According to Buddy Collette much of Mingus' *Beneath the Underdog* was fictional, such as his early interest in and command of Western classical music. See Collette with Isoardi, *Jazz Generations*, 22, 25–26. Mingus was to write years later of his membership in the L.A. Junior Philharmonic in the early to mid-1930s. However, the orchestra didn't exist at that time. Perhaps he was playing to an audience who would be impressed by such an item on his resume.

50   Tapscott, *Songs of the Unsung*, 36.

51   Tapscott, 56.

52   *Outa Sight*, Pacific Jazz, compact disc, CDP 7243 4 94849 2 4. On Anderza, see Bobby Bradford, interview by Steven Isoardi, UCLA Center for Oral History Research, 2002, 164–70, 176–78.

53   Tapscott, *Songs of the Unsung*, 37.

54   Gioia, *West Coast Jazz*, 348–59; John Litweiler, *The Freedom Principle: Jazz after 1958* (New York: Da Capo Press, 1984), 33–40; John Litweiler, *Ornette Coleman: A Harmolodic Life* (New York: William Morrow and Company, Inc., 1992), 41–68; Barry McRae, *Ornette Coleman* (London: Apollo Press Limited, 1988), 15–28; A.B. Spellman, *Four Lives in the Bebop Business* (New York: Limelight Editions, 1966), 104–25; Valerie Wilmer, *As Serious as Your Life: John Coltrane and Beyond* (London: Serpent's Tail, 1992), 68–70; Peter Niklas Wilson, *Ornette Coleman: His Life and Music* (Berkeley: Berkeley Hills Books, 1999), 14–19.

55   Tapscott, *Songs of the Unsung*, 36–37. See also Bobby Bradford's description of Ornette in those days in Bradford, UCLA interview, 138–39.

56 Bradford, UCLA interview, 150. Also 158; Harold Land, interview by Steven Isoardi, UCLA Center for Oral History Research, 2003, 48–53; and Larance Marable, interview by Steven Isoardi, UCLA Center for Oral History Research, 2001, 72.

57 Quoted in R. J. Smith, "All That L.A. Jazz," *Los Angeles Times Magazine*, 19 January 1997, 15.

58 Quoted in Litweiler, *Ornette Coleman*, 43. See also 45–46, 51, 59; and Spellman, *Four Lives*, 110–11.

59 Bradford, UCLA interview, 155. Also 158.

60 Bradford, 155; Litweiler, *Ornette Coleman*, 50; Putter Smith, interview by Alex Cline, UCLA Center for Oral History Research; and Spellman, *Four Lives*, 107.

61 Bradford, UCLA interview, 151.

62 Quoted in Vladimir Simosko and Barry Tepperman, *Eric Dolphy: A Musical Biography and Discography* (New York: Da Capo Press, 1979), 36. Litweiler in *Ornette Coleman* states that Ornette perceived a more negative reaction from Dolphy (55).

63 Don Preston, interview by Steven Isoardi, UCLA Center for Oral History Research, 2003, 58–59. During the late 1950s/early 1960s, the jam sessions at the Caprice attracted some of the best young musicians emerging throughout Los Angeles. See Preston, UCLA interview, 34–35, 40, 50–55, 93.

64 "Bobby Bradford interview with Mark Weber," *Coda*, October 1977, 3. Also Bradford, UCLA interview, 149–50.

65 Quoted in Litweiler, *Ornette Coleman*, 53.

66 Collette with Isoardi, *Jazz Generations*, 90–91.

67 Collette with Isoardi, 91.

68 Simosko and Tepperman, *Eric Dolphy*, 36–39.

69 "Interview with Billy Higgins," *Be-bop and Beyond*, 2:3 (May/June 1984): 20.

70 Curtis Amy, interview by Steven Isoardi, UCLA Center for Oral History Research, 2002, 104.

71 Anthony Ortega, interview by Steven Isoardi, UCLA Center for Oral History Research, 1997, 199. Ortega relates that he played with Bley for four or five months before Bley fired him and hired Coleman. See 194–99. Bley writes of his experiences in Los Angeles in his memoir, *Stopping Time: Paul Bley and the Transformation of Jazz* (Montreal: Vehicule Press, 1999), 54–70, but does not mention Ortega.

72 "La Monte Young and Marian Zazeela at the Dream House: In Conversation with Frank J. Oteri," in *NewMusicBox*, #54, volume 5:6 (October 2003), www.newmusicbox.org/page.nmbx?id=54fp01.

73 "American Mavericks: An Interview with La Monte Young and Marian Zazeela," www.musicmavericks.org. See also "La Monte Young and Marian Zazeela: an interview by Ian Nagoski," http://www.halana.com; and "La Monte Young and Marian Zazeela at the Dream House: In Conversation with Frank J. Oteri." On his evolution as a jazz artist in the mid-1950s, see Keith Potter, *Four Musical Minimalists: La Monte Young, Terry Riley, Steve Reich, Philip Glass* (Cambridge: Cambridge University Press, 2000), 26.

74 Tapscott, *Songs of the Unsung*, 70.

75 Tapscott, 125.

76 Paul Horn with Lee Underwood, *Inside Paul Horn: The Spiritual Odyssey of a Universal Traveler* (San Francisco: Harpercollins, 1990), 116.

77 Tapscott, *Songs of the Unsung*, 71.

78 Gioia, *West Coast Jazz*, 331.

79 Gioia, 361.

80 Peter Garland, ed., *A Lou Harrison Reader* (Santa Fe: Soundings Press, 1987), 98; and Leta Miller, notes to *Drums Along the Pacific*, New Albion Records, compact disc, NA122).

81 On Partch's life and music see: Harry Partch, *Genesis of a Music: An Account of a Creative Work, Its Roots and Its Fulfillments*, 2nd ed. (New York: Da Capo Press, 1974); and Bob Gilmore, *Harry Partch: a Biography* (New Haven: Yale University Press, 1998).

82 Michael Hicks, *Henry Cowell, Bohemian* (Urbana: University of Illinois Press, 2002), 6. John Cage has written of Cowell: "He was not attached (as Varese also was not attached) to what seemed to so many to be the important question: Whether to follow Schoenberg or Stravinsky. His early works for piano, long before Varese's *Ionization* . . . by their tone clusters and use of the piano strings, pointed towards noise and a continuum of timbre." John Cage, *Silence: Lectures and Writings* (Hanover, NH: Wesleyan University Press, 1961), 71. During the 1930s, Cage and Lou Harrison studied in San Francisco with Cowell, trowled the junk and music shops of Chinatown, attended performances of Cantonese opera, and composed and performed heavily percussive music inspired by Cowell and the Asian sounds of the city.

83 William Grant Still, "An Afro-American Composer's Point of View," in *American Composers on American Music*, ed. Henry Cowell (NY: Frederick Ungar Publishing Co., 1962; originally published 1933), 182–83.

84 Catherine Parsons Smith, *William Grant Still*, 49–51, 78. On Cowell, in addition to the Hicks biography, see Henry Cowell, *Essential Cowell: Selected Writings on Music*, ed. Dick Higgins (Kingston, NY: McPherson, 2001); and Kyle Gann, *American Music in the Twentieth Century* (Belmont, CA: Wadsworth/ Thomson Learning, 1997), 28–36.

85 Cowell, *Essential Cowell*, 188.

CHAPTER 3: LINO'S PAD

EPIGRAPH: Jayne Cortez, "Find Your Own Voice," *somewhere in advance of nowhere* (New York: Serpent's Tail, 1996), 116.

1 Bette Yarbrough Cox, *Central Avenue—Its Rise and Fall (1890–c.1955)* including the Musical Renaissance of Black Los Angeles (Los Angeles: BEEM Publications, 1996), 108.

2 Carl Burnett, interview by Steven Isoardi, UCLA Center for Oral History Research, 2007, 21–22.

3 Quoted in William Overend, "A Black Teacher Recalls Another Era," *Los Angeles Times*, 14 September 1979, IV:13.

4 Gerald Horne, *Fire This Time: The Watts Uprising and the 1960s* (Charlottesville: University Press of Virginia, 1995), 36.

5 Josh Sides, *L.A. City Limits: African American Los Angeles from the Great Depression to the Present* (Berkeley: University of California Press, 2003), 101. Sides provides an excellent overview of this struggle. See 101–6, 125–29.

6 See, for example, multiple stories and photos in the *California Eagle*: "New Bombing Threat," 20 March 1952, pp. 1, 2, 3; "Home Owner Arms Self to Guard Family," 19 June 1952, p. 3; "'White Only,' Buyer Told at Compton Housing Tract," 8 July 1954, pp. 1, 3; and "Cross Burned on Teachers' Lawn," 27 June 1957, pp. 1, 4.

7 Horne, *L.A. City Limits*, 248.

8 Horne, 47; and Bruce Michael Tyler, "Black Radicalism in Southern California, 1950–1982" (Ph.D. diss., University of California, Los Angeles, 1983), 73–74.

9 Jayne Cortez interview in D. H. Melhem, *Heroism in the New Black Poetry: Introduction and Interviews* (Lexington: The University Press of Kentucky, 1990), 198.

10 Clora Bryant, et al., eds., *Central Avenue Sounds: Jazz in Los Angeles* (Berkeley: University of California Press, 1998), 95.

11 Anthony Ortega, interview by Steven Isoardi, UCLA Center for Oral History Research, 1997, 8. See also 9, 106. Anthony also recalls instances of tagging, where various gangs would identify their territory by writing their names on whatever structures were available. See 30–33.

12 Mike Davis, *City of Quartz: Excavating the Future in Los Angeles* (London: Verso, 1990), 293. For more on L.A. gang history consult Alex Alonso, "Out of the Void: Street Gangs in Black Los Angeles," in *Black Los Angeles: American Dreams and Racial Realities*, ed. Darnell Hunt and Ana-Christina Ramón (New York: New York University Press, 2010), 140–67; "Racialized Identities and the Formation of Black Gangs in Los Angeles," *Urban Geography* 25:7 (2004): 658–74; and "Territoriality Among African American Street Gangs in Los Angeles" (M.A. thesis, University of Southern California, 1999).

13 J.K. Obatala, "The Sons of Watts: Off the Streets and into the system," *Los Angeles Times*, 13 August 1972, sec. *West Magazine*, 7.

14 Elaine Brown, interview by Steven Isoardi, 3 November 2001; Will Connell, interview by Steven Isoardi, 12, 22 March, 2 May 2001; Yusuf Jah and Sister Shah'Keyah, *Uprising: Crips and Bloods Tell the Story of America's Youth in the Crossfire* (New York: Scribner, 1995), 121; Obatala, 7; and Dadisi Sanyika, interview by Steven Isoardi, 4 January 2002.

15 Raphael J. Sonenshein, *Politics in Black and White: Race and Power in Los Angeles* (Princeton, NJ: Princeton University Press, 1993), 31.

16 Horne, *Fire This Time*, 45–46.

17 This is not to suggest that the earlier LAPD was free of racism. For example, its police chief during the 1920s was Louis Oaks, a member of the Ku Klux Klan. See Peter J. Boyer, "Bad Cops," *The New Yorker*, 21 May 2001, 63. For a

brief biography of Chief Parker, see Joe Domanick, *To Protect and to Serve: The LAPD's Century of War in the City of Dreams* (New York: Pocket Books, 1994), 85, 90–103.

18   Joe Domanick, "Police Power: Why No One Can Control the LAPD," *LA Weekly*, 16–22 February 1990, 18. Also Domanick, *To Protect*, 110–13.

19   Quoted in Domanick, *To Protect*, 19.

20   Quoted in Tyler, "Black Radicalism," 131.

21   Tyler, 132.

22   Tyler, 128. See also Sonenshein, *Politics in Black and White*, 32; and Domanick, *To Protect*, 113–16.

23   Domanick, *To Protect*, 149–53; Martin J. Schiesl, "Behind the Badge: The Police and Social Discontent in Los Angeles Since 1950," in Norman M. Klein and Martin J. Schiesl, eds., *20th Century Los Angeles: Power, Promotion, and Social Conflict* (Claremont, CA: Regina Books, 1990), 159–60; and Tyler, "Black Radicalism," 150–51.22.

24   Domanick, "Police Power," 18. See also Sonenshein, *Politics in Black and White*, 31–32.

25   Schiesl, "Behind the Badge," 156–62.

26   "Chief Parker Accused of Being 'Anti-Negro,'" *Los Angeles Times*, 12 June 1962, 24. See also Domanick, *To Protect*, 161–65.

27   Davis, *City of Quartz*, 294.

28   Paul McGee, "Avenue Businessman Protests Police Action," *Los Angeles Sentinel*, 11 November 1954, A1, A3.

29   Davis, *City of Quartz*, 294.

30   Tyler, "Black Radicalism," 173.

31   Quoted in Tyler, 180.

32   Horace Tapscott, *Songs of the Unsung: The Musical and Social Journey of Horace Tapscott*, ed. Steven Isoardi (Durham, NC: Duke University Press, 2001), 210.

33   Pan Afrikan Peoples Arkestra, liner notes, *Flight 17*, Nimbus West Records, compact disc, NS 135C.

34   Tapscott, *Songs of the Unsung*, 82.

35   Tapscott, 15.

36   Carl Burnett, personal communication, 7 July 2004. See also Burnett, UCLA interview.

37   Henry Franklin, interview by Steven Isoardi, UCLA Center for Oral History Research, 2007, 173.

38   Franklin, 174–75.

39   Tapscott, *Songs of the Unsung*, 83–84.

40   Tapscott, 84.

41   On David Bryant's early career, see Clora Bryant, et al., eds., *Central Avenue Sounds*, 164–178.

42   Horace composed a piece for Wendell titled "Ballad for Wendell Lee Black," which appeared on *At the Crossroads*, Nimbus NS-579, although misprinted as "Ballad for Window Lee Black."

43 Tapscott, *Songs of the Unsung*, 82.

44 Linda Hill, liner notes, *Lullaby for Linda*, Nimbus NS-791.

45 Hill, liner notes, *Lullaby*.

46 Hill, liner notes, *Lullaby*; and Margueritte A. Brown (Linda's oldest sister), "book research on Linda Hill," 8 July 2002, personal email.

47 Hill, liner notes, *Lullaby*.

48 See Tapscott, *Songs of the Unsung*, 102; and Zan Stewart, liner notes, *At the Crossroads*.

49 Stanley Cowell, "Horace Tapscott," 2 June 2002, personal email.

50 Tapscott, *Songs of the Unsung*, 70–71, 129–30, 134; and Marion Sherrill, interview by Steven Isoardi, 19 August 2000. Horace recorded with each of these leaders: *The Sounds of Broadway/The Sounds of Hollywood* (Palomar, 1965) with Amy and three LPs in Onzy Matthews' band, *Blues with a Touch of Elegance* (Capitol, 1964), *Sounds of the 60s* (Capitol, 1964–65), and *Tobacco Road* (Capitol, 1963) backing Lou Rawls. These recordings find him in the trombone sections. The two LPs with Blackburn, *Jazz Frontier* and *Two-Note Samba* (both on Imperial, 1963; reissued in 1999 by Fresh Sounds Records), feature Horace on piano in quintet settings. The second LP, in particular, shows his emerging command of the instrument.

51 Carmel Crunk, "Close to Freedom," Horace Tapscott Archive, UCLA.

52 Edith Hill to Patricia Hill, "Response to Inquiry RE Linda," 7 July 2002, personal email.

53 Stanley Cowell, "Horace Tapscott," 26 June 2002, personal email.

54 Horace Tapscott and Linda Hill, "Why Don't You Listen?" Tapscott Archive, UCLA.

55 Horace Tapscott and Linda Hill, "Lumumba," Tapscott Archive, UCLA.

CHAPTER 4: THE GIANT IS AWAKENED

EPIGRAPH: Ojenke, "To Mr. Charles and Sister Annie," in *From the Ashes: Voices of Watts*, ed. Budd Schulberg (New York: The New American Library, 1967), 63.

1 Patricia Rae Adler, "Watts: From Suburb to Black Ghetto" (Ph.D. diss., University of Southern California, 1976), 25–26, 55–56, 60–62, 78–81, 96–98, 233, 251, 263–64, 282; James P. Allen and Eugene Turner, *The Ethnic Quilt: Population Diversity in Southern California* (Northridge, CA: The Center for Geographical Studies, California State University, Northridge, 1997), 80; J. Max Bond, "The Negro in Los Angeles" (Ph.D. diss., University of Southern California, 1936), 87–88; Lonnie G. Bunch III, "A Past Not Necessarily Prologue: The Afro-American in Los Angeles Since 1900," in *20th Century Los Angeles: Power, Promotion, and Social Conflict*, ed. Norman M. Klein & Martin J. Schiesl (Claremont, CA: Regina Books, 1990), 115; and Lawrence B. de Graaf, "The City of Black Angels: Emergence of the Los Angeles Ghetto, 1890–1930," *Pacific Historical Review* 39 (1970): 347.

2   On the history of the Lincoln Motion Picture Company, see Thomas Cripps, *Slow Fade to Black: The Negro in American Film, 1900–1942* (Oxford: Oxford University Press, 1993), 75–89; and Jesse Algeron Rhines, *Black Film / White Money* (New Brunswick, NJ: Rutgers University Press, 1996), 18–23.

3   See Bud Goldstone and Arloa Paquin Goldstone, *The Los Angeles Watts Towers* (Los Angeles: The Getty Conservation Institute and the J. Paul Getty Museum, 1997); and William C. Seitz, *The Art of Assemblage* (New York: The Museum of Modern Art, 1961), 72–80.

4   Charles Mingus, *Beneath the Underdog*, ed. Nel King (New York: Alfred A. Knopf, 1971), 37.

5   Cecil McNeely, interview by Steven Isoardi, UCLA Center for Oral History Research, 1993, 51.

6   Mingus, *Beneath the Underdog*, 37.

7   Buddy Collette with Steven Isoardi, *Jazz Generations: A life in American music and society* (London: Continuum, 2000), 11.

8   Clora Bryant, et al., eds., *Central Avenue Sounds: Jazz in Los Angeles* (Berkeley: University of California Press, 1998), 92–93.

9   Adler, "Watts," 242.

10 Bryant, et al., eds., *Central Avenue Sounds*, 93; Floyd Levin, *Classic Jazz: A Personal View of the Music and the Musicians* (Berkeley: University of California Press, 2000), 16, 30, 34; and Phil Pastras, *Dead Man Blues: Jelly Roll Morton Way Out West* (Berkeley: University of California Press, 2001), 115–20.

11 Quoted in Adler, "Watts," 243.

12 Quoted in Adler.

13 George Lipsitz, "Introduction—Creating Dangerously: The Blues Life of Johnny Otis," in Johnny Otis, *Upside Your Head! Rhythm and Blues on Central Avenue* (Hanover: Wesleyan University Press, 1993), xxiv.

14 Quoted in press release for Eighth Annual Watts Towers Music and Arts Festival, 4 July 1984, Watts Towers Archive.

15 Nathan E. Cohen, "The Context of the Curfew Area," in *The Los Angeles Riots: A Socio-Psychological Study*, ed. Nathan Cohen (New York: Praeger Publishers, 1970), 46. Also, Adler, "Watts," 309–15; and Clay Carson, "Watts Story Covers Years 1850–1966 from 'Mudtown' to 'Symbol of Revolt,'" *Los Angeles Free Press*, 12 August 1966, 10.

16 Adler, "Watts," 276–77.

17 Stanley Crouch, *Ain't No Ambulances for No Nigguhs Tonight*. Flying Dutchman FDS-105.

18 Martin J. Schiesl, "Behind the Badge: The Police and Social Discontent in Los Angeles Since 1950," in Norman M. Klein and Martin J. Schiesl, eds., *20th Century Los Angeles: Power, Promotion, and Social Conflict* (Claremont, CA: Regina Books, 1990), 164.

19 Chester Himes, *The Quality of Hurt: The Autobiography of Chester Himes, Volume I* (Garden City, NY: Doubleday & Co., Inc., 1972), 74. For a discussion of the precipitating event, see Joe Domanick, *To Protect and to Serve: The LAPD's*

Century of War in the City of Dreams (New York: Pocket Books, 1994), 179–80; and Gerald Horne, *Fire This Time: The Watts Uprising and the 1960s* (Charlottesville, VA: University Press of Virginia, 1995), 53–60.

20 Quoted in Joe Domanick, "Police Power: Why No One Can Control the LAPD," *LA Weekly*, 16–22 February 1990, 18.

21 Quoted in Joe Domanick, 19. See also Domanick, *To Protect*, 185.

22 Horne, *Fire This Time*, 339.

23 Quoted in Adler, "Watts," 180.

24 Theomachist (Against the Gods), "How to Kill the Ku Klux," *California Eagle*, 15 October 1921, 1, 8. Other articles appeared in the issues of October 1 and 8.

25 Adler, "Watts," 330. On the weakening of the local NAACP in the years before 1965, see Horne, *Fire This Time*, 172–75.

26 See J. K. Obatala, "The Sons of Watts: Off the Streets and into the system," *Los Angeles Times*, 13 August 1972, sec. *West Magazine*, 6–9.

27 See Scot Brown, *Fighting for US: Maulana Karenga, the US Organization, and Black Cultural Nationalism* (New York: New York University Press, 2003), 82–85; and Bruce Michael Tyler, "Black Radicalism in Southern California, 1950–1982" (Ph.D. diss., University of California, Los Angeles, 1983), 311–97.

28 On Studio Watts, see also Robin D. G. Kelley, *Freedom Dreams: The Black Radical Imagination* (Boston: Beacon Press, 2002), 187; and Allan Kramer, "Studio Watts Teen Post Not a Babysitting Agency," *Los Angeles Free Press*, 1 April 1966, 1.

29 On the formation of the New Art Jazz Ensemble, see Bobby Bradford, interview by Steven Isoardi, UCLA Center for Oral History Research, 2002, 280–93; Lee Jeske, "John Carter," *Down Beat*, November 1982, 20; and Tom Williamson, interview by Steven Isoardi, UCLA Center for Oral History Research, 2002, 120–38. The band recorded three LPs during 1969–70: *Seeking* on Revelation, and *Flight for Four* and *Self Determination Music* on Flying Dutchman.

30 Quoted in Grace Glueck, "Up with the Non-Dominants," *The New York Times*, 9 April 1972, II:12.

31 Noah Purifoy, interview by Karen Anne Mason, UCLA Center for Oral History Research, 1992, 63–64. See also 58–60.

32 Quoted in Lizzetta LeFalle-Collins, "Noah Purifoy: Outside and in the Open," in *Noah Purifoy: Outside and in the Open* (Los Angeles: California Afro-American Museum Foundation, 1997), 13.

33 Noah Purifoy as told to Ted Michel, "The Art of Communication as a Creative Act," in *Junk Art: "66 Signs of Neon"* (Los Angeles: 66 Signs of Neon, n.d.)

34 John Riddle, interview by Karen Anne Mason, UCLA Center for Oral History Research, 2000, 62.

35 See *Junk Art*; and Samella Lewis, *African American Art and Artists* (Berkeley: University of California Press, 1990), 198–199.

36 Quoted in LeFalle-Collins, "Noah Purifoy," 17.

37 Purifoy, "The Art of Communication."

38 Purifoy, UCLA interview, 60.

39 LeFalle-Collins, "Noah Purifoy," 10.

40 Purifoy, UCLA interview, 69.

41 Lewis, *African American Art and Artists*, 200. See also Jane H. Carpenter with Betye Saar, *Betye Saar* (San Francisco: Pomegranate, 2003), 1–4.

42 Quoted in Lewis, *African American Art and Artists*, 204.

43 John Outterbridge, interview by Richard Candida Smith, UCLA Center for Oral History Research, 1993, 509.

44 Outterbridge, 405. Also, 376–406, 505–28.

45 Horne, *Fire This Time*, 181; and Gladwin Hill, "Watts to Hold Summer Festival on Anniversary of '65 Rioting," *The New York Times*, 7 August 1966, 48. For a fuller account of the Watts Writers Workshop see Daniel Widener, *Black Arts West: Culture and Struggle in Postwar Los Angeles* (Durham, NC: Duke University Press, 2010), 90–114.

46 Schulberg, ed., *From the Ashes*, 17–18. Also 3–18.

47 Schulberg; and *Antioch Review*, 27:2 (Fall 1967).

48 Quincy Troupe, ed., *Watts Poets: A Book of New Poetry and Essays* (n.p.: the House of Respect, 1968).

49 Erin Aubry, "Words to Live By," *Los Angeles Times*, 8 October 1995, E1.

50 See Watts Prophets, *Rappin' Black in a White World*, Acid Jazz, compact disc, JAZID CD 164.

51 For full story, see Roger Rapoport, "Meet America's Meanest Dirty Trickster," *Mother Jones* II:III (April 1977): 19–23, 59–61. See also Quincy Troupe, interview by Steven Isoardi, 24 August 2001. For an overview of the FBI program, see Ward Churchill and Jim Vander Wall, *Agents of Repression: The FBI's Secret Wars Against the Black Panther Party and the American Indian Movement* (Boston, MA: South End Press, 1990), 37–99; and Kenneth O'Reilly, *"Racial Matters": The FBI's Secret File on Black America, 1960–1972* (NY: The Free Press, 1989), 237–45, 261–324.

52 Horne, *Fire This Time*, 330; and Eliot Fremont-Smith, "TV: N.B.C. Documents 'The Angry Voices of Watts,'" *The New York Times*, 17 August 1966, 79.

53 Brown also discusses this in her autobiography, *A Taste of Power: A Black Woman's Story* (New York: Pantheon Books, 1992), 149–51.

54 Schulberg, ed., *From the Ashes*, 12–13

55 Some think Horace and Lester Robertson did the music, but a print of the film has yet to turn up to verify this and there is no substantiating evidence in the Tapscott Archive.

56 George Wesley Bourland, "A Capsule of Mafundi," *The Mafundi Potential*, 1:1 (February 1970): 4.

57 Jay Bayete, "Mafundi: A Cultural Arts Family Affair," *Neworld*, 2:2 (Winter, 1976): 35; Bourland, 4; and Jack Leonard, "Watts' Mafundi Institute Stars in Its Own Revival," *Los Angeles Times*, 24 October 1997, B5.

58 UCLA Fowler Museum of Cultural History, exhibition description of *Streetwise: The Mafundi of Dar es Salaam*. For a discussion of the meaning and role of *mafundi* in Tanzanian society, see R. Mark Livengood, "Streetwise: The

Mafundi of Dar es Salaam," in *The Cast-off Recast: Recycling and the Creative Transformation of Mass-Produced Objects*, ed. Timothy Corrigan Correll and Patrick Arthur Polk (Los Angeles: UCLA Fowler Museum of Cultural History, 1999), 81–109.

59 "Schedule for Mid-Winter Classes," *The Mafundi Potential*, 1:1 (February 1970), 3.

60 Bradford, UCLA interview, 294–95.

61 Outterbridge, UCLA interview, 251.

62 Quoted in Grace M., "African American Musical Traditions in Los Angeles: Ethnographic Portraits of Four Musicians" (master's thesis, UCLA, 1996), 95.

63 Quoted in Grace M., 95–96.

CHAPTER 5: WARRIORS ALL

EPIGRAPH: Quoted in Rudolph Porter, interview by Steven Isoardi, 5 July 2000.

1 Horace Tapscott, *Songs of the Unsung: The Musical and Social Journey of Horace Tapscott*, ed. Steven Isoardi (Durham, NC: Duke University Press, 2001), 110.

2 Tapscott, 111–12.

3 Stanley Crouch, liner notes, Horace Tapscott Quintet, *The Giant Is Awakened*, Flying Dutchman FDS-107; reissued on *West Coast Hot*, RCA Novus Series '70, compact disc, 3107-2-N.

4 Quoted in Nat Hentoff, liner notes to Leon Thomas, *Spirits Known and Unknown*, Flying Dutchman FDS-115.

5 Scot Brown, *Fighting for US: Maulana Karenga, the US Organization, and Black Cultural Nationalism* (New York: New York University Press, 2003), 83.

6 Elaine Brown, *A Taste of Power: A Black Woman's Story* (New York: Pantheon Books, 1992), 185.

7 Horace Tapscott FBI file #157-6042. According to documentation in the file, the investigation was terminated the following March after background checks on Horace and surveillance of his residence failed to turn up any incriminating information. One document also notes that neither the LAPD nor L.A. County Sheriff's Office had any record of Horace, though his recollections in *Songs of the Unsung* suggest otherwise. See pp. 118–19. Given the hostility between the LAPD and Hoover's FBI, it's doubtful that much information would have been shared. Also suggestive was Mayor Tom Bradley's announcement to a press conference in April 1975, "that the LAPD had destroyed 2 million dossiers on some fifty-five thousand individuals and organizations." Joe Domanick, *To Protect and to Serve: The LAPD's Century of War in the City of Dreams* (New York: Pocket Books, 1994), 294.

8 Tapscott, *Songs of the Unsung*, 120.

9 Tapscott, 124.

10 Quoted in "Marshall's Othello On PBS," *Los Angeles Sentinel*, 7 June 1979, B-2A. Marshall also sang a soul interpretation of *Othello* at the Ahmanson Theatre in Los Angeles in 1968, titled "Catch My Soul." Jerry Lee Lewis was

his Iago. Sylvia Jarrico, personal communication, 2 June 2004; and Barbara Mounts, "'Catch My Soul' Another Triumph for Marshall," *Los Angeles Sentinel*, 7 March 1968, B8, B10.

11 For the Kennedy Center appearance see "Douglass Speech Still Has Its Bite," *Washington Star-News*, 5 July 1974. For Marshall's appearance at the ICCC, see Victor Leo Walker, II, "The Politics of Art: A History of the Inner City Cultural Center, 1965–1986" (Ph.D. diss., University of California, Santa Barbara, 1989), 317–19. One of the longest lasting inner-city arts institutions in Los Angeles, the ICCC not only provided space for artists like Marshall, Marla Gibbs, Ted Lange, and Denzel Washington, but was also staunchly multicultural. See also Sandi Sheffey-Stinson, "The History of Theatre Productions at the Los Angeles Inner City Cultural Center: 1965–1976" (Ph.D. diss., Kent State University, 1979).

12 Tapscott, *Songs of the Unsung*, 115–16.

13 Tapscott, 115.

14 Tapscott, 112.

15 Elaine Brown, liner notes, *Seize the Time*, Vault 131.

16 "Revolutionary View of Music," *The Black Panther*, 18 October 1969, 8.

17 Brown, *A Taste of Power*, 185–86, 195–96.

18 Brown, 196.

CHAPTER 6: THE MOTHERSHIP

EPIGRAPH: Sonia Sanchez, "Catch the Fire," *Wounded in the House of a Friend* (Boston: Beacon Press, 1995), 16.

1 A riveting account of the Los Angeles Panther chapter, especially of the LAPD assault on Panther headquarters in 1969, is given by one of the Panthers inside, Wayne Pharr, in his *Nine Lives of a Black Panther: A Story of Survival* (Chicago: Lawrence Hill Books, 2014).

2 Horace Tapscott, *Songs of the Unsung: The Musical and Social Journey of Horace Tapscott*, ed. Steven Isoardi (Durham, NC: Duke University Press, 2001), 137–38.

3 Tapscott, 83.

4 For more on Grant's Music Center, see Steven L. Isoardi, *The Music Finds a Way* (Paris: Dark Tree, 2020), 70–78. This section is reproduced in *Point of Departure* 73 (December 2020), www.pointofdeparture.org.

5 Tom Williamson, interview by Steven Isoardi, UCLA Center for Oral History Research, 2002, 169.

6 Scot Brown, *Fighting for US: Maulana Karenga, the US Organization, and Black Cultural Nationalism* (New York: New York University Press, 2003), 38.

7 For an account of the Center's history, see Alfred Ligon, interview by Ranford B. Hopkins, UCLA Center for Oral History Research, 1984, 31–37, 45–46.

8 Dadisi continued teaching in the Aquarian Center tradition until his passing in 2005. See his *African Drum and Dance: The Reconnection with African Ancestral Wisdom* (Los Angeles: Golden Thread Productions, 2000).

9 Elaine Brown, "Can't Go Back," *Elaine Brown*, Black Forum BF458L.

10 Tapscott, *Songs of the Unsung*, 137.

11 Elaine Brown, "I Know Who You Are," *Elaine Brown*.

12 In *A Taste of Power: A Black Woman's Story* (New York: Pantheon Books, 1992), 305–6, 310–12, Brown describes planning for the record and her contact with Suzanne de Passe, head of Motown's Creative Department.

13 Kamau Daáood, "Liberator of the Spirit," *The Language of Saxophones* (San Francisco, CA: City Lights, 2005), 35.

14 Williamson, UCLA interview, 154.

15 Quoted in Tapscott, *Songs of the Unsung*, 143.

16 See also Horace's recollection of the concert in *Songs of the Unsung*, 145–46.

17 See also *Life Is a Saxophone: Kamau Daáood, The Word Musician*, prod. and dir. Saundra Sharp, 58 min., A Sharp Show, 2013, DVD, which includes a martial arts improvisation by Dadisi.

18 Quincy Troupe, "Ode to John Coltrane," *Skulls Along the River* (New York: I. Reed Books, 1984), 37.

19 Ojenke, "Legacy of the Word," in Quincy Troupe, ed., *Watts Poets: A Book of New Poetry and Essays* (n.p.: the House of Respect, 1968), 19.

20 Kamau Daáood, personal communication with Steven Isoardi, 2002.

21 On Crouch's evolution as a drummer, see Peter Occhiogrosso, "Profile: Stanley Crouch, David Murray," *Down Beat*, 25 March 1976, 38–39.

22 Bobby Bradford, interview by Steven Isoardi, UCLA Center for Oral History Research, 318.

23 See also Horace Mansfield, Jr., "Newton's Law: A Discussion of Musical Forces with the World-Renowned Flutist," *Be-bop and Beyond* 1:5 (September/October 1983): 14–15.

24 Most of the classes were audio-taped by UGMAA archivist Michael Dett Wilcots and are in the Tapscott Archive at UCLA. A detailed presentation of that material is in Steven L. Isoardi and Michael Dett Wilcots, "Black Experience in the Fine Arts: An African American Community Arts Movement in a University Setting," *Current Research in Jazz* 6 (2014), www.crj-online.org.

CHAPTER 7: TO THE GREAT HOUSE

EPIGRAPH: Adele Sebastian, interview by Steve Buchanan, KCRW Radio, 18 August 1980; James Andrews, interview by Steven Isoardi, 6 December 2015.

1 Adele Sebastian, interview by John Breckow, KPFK Radio, 1981.

2 Adele Sebastian, interview by Steve Buchanan, KCRW Radio, 18 August 1980.

3 Ben Caldwell, interview by Steven Isoardi, 12 December 1998, for *Leimert Park: the Story of a Village in South Central Los Angeles*, produced and directed by Jeannette Lindsay, DVD, 2008; Larry Clark, interview by Steven Isoardi, 13 December 2000; and Ntongela Masilela, "The Los Angeles School of Black Filmmakers," in *Black American Cinema*, ed. Manthia Diawara (New York: Routledge, 1993), 107–17. Essays and interviews on the L.A. Rebellion

are in a collection edited by Allyson Nadia Field, Jan-Christpoher Horak, and Jacqueline Najuma Stewart, *L.A. Rebellion: Creating a New Black Cinema* (Berkeley: University of California Press, 2015).

4 Caldwell interview, *Leimert Park*.

5 Quoted in Larry Clark, interview by Steven Isoardi, 13 December 2000. Muse would appear in one more film, *The Black Stallion*, before his death in 1979.

6 Horace Tapscott, *Songs of the Unsung: The Musical and Social Journey of Horace Tapscott*, ed. Steven Isoardi (Durham, NC: Duke University Press, 2001), 178.

7 Tapscott comments in "H.T. Solo Piano in Concert," audio cassette tape, Tapscott Archive.

8 Letter of March 8, 1974, Sixth Pan African Congress, Tapscott Archive.

9 Adele Sebastian, interview by Steve Buchanan, KCRW Radio, 18 August 1980.

10 Sebastian, interview by Steve Buchanan.

11 Pan Afrikan Peoples Arkestra, "Quagmire Manor at 5 A.M.," *The Call*, Nimbus NS-246.

12 Adele Sebastian, interview by Steve Buchanan, KCRW Radio, 18 August 1980.

13 Billie Harris, liner notes, *I Want Some Water*, Nimbus West, compact disc, NS 510C.

14 Henry Franklin, interview by Steven Isoardi, UCLA Center for Oral History Research, 2007, 134.

15 Michael E. Veal, *Fela: The Life and Times of an African Musical Icon* (Philadelphia: Temple University Press, 2000), 151.

16 Tapscott, *Songs of the Unsung*, 179–80.

CHAPTER 8: THOUGHTS OF DAR ES SALAAM

EPIGRAPH: Chris Abani, "Orders," *Daphne's Lot* (Los Angeles: Red Hen Press, 2003), 93.

1 See Sabir Mateen Trio, *Divine Mad Love*, Eremite, compact disc, MTE011.

2 "Articles of Incorp," Tapscott Archive.

3 Michael Dett Wilcots, interviews by Steven Isoardi, 10 November 2001–20 April 2002.

4 "UGMAA Foundation Project Planning Document, A Public Agency: History," Tapscott Archive.

5 Unfortunately, no documentation of these other groups has been found.

6 Elizabeth Gray, "CETA & 'The Arts,'" *Neworld* 4:4 (1978—No. 3): 14–18. See also Victor Leo Walker, II, "The Politics of Art: A History of the Inner City Cultural Center, 1965–1986" (Ph.D. diss., University of California, Santa Barbara, 1989), 195–98.

7 "Agreement or Contract," June 5, 1976, Tapscott Archive.

8 See also "Department, Workshops and Program Activities," 30 June 1977; "UGMAA Foundation Workshops," 22 July 1976; and minutes/agendas from Board and Administrative staff meetings, 13 December 1976–14 February 1977, Tapscott Archive.

9 "Department, Workshops and Program Activities," 30, June 1977; and "Goals and Objectives" of the ECD Program, Tapscott Archive.

10 Grant letter of 16 August 1977; and "Contract," 8 September 1977, Tapscott Archive.

11 Press releases and flyers, Watts Towers Arts Center Archive.

12 Leonard Feather, "Pan-Afrikan Arkestra: Broad in Scope," *Los Angeles Times*, 16 October 1976, II:7. Feather had earlier reviewed a performance of Horace's Quintet and the Voice of UGMAA in 1970. See "Tapscott Ensemble Plays at Museum," *Los Angeles Times*, 22 July 1970, IV:12.

13 Bobby Bradford, interview by Steven Isoardi, UCLA Center for Oral History Research, 2002, 389.

14 Bradford, 326, 386–89, 391, 393, 435.

15 Nels Cline, interview by Steven Isoardi, UCLA Center for Oral History Research, 2007, 232.

16 Cline, 232.

17 See Horace Tapscott, *Songs of the Unsung: The Musical and Social Journey of Horace Tapscott*, ed. Steven Isoardi (Durham, NC: Duke University Press, 2001), 114–16.

18 Tapscott, *Songs of the Unsung*, 175–76.

19 Tom Albach, interview by John Breckow, KPFK Radio, 1981.

20 That first piece, "Inception," is now available on the CD re-issue of *Live at Lobero, Volume 1*. Nimbus West, NS2370 C, 2006.

21 Adele Sebastian, interview by Steve Buchanan, KCRW Radio, 18 August 1980.

22 Raspoeter Ojenke, "Sun Ra: Mystery of Mister Ra," SOUL, 1978.

23 See Walker, "Politics of Art," 135–39.

CHAPTER 9: AT THE CROSSROADS

EPIGRAPH: Wanda Coleman, "American Sonnet (4)," *Hand Dance* (Santa Rosa, CA: Black Sparrow Press, 1993), 93.

1 Eugene Grigsby, "The Rise and Decline of Black Neighborhoods in Los Angeles," *UCLA CAAS Report* 12:1&2 (Spring/Fall 1989): 17.

2 Ron Curran, "Malign Neglect: The Roots of an Urban War Zone," *L.A. Weekly*, 30 December 1988–5 January 1989, 8; Shawn Hubler, "South L.A.'s Poverty Rate Worse Than '65," *Los Angeles Times*, 11 May 1992, 1, 22; and Peter Kwong "The First Multicultural Riots," *Village Voice*, 9 June 1992, 31.

3 Francis Ward, "Permanent 'Underclass' of Jobless Blacks Feared," *Los Angeles Times*, 5 April 1976, 5.

4 Austin Scott, "Black Youths' Jobs Picture Still Bleak," *Los Angeles Times*, 24 December 1978, 8. An Urban League study, released a few months later, claimed that when part-time, temporary, and discouraged workers are factored in, the total was closer to sixty percent. "Black Youth Jobless Rate Put at 60%," *Los Angeles Times*, 26 July 1979, 24. See also Black Partnership Development Council, *The Black Community of Greater Los Angeles: A Community in Transition*

(United Way of Greater Los Angeles, October 16, 1991), 3.1–3.2. On deindustri-
alization, see James P. Allen and Eugene Turner, *The Ethnic Quilt: Population
Diversity in Southern California* (Northridge, CA: The Center for Geograph-
ical Studies, California State University, Northridge, 1997), 81; and Barry
Bluestone and Bennett Harrison, *The Deindustrialization of America: Plant
Closings, Community Abandonment, and the Dismantling of Basic Industry*
(New York: Basic Books, Inc., Publishers, 1992), 35–40.

5 Joe Domanick, *To Protect and to Serve: The LAPD's Century of War in the City
of Dreams* (New York: Pocket Books, 1994), 286.

6 Horace Tapscott, *Songs of the Unsung: The Musical and Social Journey of Horace Tapscott*, ed. Steven Isoardi (Durham, NC: Duke University Press, 2001),
205.

7 Grigsby, "Rise and Decline of Black Neighborhoods," 17. See also Black
Partnership Development Council, *Black Community of Greater Los Angeles*,
2.3–2.4.

8 Elaine Brown, *The Condemnation of Little B* (Boston: Beacon Press, 2002), 165.

9 Quoted in Ed Boyer and Ron Finney, "Black Youth—Changing Generation,"
Los Angeles Times, 5 September 1982, 1. See also Black Partnership Development Council, *Black Community of Greater Los Angeles*, 3.15; Mike Davis, *City
of Quartz: Excavating the Future in Los Angeles* (London: Verso, 1990), 270;
and Joe Domanick, "Police Power: Why No One Can Control the LAPD," *LA
Weekly*, 16–22 February 1990, 20.

10 Brown, *Condemnation of Little B*, 165–66.

11 Domanick, *To Protect*, 311. On the origins of the Crips and Bloods see Donald
Bakeer, CRIPS (Los Angeles: Precocious Publishing, 1992), 12–13; Davis, *City of
Quartz*, 298–300; Yusuf Jah and Sister Shah'Keyah, *Uprising: Crips and Bloods
Tell the Story of America's Youth in the Crossfire* (New York: Scribner, 1995),
45–54, 121–24; and Jenifer Warren and Dan Morain, "Crips Target of Prison
Lockdown," *Los Angeles Times*, 1 July 2003, B1, 7.

12 Tapscott, *Songs of the Unsung*, 207.

13 See the following articles in the *San Jose Mercury News*: "'Crack' plague's roots
are in Nicaraguan War," 18 August 1996, 1A, 16A–17A; "Odd trio created mass
market for 'crack,'" 19 August 1996, 1A, 10A–11A; and "War on drugs' unequal impact on U.S. blacks," 20 August 1996, 1A, 10A. Webb presents a more
detailed argument and further research in his subsequent *Dark Alliance: The
CIA, the Contras, and the Crack Cocaine Explosion* (New York: Seven Stories
Press, 1998).

14 Brown, *Condemnation of Little B*, 167.

15 Robin D. G. Kelley, *Yo' Mama's Disfunktional! Fighting the Culture Wars in
Urban America* (Boston: Beacon Press, 1997), 47.

16 Kelley, 52.

17 See Horace Mansfield, Jr., "Newton's Law: A Discussion of Musical Forces
with the World-Renowned Flutist," *Be-bop and Beyond* 1:5 (September/Oc-
tober 1983): 17; John Green, "The Seeds Are Set: Wind College," *Be-bop and*

Beyond 1:5 (September/October 1983): 8–9; and Lee Jeske, "John Carter," *Down Beat*, November 1982, 18–19.

Ron LaRue, "Obituary: Remembering Ray Draper," *Be-bop and Beyond* 1:1 (January/February 1983): 3.

D. Jean Collins, "Interview with Adele Sebastian," *Uraeus: The Journal of Unconscious Life* 2:4, 38.

For a discussion of the Nigerian government's assault on the compound, see Michael E. Veal, *Fela: The Life and Times of an African Musical Icon* (Philadelphia: Temple University Press, 2000), 155–57.

Don Snowden, "3 Jazz Pianists in a Concert Setting," *Los Angeles Times*, 14 February 1984, VI:3.

See also Elaine Cohen, "Tapscott/Hill/Weston," *Down Beat*, June 1984, 60–61; and Horace Mansfield, Jr., "World Piano Summit: Tapscott, Hill and Weston rise to this historic occasion," *Be-bop and Beyond* 2:2 (March/April 1984): 22–23.

Hans Falb, 21 February 2017, personal email.

On the history of Leimert Park, see Fathia Beatrice Macauley, "Leimert Park: Preserving African American Culture Through the Built Environment" (master's thesis, UCLA, 1997).

Dale Davis, interview by Steven Isoardi, 3 March 2001, for *Leimert Park: the Story of a Village in South Central Los Angeles*, produced and directed by Jeannette Lindsay, DVD, 2008.

On the Brockman Gallery and Brockman Productions, see also Kinshasha Holman Conwill, interview by Karen Anne Mason, UCLA Center for Oral History Research, 1996, 51–52; Alonzo Davis, interview by Karen Anne Mason, UCLA Center for Oral History Research, 1994, 142–53, 257–59; Noah Purifoy, interview by Karen Anne Mason, UCLA Center for Oral History Research, 47–54; and John Outterbridge, interview by Richard Candida Smith, UCLA Center for Oral History Research, 289–93. Other galleries soon emerged in other locations to foster and celebrate African American art, including Suzanne Jackson's Gallery 32, Dr. Samella Lewis' Contemporary Crafts, and Art West Associated, of which Ruth Waddy was at one time president. The Black Arts Council also brought together many artists and administrators to further the cause of black art and gain more support and visibility. The council not only organized exhibitions but was instrumental in founding the Afro-American Museum in Exposition Park. See Jane H. Carpenter with Betye Saar, *Betye Saar* (San Francisco: Pomegranate, 2003), 25–26; Cecil Fergerson, interview by Karen Anne Mason, UCLA Center for Oral History Research, 1996, 166–79; Suzanne Jackson, interview by Karen Anne Mason, UCLA Center for Oral History Research, 1998, 102–48, 253; Outterbridge, UCLA interview, 268–95, 326–28; Betye Saar, interview by Karen Anne Mason, UCLA Center for Oral History Research, 1996, 102–03; Ruth Waddy, interview by Karen Anne Mason, UCLA Center for Oral History Research, 1993, 55–60, 118–19.

Carl Burnett, interview by Steven Isoardi, UCLA Center for Oral History Research, 2007, 179–206.

—NOTES TO CHAPTER 9

28 Burnett, 186.

29 Richard Fulton interview by Steven Isoardi, 1 May 1999, for *Leimert Park: the Story of a Village in South Central Los Angeles*, produced and directed by Jeannette Lindsay, DVD, 2008.

CHAPTER 10: THE HERO'S LAST DANCE

EPIGRAPH: Kamau Daáood, "Leimert Park," *The Language of Saxophones* (San Francisco, CA: City Lights, 2005), 69.

1   See "Bloods/Crips Proposal for LA's Face-Lift," in *Why L.A. Happened: Implications of the '92 Los Angeles Rebellion*, ed. Haki R. Madhubuti (Chicago: Third World Press, 1993), 274–82.

2   Ice-T, "Escape from the Killing Fields," *O.G.—The Original Gangster Video*, Warner Reprise, 1991, videocassette.

3   NWA, "Fuck Tha Police," *Straight Outta Compton*, Ruthless Records, compact disc, CDL57102.

4   Quoted in John L. Mitchell, "Many Blacks Fear Police Are the Enemy," *Los Angeles Times*, 27 August 1982, 3. On gangsta rap in Los Angeles, see Todd Boyd, *Am I Black Enough for You? Popular Culture from the 'Hood and Beyond* (Bloomington: Indiana University Press, 1997), 70–82; Brian Cross, *It's Not About a Salary . . . Rap, Race and Resistance in Los Angeles* (London: Verso, 1993), 24–39, 54–64; Robin D. G. Kelley, *Race Rebels: Culture, Politics, and the Black Working Class* (New York: The Free Press, 1994), 183–227; and Ice T as told to Heidi Siegmund, *The Ice Opinion: Who Gives a Fuck?* (New York: St. Martin's Press, 1994), 3–67, 147–60.

5   Joe Domanick, "Police Power: Why No One Can Control the LAPD," *LA Weekly*, 16–22 February 1990, 20.

6   Domanick, 21.

7   Joe Domanick, *To Protect and to Serve: The LAPD's Century of War in the City of Dreams* (New York: Pocket Books, 1994), 262.

8   John Gregory Dunne, "Law and Disorder in LA: Part Two," *The New York Review of Books*, 24 October 1991, 66.

9   David Parrish and Beth Barrett, "LAPD fires few in shootings," *Daily News*, 12 May 1991, 12. See also Domanick, *To Protect*, 334–42.

10 Mitchell, "Many Blacks Fear Police Are the Enemy," 1.

11 Chester Himes, *The Quality of Hurt: The Autobiography of Chester Himes, Volume I* (Garden City, NY: Doubleday & Company, Inc., 1972), 74.

12 "Young Black Men," *The New York Times*, editorial, 7 May 1992.

13 Richard Fulton interview by Steven Isoardi, 1 May 1999, for *Leimert Park: the Story of a Village in South Central Los Angeles*, produced and directed by Jeannette Lindsay, DVD, 2008.

14 Aceyalone, "Project Blowed," *Accepted Eclectic*, Ground Control Records, compact disc, GCR 7045-2.

15 Daáood, "Leimert Park," *Language of Saxophones*, 67.

16 Documents in the Tapscott Archive dated 1988, January 1989, 17 January 1989, 15 June 1989, and 30 October 1990.

17 Quoted in Joshua Spiegelman (Yaakov Levy), interview by Steven Isoardi, 31 March 2002.

18 David Whiteis, "Chicago Jazz Festival," *Down Beat*, December 1993, 58.

19 Horace Tapscott, *Songs of the Unsung: The Musical and Social Journey of Horace Tapscott*, ed. Steven Isoardi (Durham, NC: Duke University Press, 2001), 185.

20 Watts Prophets Community Education Association, Inc., "Our Mission," in program for UCLA Performing Arts at Royce Hall, 5 October 2001. See also Concerned Artists Action Group of Watts at www.forests.com/caaghist.html.

21 Quoted in "Two Shades of Soul: The 17th Asian American Jazz Festival Features Jon Jang Quintet and Horace Tapscott," *KSW News* 3:4 (Spring 1998), 1.

22 Quoted in "Playing for Horace: A Tribute to the Music of Rebellion," *Revolutionary Worker*, 4 July 1999, 5.

23 See text in Tapscott, *Songs of the Unsung*, 213.

CHAPTER 11: *AIEE! THE PHANTOM*

EPIGRAPH: Kamau Daáood, "Papa, the Lean Griot," *The Language of Saxophones* (San Francisco, CA: City Lights, 2005), 95.

1 Horace Tapscott, *Songs of the Unsung: The Musical and Social Journey of Horace Tapscott*, ed. Steven Isoardi (Durham, NC: Duke University Press, 2001), 211.

2 "The UGMAA Foundation," Tapscott Archive.

3 LeRoi Jones (Amiri Baraka), *Blues People: Negro Music in White America* (New York: William Morrow, 1963), 213.

4 Tapscott, *Songs of the Unsung*, 77–78.

5 Tapscott, 179.

6 Tapscott, 200–201.

7 Quoted in Grace M., "African American Musical Traditions in Los Angeles: Ethnographic Portraits of Four Musicians" (master's thesis, UCLA, 1996), 104.

8 Adele Sebastian, interview by John Breckow, KPFK Radio, 1981.

9 Tapscott, *Songs of the Unsung*, 178.

10 For an explanation of conduction, see Lawrence D. "Butch" Morris, *The Art of Conduction: A Conduction Workbook*, ed. Daniela Veronesi (New York: Karma with Tilton Gallery and Pozitif, 2017), and the accompanying booklet to Lawrence D. "Butch" Morris, *Testament: A Conduction Collection*, New World Records, compact discs, 80478-2. See also Ben Ratliff, "Taking Charge: Conductor Butch Morris' Structured Chaos," *Option* (November/December 1991): 43–46.

11 Tapscott, *Songs of the Unsung*, 74.

12 "Lawrence 'Butch' Morris Interview," *Cadence* (July 1989): 15. For Horace's influence on Butch, see Howard Mandel, "Butch Morris," *Down Beat*, October, 1986, 26–27.

13 Tapscott, *Songs of the Unsung*, 109.

EPIGRAPH: Otto René Castillo, "Before the Scales, Tomorrow," *Let's Go!* trans. Margaret Randall (New York: Cape Goliard Press, 1971), n.p.

1 Quoted in Robert Farris Thompson, *Flash of the Spirit: African and Afro-American Art and Philosophy* (New York: Vintage Books, 1984), ix.
2 Adele Sebastian, interview by Steve Buchanan, KCRW Radio, 18 August 1980.
3 "Tapscott Memorial—NYC," Knitting Factory, New York.,163 mins., 1999, videocassette.
4 "A Special Tribute to Horace Tapscott," *Jazz and Poetry in Motion*, prod. and dir. by Annya Bell, 29 min., MediaOne TV, 17 February 1999, videocassette.
5 Amina Amatullah, interview by Tobi Knight, KOST Radio, 18 February 2001.
6 See Buddy Collette with Steven Isoardi, *Jazz Generations: A Life in American Music and Society* (London: Continuum, 2000), 170–71, for an illustrative example from Buddy's experience playing with Ellington's band.
7 Horace Tapscott, *Songs of the Unsung: The Musical and Social Journey of Horace Tapscott*, ed. Steven Isoardi (Durham, NC: Duke University Press, 2001), 159.
8 Jean Williams, "Soul Sauce: Tapscott Taps Out a New System," *Billboard*, 10 April 1976, 22.
9 Titus Levi, "Pianist Horace Tapscott: Keeping It Lit," *Option* (September/October 1986): 37.
10 Vinny Golia, "Arkestra Book," 6 June 2004, personal email. See also Vinny Golia, interview by Steven Isoardi, UCLA Center for Oral History Research, 2008, vol. 2, 551.
11 Levi, "Pianist Horace Tapscott," 38.
12 Yaakov qualifies this ethnic characterization: "In terms of my ethnicity, for a long time I haven't considered myself white, because I'm very much a Jewish person and I know my history as a Jewish person. . . . There's a lot of Jewish people who feel a profound sense of connection with African Americans and African-American culture. It comes from several reasons. The Jewish people became a nation during our exile (sojourn and enslavement) in Egypt. We're from Israel, which is next to Africa. I remember, specifically, hearing Trane's records when I was in junior high and early high school, and thinking that some of his pieces sounded like the prayer music I'd heard in the synagogue getting ready for my bar mitzvah. Hearing Trane, like he was playing cantorial music, was very profound for me. A piece like 'The Promise' is a very Jewish sounding piece both in theme as well as in melody, even 'Afro-Blue' or the last part of *A Love Supreme*, in particular. There are certain motifs that he uses that are very Jewish, and I remember thinking that Trane was showing me how to pray on the saxophone."
13 Jon Jang, "Horace Tapscott," 22 May 2001, personal email.
14 Quoted in Robert Lloyd, "This Ain't No Juilliard! Life and Violins at the Silverlake Conservatory of Music, The School that Flea Built," *LA Weekly*, 4–10 October 2002, 32.

15 Quetzal Flores, personal communication, 5 April 2004.

16 José Ramirez, "Horace Tapscott," 11 February 2004, personal email.

17 D. Jean Collins, "Interview with Adele Sebastian," *Uraeus: The Journal of Unconscious Life* 2:4, 41–42.

18 Theodor W. Adorno, *Philosophy of Modern Music*, trans. by Anne G. Mitchell and Wesley V. Blomster (New York: The Seabury Press, 1980), 105–06.

19 Andre Breton and Diego Rivera, "Manifesto: Towards a Free Revolutionary Art," in Leon Trotsky, *Culture & Socialism and a Manifesto: Art and Revolution* (London: New Park Publications, 1975), 31. Emphasis theirs.

20 Leon Trotsky, *Literature and Revolution*, trans. Rose Strunsky (Ann Arbor: University of Michigan Press, 1960), 192–93.

EPILOGUE

EPIGRAPH: Quoted in Michael Session, interview by Steven Isoardi, 29 July 1999.

1 Executive Director, "Address of State to UGMAA Members," PAPA@UGMAA *Newsletter*, Vol. 1 (November 2000), 1.

BIBLIOGRAPHY

INTERVIEWS CONDUCTED FOR THIS BOOK

The following interviews, conducted and transcribed by the author, are not individually cited in the notes to the text.

Abdul-Khaliq, Fuasi. 21 December 2001.
Agindotan, Najite. 1 September 2001.
Alade, Baba. 29 December 2000.
Albach, Tom. 21 January 2001.
Ali, Kaeef. 16 June 2001.
Amatullah, Amina. 2, 19 December 2000, 20 January 2001.
Amde, Father. 27 August 2001.
Andrews, James. 8, 13 December 2015, 21 February 2016.
Andrews, Reggie. 9 December 2001.
Avotcja. 7 September, 19 October 2003.
Bias, Gary. 23 August 2001.
Bidlack, Bruce. 2 January 2002.
Black, Wendell Lee. 8 November 1998.
Blythe, Arthur. 12 July 2000.
Brown, Elaine. 3 November 2001.
Brown, Everett, Jr. 4, 9 September 2000.
Bryant, David. 14 November 1998.
Byrd, Robbie Tapscott. 15 November, 30 December 1998.
Caliman, Hadley. 14 September 2003.
Chandler, Charles. 23 November 2019.
Childs, Billy. 25 February 2002.
Clark, Larry. 13 December 2000.
Cline, Alex. 14 August 2001.
Connell, Will. 12, 22 March, 2 May 2001.
Cortez, Jayne. 1 December 2001.

Crouch, Stanley. 29 November 2000.

Daáood, Kamau. 27 January, 6 April 2000, 5 March 2015

Daniel, Conga Mike. 26 May 2001.

Dean, Donald. 2 August 2000.

Dedeaux, Richard. 30 August 2001.

Delone, Amos. 25 July 2001.

Gibbs, Marla. 30 December 2000.

Golia, Vinny. 3 August 2001.

Harris, Billie. 27 July 2000.

Hart, Aubrey. 23, 25, 27 January 2022.

Hill, Leland. 14 June 2001.

Hines, Alan. 22 November 1998.

Jang, Jon. 21 May 2001.

Jarrico, Sylvia. 10 September 2003.

Jihad, Ali. 23 July 2001.

Johnson, Jai Jae. 20 November 2003.

Keller, David. 16 December 2001.

Kelly, Rickey. 21 February 2001.

Komolafe, Dadisi. 21 April, 12 May 2001.

Kufahamu, Aman. 25 January 2001.

Lange, Ted. 7 September 2001.

Lawrence, Azar. 18 August 2001.

Legohn, Fundi. 28 July 2000.

Levy, Yaakov. 31 March 2002.

Madison, Bill. 10 November 1999.

Marshall, William, and Sylvia Jarrico. 8 April 1999.

Mateen, Sabir. 15 January 2001.

Meeks, Steven. 17 August 2000.

Miranda, Roberto. 24, 30 March, 15 April 1999.

Moody, Dennis. 27 August 2001.

Morgan, Nate. 5 April 2000, 20 November 2001.

Morris, Butch. 3 September 2001.

Morris, Wilber. 21 September 2000.

Muhammad, Abdul-Salaam. 2 February 2002.

Murray, David. 13 September 2000.

Newton, James. 17 August 2001.

Ojenke. 5 May 2001.

Olivier, Rufus. 7 January 2001.

O'Solomon, Otis. 9 September 2001.

Outterbridge, John. 24 February 2001.

Owens, Charles. 5 July 2000.

Peet, Wayne. 16 August 2001.

Pleasant, Edwin. 14 July 1999.

Porter, Rudolph. 5 July 2000.

Priestley, Eric. 13 October 2001.
Ranelin, Phil. 6 August 2001.
Rhodes, Cecil. 4 May 2001.
Roberts, Kafi. 19 June 2000.
Roberts, Vicky. 30 October 2003.
Romero, Danyel. 25 January 2001.
Roper, William. 8 August 2001.
Sanyika, Dadisi. 4 January 2002.
Savage, Walter. 27 February, 16 April 2001.
Session, Michael. 22, 29 July 1999.
Sharps, Jesse. 24, 26 August 1999.
Sherrill, Marion. 19 August 2000.
Smith, Steven. 20 June 2000.
Stephenson, Mickey. 17 February 2001.
Straughter, Ernest. 8 October 2006.
Straughter, Ray. 27 October 2007.
Taumbu. 7 August 2001.
Theus, Sonship. 9 March 2000.
Tribble, Denise. 23 January 2000.
Trible, Dwight. 23 January 2000.
Troupe, Quincy. 24 August 2001.
Trujillo, Tommy. 7 June 2001.
Wainwright, E. W. 11 March 2001.
Watt, Robert. 18 January 2001.
West, Bobby. 24 August 2001.
Wilcots, Michael Dett. 10 November 2001–20 April 2002.
Williams, Jon. 24 July 2001.
Williams, Wendell C. 4 May 2002.
Wise, Fritz. 9 January and 4 March 2000.

OTHER UNPUBLISHED INTERVIEWS

The following were conducted by the author unless otherwise indicated. Interviews for the UCLA Center for Oral History Research were transcribed by the UCLA Center for Oral History Research; they are identified by the abbreviations AAALA ("African American Artists of Los Angeles" Project), BC ("Beyond Central" Project), and CAS ("Central Avenue Sounds" Project). Interviews for the documentary film, *Leimert Park: The Story of a Village in South Central Los Angeles*, produced and directed by Jeannette Lindsay, DVD 2008, are marked LP.

Albach, Tom. Interview by John Breckow. KPFK Radio, 1981.
Amatullah, Amina. Interview by Tobi Knight. KOST Radio, 18 February 2001.
Amy, Curtis. 2002. BC.
Bihari, Joseph. 1997. CAS.
Bradford, Bobby. 2002. BC.

Burnett, Carl. 2007. BC.

Caldwell, Ben. 12 December 1998. LP

Cline, Nels. 2007. BC.

Conwill, Kinshasha Holman. Interview by Karen Anne Mason, 1996. AAALA.

Davis, Alonzo. Interview by Karen Anne Mason, 1994. AAALA.

Davis, Dale. 3 March 2001. LP.

Fergerson, Cecil. Interview by Karen Anne Mason, 1996. AAALA.

Franklin, Henry. 2007. BC.

Fulton, Richard. 1 May 1999. LP.

Golia, Vinny. 2008. BC.

Hurte, Leroy. 1997. CAS.

Jackson, Suzanne. Interview by Karen Anne Mason, 1998. AAALA.

Land, Harold. 2003. BC.

Ligon, Alfred. Interview by Ranford B. Hopkins. UCLA Center for Oral History Research. 1984.

Marable, Larance. 2001. CAS.

McNeely, Cecil. 1993. CAS.

Morgan, Frank. 1996. CAS.

Ortega, Anthony. 1997. CAS.

Outterbridge, John. Interview by Richard Candida Smith, 1993. AAALA.

Preston, Don. 2003. BC.

Purifoy, Noah. Interview by Karen Anne Mason, 1992. AAALA.

Redd, Vi. 2004. CAS.

Riddle, John. Interview by Karen Anne Mason, 2000. AAALA.

Saar, Betye. Interview by Karen Anne Mason, 1996. AAALA.

Sebastian, Adele. Interview by John Breckow. KPFK Radio, 1981.

Sebastian, Adele. Interview by Steve Buchanan. KCRW Radio, 18 August 1980.

Smith, Putter. Interview by Alex Cline. BC

Solomon, Clifford. 2000. CAS.

Waddy, Ruth. Interview by Karen Anne Mason, 1993. AAALA.

Williamson, Tom. 2002. BC.

ARTICLES, BOOKS, AND ONLINE SOURCES

Abani, Chris. *Daphne's Lot.* Los Angeles: Red Hen Press, 2003.

Abbott, Lynn, and Doug Seroff. *Out of Sight: The Rise of African American Popular Music, 1889–1895.* Jackson: University Press of Mississippi, 2002.

Abiodun, Rowland, Henry J. Drewal, and John Pemberton III, eds. *The Yoruba Artist: New Theoretical Perspectives on African Arts.* Washington: Smithsonian Institution Press, 1994.

Adler, Nancy J. "Arts Center Born after Watts Riot." *The New York Times,* 19 March 1967, 92.

Adler, Patricia Rae. "Watts: From Suburb to Black Ghetto." Ph.D. diss., University of Southern California, 1976.

Adorno, Theodor W. *Philosophy of Modern Music*. Translated by Anne G. Mitchell and Wesley V. Blomster. NY: The Seabury Press, 1980.

Agawu, Kofi. *Representing African Music: Postcolonial Notes, Queries, Positions*. New York: Routledge, 2003.

Allen, James P., and Eugene Turner. *The Ethnic Quilt: Population Diversity in Southern California*. Northridge, CA: The Center for Geographical Studies, California State University, Northridge, 1997.

Alonso, Alex. "Out of the Void: Street Gangs in Black Los Angeles." In *Black Los Angeles: American Dreams and Racial Realities*, 140–67. Edited by Darnell Hunt and Ana-Christina Ramón. New York: New York University Press, 2010.

Alonso, Alex. "Racialized Identities and the Formation of Black Gangs in Los Angeles," *Urban Geography* 25:7 (2004): 658–74.

Alonso, Alex. "Territoriality Among African American Street Gangs in Los Angeles." M.A. thesis, University of Southern California, 1999.

"American Mavericks: An Interview with La Monte Young and Marian Zazeela." www.musicmavericks.org

Ames, David W. "A Sociocultural View of Hausa Musical Activity." In *The Traditional Artist in African Societies*, 128–61. Edited by Warren L. d'Azevedo. Bloomington: Indiana University Press, 1973.

Aubry, Erin. "Words to Live By." *Los Angeles Times*, 8 October 1995, sec. E.

Bakeer, Donald. CRIPS. Los Angeles: Precocious Publishing, 1992.

Bascom, William. *African Art in Cultural Perspective: An Introduction*. New York: W. W. Norton & Company, 1973.

Bayete, Jay. "Mafundi: A Cultural Arts Family Affair." *Neworld* 2:2 (Winter, 1976): 32–36.

Black Partnership Development Council. *The Black Community of Greater Los Angeles: A Community in Transition*. United Way of Greater Los Angeles, 16 October 1991.

"Black Youth Jobless Rate Put at 60%." *Los Angeles Times*, 26 July 1979, 24.

Blassingame, John W. *The Slave Community: Plantation Life in the Antebellum South*. Rev. ed. New York: Oxford University Press, 1979.

Bley, Paul, with David Lee. *Stopping Time: Paul Bley and the Transformation of Jazz*. Canada: Vehicule Press, 1999.

Blier, Suzanne Preston. *The Royal Arts of Africa: The Majesty of Form*. New York: Harry N. Abrams, Inc., 1998.

Bluestone, Barry, and Bennett Harrison. *The Deindustrialization of America: Plant Closings, Community Abandonment, and the Dismantling of Basic Industry*. New York: Basic Books, Inc., Publishers, 1992.

"Bobby Bradford interview with Mark Weber." *Coda*, October 1977, 2–5.

Bond, J. Max. "The Negro in Los Angeles." Ph.D. diss., University of Southern California, 1936.

Bontemps, Arna. *Black Thunder*. Boston: Beacon Press, 1968.

Bontemps, Arna, and Jack Conroy. *Anyplace But Here*. New York: Hill and Wang, 1966.

Bourland, George Wesley. "A Capsule of Mafundi," *The Mafundi Potential*, 1:1 (February 1970): 4.

Boyd, Todd. *Am I Black Enough for You? Popular Culture from the 'Hood and Beyond*. Bloomington: Indiana University Press, 1997.

Boyer, Ed, and Ron Finney. "Black Youth—Changing Generation." *Los Angeles Times*, 5 September 1982, 1, 3, 9.

Boyer, Peter J. "Bad Cops." *The New Yorker*, 21 May 2001, 60–77.

Braxton, Anthony. *Tri-Axium Writings I*. N.p.: Synthesis Music, 1985.

Breton, Andre, and Diego Rivera. "Manifesto: Towards a Free Revolutionary Art." In Leon Trotsky, *Culture and Socialism and a Manifesto: Art and Revolution*. London: New Park Publications, 1975.

Brown, Elaine. *The Condemnation of Little B*. Boston: Beacon Press, 2002.

Brown, Elaine. *A Taste of Power: A Black Woman's Story*. New York: Pantheon Books, 1992.

Brown, Scot. *Fighting for US: Maulana Karenga, the US Organization, and Black Cultural Nationalism*. New York: New York University Press, 2003.

Bryant, Clora, et al., eds. *Central Avenue Sounds: Jazz in Los Angeles*. Berkeley: University of California Press, 1998.

Bunch, Lonnie G. "A Past Not Necessarily Prologue: The Afro-American in Los Angeles." In *20th Century Los Angeles: Power, Promotion, and Social Conflict*, 100–30. Edited by Norman M. Klein and Martin J. Schiesl. Claremont, CA: Regina Books, 1990.

Cage, John. *Silence: Lectures and Writings*. Hanover, NH: Wesleyan University Press, 1961.

Carpenter, Jane H., with Betye Saar. *Betye Saar*. San Francisco: Pomegranate, 2003.

Carson, Clay. "Watts Story Covers Years 1850–1966 from 'Mudtown' to 'Symbol of Revolt.'" *Los Angeles Free Press*, August 12, 1966, 3, 10.

Castillo, Otto René. *Let's Go!* Translated by Margaret Randall. New York: Cape Goliard Press, 1971.

Chambers, Douglas Brent. "'He Gwine Sing He Country': Africans, Afro-Virginians, and the Development of Slave Culture in the Virginia, 1690–1810." Ph.D. diss., University of Virginia, 1996.

"Chief Parker Accused of Being 'Anti-Negro.'" *Los Angeles Times*, 12 June 1962, 24.

Churchill, Ward, and Jim Vander Wall. *Agents of Repression: The FBI's Secret Wars Against the Black Panther Party and the American Indian Movement*. Boston, MA: South End Press, 1990.

Cohen, Elaine. "Tapscott/Hill/Weston." *Down Beat*, June 1984, 60–61.

Cohen, Nathan E. "The Context of the Curfew Area." In *The Los Angeles Riots: A Socio-Psychological Study*, 41–80. Edited by Nathan Cohen. New York: Praeger Publishers, 1970.

Cohen, Noal, and Michael Fitzgerald. *Rat Race Blues: The Musical Life of Gigi Gryce*. Berkeley: Berkeley Hill Books, 2002.

Cole, Herbert M., and Chike C. Aniakor. *Igbo Arts: Community and Cosmos*. Los Angeles: UCLA Museum of Cultural History, 1984.

Coleman, Wanda. *Hand Dance.* Santa Rosa, CA: Black Sparrow Press, 1993.

Collette, Buddy, with Steven Isoardi. *Jazz Generations: A Life in American Music and Society.* London: Continuum, 2000.

Collins, D. Jean. "Interview with Adele Sebastian." *Uraeus: The Journal of Unconscious Life* 2:4, 36–43.

Collins, Willie R. "California Rhythm and Blues Recordings, 1942–1972: A Diversity of Styles." In *California Soul: Music of African Americans in the West,* 213–43. Edited by Jacqueline Cogdell DjeDje and Eddie S. Meadows. Berkeley: University of California Press, 1998.

Concerned Artists Action Group of Watts. www.forests.com/caaghist.html

Coolen, Michael T. "Senegambian Influences on Afro-American Musical Culture." *Black Music Research Journal* 11:1 (Spring, 1991): 1–18.

Coquet, Michele. *African Royal Court Art.* Translated by Jane Marie Todd. Chicago: University of Chicago Press, 1998.

Cortez, Jayne. *somewhere in advance of nowhere.* New York: Serpent's Tail, 1996.

Cowell, Henry. *Essential Cowell: Selected Writings on Music.* Edited by Dick Higgins. Kingston, NY: McPherson & Company, 2001.

Cox, Bette Yarbrough. *Central Avenue—Its Rise and Fall (1890–c.1955); Including the Musical Renaissance of Black Los Angeles.* Los Angeles: BEEM Publications, 1996.

"'Crack' plague's roots are in Nicaraguan War." *San Jose Mercury News,* 18 August 1996, 1A, 16A, 17A.

Cripps, Thomas. *Slow Fade to Black: The Negro in American Film, 1900–1942.* Oxford: Oxford University Press, 1993.

Cross, Brian. *It's Not About a Salary . . . Rap, Race and Resistance in Los Angeles.* London: Verso, 1993.

Curran, Ron. "Malign Neglect: The Roots of an Urban War Zone." *L.A. Weekly,* 30 December 1988–5 January 1989, 8–20.

Daáood, Kamau. *The Language of Saxophones.* San Francisco, CA: City Lights, 2005.

Darensbourg, Joe, as told to Peter Vacher. *Jazz Odyssey: The Autobiography of Joe Darensbourg.* Baton Rouge: Louisiana State University Press, 1987.

Davis, Mike. *City of Quartz: Excavating the Future in Los Angeles.* London: Verso, 1990.

Dawson, Jim. *Nervous Man Nervous: Big Jay McNeely and the Rise of the Honking Tenor Sax.* Milford, NH: Big Nickel Publications, 1994.

de Graaf, Lawrence B. "The City of Black Angels: Emergence of the Los Angeles Ghetto, 1890–1930." *Pacific Historical Review* 39 (1970): 323–52.

de Grunne, Bernard. *The Birth of Art in Africa: Nok Statuary in Nigeria.* Luxembourg: Adam Biro, 1998.

Dickerson, Lowell Dwight. "Central Avenue Meets Hollywood: The Amalgamation of the Black and White Musicians' Unions in Los Angeles." Ph.D. diss., University of California, Los Angeles, 1998.

Domanick, Joe. "Police Power: Why No One Can Control the LAPD." *LA Weekly,* 16–22 February 1990, 16–27.

Domanick, Joe. *To Protect and to Serve: The LAPD's Century of War in the City of Dreams.* New York: Pocket Books, 1994.

"Douglass Speech Still Has Its Bite." *Washington Star-News*, 5 July 1974.

Drewal, Henry John, and John Pemberton III with Roland Abiodun. *Yoruba: Nine Centuries of African Art and Thought.* Edited by Allen Wardell. New York: The Center for African Art in association with Harry N. Abrams, Inc., 1989.

Du Bois, W. E. B. *The Souls of Black Folk.* New York: Dover Publications, Inc., 1994.

Dunne, John Gregory. "Law and Disorder in LA: Part Two." *The New York Review of Books*, 24 October 1991, 62–70.

Eastman, Ralph. "Central Avenue Blues: The Making of Los Angeles Rhythm and Blues, 1942–1947." *Black Music Research Journal* 9:1 (Spring, 1989): 19–33.

Ebron, Paulla A. *Performing Africa.* Princeton: Princeton University Press, 2002.

Feather, Leonard. "Pan-Afrikan Arkestra: Broad in Scope." *Los Angeles Times*, 16 October 1976, II:7.

Feather, Leonard. "Tapscott Ensemble Plays at Museum." *Los Angeles Times*, 22 July 1970, IV:12.

Fernandez, James. "The Exposition and Imposition of Order: Artistic Expression in Fang Culture." In *The Traditional Artist in African Societies*, 194–220. Edited by Warren L. d'Azevedo. Bloomington: Indiana University Press, 1973.

Field, Allyson Nadia, Jan-Christpoher Horak, and Jacqueline Najuma Stewart, eds. *L.A. Rebellion: Creating a New Black Cinema.* Berkeley: University of California Press, 2015.

Finnegan, Ruth. *Oral Literature in Africa.* Oxford: Oxford University Press, 1970.

Fisher, Miles Mark. *Negro Slave Songs in the United States.* New York: The Citadel Press, 1963.

Floyd, Samuel A., Jr. *The Power of Black Music: Interpreting Its History from Africa to the United States.* New York: Oxford University Press, 1995.

Folkart, Burt A. "S.R. Browne, Pioneer Black Teacher, Dies." *Los Angeles Times*, 20 November 1991, B8.

"Former Lunceford Trumpeter in Rehearsal with New Swing Band." *California Eagle*, 12 October 1944, 12.

Frankel, Noralee. "Breaking the Chains: 1860–1880." In *To Make Our World Anew: A History of African Americans*, 227–80. Edited by Robin D.G. Kelley and Earl Lewis. Oxford: Oxford University Press, 2000.

Franklin, John Hope, and Alfred A. Moss, Jr. *From Slavery to Freedom: A History of African Americans.* 8th ed. New York: Alfred A. Knopf, 2000.

Fremont-Smith, Eliot. "TV: N.B.C. Documents 'The Angry Voices of Watts.'" *The New York Times*, 17 August 1966, 79.

From the Executive Director. "Address of State to UGMAA Members." *PAPA@ UGMAA Newsletter*, Vol. 1, November 2000, 1.

Gann, Kyle. *American Music in the Twentieth Century.* Belmont, CA: Wadsworth/ Thomson Learning, 1997.

Garland, Peter, ed. *A Lou Harrison Reader.* Santa Fe, NM: Soundings Press, 1987.

Gilmore, Bob. *Harry Partch: A Biography.* New Haven, CT: Yale University Press, 1998.

Gioia, Ted. *West Coast Jazz: Modern Jazz in California 1945–1960*. New York: Oxford University Press, 1992.

Glueck, Grace. "Up with the Non-Dominants." *The New York Times*, 9 April 1972, II:12.

Goldstone, Bud, and Arloa Paquin Goldstone. *The Los Angeles Watts Towers*. Los Angeles: The Getty Conservation Institute and the J. Paul Getty Museum, 1997.

Gordon, Robert. *Jazz West Coast: The Los Angeles Jazz Scene of the 1950s*. London: Quartet Books, 1986.

Gray, Elizabeth. "CETA & 'The Arts.'" *Neworld*, 4:4 (1978—no. 3): 14–18.

Green, John. "The Seeds Are Set: Wind College." *Be-bop and Beyond* 1:5 (September/October 1983): 8–9.

Grigsby, Eugene. "The Rise and Decline of Black Neighborhoods in Los Angeles." *UCLA CAAS Report* 12:1&2 (Spring/Fall 1989): 16–17, 44.

Grossman, James R. "A Chance to Make Good: 1900–1929." In *To Make Our World Anew: A History of African Americans*, 345–408. Edited by Robin D.G. Kelley and Earl Lewis. Oxford: Oxford University Press, 2000.

Hale, Thomas. *Griots and Griottes: Masters of Words and Music*. Bloomington: Indiana University Press, 1998.

Halker, Clark. "A History of Local 208 and the Struggle for Racial Equality in the American Federation of Musicians." *Black Music Research Journal* 8:2 (Fall, 1988): 207–23.

Hicks, Michael. *Henry Cowell, Bohemian*. Urbana: University of Illinois Press, 2002.

Hill, Gladwin. "Watts to Hold Summer Festival on Anniversary of '65 Rioting." *The New York Times*, 7 August 1966, 48.

Himes, Chester. *The Quality of Hurt: The Autobiography of Chester Himes, Volume I*. Garden City, NY: Doubleday & Company, Inc., 1972.

Horn, Paul, with Lee Underwood. *Inside Paul Horn: The Spiritual Odyssey of a Universal Traveler*. N.p.: HarperSanFrancisco, 1990.

Horne, Gerald. *Fire This Time: The Watts Uprising and the 1960s*. Charlottesville: University Press of Virginia, 1995.

Horricks, Raymond. *The Importance of Being Eric Dolphy*. Tumbridge Wells, Great Britain: D J Costello (Publishers) Ltd., 1989.

Hubler, Shawn. "South L.A.'s Poverty Rate Worse Than '65." *Los Angeles Times*, 11 May 1992, 1, 22.

Hughes, Langston. *The Collected Poems of Langston Hughes*. Edited by Arnold Rampersad and David Roessel. New York: Alfred A. Knopf, 1995.

Hurte, Leroy E. *The Magic of Music: An Autobiography*. Apple Valley, CA: Bronze-Lyric Publishing Co., 1997.

Ice T, as told to Heidi Siegmund. *The Ice Opinion: Who Gives a Fuck?* New York: St. Martin's Press, 1994.

"Interview with Billy Higgins." *Be-bop and Beyond* 2:3 (May/June 1984): 16–21.

Isoardi, Steven L. Horace Tapscott website—a work in progress. https://horacetapscott.free-jazz.net

Isoardi, Steven L. *The Music Finds a Way: A PAPA/UGMAA Oral History of Growing Up in Postwar South Central Los Angeles.* Paris, France: Dark Tree, 2020.

Isoardi, Steven L., and Michael Dett Wilcots. "Black Experience in the Fine Arts: An African American Community Arts Movement in a University Setting." *Current Research in Jazz* 6, 2014. www.crj-online.org

Jah, Yusuf, and Sister Shah'Keyah. *Uprising: Crips and Bloods Tell the Story of America's Youth in the Crossfire.* New York: Scribner, 1995.

Jeske, Lee. "John Carter." *Down Beat*, November 1982, 18–20.

Jones, K. Maurice. *Say It Loud! The Story of Rap Music.* Brookfield, CT: The Millbrook Press, 1994.

Jones, LeRoi (Amiri Baraka). *Blues People: Negro Music in White America.* New York: William Morrow, 1963.

Jost, Ekkehard. *Free Jazz.* New York: Da Capo Press, 1994.

Keepnews, Peter. "What is the CBAE?" *Down Beat*, 28 February 1974, 10.

Kelley, Robin D. G. *Freedom Dreams: The Black Radical Imagination.* Boston: Beacon Press, 2002.

Kelley, Robin D.G. *Race Rebels: Culture, Politics, and the Black Working Class.* New York: The Free Press, 1994.

Kelley, Robin D. G. *Yo' Mama's Disfunktional! Fighting the Culture Wars in Urban America.* Boston: Beacon Press, 1997.

Keyes, Cheryl L. *Rap Music and Street Consciousness.* Urbana: University of Illinois Press, 2002.

Kramer, Allan. "Studio Watts Teen Post Not a Babysitting Agency." *Los Angeles Free Press*, 1 April 1966, 1.

Kwong, Peter. "The First Multicultural Riots." *Village Voice*, 9 June 1992, 29–32.

"La Monte Young and Marian Zazeela: an interview by Ian Nagoski." http://www .halana.com

"La Monte Young and Marian Zazeela at the Dream House: In Conversation with Frank J. Oteri." In *NewMusicBox.* #54, volume 5:6 (October 2003). www .newmusicbox.org/page.nmbx?id=54fp01)

LaRue, Ron. "Obituary: Remembering Ray Draper." *Be-bop and Beyond* 1:1 (January/February 1983): 3.

Laude, Jean. *The Arts of Black Africa.* Translated by Jean Decock. Berkeley: University of California Press, 1971.

"Lawrence 'Butch' Morris Interview." *Cadence* (July 1989): 15.

LeFalle-Collins, Lizzetta. "Noah Purifoy: Outside and in the Open." In *Noah Purifoy: Outside and in The Open*, 7–61. Los Angeles: California Afro-American Museum Foundation, 1997.

Leonard, Jack. "Watts' Mafundi Institute Stars in Its Own Revival." *Los Angeles Times*, 24 October 1997, B1, B5.

Levi, Titus. "Pianist Horace Tapscott: Keeping It Lit." *Option* (September/October 1986): 37–38.

Levin, Floyd. *Classic Jazz: A Personal View of the Music and the Musicians.* Berkeley: University of California Press, 2000.

Levin, Floyd. "Kid Ory's Legendary Nordskog/Sunshine Recordings." *Jazz Journal International* 46:7 (July 1993): 6–10.

Levin, Floyd. "The Spikes Brothers—A Los Angeles Saga." *Jazz Journal* 4:12 (December 1951): 12–14.

Levin, Robert. "The Jazz Composers Guild: An Assertion of Dignity." *Down Beat*, 6 May 1965, 17–18.

Levin, Robert. "The Third World: Anthony Braxton and the Third Generation." *Jazz & Pop* 9:10 (October 1970): 12–14.

Levine, Lawrence W. *Black Culture and Black Consciousness: Afro-American Folk Thought from Slavery to Freedom.* Oxford: Oxford University Press, 1977.

Lewis, Earl. *In Their Own Interests: Race, Class, and Power in Twentieth-Century Norfolk, Virginia.* Berkeley: University of California Press, 1991.

Lewis, George E. *A Power Stronger Than Itself: The AACM and American Experimental Music.* Chicago: University of Chicago Press, 2008.

Lewis, Samella. *African American Art and Artists.* Berkeley: University of California Press, 1990.

Lipsitz, George. "Introduction—Creating Dangerously: The Blues Life of Johnny Otis." In Johnny Otis, *Upside Your Head! Rhythm and Blues on Central Avenue.* Hanover, NH: Wesleyan University Press, 1993.

Lipsitz, George. "Like a Weed in a Vacant Lot: The Black Artists Group in St. Louis." Revised February 1999 from earlier version in Sue-Ellen Case, Philip Brett, and Susan Leigh Foster, eds. *Decomposition: Post Disciplinary Performance.* Bloomington: Indiana University Press, 2000.

Litweiler, John. "AACM at 30: A Chicago Free Jazz Survey." *Coda Magazine* 267 (May/June 1996): 10–13.

Litweiler, John. *The Freedom Principle: Jazz after 1958.* New York: Da Capo Press, Inc., 1984.

Litweiler, John. *Ornette Coleman: A Harmolodic Life.* New York: William Morrow and Company, 1992.

Livengood, R. Mark. "Streetwise: The *Mafundi* of Dar es Salaam." In *The Cast-off Recast: Recycling and the Creative Transformation of Mass-Produced Objects,* 81–109. Edited by Timothy Corrigan Correll and Patrick Arthur Polk. Los Angeles: UCLA Fowler Museum of Cultural History, 1999.

Lloyd, Robert. "This Ain't No Juilliard! Life and Violins at the Silverlake Conservatory of Music, The School that Flea Built." *LA Weekly,* 4–10 October 2002, 32.

Lock, Graham. *Blutopia: Visions of the Future and Revisions of the Past in the Work of Sun Ra, Duke Ellington, and Anthony Braxton.* Durham, NC: Duke University Press, 1999.

M., Grace. "African American Musical Traditions in Los Angeles: Ethnographic Portraits of Four Musicians." M.A. thesis, University of California, Los Angeles, 1996.

Macauley, Fathia Beatrice. "Leimert Park: Preserving African American Culture Through the Built Environment." M.A. thesis, University of California, Los Angeles, 1997.

Madhubuti, Haki R., ed. *Why L.A. Happened: Implications of the '92 Los Angeles Rebellion*. Chicago: Third World Press, 1993.

Mandel, Howard. "Butch Morris." *Down Beat*, October 1986, 26–28, 61.

Mansfield, Horace, Jr. "Newton's Law: A Discussion of Musical Forces with the World-Renowned Flutist." *Be-bop and Beyond* 1:5 (September/October 1983): 11–17.

Mansfield, Horace, Jr. "World Piano Summit: Tapscott, Hill and Weston rise to this historic occasion." *Be-bop and Beyond* 2:2 (March/April 1984): 22–23.

"Marshall's Othello on PBS." *Los Angeles Sentinel*, 7 June 1979, B-2A.

Masilela, Ntongela. "The Los Angeles School of Black Filmmakers." In *Black American Cinema*, 107–17. Edited by Manthia Diawara. New York: Routledge, 1993.

McNaughton, Patrick R. *The Mande Blacksmiths: Knowledge, Power, and Art in West Africa*. Bloomington: Indiana University Press, 1988.

McRae, Barry. *Ornette Coleman*. London: Apollo Press Limited, 1988.

Melhem, D. H. *Heroism in the New Black Poetry: Introduction and Interviews*. Lexington: University Press of Kentucky, 1990.

Meyer, Laure. *African Forms: Art and Rituals*. New York: Assouline, 2001.

Mingus, Charles. *Beneath the Underdog*. Edited by Nel King. New York: Alfred A. Knopf, 1971.

Mitchell, John L. "Many Blacks Fear Police Are the Enemy." *Los Angeles Times*, 27 August 1982, 1, 3, 16.

Muni, Kai. "AACM: Continuing the Tradition." *Be-bop & Beyond* 4:2 (March/April 1986): 8–12.

Niane, D.T. *Sundiata: An Epic of Old Mali*. Translated by G. D. Pickett. Essex: Longman, 1965.

Nketia, J. H. Kwabena. "The Musician in Akan Society." In *The Traditional Artist in African Societies*, 79–100. Edited by Warren L. d'Azevedo. Bloomington: Indiana University Press, 1973.

Obatala, J. K. "The Sons of Watts: Off the Streets and into the system." *Los Angeles Times*, 13 August 1972, sec. *West Magazine*, 6–9.

Occhiogrosso, Peter. "Profile: Stanley Crouch, David Murray." *Down Beat*, 25 March 1976, 38–39.

"Odd Trio Created Mass Market for 'Crack.'" *San Jose Mercury News*, 19 August 1996, 1A, 10A–11A.

Ojenke. "To Mr. Charles and Sister Annie." In *From the Ashes: Voices of Watts*, 63–65. Edited by Budd Schulberg. New York: The New American Library, 1967.

Ojenke, Raspoeter. "Sun Ra: Mystery or Mister Ra." *Soul*, 1978.

Oliver, Paul. *Savannah Syncopators: African Retentions in the Blues*. New York: Stein and Day Publishers, 1970.

O'Reilly, Kenneth. *"Racial Matters": The FBI's Secret File on Black America, 1960–1972*. New York: The Free Press, 1989.

Otis, Johnny. *Upside Your Head! Rhythm and Blues on Central Avenue*. Hanover, NH: Wesleyan University Press, 1993.

Overend, William. "A Black Teacher Recalls Another Era." *Los Angeles Times*, 14 September 1979, IV:1, 12–13, 22.

Parrish, David, and Beth Barrett. "LAPD fires few in shootings." *Daily News*, 12 May 1991, 1, 12–13.

Partch, Harry. *Genesis of a Music: An Account of a Creative Work, Its Roots and Its Fulfillments*. 2nd ed. New York: Da Capo Press, 1974.

Pastras, Phil. *Dead Man Blues: Jelly Roll Morton Way Out West*. Berkeley: University of California Press, 2001.

Pharr, Wayne. *Nine Lives of a Black Panther: A Story of Survival*. Chicago: Lawrence Hill Books, 2014.

"Pickets Store, Gets Arrested but Released." *California Eagle*, 26 January 1934, 1.

"Playing for Horace: A Tribute to the Music of Rebellion," *Revolutionary Worker*, 4 July 1999, 5.

Porter, Eric. *What Is This Thing Called Jazz? African American Musicians as Artists, Critics, and Activists*. Berkeley: University of California Press, 2002.

Potter, Keith. *Four Musical Minimalists: La Monte Young, Terry Riley, Steve Reich, Philip Glass*. Cambridge: Cambridge University Press, 2000.

Priestley, Brian. *Mingus: A Critical Biography*. New York: Da Capo Press, 1983.

Purifoy, Noah, as told to Ted Michel. "The Art of Communication as a Creative Act." In *Junk Art: "66 Signs of Neon."* Los Angeles: 66 Signs of Neon, n.d.

Radano, Ronald M. *New Musical Figurations: Anthony Braxton's Cultural Critique*. Chicago: University of Chicago Press, 1993.

Rapoport, Roger. "Meet America's Meanest Dirty Trickster." *Mother Jones* II:III (April 1977): 19–23, 59–61.

Ratliff, Ben. "Taking Charge: Conductor Butch Morris' Structured Chaos." *Option* (November/December 1991): 43–46.

"Revolutionary View of Music." *The Black Panther*, 18 October 1969, 8.

Rhines, Jesse Algeron. *Black Film / White Money*. New Brunswick, NJ: Rutgers University Press, 1996.

Rosner, Lora. "Billy Higgins: Making the Music One." *Modern Drummer* 16 (February 1992): 26–29, 102–09.

Sanchez, Sonia. *Wounded in the House of a Friend*. Boston: Beacon Press, 1995.

Santoro, Gene. *When I Am Real: The Life and Music of Charles Mingus*. Oxford: Oxford University Press, 2000.

Sanyika, Dadisi. *African Drum and Dance: The Reconnection with African Ancestral Wisdom*. Los Angeles: Golden Thread Productions, 2000.

"Schedule for Mid-Winter Classes." *The Mafundi Potential* 1:1 (February 1970), 3.

Schiesl, Martin J. "Behind the Badge: The Police and Social Discontent in Los Angeles Since 1950." In *20th Century Los Angeles: Power, Promotion, and Social Conflict*, 153–94. Edited by Norman M. Klein and Martin J. Schiesl. Claremont, CA: Regina Books, 1990.

Scott, Austin. "Black Youths' Jobs Picture Still Bleak." *Los Angeles Times*, 24 December 1978, 1, 8.

Seitz, William C. *The Art of Assemblage*. New York: The Museum of Modern Art, 1961.

Seltzer, George. *Music Matters: The Performer and the American Federation of Musicians.* Metuchen, NJ: The Scarecrow Press, Inc., 1989.

Shaw, Arnold. *Honkers and Shouters: The Golden Years of Rhythm and Blues.* New York: Macmillan Publishing Company, 1978.

Sheffey-Stinson, Sandi. "The History of Theatre Productions at the Los Angeles Inner City Cultural Center: 1965–1976." Ph.D. diss., Kent State University, 1979.

Sides, Josh. *L.A. City Limits: African American Los Angeles from the Great Depression to the Present.* Berkeley: University of California Press, 2003.

Simosko, Vladimir, and Barry Tepperman. *Eric Dolphy: A Musical Biography and Discography.* Washington, D.C.: Smithsonian Institution Press, 1974; reprint ed., New York: Da Capo Press, 1979.

Smith, Arnold Jay. "Billy Taylor and Dave Bailey: Magnetizing the Arts." *Down Beat*, 1 December 1977, 14–15.

Smith, Catherine Parsons. *William Grant Still: A Study in Contradictions.* Berkeley: University of California Press, 2000.

Smith, R. J. "All That L.A. Jazz," *Los Angeles Times Magazine*, 19 January 1997, 12–17.

Smith, R. J. *The Great Black Way: L.A. in the 1940s and the Lost African-American Renaissance.* New York: Public Affairs, 2006.

Snowden, Don. "Horace Tapscott at the Lighthouse." *Los Angeles Times*, 17 November 1979, II:11.

Snowden, Don. "3 Jazz Pianists in a Concert Setting." *Los Angeles Times*, 14, February 1984, VI:3.

Sonenshein, Raphael J. *Politics in Black and White: Race and Power in Los Angeles.* Princeton, NJ: Princeton University Press, 1993.

Southern, Eileen. *The Music of Black Americans.* 3rd ed. New York: W. W. Norton, 1997.

Spellman, A. B. *Four Lives in the Bebop Business.* New York: Limelight Editions, 1966.

Still, William Grant. "An Afro-American Composer's Point of View." In *American Composers on American Music*, 182–83. Edited by Henry Cowell. NY: Frederick Ungar Publishing Co., 1962, 1933.

Such, David G. *Avant-Garde Jazz Musicians Performing 'Out There.'* Iowa City: University of Iowa Press, 1993.

Szwed, John. *Space Is the Place: The Lives and Times of Sun Ra.* New York: Pantheon Books, 1997.

Tapscott, Horace. *Songs of the Unsung: The Musical and Social Journey of Horace Tapscott.* Edited by Steven Isoardi. Durham, NC: Duke University Press, 2001.

Theomachist (Against the Gods). "How to Kill the Ku Klux." *California Eagle*, 15 October 1921, 1, 8.

Thompson, Robert Farris. *Flash of the Spirit: African and Afro-American Art and Philosophy.* New York: Vintage Books, 1984.

Thompson, Robert Farris. "Kongo Influences on African-American Artistic Culture." In *Africanisms in American Culture*, 148–84. Edited by Joseph E. Holloway. Bloomington: Indiana University Press, 1990.

Toop, David. *Rap Attack 2: African Rap to Global Hip Hop.* London: Serpent's Tail, 1991.

Trotsky, Leon. *Literature and Revolution*. Translated by Rose Strunsky. Ann Arbor: University of Michigan Press, 1960.

Troupe, Quincy. *Skulls Along the River*. New York: I. Reed Books, 1984.

Troupe, Quincy, ed. *Watts Poets: A Book of New Poetry and Essays*. N.p.: the House of Respect, 1968.

"Two Shades of Soul: The 17th Asian American Jazz Festival Features Jon Jang Quintet and Horace Tapscott." KSW *News* 3:4 (Spring 1998): 1, 7.

Tyler, Bruce Michael. "Black Radicalism in Southern California, 1950–1982." Ph.D. diss., University of California, Los Angeles, 1983.

Tyler, Bruce Michael. *From Harlem to Hollywood: The Struggle for Racial and Cultural Democracy 1920–1943*. New York: Garland Publishing, Inc., 1992.

Tyler, Bruce Michael. "The Rise and Decline of the Watts Summer Festival, 1965 to 1986." *American Studies* 31:2 (Fall 1990): 61–81.

Veal, Michael E. *Fela: The Life and Times of an African Musical Icon*. Philadelphia: Temple University Press, 2000.

Vernon-Central Revisited; A Capsule History. Washington, D.C.: A Neighbor-Works Publication, 1989.

Walker, Victor Leo, II. "The Politics of Art: A History of the Inner City Cultural Center, 1965–1986." Ph.D. diss., University of California, Santa Barbara, 1989.

"War on drugs' unequal impact on U.S. blacks." *San Jose Mercury News*, 20 August 1966, 1A, 10A.

Ward, Francis. "Permanent 'Underclass' of Jobless Blacks Feared." *Los Angeles Times*, 5 April 1976, 1, 5.

Warren, Fred. *The Music of Africa: An Introduction*. Englewood Cliffs, NJ: Prentice-Hall, Inc., 1970.

Warren, Jenifer, and Dan Morain. "Crips Target of Prison Lockdown." *Los Angeles Times*, 1 July 2003, B1, B7.

Watts Prophets Community Education Association, Inc. "Our Mission." Program, UCLA Performing Arts at Royce Hall, 5 October 2001.

"The Watts Writers Workshop." *The Antioch Review* 27:2 (Fall 1967).

Webb, Gary. *Dark Alliance: The CIA, the Contras, and the Crack Cocaine Explosion*. New York: Seven Stories Press, 1998.

"Wendell Harrison, Phil Ranelin and Tribe." *JazzTimes*, September 2001, 34–37.

White, Deborah Gray. "Let My People Go: 1804–1860." In *To Make Our World Anew: A History of African Americans*, 169–226. Edited by Robin D.G. Kelley and Earl Lewis. Oxford: Oxford University Press, 2000.

Whiteis, David. "Chicago Jazz Festival." *Down Beat*, December 1993, 58.

Widener, Daniel L. *Black Arts West: Culture and Struggle in Postwar Los Angeles*. Durham, NC: Duke University Press, 2010.

Widener, Daniel L. "'Way Out West': Expressive Art, Music, and Culture in Black LA." *Emergences* 9:2 (1999): 271–89.

Williams, Jean. "Soul Sauce: Tapscott Taps Out a New System." *Billboard*, 10 April 1976, 22–23.

Wilmer, Valerie. *As Serious as Your Life: John Coltrane and Beyond*. London: Serpent's Tail, 1992.

Wilson, Peter Niklas. *Ornette Coleman: His Life and Music*. Berkeley: Berkeley Hills Books, 1999.

Wood, Peter. "Strange New Land: 1619–1776." In *To Make Our World Anew: A History of African Americans*, 53–102. Edited by Robin D.G. Kelley and Earl Lewis. Oxford: Oxford University Press, 2000.

"Young Black Men." *The New York Times*, 7 May 1992.

RECORDINGS AND FILMS

Aceyalone. *Accepted Eclectic*. Ground Control Records compact disc GCR 7045-2.

Anderza, Earl. *Outa Sight*. Pacific Jazz compact disc CDP 7243 4 94849 2 4.

Brown, Elaine. *Elaine Brown*. Black Forum BF458L.

Brown, Elaine. *Seize the Time*. Vault 131.

Central Avenue Sounds: Jazz in Los Angeles (1921–1956). Rhino Entertainment Company compact discs R2 75872.

Crouch, Stanley. *Ain't No Ambulances for No Nigguhs Tonight*. Flying Dutchman FDS-105.

Daáood, Kamau. *Leimert Park*. MAMA Foundation compact disc MAMA1019.

Drums Along the Pacific. New Albion Records compact disc NA122.

Harris, Billie. *I Want Some Water*. Nimbus West compact disc NS 510C.

Hill, Linda. *Lullaby for Linda*. Nimbus NS-791.

Horace Tapscott Quintet. *The Giant Is Awakened*. Flying Dutchman FDS-107. Reissued on *West Coast Hot*. RCA Novus Series '70 compact disc 3107-2-N.

Ice-T. OG *The Original Gangster Video*. 70 min. Warner Reprise, 1991. Videocassette.

Last Date: Eric Dolphy. Produced by Marian Brouwer and directed by Hans Hylkema. 92 min. Rhapsody Films Inc., 1991. Videocassette.

Leimert Park: The Story of a Village in South Central Los Angeles. Produced and directed by Jeannette Lindsay. 87 min. 2008. DVD.

Life Is a Saxophone: Kamau Daáood, The Word Musician. Produced and directed by Saundra Sharp. 58 min. A Sharp Show, 2013. DVD.

Message from the Tribe—An Anthology of Tribe Records: 1972–1977. Universal Sound compact discs US CD 5.

Morris, Lawrence D. "Butch." *Testament: A Conduction Collection*. New World Records compact discs 80478-2.

NWA *Flight 17*. Nimbus West Records compact disc NS 135 C.

NWA. *Straight Outta Compton*. Ruthless Records compact disc CDL57102.

Pan Afrikan Peoples Arkestra. *The Call*. Nimbus NS-246.

Ranelin, Phil. *The Time Is Now!* Hefty Records compact disc Hefty32.

rhythms of life, songs of wisdom: akan music from ghana, west africa. Smithsonian/Folkways Recordings compact disc SF CD 40463.

"A Special Tribute to Horace Tapscott." *Jazz and Poetry in Motion*. Produced and directed by Annya Bell. 29 min. MediaOne TV, 17 February 1999. Videocassette.

Sun Ra: A Joyful Noise. Produced and directed by Robert Mugge. 60 min. Rhapsody Films Inc., 1986. Videocassette.

Tapscott, Horace. *At the Crossroads.* Nimbus NS-579.

"Tapscott Memorial—NYC." Knitting Factory, New York. 163 mins. 1999. Videocassette.

Thomas, Leon. *Spirits Known and Unknown.* Flying Dutchman FDS-115.

The Watts Prophets. *Rappin' Black in a White World.* Acid Jazz compact disc JAZID CD 164.

Peet, Wayne, 228, 230, 299, 303, 326, 328, 356–57
Pepper, Art, 62, 119, 356
Performing Arts Society of Los Angeles (PASLA), 89, 191, 223
Perry, Darthard, 89–90, 169
Person-Lynn, Kwaku, 169
Pharoah's Den, 15
Phillips, Little Esther, 72
Plantation Club, 71–72
Pleasant, Edwin, 63, 333, 344, 347, 366, 370
Polk, Kamonta, 181, 183, 216
Porter, Roy, 28, 31, 40
Porter, Rudolph, 121, 128, 136–37, 170–71, 366
Powell, Adam Clayton, 56
Powell, Benny, 229
Powell, Judson, 73, 79, 81
Pratt, Geronimo, 153–54, 295
Preston, Don, 34, 35, 36
Previn, André, 324
Priestley, Eric, 85–87, 163, 319
Progressive Musicians Organization, 25
Project Blowed, 290, 301
Proposition 13, 261
Pullen, Don, 328
Purifoy, Noah, 73, 79, 81–83, 169, 279, 320

Quagmire Manor, 201, 203
"Quagmire Manor at 5 a.m.," 203–4
Quant, George, 173
Quetzal (band), 358

Rachmaninoff, Sergei, 276
Ramirez, José, 358–59
Ramsess, 281
Ranelin, Phil, 17, 298, 305, 329
Rap music, 4, 28, 260, 280, 286–87, 290, 300–301
Rapson, John, 228, 230, 294
Reagan, Ronald, 260, 263, 288
Redd, Alton, 24
Redd, Vi, 24–25
Reese, Lloyd, 24, 31–34, 37, 44, 325
Reiter, Louis, 287
René, Leon, 27, 192
René, Otis, 27, 192
Rhodes, Cecil, 38, 145, 187
Rhythm and Blues (R&B), 26–28, 49, 72–73
Riddle, John, 79, 81, 83, 279

Riggs, Ed. *See* Perry, Darthard
Riley, Herman, 51
Roach, Max, 13
Roberson, Stanley "Chico," 56, 146
Roberts, Ernest. *See* Abdul-Khaliq, Fuasi
Roberts, Kafi, 218, 233–34, 277–78, 337; with Ark, 194, 198; background of, 183; as community artist, 346; with Medi-Music, 225; with Panthers, 188
Roberts, Kachina, 181, 188, 202–3, 205, 207, 267, 360
Robertson, Lester "Lately," 60, 117, 139; with Ark, 298, 349; death of, 265; with Eric Dolphy, 37, 51–52; with Melodic Dots, 24–25; as teacher, 250–51
Robins, The, 72–73
Robinson, Leroy "Sweet Pea," 26, 29
Rodia, Simon, 71–72, 81, 82, 226
Rogers, Bob, 80
Rogers, Shorty, 40
Romero, Carmencita, 80
Romero, Danyel, 59–60, 63, 297, 313, 340
Room 227, 224
Roosevelt Park Cemetery, 308
Roper, William, 294–95, 296, 299, 336, 372
Roy, Robert. *See* Muhammad, Abdul-Salaam
Royal, Ernest, 24
Royal, Ernie, 24
Royal, Marshal, 24
Royal, Marshal, Sr., 24
Rudolph's Fine Art Center, 168, 170–71

Saar, Betye, 83, 279
Sample, Joe, 152
Sanchez, Sonia: poetry of, 141
Sanders, Pharoah, 63
Sanford and Son, 192
San Francisco Opera Orchestra and Ballet, 184–85, 324, 354
San Francisco Symphony, 184, 218
Sanyika, Dadisi, 156, 163, 165, 168–69, 225, 237, 343–46
Savage, Walter, 62, 90–91, 126, 132, 135–36, 171, 210–11, 330
Saxon, Alvin, Jr. *See* Ojenke
Schoenberg, Arnold, 31
Schulberg, Budd, 84–85, 91
Screen Actors Guild, 192
Seale, Bobby, 124, 126, 180

272–73, 303; with Pan Asian Arkestra, 301–2, 358; as "Papa," 63; personality of, 312–19; as Phantom, 316–17; as pianist, 275–76, 325–29, 375–76; political views, 66–67; at prisons, 199–200, 300; Quintet of, 132–33; and rap music, 300–301; recordings of, 230–35, 275–78, 299–301, 317; recruits from community, 346–48; rehearsals, 48, 51–53, 296, 335–36; rejects commercialism, 2, 53, 341–42, 346–47, 360–61; at Riverside, 173–74; with Samuel Browne, 23–24, 50; starts band, 2, 51–54; tribute to, 311–12; views on African culture, 156–58; views on name changes, 157–58; in Watts, 69; with William Marshall, 129–30, 163; and women, 318–19

Taumbu, 124–25, 136, 207–8, 293–94, 366

Taylor, Billy, 16

Taylor, Cecil, 14, 181, 273–75

Taylor Nathaniel, 191–92

Taylor Pat, 290

Theus, Sonship, 128, 211, 218–19, 234–35, 271, 328, 330–31

Thiele, Bob, 122

Thomas, Leon, 94, 161

Thommen, Anke, 367

Thornton, Big Mama, 73

"Thoughts of Dar es Salaam," 66, 174, 298, 321, 323

Thoughts of Dar es Salaam (album), 300

Together Again Band, 274–75

Trembley, George, 31

Tribble, Denise, 297, 321, 337

Tribe (group), 17, 298

Trible, Dwight, 280, 282–83, 289, 296–97, 303, 320–21, 327, 366

Troubadour (club), 38–39, 218, 227

Troupe, Quincy, 85–88, 91, 128, 165, 169, 357–58

Trujillo, Tommy, 64, 121, 125, 137, 215, 339

Tubman, Harriet, 3, 359

Tut (language), 9

Two Shades of Soul, 302

Tyner, McCoy, 20, 127, 152, 161, 217, 219, 277, 339

Ueberoth, Peter, 293

Underground Musicians Assocation (UGMA): and black nationalism, 124–26; change to UGMAA, 142–43; drugs in, 64; houses of, 54–55, 59–60, 135–40; music and, 54–59, 118, 136–39; origins of, 37, 50–59; police and, 138; political alignments, 65–67, 123–27; recordings of, 131–35; in South Park, 130–31; in Watts, 69, 90–91, 117–18, 127–29; women in, 61–62

Underwood, Earl, 290, 365

Union of God's Musicians and Artists Ascension (UGMAA): and black history, 155–56; cultural activities, 224–25; expansion of, 173; film projects, 189–93; Foundation of, 220–21; grants for, 302; houses of, 162–63, 180, 201–7, 264; institutionalization of, 215–16, 220–26; lifestyles of, 154, 158–59; new recruits, 180–81; political views, 154–55, 158–60, 187–89, 360–61; printing business, 223–24; at prisons, 199–201; reduction of activities, 238–39; setbacks, 260; start of, 142–44; universality of, 355–59

United Clergymen of Central Los Angeles, 48–49

Universal Order of Black Expression, 145–46

University of California at Riverside, 173–74, 183, 375

University of Southern California, 58, 144, 152

Urban League, 21, 74

US Organizaation, 78, 123–26, 142, 146, 156, 188

Utterbach, Cynthia, 280

Varese, Edgar, 41

Venice, California, 207–8

Venture Records, 175

Vereen, Lady Walquer, 290

Vietnam War, 120, 128, 147–48, 154, 178, 179, 188–89, 205

Vieux, Phil, 297, 299

Village, The, 367

Village Vanguard, 272–73

Vision Theater, 281

Voice of UGMA, 122, 124, 136

Voice of UGMAA, 153, 176, 296–97, 302–4

von Essen, Eric, 228–30

Voting Rights Act of 1965, 3

Wainwright, E. W., 120–122, 125–28, 131, 138, 177, 217, 314, 359

Waldron, Mal, 271